DATE DUE

MY 16 97			
AP 01 06			

DEMCO 38-296

THE JEW IN THE TEXT

E. Belmann, *Un Juif*, Salon of 1889 (*see pp. 27–8*)

Edited and Introduced by
Linda Nochlin & Tamar Garb

THE JEW
IN THE TEXT

Modernity and the
Construction of Identity

With 72 illustrations

THAMES AND HUDSON

mothers,
the late Elka Heller,
to whom we each owe not only our Jewishness but our
differing conceptions of its meaning

Illustration Acknowledgments

References are to page numbers; *a* = above,
b = below, *c* = center, *l* = left, *r* = right.

Josse Bernheim-Jeune Collection, Paris, stolen by German troops in 1944 61*r*; Jerusalem: National Library, Hebrew University, Givat Ram 193, Israel Museum, The Boris and Lisa Aronson Collection, purchased through a bequest from Mrs. Dvora Cohen, Afeka, Israel, 1989 197; Daniel Libeskind 198; London: BFI Stills, Posters and Designs 285, 287, 290, Tate Gallery 88, 89, 92, 93; New York: The Jewish Museum 67; Paris: Bibliothèque Nationale de France 13–15, 17, 56, 63, 66, 71, 74, 78*r*, 123–5, 130, 131, 133*a*, 134, 136, 185, 277, Cabinet des Estampes, Bibliothèque Nationale de France (photo Lauros-Giraudon) 133*br*, Centre de Documentation Juive Contemporaine 178, 179, Musée Carnavalet (photo Lauros-Giraudon) 133*bl*, Musée du Petit Palais (photo Musées de la Ville de Paris) 137; © Pei Cobb Freed & Partners 298, 299; private collections (Photo-Services, Cornell University) 98, 99, 103, 112, 113, photo by courtesy of the National Portrait Gallery, London 87; photo Adrian Rifkin 281, 282; photo courtesy Verlag der Kunst, Dresden 199.

© 1995 Thames and Hudson Ltd, London

Text © Linda Nochlin and Tamar Garb, and
the several authors appearing in the Contents list opposite

First published in the United States of America in 1996 by
Thames and Hudson Inc., 500 Fifth Avenue,
New York, New York 10110

Library of Congress Catalog Card Number 95–60275
ISBN 0–500–01667–4

Printed and bound in Slovenia

Contents

Preface and Acknowledgments

This book was born of long conversations between friends. It had struck us, and not surprisingly many others at around the same time, that the category of the "Jew," not the history of Jews, Judaism, or Jewish culture, but the way in which the "Jew" had been perceived in modern culture, was relatively unexplored. While issues surrounding race, identity, colonialism, and Eurocentrism have become the focus of endless debate and scrutiny, the "Jew" had been largely left out. It is as if the issue of the "Jew" is just as much an embarrassment to contemporary cultural theorists as it was to their European ancestors. The time, we thought, was ripe to explore through a number of case studies, whether from art, literature, or popular culture, the complex issues raised by the way the "Jew" is constructed and represented in modern times, and to use some of the tools of the recent theorization of "identity"—racial, sexual, political. Our contributors responded magnificently to our requests for papers. They submitted to badgering, encouragement, and criticism (from both sides of the Atlantic, and not always at the same time) with good grace and we thank them warmly for this. Our friends and families have had to put up with the usual authorial groans, exacerbated by long-distance calls, midnight faxes, and prolonged absences.

We should like to extend our thanks to Elie Szapiro for generously sharing his information and insights about the nineteenth-century printmaker Alphonse Lévy; thanks are also due to: Rachel Esner, Benjamin David, Paul Jackson, Louis Mitelberg (the French political cartoonist Tim), Rasaad Jamie, Briony Fer, and Andrew Hemingway.

Linda Nochlin and Tamar Garb, New York and London, 1995

Introduction

Starting with the Self: Jewish Identity and its Representation

LINDA NOCHLIN

"Why do they hate us so much?" This is not merely an anguished cry torn from the heart—although, of course, it is that, too—but rather a perfectly rational question to ask in the face of the plethora of hostile, denigrating, and debasing representations of Jews—the Jew, Jewishness—collected and analyzed in the texts of this volume. That these representations are often contradictory—Jews are too smart and innately incapable of genius; Jewish women are natural wantons and asexual or frigid; Jews underhandedly control the international banking community and yet pollute the great cities with their fetid, crime-ridden slums; Jews are over-intellectual but over-emotional, hyper-rational but superstitious—does nothing to mitigate the force of their collective assault. On the contrary, it would seem to imply that we are and have been so hated that *only* mutually exclusive categories would seem large enough to encompass the totality of our iniquity. A language of excess seems the natural vehicle for such vileness.

Sometimes, reading these texts and the myriad others detailing the dark face of anti-Semitic representation, I have actually felt compelled to run to the mirror. To what extent do I conform to the Jewish stereotypes reiterated time after time in these pages and detailed in Sander Gilman's book *The Jew's Body*?[1] While it is true that my ears do not stick out, my nose is far from hooked, and my lips are thin rather than thick and coarse, I do have flat feet and rounded shoulders (I remember gratefully that my husband, equally Jewish, had such high arches that as a child, he had to wear orthopedic shoes and do detestable exercises to correct them, and that he had shoulders so broad that he had trouble finding suits to fit; but, I remembered, his nose *was* slightly aquiline). While I had always associated my red hair and freckles with the Gentile world—Irish, perhaps, or Scottish—I learned that these were particularly ascribed to the diabolic or demonic aspects of Jewishness: Gauguin, for example, depicts the Dutch Jewish artist Meyer de Haan with red hair, red beard, and a cloven hoof in place of a hand, and the image is not merely his invention. At times, I would find myself surreptitiously looking at people on the street in my neighborhood on the Upper West Side of Manhatten or at a concert or movie or, more to the point, emerging from the local synagogue. Some of them, indeed—the older ones mostly—bore the stigmata of stereotypical Jewishness: the frog-like mouths, the large, uncomely noses, the squinty eyes, and the weak, hunched-over physiognomies of the classical anti-Semitic caricature. How delighted I was to see that the young people, on the contrary, even the ones walking to the Orthodox synagogue around the corner, were often tall, broad-shouldered, and fit beneath their prayer-shawls and yarmulkes, the young women fashionably if conservatively dressed: no hint of caricature here!

The terrible thing about the voluminous literature representing the Jew as excessive is the way it sticks in the mind, seeps into the unconscious, embeds itself in the deepest levels of my being even if I detest its assertions and, on the rational level, I realize its total irrationality. But I am irrational, too, or not merely rational. I am ashamed of myself for subscribing to these hateful, phantasmagoric pseudo-identities for even an instant; but something deep inside me cannot be gainsaid. Centuries of negative stereotyping cannot be erased so easily—not even in the minds of those who would discredit the anti-Semites and defend the Jews. Figures as intelligent and anti-anti-Semitic as Sartre may unconsciously subscribe to stereotypical notions of "the Jew," as Susan Suleiman points out in her perceptive essay in this volume. The minds of Jews who are not particularly "self-hating" themselves may share some of the anti-Semites' attitudes about Jewish "Others"—German Jews about Ashkenazis, for instance, or Jews with rural origins about their urban co-religionists. The almost universal opprobrium felt by Christian Europe for Jews and Jewishness, epitomized in the stereotypical construction of "The Jew," seeps into the most hidden layers of even the most enlightened and self-confident psyche, where it lies dormant until stimulated, roused to consciousness by an experience like working on this book.

If, as William James said, "The deepest principle in human nature is the craving to be appreciated,"[2] then the historical representation of the Jew as irredeemably detestable, corrupt, and physically and morally loathsome is destructive of this "deepest principle," for it denies all appreciation to any member of this alienated group simply by virtue of being born to it. Why do they hate *me* so much, when they, the anti-Semitic perpetrators of the articles, stories, and images discussed by our authors, don't even know me? I am unappreciated, made abject *a priori* simply because I am one of them. And the consequences of this belief have been more terrible than mere lack of appreciation. They have been extermination.

Hovering, unspoken for the most part, above the discourse about Jewish identity and representation after the middle of the twentieth century is the shadow of the Holocaust. It is hard to consider a character like Fagin objectively, to think of Lautrec's illustrations to *Au Pieds du Sinaï* within a limited historical context, because the thought of the terrible consequences, the ultimate corollary, of the "representation of the Jew as excess," inevitably intervenes; it may be brushed aside or taken into consideration—but cannot be dismissed.

For me, who had always taken for granted that I was Jewish, who had grown up in an almost completely Jewish community in Brooklyn, New York, during the thirties and forties, but had never particularly considered the content of that Jewish identity until I undertook the editing of this book, visiting Prague this summer was a revelation. I made the obligatory pilgrimage to the cramped "Jewish Quarter," now a tourist Mecca for Jews from all over the world, mainly, I suspect, from the United States. Cravenly avoiding the exhibition of children's art from Theresienstadt, I threaded my way through the old Jewish Cemetery, the oldest in Europe I understand, with its rows and layers of crooked and tilted grave stones (like the rounded shoulders of Jewish stereotype) and entered the so-called Pinkas School or Synagogue, founded in the sixteenth century. There was a sign asking for silence. Inside the building, a small group of dedicated young people were painstakingly recopying the names of the 77,000 or so Jewish victims of the Holocaust from the region who had been murdered by the Nazis, names that had been inscribed on the walls right after the war and then effaced in a so-called cleaning process by the Soviet invaders.[3] Reading the long lists of names, row after row of them, transcribed in colored pigment on the whitewashed walls of the synagogue, humble forerunners of the more monumental inscription on the bronze surface of the Vietnam Memorial in Washington, D.C., I was struck by the familiarity of the names I was reading: Ableman, Bruckenfeld, Anbinder, Cohen—this could have been the Brooklyn telephone directory of my youth. People with the same names as these were the ones I was telephoning, playing with, visiting, or complaining to about rationing at the very time the bearers of these Jewish names in Prague, the members of *these* families, were being brutally taken from their homes, piled into box cars, and killed in the gas chambers. It was not that I didn't know such things before, but the walls of the Pinkas Synagogue suddenly made them concrete, gave specificity and recognizable identities to the anonymous "victims" in a way that made their fate all the more terrible in that the lists were so "ordinary," so much part of my childhood experience, and yet, at the same time, so horrifically different. More powerfully than any representation, the names, in their naked indexicality, an indexicality which here denied the very possibility of communication through an icon of the Holocaust, bore concrete witness to Jewish identity and its destruction. Consciously or not, the Hebrew interdiction against the graven image was in effect, and powerfully effective. Here, on the walls of the Pinkas Synagogue, the Jew and the text coincide absolutely and literally.

There too, in Prague, I read briefly the history of the Jews in the city: an ancient history, dating back to the Middle Ages, a familiar narrative of brief periods of acceptance—extremely circumscribed—followed by exiles or even pogroms, a rebuilding of the community, success, and security, followed by recurrent difficulty and renewed oppression and exile. There was almost no place in Europe where Jews could live with equanimity, in peace and security long enough to establish deep roots; no place where they could own land over a period of time; no place where they could have equal access to all the trades and professions, until well after the French Revolution. In Christian Europe, they were the irrevocable other, endowed with all the negative characteristics the Christian majority most hated and despised—in themselves primarily. Paranoid fantasies could always be fueled by selective fact-finding, heightened by vicious and exaggerated representation.

"Why do and did they hate us?" can be answered on the simplest level by replying "Because we were the ones singled out to be objects of hatred." Jews have always been the hated other since the beginning of the Christian era. Not only were they the Christ Killers, but they stubbornly refused to see the light of Christian salvation and stuck to the old dispensation. It is the shapes this hatred assumes, the substance of the paranoid fantasies, the social role played by the "phantasmagoric" Jew of racial abjection that varies, that is at once interesting and abhorrent.

The modern construction of the Jew and the establishing of a coherent Jewish identity may be said to have begun with the construction of modernity itself, in the nineteenth century. This construction is almost synchronous with, though hardly identical to, the growth of mass communication and the possibility of popular representation on a large scale. This fabric of Jewish identity is interwoven with the complex formation of anti-Semitism as an ideological position. Indeed, one might say that Jewish identity and the Jew of anti-Semitism are brought into being by the same representational trajectory. What we are interested in here is not some "real," essential Jewishness lurking beneath a surface of lies and clichés, a reduced essence beyond the excessiveness of the stereotypical Jewish persona of art, literature, and propaganda, but rather that excessiveness itself; the almost hysterical repetitiveness of myths and exaggerations, black or white, and the ambivalent fluctuations between these two poles, revealed in a subtle analysis like the one to which Bryan Cheyette's submits colonialist Jewish representation, which constitutes the repertory of represented Jewishness in modern times.

It may be the ultimate irony in the history of Jewish identity and the representation of the Jew that successful assimilation, in France and Germany during the "benign" nineteenth century, should be so intimately, indeed necessarily, connected with the formation of modern anti-Semitic stereo-types. "Anti-Semitism turned racist only on the fateful day, when, as a con-sequence of Emancipation, you could no longer pick Jews out of a crowd at first glance," declares Alain Finkielkraut in his provocative study of mod-ern anti-Semitism and its variants, *The Imaginary Jew*.[4] Continues Finkielkraut: "Since the Jews—those revolting mimics—were no longer distinguishable by any particular trait, they were graced with a distinct men-tality. Science was charged with succeeding where the gaze had failed, asked to make sure that the adversary remained foreign, to stigmatize the nation of Israel by enclosing it within a Jewish reality. . . . Racial hatred and its blind rage were essentially the Jews' punishment for no longer placing their dif-ference on display."[5]

Jewish Identity and the Ambiguities of Visual Representation

If the terrible consequences of a politics of Jewish identity in the mid-twentieth century are brutally legible in the names of murdered victims inscribed on the wall of the Pinkas Synagogue, the relationship between Jewish identity and visual representation in the modern period as a whole is far more ambiguous. Although the coarse anti-Semitic caricatures dis-cussed by Michèle Cone in her essay on anti-Semitism and art criticism under Vichy seem unequivocal in their visual venom, in other cases the rep-resentational spectrum and its variables present themselves with far greater complexity. Much depends on the position of the artist—Jewish or non-Jewish, more or less sympathetic to Jews, "neutral" or hostile—as well as the position of the viewer in relation to represented Jewishness. In the lat-ter case, we might turn to the interesting example provided by Kathleen Adler in her essay on Sargent's portraits of the Wertheimer family: these portraits might well be taken for overt or covert anti-Semitic caricatures by viewers with varied attitudes towards "the Jews" themselves. Nevertheless, both the artist and his Jewish sitters saw them as extremely sympathetic, vital images of the wealthy art dealer and his family. For them, the portrait of Asher Wertheimer "served both as a likeness which satisfied the family and as an image which proclaimed the sitter's identity as a Jew—a Jew of a particular class, distinguished by his wealth."[6]

CONTRAST AND COMPARE: TWO REPRESENTATIONS OF JEWS

How then is "Jewishness" constituted as a visual trope in the modern per-iod? Can the artist establish a Jewish typology which is generally readable as Jewish without resorting to caricature or "negative" (I use the term prov-isionally and warily) imagery? How can we—and who are "we" *vis-à-vis* Jewish identity anyway?—distinguish between an image of Jews which is anti-Semitic and one which is "positive" (again, I use the other term of the dichotomy with extreme reluctance)? A detailed comparison of two nine-teenth-century representations of very similar Jewish subjects reveals the complexity involved in attempting to separate "good" and "bad" images of Jews. The comparison will put up the work of the German artist Ludwig Knaus (1829–1910) against that of the French Jew Alphonse Lévy (1843–1918). Both Knaus's *Solomonic Wisdom* of 1878 and Lévy's *The Hebrew Lesson: The Portion*, one of the artist's most celebrated lithographs, first pub-lished in the periodical *La Plume* in 1895,[7] represent an older Jewish man transmitting the traditional wisdom of his people to a younger disciple.

Solomonic Wisdom is one of a group of genre paintings Knaus devoted to marginal groups, Gypsies as well as Jews. Although at first sight the image is a benign one, the ironic title directs the viewer to more or less subtle clues undermining the apparent coziness of the scene. The benign old man, tak-ing his ease with his pipe, is not really benign; his dignity is farcical. This is a Jewish old-clothes dealer (a fairly common trade for Jews, deprived as they were of access to more dignified professions), teaching an unsavory young disciple, whose animalistic features and "typical" red hair betray his racial origins, the tricks of the trade, the sharp practices characteristic of the race.[8]

The old man's unchristian pride in profiting off the misery of others (Gentiles), the young man's unseemly avidity in absorbing the sordid les-son, are underlined by the abjectness of the setting—a squalid basement full of rags. The Jews, of course, are depicted as unaware of this squalor since it is their natural environment. Yet if the image is an anti-Semitic one, it is, at least for the modern viewer, a relatively subtle one, its ironic vision of Jewish domesticity directed to our attention as much by the title as by out-right exaggeration of physiognomy, gesture, or setting. To a viewer of Knaus's day, however, like the art historian and critic Ludwig Pfau, this was an easily readable satire of Jewish sharp practices.[9] Looking back at the painting ten years later, in 1888, Pfau describes it as follows: "A gray-haired old-clothes dealer gives his redheaded offspring theoretical advice about how to get rich. The harmony between these two noble souls, for whom haggling has all the fascination of an art form, the cozy air of superiority of the smoking old man, who feels himself as completely at home in his over-crowded den as Mephistopheles in the witches' kitchen, and the knowing grin of the youth, whose eyes glisten like those of a cat when he hears a mouse rustling, are products of an extraordinary art of expression."[10] Once more, irony puts these Jewish figures in their place and bears witness to the skill of the artist who can convey the underlying racial character of the group with such authenticity.

But what are "we" (and by this I mean the modern, visually sophisticated spectator, Jewish or non-Jewish, interested in reading the inscription of

Alphonse Lévy, *The Hebrew Lesson: The Portion,* 1895

value in visual imagery) to make of Alphonse Lévy's construction of Jewishness in *The Hebrew Lesson?* Clearly this is meant to be, and to some extent works as, a "positive" image. The old Hebrew teacher, a rabbi, teaches a young pupil to read the time-honored language of his people, thereby contributing to the continuation of Jewish identity in diaspora. Given the age of the pupil, it is possible, and probable, that this is a bar mitzvah portion: the boy is imbibing not merely an identifying language, but also the traditional wisdom that will enable him to take his place as an adult member of the Jewish community—to become a Jewish man, in short. The instruction represented, rather than being a training in stealth and abjection, a "negative" image, such as that depicted by the German Knaus, is the transmission of traditional religious wisdom (the very opposite, in its purity and unworldliness, from the ironically designated "Wisdom" of Knaus's denomination), "positive" in the best sense of the word.

But when we consider the representation as a representation, and not merely its iconography, the case is much less clear. Indeed, it constitutes a case of that representational ambiguity to which I have referred. What we have here is a gap-toothed, large-nosed old man, positioned close to the

Alphonse Lévy,
*Anniversary in the
Cemetery*, c.1900

surface of the print in a pose of authority vaguely reminiscent of that
established by Titian in his papal portraits, and his less than attractive, or
even intelligent, young pupil with cap pulled low over his eyes as he struggles over the text, presented in close-up within a dark interior unmistakably
shown as Jewish by the Hebrew inscription and seven-branched lamp
hanging from the ceiling. It would seem to be no accident that the Lévy
image at one time was included in what one authority on the artist, Elie
Szapiro, has termed a "véritable anthologie antisémite," Furst's *Die Juden in
der Karikatur* of 1923, and yet at another time served as the cover illustration
for a special number of *La Vie illustrée* consecrated to the "Jewish world" on
the occasion of the 1902 Zionist Congress in Basel.[11]

It seems to me that *The Hebrew Lesson* must be further contextualized,
within both the frame of Lévy's production and that provided by his own
statement of his intentions in a representation such as this. Alphonse Lévy
made his reputation, and it was a considerable one in France in the latter
part of the nineteenth century, as a purveyor of Jewish customs and folklore. He exhibited regularly in the Salon, but was best known for his lithographs and illustrations of Jewish family life and religious practice in
Alsace, scenes already old-fashioned and replete with nostalgia when he
depicted them.[12] Lévy was a draftsman of considerable skill, whose efforts

Alphonse Lévy,
*Preparations for
Passover*, c.1900

were consecrated by an exhibition on the premises of *La Plume* in 1897. He
was capable of work of considerable dignity and formal inventiveness, like
the forceful poster of a man in a prayer shawl advertising the exhibition of
his work, or the humorous but still effective *Preparations for Passover*, depicting an Alsatian-Jewish housewife putting herbs in the holiday soup as she
looks out at the spectator challengingly from the bailiwick of her resplendent kitchen; still other works, less formally distinguished but not without
pictorial interest, represent *Saturday Prayer; The Meeting with the Rabbi*, an out-
door scene indicating the Alsatian architecture in the background; *The
Kapora Ceremony*, representing the swinging of a chicken over the heads of
some startled children on the Eve of Yom Kippur; *The Matzo Balls*, also
titled *The Good Jewish Housewife*, showing a buxom matron rubbing her hands
with satisfaction, or flour, as she pauses to look up at the spectator in the
midst of Passover food preparation; and a whole series of representations
of the Jews of Algiers to whom Lévy turned for subject matter later in his
life.[13] Lévy made his intention to celebrate rather than satirize Jewish family
customs and religious practices explicit in a letter he published in *La Plume*
in August, 1895. His inspiration, Lévy declares, was "the beauty, the charms
of the religious group to which I belonged. It is in taking notice of all its
picturesque qualities that I decided to depict it with my feeble talents."

But Lévy buys his benign image of Judaism at a price: the price of difference. By distinguishing between his "good" Jews—"I chose my models among the humble folk, the naively pious villagers for whom the tricks of our over-civilized society were still a mystery"—and the corrupt nogoodniks of the modern city, he makes it clear that he has no truck with the ambitious assimilationists of Paris. "Raised in a simple, humble milieu," the artist declares, "I was able to observe in my childhood the scenes that I try to represent . . . mores and character-types of a race still unspoiled by contact with the great centers. My models have not yet crossed the borders of the villages in Alsace or Lorraine; they are the ancestors of those whom Drumont attacks so vehemently today." And he continues with his apologia for his (rural) Jewish subjects: "The race is valiant, strong in its family virtues, its sobriety, its tenacity . . . and all these virtues are annihilated, are transformed by the emigration to the great cities."[14]

No more than Lautrec, in his poster for the outspokenly anti-Semitic novel of Victor Joze, would Lévy, apparently, look to the urban Jewish financier or businessman for sympathetic models.[15] Like the Mennonites, or Pennsylvania Dutch in the United States, or the country folk represented in the peasant novels of George Sand earlier in the century, called up to support the enterprise of Lévy's literary confrère Daniel Stauben in his *Scenes of Jewish Life in Alsace* in the 1850's, these quaint, marginal, nostalgically isolated Jews of the countryside seem to have been constructed almost explicitly to countervene the hostile representation of the Jews by the French anti-Semites of the period. Above all, Lévy's Jews are harmless and open about their identity—and they belong to the past. They would never try to "mingle," he implies, or to "get above themselves."

One might say that Lévy's representation of his Jewish subjects is in fact a sub-category of a broader representational formation: that reassuring nineteenth-century trope of difference which reconstructs the rural as the timeless, the pious, and the quaintly picturesque in the wake of the various Revolutions—1789, 1830, and 1848—in which portions of the peasantry had played an active and threatening role. Just as the picturesque and timeless peasant was called into representational play in an endless stream of banal Salon paintings during the period, so the "good rural Jew" with his or her charming, timeless customs, superstitions, and folkloristic idiosyncrasies, is summoned up to meet the perceived threat of the assimilated, smart, successful urban Jew, represented so unflatteringly by Lautrec in his Joze posters, or, on a more sinister level, by anti-Semitic caricaturists. One might even think of Chagall's earlier work, combining astutely measured dosages of fantasy, *shtetl* memories, and Cubist formal structure, as providing a Modernist version of this strategy of difference within Jewish representation.

Alphonse Lévy,
The Matzo Balls,
c.1900

I do not mean to imply that the only good Jew in modern representation
is the rural Jew: far from it. The writer Israel Zangwill's popular *Children of
the Ghetto*, as well as the important novel of Henry Roth, *Call It Sleep*, focus
with enormous sympathy, and a sense of the human complexity, on the
plight of the newly transplanted urban Jews of the late nineteenth and early
twentieth century. Indeed, in the construction of Modernity, the shift from
restrictive rural societies, no matter how picturesque, to open, urban ones,
no matter how risky, can be viewed more fruitfully as a liberation rather
than a corruption, for Jews as well as Gentiles, as Marshall Berman has
pointed out in his classic examination of Modernism and Modernity *All
that Is Solid Melts into Air*[16] and as he implies in his analysis of the apocalyptic
final scenes of *Call It Sleep* in this volume.

THE NATURE OF THE CRITERIA

But, to return to our analysis of the specific work of Lévy with which we
started, *The Hebrew Lesson: The Portion*, and the representational ambiguities
that it offers to the interpreter: it seems to me that before we can deal properly with the idea of "ambiguous" semiology in Jewish representation, we
must examine carefully what we have in mind when we talk about a "positive" or a "negative" image of a Jew. We need, that is, to consider the nature

of the criteria themselves, and who has established them, rather than taking for granted that such and such a lithograph is a "good" one or another a "bad" one: we must also take account of the fact that the same image can be put to different uses.

While it is true that the Jew-as-Vampire caricatures discussed by Michèle Cone can only be read as unequivocally negative, since the Jew in question is constructed as the signifier of an allegory of greed, and can be read in no other way, in the case of Lévy's *The Hebrew Lesson*, we must examine the all too easily taken for granted bias in criteria of Jewish negativity itself. Why, for example, does an image which represents a Jew as an old man with a single tooth and a big nose necessarily constitute a "negative" representation or, to put it more forcefully, an "anti-Semitic" one? Doesn't this notion of negativity itself derive from a certain deeply implanted, universalist notion of the "normal" (or more strongly, of the "beautiful"), deriving ultimately from Greek classicism, which condemns all other types to the realm of "otherness" or "deviance?"[17] Similar deviations have been read into the thick lips and dark skin of the Black or even, in the eyes of Winckelmann and his more extreme, gynophobic followers, into the curving breasts and bulging hips of women which "deviate" from the masculine ideal type.[18]

Here, it seems to me, we are forced to take into account the role played by both intentionality and contextuality in the construction of Jewish representation. To what else can we resort when the criteria of judgment are themselves ambiguous or even suspect? It seems to me that in such cases, the intention of the artist, suspect though it has been held in sophisticated critical discourse, as well as the context within which the work was created, must then be called into play. In a work like Lévy's *The Hebrew Lesson*, intentionality must be summoned to assist in the reading of the image. First of all, one needs to know that this is a Jew, a scene of Jewish life, and a scene of Jewish life created by a Jewish artist, for it to assume a sinister or contrarily, a benign, implication. Once one knows that the Jewish artist, Lévy, intended it as one of a series of representations of the practices of the rapidly vanishing Jewish communities of rural Alsace in the nineteenth century, communities which to a large extent ceased to exist after the German occupation of 1871, and which he clearly regarded with the same nostalgia that American Jews lavished on life in the *shtetl*, and that he devoted a great deal of time, warmth, and energy to his creation of *Scènes familiales juives*, we inevitably look at the work somewhat otherwise than if it had been intended as an anti-Semitic caricature.[19] And this is true even when we discover that Lévy, in this series of lithographs, often seems to find caricature "irresistible," while at other times his "tenderness" towards his subjects seems evident.[20]

And much also depends on the eye of the beholder. To the Jewish viewer, especially the religious Jew, or the Jew nostalgic about the vanished life of the rural Jewish communities of Europe, this may seem merely an accurate and basically sympathetic record of how poor (toothless, big-nosed) rabbis and their youthful students looked and behaved in the past. The passing down of Jewish wisdom from one generation to another seems an honorable and praiseworthy practice, certainly one that is completely harmless to non-Jews. To the non-Jew, and above all, to the anti-Semitic observer, who sees otherness as a threat and an insult, such an image might seem to bear witness to Jewish "conspiracy"; how "they" plot to maintain their special difference and apartness, or, more paranoid still, how "they"—ugly, hook-nosed, deformed, clannish—conspire to undermine Gentile hegemony with their secret language and nefarious rituals.

In conclusion, one might say that, as opposed to the implacable simplicity of the names inscribed on the wall of the Pinkas Synagogue, or the grotesqueries of out-and-out anti-Semitic caricature, when it comes to representing Jews, there are no simple formulae to be adopted, no good versus bad representations, and, more germane to the point of this collection, no one-dimensional modes of interpretation that may satisfactorily explicate or exhaust the meanings of representations of Jews and Jewishness—any more than there is a single, simple essential Jewish identity which exists waiting to be discovered. Admittedly, it is more difficult to find work in the visual arts which deliberately problematizes the issue of Jewish identity (rather than merely rendering it problematic by unconscious ambiguities of expression), than in the realm of literature. I am thinking, of course, of the examples of such deliberate refusal of narrative simplicity offered by Joyce and Proust, discussed by Connor and Kristeva respectively here. Nevertheless, certain examples of such problematization, often inscribed by foregrounding the formal structure or visual language of the work in question, immediately come to mind: Claude Lanzmann's film *Shoah*, for example, which refuses the easy pathos of realism; some of the Holocaust memorials described by James Young in his *The Texture of Memory: Holocaust Memorials and Meaning*, like the range of broken shards at Treblinka or the Memorial Tent at Yad Vashem ("stone heaviness on the outside, dark absence inside");[21] or the ambiguously resonant work of the artist Kitaj, one of whose works is reproduced on our cover—all refuse an easy representation of Jewish identity or experience. It is to be hoped that the essays in this volume, like this adventurous work in art and literature, rather than attempting to provide interpretative solutions or reductions of meaning, to foreclose the possibilities of significance, will, on the contrary, problematize the vexed issue of representing Jews or Jewishness by pointing out the multiplicity of possible meanings and the variety of interpretative strategies at the disposal of both authors and audience.

Introduction
Modernity, Identity, Textuality

TAMAR GARB

Modernity and the Jew—Framing the Issues

It is not surprising that the Jew appears as a key figure in so many of the literary, philosophical, and visual products of modern European culture. In the complex and contradictory fabric of Western Christian culture, with all its fissures, divisions, and internal conflicts, the Jew has functioned alternately as its conscience, its alter ego, its abject, its Other. Placed at the source and origin of Christianity whilst representing an eternal witness to the possibility of its denial, the Jew has provided a crucial point of differentiation for Christian theologies, a referent in relation to which the specificity of Christian belief and practice has been demarcated and defined. Unavoidably part of the Christian narrative of self, the Jew also marks the point of rupture which is Christianity's founding moment. Stubborn, recalcitrant, and blind, the Jew has had to be punished not only for the original sin of deicide but also for "his" continued refusal to acknowledge the truth of Christianity and to relinquish "his" own distinctness. The Jew has provided, therefore, a crucial marker of difference both in the master texts of Christian Europe and in some of their most high-minded critiques. Allegorized, abstracted, and reified, the Jew marks the blind spot of the text even as "he" is projected as its non-seeing narrative focus.[1]

Physically too, Jews, in pre- and early modern times, were both a part of and apart from the wider culture, usually living in demarcated areas but engaging in commercial and mercantile practices that brought them into contact with the wider community.[2] Ever present in Christian cities, but physically separated and culturally distinct, the Jew haunted the Gentile imagination. "He" was the stranger within, alternately idealized and vilified, tolerated and condemned.

Ambivalence has been the salient attitude toward the Jew in Christian consciousness. The boundary between Judaism and Christianity could never be firmly policed. The Jew could not function in Christian mythology simply as an object of scorn and hatred. If anything "he" was owed a debt. Christ's own Jewishness had to be acknowledged, and the understanding of Christianity's origins in the Hebrew Bible produced a dependence on the

Jew which fostered its own anxiety-ridden representations. The Jew was the thorn in the flesh of Christian culture, for it could neither completely rid itself of "him" nor accept "his" difference as legitimate and permanent. Christianity needed its Jews to make sense of its own redemptive mission but this usually involved a fantasy of annihilation, if not of Jews themselves then of Jewishness as a system of belief and a code of behavior. Christian Judeophobia was always therefore conflicted: even as it vilified the Jews it recognized their indispensability, both for its own origins and for the possibility of a Second Coming when all differences would disappear in the utopian realization of a universalized Christian paradise.

Amongst the various groups and factions making up that political and geographical terrain that we have come to know as early modern Europe, the Jews occupied a special position. For the most part they were separated, expelled, persecuted, and converted. Brief moments of glorious cultural and religious freedom were flanked by horrendous persecution. Laws regarding their status and rights were alternately liberalized and tightened up. Always they were subject to the whims and caprices of the oligarchies. Visibly different through their dress, language, occupations, and religious practices, most Jews seemed like an alien and strange people to their Gentile neighbors. Ghettoized and circumscribed by local laws, restricted in access to professions and educational establishments, Jewish life in pre- and early modern Europe developed its own communal identity grounded in Jewish ritual practice, the study of the Scriptures, Yiddish cultural expression, and trade. Suspicion surrounded Jewish ethics and religion and a stock supply of images of the Jew—the usurer, the horned devil, the seducer, the drinker of Christian blood, the parasite—became part of Christian folklore and high culture alike. For most Christians, actual Jews were mediated via these stock images, many of which, as we shall see in the essays collected in this book, far outlived the theological worldview and material circumstances of their invention. Indeed, it is the recurrence of these same images in the supposedly secular world of modernity and their terrifying endurability, even today, in the consciousness of post-Soviet Eastern Europeans, for example, that alert us to their continuing power as projection and fantasy. In a world before mechanical reproduction, mass media, and the modern technologies of propaganda, it was through songs and sermons, folk tales, prints, and pamphlets that an image of the Jew was formulated, circulated, and perpetuated. With the advent of mass literacy and the increased possibilities of reproducing and circulating imagery in modern times, these images continued to provide the source material for the anti-Semitic imagination.[3]

For all its suspicion of the Jew's difference, Christian Judeophobia, at least in theory, always retained the possibility of the Jew's redemption.

Conversion could deliver the Jews from their delusions and show them the true path so that their Judaism could be overcome. But baptized Jews, although allowed access to power and wealth, had to behave as Gentiles and confirm the attitudes toward Jews promoted by Christian cultures. They were required to testify to the deficiencies of an anachronistic Judaism which had long outlived its function; as such, they performed a very useful role for the Christian establishment. However, if conversion could deliver the medieval and early modern Jews from the stigma of their identity, this was not the case for Jews in the modern period. Now Jewishness came to be conceived not as a matter of belief but as a racial identity, one which could be observed, measured, understood, and patholo-gized. The construction of the Jew moves, with modernization, from the language of religion to the pseudoscientific mobilization of the category of race in the new nineteenth-century disciplines of anthropology, ethnology, and biology. In one powerful and highly influential strand of the new ratio-nalist discourse of modernity—for all its cosmopolitan rhetoric and emphasis on the rights of the individual—the old feudal hierarchies, which had grounded the superiority of the aristocracy in class and birthright, became replaced by a system of hierarchy based on race. Racial difference came to be perceived as a "fact of nature," one which could be demonstrat-ed and displayed. The new rationalist theorists of modernity set out to trace and account for the physical and cultural changes from the savagery of pre-historic times, conceived as a state of nature, to the present state of civiliza-tion, conceived as a triumph of culture. Needless to say, it was the white Christian male (whether British, German, or French depended on the nationality of the writer in question) who came to represent the apogee of civilization, the most evolved of *homo sapiens*.[4] While the "Negro" was placed at the bottom of the evolutionary scale, Jews were ambivalently placed between the extreme antinomies of blackness and whiteness, always tainted with the one, never quite embraced within the other. Jewishness, unlike Judaism, could not be discarded.[5] It was neither a matter of belief nor custom. It was an essential property of the Jews, their ineradicable nature, rooted in their biology, their psychological make-up, and their cul-tural heritage. Indelibly Other, the Jews' difference became a necessity to the projections of Gentile culture. It was the Jews (amongst others) who could embody the atavistic, animalistic, and affective qualities which civil-ization repressed in the name of a new rational, controlled, and purposeful self and it was they who served as one repository for the violent and sadis-tic fantasies which reasonable behavior disallowed. As such, the Jew func-tioned as an object of projection and potential punishment, providing a legitimate outlet for the enactment of those very fantasies which civiliza-tion forbade.[6]

The transition from the theological paradigm of premodern times to the scientist paradigm of modernity was negotiated via the Enlightenment. The specifically racist attitudes based on the Jews' purported biological difference that emerged during this period came to be called anti-Semitism, the modern form of traditional theological anti-Judaism, now transformed by the ideological appropriation of science and the apparatuses of reason. The racialized construction of the Jews which modernity bequeathed centered as much around their irreducible otherness as their inferiority. This otherness expressed itself in the stigmata of difference which were inscribed on the Jewish body, in the language that Jews spoke, the manner of their thinking, and the patterns of their behavior.[7] In the racialized body of the Jew was expressed "his" cultural and psychic otherness, an otherness which would persist even when the disguises of assimilation and integration had rid the body of its outward signifiers of difference. In the mind of the anti-Semite, nothing, not even the most accomplished performances of the assimilated cosmopolitans of the modern period, could eradicate their essential identity as Jews.

The Enlightenment, or Haskalah as it was called by Jewish thinkers, had for a time held out a promise of liberation from the entrapment of cultural determinism. In its elaboration of the ideals of a true cosmopolitanism based on rights for individuals and nations, it promised the Jews emancipation from the circumscribed life of the ghetto, which came to be associated with the superstitious, mystificatory beliefs of a discredited irrationalism. In the formation of the modern state, with its centralist imperatives and rationalization of resources and workforce, it would have been impossible to allow a semi-autonomous economic community to flourish governed by its own religious courts and laws. Physically liberated from the urban ghettos and *shtetls* (market towns) in which Yiddish culture had developed and flourished, but which were widely regarded as regressive, insular, and second-rate, the Jews would, the protagonists of emancipation argued, be able to participate in the universalizing project of modernity and contribute to the wider culture while benefiting themselves, both culturally and materially. Jews would be granted civil rights for the first time, allowed to move freely in the metropolitan centers of Europe, granted entry to selective educational establishments and professions. Worship and religious practices would become private affairs, confined to the home, the synagogue, and the church. In the polis, everyone would be the same. It was this utopian secularist vision—democratic, anti-feudal, and egalitarian—that provided an impetus for some of the most important revolutionary movements of the modern period, while simultaneously creating the conditions for some of its most reactionary and disastrous consequences.

For liberal Enlightenment protagonists, the common humanity of all subjects far outweighed the specificity of their cultural differences. It was this common humanity that would be allowed to flourish when difference was eradicated. Enlightenment thinkers drew on the universalist fantasies which constituted both the best and the worst of Christian theology, and in which name both its most noble and most scurrilous deeds have been performed, while they envisaged a secular, modern society governed by consensus and conformity, free of the stranglehold of the Church.[8] But this dream was flawed on at least two counts. For one thing, the very rationalism that underpinned the theorization of the new political and social order, and the erosion of old systems of privilege, also provided the basis for the development of those disciplines that erected their own systems of hierarchy and classification, ones that safeguarded the privileges of a white Christian patriarchy even though they based their claims to superiority on the apparently objective findings of science. While this criticism does not discredit reason as such, it certainly throws into question the uses to which it can be put. Secondly, the secularizing and universalizing dream of emancipation, whilst purporting to be inclusive and democratizing, resembled the proselytizing ethos of the Christian missionaries in a fundamental way. It was premised on an eradication of difference that was by no means reciprocal. There was no negotiation of a new shared culture for Christians and Jews, involving a give and take, a symbiosis, or a mutual respect. Rather, Jews were expected to discard their own cultural specificity for a more "rational," "modern," "universal" identity and thereby enter into the "common culture of Man." This involved the relinquishing of language, dress, and religious and cultural expressions of difference in favor of the dominant cultural modes. In the process, the practices of Jews were devalued, parochialized, and stigmatized, those of the wider Christian communities valorized and made to stand for rational, universal values. There were, of course, huge tensions between church and state that precipitated crises of identity for Christian and secular subjects too, but these were not visibly expressed on the body in the same tangible way as they were for Jews. Emancipated Christians were not required visibly to alter their behavior, dress, speech, or manners, either in public or in private.

For the Jews it was different. Even for the most liberal of Enlightenment thinkers like Kant and Herder, the necessary price of emancipation was the destruction of difference. They demanded of Jews that they "alter their natures and give up their way of living."[9] Only then would they themselves be transformed and the wider culture liberated from what Kant called "the vampires of society."[10] Others saw no hope even in this transformative process. Fichte advocated forced removal of Jews to the Holy Land, Voltaire blamed Judaism for everything that was bad in Christianity and held contemporary Jews responsible. Optimistically, many of the Jews of Europe believed that their redemption lay in the renunciation of their identity. They were ready to suppress their Jewishness if it was going to buy them "an admission ticket to Western culture," as Heinrich Heine put it.[11] Progressive Jews in Western Europe embraced their newly won access to the "common culture" and became some of its principal theoreticians and most eloquent critics. They modernized, they transformed Judaism itself so that it would conform to the expectations of Enlightenment culture, they converted, they colluded, they disavowed, and even then, they were trapped by the perverse distortions of that ostensibly rationalist dream that had offered them redemption: they were measured, classified, contained, and eventually exterminated. In the words of Theodor Adorno and Max Horkheimer, writing in 1944, "Those who proclaimed individualism, abstract justice, and the notion of the person are now degraded to the condition of a species."[12] Paradoxically, some of modernity's most avid apologists had become its most abject victims.

Those who discarded Europe and went to America enacted the transition from the Old World to the New World in a physical journey, the journey made memorable in El Lissitzky's "Shifs Carta" and given literary form in the fiction of Henry Roth, Chaim Potok, Bernard Malamud, and others. Tensions between old and new, tradition and modernity, identification and assimilation, become the leitmotifs of Jewish American cultural expression, now made vivid in the novels of Philip Roth and Saul Bellow, now repressed in the illusory dream world of a shared culture as promoted by Hollywood's Jewish cinema moguls.

If in the conditions of modernity the Nation subsumed all its citizens into the formation of a shared, secular culture, it proclaimed this under the rubric of the "Rights of Man," an apparently universal slogan that, in fact, precluded both women and people of color. There were, of course, those who vociferously protested that the category "man" should be an inclusive one, but if legislation, franchise, and civic rights are to be the means by which we judge this ideal, it took a long time for their view to prevail. The Jew's position in this scenario was an awkward one. As I showed earlier, in some versions of nineteenth-century racial science the Jew was "black," the syphilitic representative of a mongrel race, radically different from the healthy "white" nations which "he" threatened to corrupt.[13] Paradoxically, in British imperial discourse the Jew could be embraced in the construction of a Judeo-Christian "common culture" whose mission it was to civilize the world and, simultaneously, could be figured as its dark other, the savage within European consciousness. Indeed, as Bryan Cheyette has argued, it is the radical instability of the construction of the Jew which makes "him" the perfect vehicle through which a self-conscious literary modernism can "explore the limits of its own foundations."[14] It is possible to move, therefore, as we do in this collection, from the excessive stereotyping of Dickens' Jew, Fagin, which articulates so consummately the fears and, despite itself, the desires of mid nineteenth-century England via the screen of realist "objectivity," to the anguished self-reflexiveness of Joyce and Proust in which identity is never a given but always a question posed by the text. In the first, the characterization of the Jew provides a vehicle for a critique of contemporary society, in the second the problematic natures of identity and narration itself are juxtaposed so that neither can be comfortably secured or fixed.

The identity (racial, religious, or whatever) of the Jew made "his" participation in the "family of man" a complicated affair. For female Jews this was even more complex. The Jew as abstraction is always constructed in the masculine; the Jewess, when differentiated as such, invokes fantasies of desire, exoticism, and guilt that specifically address a racialized femininity and an embodied subjectivity. Stereotypes of the male Jew were not all negative. Jewish intelligence and emotionalism could occasionally figure as positive "Jewish traits," but they could just as easily feed into a mythology of the Jew as excessive, dangerous, and suspect. Indeed, the overriding perception of the Jew's captivity in his own body, his physicality, functioned as a symbol of his baseness in the European imagination. Locked in his body, unable to transcend the flesh, be becomes feminized, castrated, weak.[15] Caricatured in the illustrations to Victor Jose by Toulouse-Lautrec or in the propaganda of Vichy and Nazi Germany alike, the lecherous, swarthy body of the male Jew has functioned as a physical manifestation of the baseness of his character, of his incapacity for transcendence, and of his orientation toward worldly rewards. Indeed, the figure of the art dealer, to which so many of the articles in this collection allude, became the archetypal modern male Jew, parasitically existing on the margins of culture without being one of its practitioners: materialistic, interested, and exploitative. Aesthetically limited but financially astute, the Jew could profit from art even though he was incapable of understanding its finer qualities or transcendent value. His monetary machinations diminished Art, subsuming it into the vulgar world of Capital and commerce. He tainted everything that he touched.

The physicality of the male Jew is generally an object of scorn and repulsion. Not so the image of the Jewess. If anything the sexualization of the female Jew involves an idealization that confers upon her an exotic otherness, a sensuality, and beauty, which make her an object of erotic fascination and protect her from some of the more virulent and overt animosity suffered by her male coreligionists. If the Jewess is debased it is via the reduction of her being to her sex, but this often passes as adoration or fascination. While a rootedness in the body involves a diminishing for masculine subjectivity, it provides the appropriate locus for a desirable, if sometimes excessively sexualized, femininity. The image of *la belle juive*, the sensuous, oriental, and beautiful Jewess, is linked to the women of the Old Testament, the Bathshebas, Salomes, and Suzannas who have fed the erotic fantasies of generations of male artists and writers. Specific Jewish women, the sitters of portraits by Ingres and Sargent, as Carol Ockman and Kathleen Adler have shown, or fictitious characters shrouded in the warm glow of pinkness and redness, as Julia Kristeva demonstrates in relation to Proust's "Gilberte" and "Odette," seem to radiate a warm physicality, a liveliness that is neither decorous nor virtuous.[16]

Juxtaposed with the modest abstinence of the chaste Christian woman, the Jewess can stand for warmth, love, and sensuality, a constellation of characteristics that always threatens to spill over into excess. In the Christian imagination, the sexuality of the Jewess is both dangerous and desirable. Modern day Judiths and Salomes, they always threaten to become eternal seductresses, wild, wilful, and untrustworthy. The construction of Jewishness that characterizes the modern period is highly gendered, therefore, despite the widespread mobilization of an apparently non-gender-specific category "the Jew" in both anti- and philo-Semitic discourse. The Jewess invokes a particular set of racist and misogynist fantasies, which involve a double "othering" and consequently a double silencing. To speak as an actual Jewish woman in the face of the dead weight of phantasmatic projections that circulated around the category Jewess was difficult, if not impossible.

The "Jew in the Text" of Western culture covers up the silence and permeates the speech of actual Jews, those men and women negotiating the crisis of modernity from their position as Jewish subjects, speaking in either a devalorized or a borrowed tongue and from a body on which was inscribed their ineluctable difference.

Who is the Jew in the Text?

At the Paris Salon of 1889, E. Belmann, a now forgotten French painter, exhibited a portrait of a gray-bearded man wearing an "oriental" skull-cap, his hunched body bent over a table on which are arrayed various coins, a small metallic vase, ornaments, and a couple of books. In his left hand is poised a small magnifying glass through which he scrutinizes a figurine, held firmly in the right hand (see the frontispiece). The brow is creased, the eyes focused on the hands and object. Half of the face is in shadow, the other half brightly illuminated as if under a spotlight, drawing attention to the one open eye which peers interestedly through the glass, the prominent nose which carries the shaft of light downwards, the busy hands, the objects, and the coins. The discerning gaze of the figure, his self-absorbed demeanor, and obvious preoccupation seal him off from the viewer, containing him within the pictorial world he inhabits. Juxtaposed with the strange buddha-like figure on his table and paralleling him in age and exoticism, the difference of the old man is underlined and emphasized. Represented in oil on canvas, exhibited in a prestigious public art exhibition, reproduced photographically, and circulated as a cover image of the art magazine *L'Art français*, the figure is legible as a Jew even without the apparently neutral "Un Juif" which accompanies it on the reproduced page and in the published Salon catalogue. For this is no particular Jew. This is "un juif," any "juif," any representative of the class of "juifs" which makes sense to the consumers of *art français*. Genre subject rather than individual sitter, he functions in the arena of the typical, the generic. As such he seems to embody, without conflict, that set of characteristics that fix his identity and locate him safely in his own specificity. Rooted in this world, fleshly, materialistic, earthbound, the Jew here concerns himself with objects, assessing their value, scrutinizing their worth, fixing their price. Fixed textually and iconically, he provides a discreet image of difference, one which is kept separate from the Frenchness which frames him, encasing him in a language which describes him and yet which is not his own.

The Jew here is iconically and verbally fixed. In the specificity of this text, he is readable as a Jew. He functions as an aggregate of the stereotypical projections of the culture, which depicts, displays, and reproduces him. Redolent of an "old world," the preemancipatory world of a ghettoized Europe, this image of apparent calm and repose, is simultaneously comforting and potentially explosive. On the one hand, this is an image of the Jew which is reassuringly "old-fashioned," a familiar figure in a changing world, one who is secured in his difference from the "Frenchness" that surrounds him on the page and in the world. On the other hand, this Jew (any Jew) could potentially invoke the fear of contamination, of seepage beyond the boundaries of his Otherness which would put that very Frenchness at risk and call into question the boundary between Self and Other, held in such fragile balance. In 1889, the year of the Universal Exhibition, when France was proclaiming its modernity to the world, the presence of the atavistic, old-fashioned Jew could serve as a pointed reminder that beneath the veil of emancipation of the modern bourgeois Jew lay an irredeemable Jewish character that was not to be trusted. He was not "one of us." Art performed its own function in naturalizing racial, regional, and cultural differences, and in concealing its own ideological agenda behind the veneer of realism and reportage.

The Jew is both in the text and of the text. But the text itself is not confined to those words and images that confront us on the page or on the gallery wall. The text is both specific and general. It refers to the individual works of art and literature—the essays, paintings, objects, and spaces that create an image of the Jew—and to the larger ideas that inform them, to the subtexts, contexts, and metatexts that provide the very framework of signification from which the work is drawn. The images of Toulouse-Lautrec, Lissitzky, and Sargent, the novels of Proust, Dickens, Joyce, and Roth, the philosophies of Sartre and Levinas, the criticism of Rebatet and Mauclair or the Jewish graves at Père Lachaise cemetery are all texts that are saturated with notions of Jewishness and its embodiment in the figure of the Jew. Verbal description constructs a visual image. Pictorial representation draws on ideas elaborated in language. And every text is implicated in that complex fabric of texts that precede it and which create dominant patterns of thought at any given moment. It is that larger text, those broad cultural assumptions that accrue over time and undergo their own mutations and alterations, in relation to which the individual work can be measured and understood.

The Jew in Belmann's text is both a specific image (this Jew in this picture, exhibited, reproduced, and circulated) and signifies in relation to a broader set of assumptions about Jewishness, masculinity, Frenchness, commerce. The Jew in the text retains its specificity, its character as representation, while referring to the wider field of textuality of which it is constituted and to which it, in turn, contributes. We are not here trying to discover "real Jews," "authentic Jews," "good" or "bad Jews." In *The Jew in the Text* our concern is to focus attention on a number of specific instances in which a complex, sometimes contradictory construction of Jewishness, Jewish history, or Jewish memory either forms the central theme or motif of a work or problematizes its very mode of address. The work's identity is implicated in the textual configuring of its Jews, and the Jew's identity is posed as an effect of his or her representation in the work.

The focus of this book is on the representation of the Jew in modern Western culture, but this concern by no means diminishes the experiences of actual Jews in the world. The momentous events of modernity, the conflicts of assimilation and acculturation, the pain and promise of exile and immigration, the horrors of genocide, have all been negotiated and endured, internalized, or disavowed by actual Jews. But the records that we have of these experiences, their traces in peoples' lives, come to us via language and image, embedded in the material culture that we have inherited and generative of their own meanings and interpretations. Whether we examine the deliberate and self-conscious inscribings of identity on the graves at Père Lachaise, the didactic and commemorative installations at the Holocaust Museum in Washington, D.C. the monumental memoirs of Primo Levi, the ambivalent imagery of El Lissitzky, the linguistic and narrative structures of *Call It Sleep*, or the critical reception of Sarah

Bernhardt's performances, we are faced with representations of Jewish experience in modern times which are neither monolithic nor uniform. What it means to be Jewish, despite the claims of the racial essentialists of the nineteenth century or the Fascists of the twentieth century, remains an open question. From the confident self-assertion of Marshall Berman, comfortable in the biblical and secular narratives of Jewish experience that he celebrates here, to the agonizing self-reflexiveness of Adrian Rifkin, worried by the homophobia of traditional Judaism as much as by the anti-Semitism of French culture, there is a world apart. Each has its place in the interrogation of identity which the project of modernity and the history of Jewish experience have bequeathed us.

The situating of the Jew in the text does not deny his or her experience in the world. Indeed, in so far as the text is of the world, in its material as well as its symbolic manifestations, to situate the Jew in the text is both a refusal of some preexisting known and uncontested Jewish identity, which we either accept or reject, and an assertion that it is in the world (and the symbolic systems through which we try to understand it, indeed articulate it at all) that identity is formed. Nor does the negotiation of Jewish identity in the world happen in isolation. It is implicated and inflected by considerations of gender and sexuality, by notions of nation and class. European patriarchal culture has needed its own feminized Jews and exoticized Jewesses, its Fagins and Salomes, and Jews in turn have negotiated these stereotypes whether in the self-parodying mode of Woody Allen, or the outrageous, theatrical gestures of Sandra Bernhard. "Real" Jews and "fictitious" Jews occupy the same representational theater, one in which the masquerades of performative subjectivity can just as easily take their cues from fiction as the characterizations and codes of art can call upon life as their model and source.

In the case of the cover of *L'Art français*, the "Jew in the Text" is both Belmann's model as represented in the painting, its life as a reproduced image on the cover of a prestigious French art magazine, and the framing ideas that brought these into being and made them legible to their contemporary audience. Further, that mediocre and now forgotten image, useful for its banal typicality, is now asked to do more work in this volume of critical essays, a book that seeks to explore those fantasies, fictions, and desires which have constituted the text of represented Jewishness in modern culture. That their consequences have reached far beyond the text, into the lives and deaths of men and women in our time, makes them all the more urgently the product of a culture that we have a responsibility to try to understand.

1

Neither Black Nor White: The Figure of "the Jew" in Imperial British Literature

BRYAN CHEYETTE

At the beginning of his anonymous *Nina Balatka* (1867), Anthony Trollope introduces his Jewish hero, Anton Trendellsohn, with the following description: "He was very dark—dark as a man can be and yet show no sign of colour in his blood. No white man could be more dark and swarthy than Anton Trendellsohn" (11).[1] Trendellsohn is, equivocally, as "dark" as a man can be who happens also to be "white." It is precisely this uncertainty about where the borders lie between a racialized black and white that is the subject of this essay. That Trollope should have chosen what he calls a "very Jew among Jews" (11) to illustrate this indeterminacy is not, I believe, a coincidence. What I want to show is that the figure of "the Jew" exposes widespread tensions in imperial culture concerning the whiteness and racial purity of British society.

Martin Bernal, the author of the controversial book *Black Athena* (1987), has documented the prevailing anxieties which have historically been associated with the Afroasiatic roots of European classical civilization. He has demonstrated, comprehensively, that a good deal of the racial discourse surrounding a supposedly irredeemable black inferiority is implicitly concerned with the presumed whiteness of European culture. The apprehension in Victorian Britain concerning the color of the ancient Egyptians or the race of the Semites was, Bernal believes, a bid to expunge its seemingly impure racial history.[2] What I will attempt to establish is that the figure of "the Jew" had a specific role in relation to this quest for national or European purity. The inability of British culture to categorize Jews as either black or white was, I will argue, an important aspect of this larger anxiety.

My approach specifically opposes postcolonial theorists who maintain that there was, historically, a homogenous and dominant white "Western Judeo-Christian" culture. Edward Said, in his *Culture and Imperialism* (1993), has followed the theorist Henry Louis Gates in reinforcing this contention. It is undoubtedly the case that colonialists invariably resembled Benjamin Disraeli, the founding father of the British Empire, in arguing that imperialism enacted the superiority of Judeo-Christian values throughout the world. There is a danger, however, in simply reinforcing Disraeli's belief that Judeo-Christianity was a homogenous "common culture."[3] As the literature under disucussion will show, many imperialists were unable to contain "the Jew" within their rigid racial hierarchies. As opposed to postcolonial theory, many colonial writers, in fact, found it impossible to subsume unproblematically "the Jew" as a facile aspect of dominant white oppression. What is interesting about these colonial writers is the transparent difficulties that they had in making Jews unambivalent—fixed in their whiteness or Judeo-Christian superiority. My hope is that by concentrating on the ambivalence of "the Jew," I will make it easier to historicize the kind of unstable and promiscuous identities, and multiple and impure national traditions, that all agree are needed to rethink the certainties of the West. I will begin with a detailed reading of one of the most ambivalent imperial writers, John Buchan.

At one point in Buchan's *Prester John* (1910), the Reverend John Laputa, presumed heir to Prester John, attempts to gain African independence and makes a priestly intercession on behalf of his people. Buchan's colonial persona comments as follows:

> He prayed—prayed as I never heard man pray before—and to the God of Israel! It was no heathen fetish he was invoking, but the God of whom he had often preached in Christian kirks. . . . He pled with God to forget the sins of his people, to recall the bondage of Zion. It was amazing to hear these bloodthirsty savages consecrated by their leader to the meek service of Christ. An enthusiast may deceive himself, and I did not question his sincerity. I knew his heart, black with all the lusts of paganism. I knew that his purpose was to deluge the land with blood. But I knew also that in his eyes his mission was divine, and that he felt behind him all the armies of Heaven. (106)

Elsewhere in the novel Laputa is described as a "commanding" figure whose "voice was the most wonderful thing that ever came out of a human mouth" (25). Rather like George Du Maurier's evil genius Svengali, who is musically gifted but racially depraved, Laputa has both a "divine" mission and is a "bloodthirsty savage." This typical Buchan duality is indicated specifically with reference to Laputa's Judeo-Christianity. The "God of Israel" and the "bondage of Zion" are pointedly a key aspect of Laputa's pseudo-Calvinist rhetoric that threatens to undermine the colonial Church of Empire in Africa. What is more, Laputa is said to have "none of the squat and preposterous Negro lineaments, but a hawk nose like an Arab, dark flashing eyes and a cruel and resolute mouth" (25). Disraeli, whom Buchan much admired, had long since argued that Jewish and Arab "semites" were in fact white "aryans" or "purer caucasians."[4] By emphasizing Laputa's "Arab" features, Buchan follows Disraeli and places Laputa at the top of his crude imperial hierarchy. The uneasy location of Laputa on the borders of Africa and Europe is summarized in the following formula: "[Laputa] was black as my hat, but for the rest he might have sat for a figure of a Crusader" (25). Identified with both the history of colonizing European Crusaders and an inferior black Africa, Laputa has the characteristic ambivalent qualities of many of Buchan's most terrifying villains.

What is interesting about Laputa, in terms of my argument, is the extent to which he is partially transformed by Buchan into a Semitic figure which signifies, above all, his threat to Empire. Only by employing the divine rhetoric of Judeo-Christianity is Laputa able to bring about African independence. Laputa is, moreover, Semitic in Disraeli's terms of being a natural aristocrat. Thus, we are told that Laputa is "a born leader of men and as brave as a lion . . . there's fineness and nobility in him . . . He has the heart of a poet and a king" (79). But it is precisely when these aristocratic qualities become overly attractive that Laputa is most violently stereotyped. In the end, he is consistently described as a "blustering savage" (147) or a "savage transported in the presence of his fetish" (157), and any identification with Laputa is replaced by repulsion. There is throughout a tension between Buchan's self-conscious use of the language of Judeo-Christianity (with Laputa, at one point, assuming the role of a latter-day Samuel) and a racial discourse which deems Africa to be the savage Other of Western civilization. Buchan's colonial narrator is said to have "looked into the heart of darkness and the sight terrified me" (112), and it is these racialized fears of African independence that, finally, results in the absolute differentiation between the narrator and Laputa.

Laputa's equivocal characterization also feeds into the more general ambivalence of Buchan's Judeo-Christian vocabulary which is, in turn, split between laudatory biblical references to the Old Testament and racialized references to contemporary Jews. Buchan's colonial narrator views himself as being "in the hands of my Maker, watching, like the Jews of old, for a sign" (156). At the same time, he conspicuously "lusts" for "treasure of jewels and gold" (97) and pointedly ends his narrative with a "very considerable fortune" (200). However, in case this makes Buchan's narrator too stereotypically "Jewish," we are warned from the beginning that "Jew and Portugese traders" dealt in stolen diamonds and that the British have "a lot of trouble with the vermin" (31) who profit from these thefts. Just as Laputa's desirable Semitic depths and noble lineage are juxtaposed with references to him as a "savage," the novel's Judeo-Christianity is similarly undermined by references to these contemporary "vermin."

The flawed transformation of Laputa into a Semite indicates the extent to which the figure of the Jew, more typically, could provide a peculiarly radical form of ambivalence in relation to the Empire. Laputa's simultaneous attraction and repulsion is specifically related to the Disraelian formulation of imperialism as the living embodiment of civilizing Judeo-Christian values. Buchan's equivocation toward Laputa is also reflected in his distinct unease with the Judaic dimension of empire. This can be especially illustrated in a story originally published in the same year as *Prester John* called "The Grove of Ashtaroth" (1910) and collected in *The Moon Endureth: Tales and Fancies* (1912). In this story, Buchan explicitly rewrites Laputa as a Jew. The problem for Buchan is in his representation of Jews as unequivocally white so that they can fit straightforwardly into his ethnocentric notions of what constitutes European history. Just as Laputa needed to be whitened, so that he could be a leader who seriously threatened the Empire, Jews were often situated uneasily on the borderline between black and white.

This racial uncertainty is at the heart of "The Grove of Ashtaroth," which is about a supposedly unmistakably white Jew named Lawson, who is a "born colonial at heart," although, we are told, he does not "propose to become the conventional English gentleman" (100). Lawson is one of many colonial financiers in southern Africa but his unusual racial "pedigree," especially signified in his eyes, "marked him out from the ordinary blonde type of our countrymen." His eyes, we are told, "were large and brown and mysterious, and the light of another race was in their odd depths" (100). It turns out that Lawson had a "grandfather who sold antiques in a back street at Brighton [who] still frequented the synagogue," and a mother who was "a blonde Saxon from the Midlands" (100–01). This Semitic dimension causes Lawson to be possessed by the goddess Ashtaroth when he builds a house in a desolate grove in southern Africa. By the end of the story, Lawson is turned from a "gentleman" into a "brute" (109):

> Ashtaroth was the old goddess of the East. Was it not possible that in all Semitic blood there remained, transmitted through the dim generations, some craving for her spell? I thought of the grandfather in the back street at Brighton and of those burning eyes upstairs. (116)

In this regressive racial state, Lawson indulges in grotesque pagan rites akin to "black magic": "the dance grew swifter and fierce. I saw the blood dripping from Lawson's body, and his face ghastly white above his scarred breast" (119). Here Lawson is indistinguishable from Laputa in *Prester John* who, as we have seen, similarly prays to the "God of Israel" with his heart "black with the lusts of paganism." Whereas Laputa is Europeanized so that he can become an African leader, Lawson, his mirror image, is blackened to show that all but the purest of Anglo-Saxon races can potentially pose a threat to the Empire. In another story called "The Kings of Orion," also collected in *The Moon Endureth*, Buchan continues to reinforce the idea of "the Jew," however assimilated into British culture, as being precariously on the borders of whiteness. In this story, in fact, Jews are specifically "Levantine" and are most explicitly associated with imperiling the Empire in eastern Africa. Buchan's narrator is quite blunt about the dangers of Jewish colonialists:

> For our sins we got a brand of Levantine Jew, who was fit for nothing but making money and making trouble. They were always defying the law, and then, when they got into a hole, they squealed to the Government for help, and started a racket in the papers about the weakness of the Imperial power. (243)

When the behavior of these Levantine Jews did eventually cause chaos in eastern Africa, Buchan's narrator takes his *sjambok* (club) to one of them so that he becomes "soap and butter" (246) in his hands. An ordinary "Tommy" then goes on to discover the greatness of the Kings of Orion by singlehandedly putting down the native uprising. As part of the uprising, "fat Jew boys, with diamond rings on dirty fingers and greasy linen cuffs, kept staring at us with twitching lips; and one or two smarter fellows . . . tried to show their pluck by [making] nervous jokes" (259). There is no doubt about the unequivocal "blackness" of the Levantine Jews in this story, as they are all absolutely cowardly and treacherous. The extreme ambivalence of Lawson in "The Grove of Ashtaroth" is here resolved in a series of crude racial stereotypes that is not unlike the reduction of Laputa to a "savage" at the end of *Prester John*. During his heroic exploits, Buchan's Tommy pointedly prays to the "God of Israel" (259) to show just how far the deceitful "fat Jew boys" have departed from their biblical origins.

The close juxtaposition of "The Kings of Orion" and "The Grove of Ashtaroth" in *The Moon Endureth* shows the extent to which Jews could be represented simultaneously as both black and white or, in other words, as racial inferiors and ideal colonialists. It is precisely this racial uncertainty that makes "the Jew" such an unsettling imperial presence. Buchan, because of his lifelong admiration for Disraeli, was the first to acknowledge when a character was, as he put it *The Three Hostages* (1924), "the whitest Jew since the Apostle Paul" (17). But, as the figure of Lawson demonstrates, such white Jews were often indistinguishable in Buchan's fiction from their black counterparts.

Other writers, such as Rudyard Kipling and Henry Rider Haggard, who had some slight knowledge of Ethiopian Jews in Africa, or of Jewish communities in India, were less inclined to whiten even Jewish colonialists. In his novel *Queen Sheba's Ring* (1910), Rider Haggard, for instance, portrays "Abyssinian Jews" (19), known as the Abati, in the following terms: "they look something like Jews, practise a very debased form of the Jewish religion ... but are in the last stage of decadence from interbreeding" (19). In this novel, Jews and Africans are in fact indistinguishable and provide a telling contrast with white colonial Jews who were helping to build up the Empire in Africa. What is interesting about Haggard's novel is his use of the Abati, the professed offspring of Soloman and Sheba, as an allegory for the potential unpreparedness of Britain in the lead up to the First World War. The Abati are, like the British, a once great nation who have since become depraved due to a growing cowardice, materialism, and hedonism.[5] Their leader, Maqueda, makes it clear why she cannot help the British against the militaristic Fung (who echo contemporary stereotypes of the Teuton): "My people are worn out; they have forgot their faith and gone astray, as did Israel" (106). The contrast between a decadent contemporary Israel, and its illustrious biblical counterparts, proves to be a fruitful analogy with the imperial British who are, like the Jews, in danger of rejecting their "chosen" role as civilizing colonialists. This analogy, in fact, achieved an early popular appeal in the well-known fourth stanza of Kipling's poem "Recessional" (1897):

> If, drunk with sight of power, we loose
>   Wild tongues that have not Thee in awe,
> Such boastings as the Gentiles use,
>   Or lesser breeds without the Law—
> Lord God of Hosts, be with us yet,
> Lest we forget—lest we forget!

As in *Queen Sheba's Ring*, the imperial race in this stanza is identified with the biblically chosen Jews—as opposed to the boastful "Gentiles"—who have subsequently become "drunk with sight of power." By ignoring the responsibilities that go with their superior racial destiny, the "chosen" English nation threatens to deteriorate into "lesser breeds without the Law." Haggard's use of the Abati, as an example of how a once great civilization has become indistinguishable from these "lesser breeds," results in a good deal of unresolved racial anxiety in *Queen Sheba's Ring*.

On the one hand, the novel's plot can be crudely summarized in relation to a fixed racial hierarchy: "we are three white men here consorting with a mob of quarter-bred African Jews and one real lady" (136). But the reference to "quarter-bred African Jews" gives some idea of the arbitrary racial categorization of the Abati in the novel. The Abati are the progeny of the "lost tribes of Israel" (18) but they have, over the centuries, interbred with the local population. Throughout the novel they are therefore both part of the "lesser breeds without the Law" as well as living remnants of a superior Judeo-Christianity. When Sergeant Quick describes the latter-day Queen of Sheba, Maqueda, as a "nigger woman," his master Oliver Orme replies: "I never used such words . . . Good heavens! It's a desecration" (153). The rough-hewn Quick, accepting his master's caveat, promptly concludes that "although she is half a Jew, and I never could abide the Jews, [she] is the sweetest and loveliest and the best and the bravest little woman that ever walked God's earth" (153). Within a page, the contemporary Queen of Sheba has been transformed from a "nigger woman" into "the bravest little woman that ever walked God's earth." Such incommensurable representations are to be found throughout *Queen Sheba's Ring*.

The fact that Haggard is unable to categorize the Abati in any stable way clearly undermines his all-important subtext that the Abati signify the dangers of England dropping its imperial guard. The Abati are both "Jews" and "niggers" who belong simultaneously to Israel and Africa. This irresolvable uncertainty eventually resulted in Haggard calling for a Jewish Napoleon to lead Jews into Palestine, as well as his promotion of a Jewish conspiracy theory where the Jews were cast as the destroyers of empire.[6] This inability to categorize Jews as white or black, good or evil—so that they could be safely placed within a manichean law of colonialism—is a theme taken up by Kipling with particular regard to the Jews of India. In two stories, "Jews in Shushan" and "His Chance in Life," Kipling illustrates the difficulties of trying to subsume Indian Jews within imperial "law."

Originally collected in *Life's Handicap* (1891), "Jews in Shushan" centers around the figure of "Ephraim the Jew," as he is known to the natives of Shushan. He is introduced initially as a rather "meek" debt collector who wishes to build a synagogue in Shushan by forming a prayer quorum of ten Jews. After his initial "meek" appearance—"never was Jew more unlike his dread breed" (338)—Ephraim is, however, quickly transformed into a "dread" example of the dangers of Judaic particularism. When the door is opened, which shuts Ephraim "off from the world of the Gentile" (341), he is seen holding a "half-maddened sheep" as the "butcher to our [Jewish] people":

> He was attired in strange raiment . . . and a knife was in his mouth. As he struggled with the animal between the walls, the breath came from him in thick sobs, and the nature of the man seemed changed . . . A glimpse of Ephraim busied in one of his religious capacities was no thing to be desired twice. (339–40)

As with the "black magic" rituals of Lawson and Laputa, Ephraim is here situated outside the Judeo-Christian values of empire and is, thus, able to unleash all kinds of "primitive" destablizing forces. Kipling comments rather po-facedly that Ephraim "set at naught the sanitary regulations of a large, flourishing, and remarkably well-governed Empire" (341). Ephraim's quest to build a Jewish community in Shushan is thwarted by the death of his children and the other congregants, so disobeying the Law of empire is severely punished in this story. What is more, "Jews in Shushan" ends on the disparaging racial note of a subaltern whistling "Ten Little Nigger Boys," which is described as the "dirge of the Jews of Shushan" (342). This is an obvious allusion to Ephraim's quest to form a prayer quorum of ten Jews in Shushan. The subaltern's abusive point of closure conspicuously brings together "the Jew" and "the nigger" as racial primitives who need to be governed by a superior colonial power.

In "His Chance in Life," which is collected in *Plain Tales From the Hills* (1888), the unequivocal blackness of Ephraim is reversed by Kipling when a black Jew is momentarily transformed into a white man. Set on the racial borderline where "the last drop of White blood ends and the full Black tide sets in" (71), the story concerns the "very black" Michele D'Cruze who has only "seven-eighths native blood in his veins." The other blood in him is part Portuguese, part "Yorkshire platelayer," and part "black Jew of Cochin" (73). In the divided racial context of Kipling's Indian stories, D'Cruze finds himself confronted with a native riot and a local police inspector who regards him as a "Sahib" because of the "old race-instinct which recognizes a drop of White blood as far as it can be diluted" (75). Kipling notes caustically that "the man with the Cochin Jew and the menial uncle in his pedigree" was "the only representative of English authority in the place" (75). By bowing to this "authority" and sending for the British Army to stem the riot, D'Cruze's heart becomes "big and white in his breast" (76) and he learns to love a woman who is his social superior. But when faced with the authentic sign of "Our Authority" (74), a young English officer, D'Cruze "felt himself slipping back more and more into the native" as the "white drop" of blood in "his veins" began to "die out" (77).

What is clear from "His Chance in Life" and "Jews in Shushan" is that whether a Jew was white or black depended ultimately on a wider relationship to an exclusively British imperial authority. This law applied especially to "dark Israel" because of its dangerous indeterminacy which meant that it could be both white and black at the same time. That D'Cruze was to end up earning an imperial salary of 66 rupees, to pay for his fiancée's dowry, contrasts markedly with Ephraim's loss of his family and friends for daring to practise Judaism in the face of the law of empire. Such were the stark options open to Kipling's Indian Jews situated awkwardly on the borderline between white and black.

In *The Light That Failed* (1891), Kipling's artist hero, Dick Heldar, describes a passenger on a train as "a sort of Negroid-Jewess-Cuban, with morals to match" (131). Having said that, the racial categorization of "Negroid-Jews" was a commonplace in European society from the mid-nineteenth century onwards.[7] The fiction of Buchan, Haggard, and Kipling all shows the extent to which Jews could be deemed to be black, even in relation to a Judeo-Christian tradition that was apparently at the heart of empire. But one should not, in fact, underestimate the intense arbitrariness of Semitic racial designations in imperial culture. G. K. Chesterton, for example, wrote a story called "The Queer Feet," collected originally in *The Innocence of Father Brown* (1911), in which Lever, Chesterton's acculturated Jewish villain, physically changes in relation to his misdeeds. As the story progresses, Lever speaks with a "deepening accent" (74) and his skin turns from a "genial copperbrown" into a "sickly yellow" (73). Chesterton, who often portrayed a supposedly Jewish "negro vitality," wanted to show that however assimilated "the Jews" were, their innate racial characteristics would eventually come to the surface.[8] For British imperialist writers, the very changeability of these characteristics could threaten the fixed hierarchies that, above all, defined the Empire.

It is clear from these examples that the racial identity of "the Jew" was not simply determined biologically but varied radically within and between individual cultural and political contexts. The racial indeterminacy of "the Jew" can, thus, also be illustrated in settings which contrast starkly with the imperial realm of Buchan, Haggard, and Kipling. In Dorothy Richardson's *Pilgrimage* sequence of novels, for example, written between 1914 and 1938, various Jewish characters become identified with Miriam Henderson, the alienated and diasporic heroine of the novels. Although Richardson is writing from a radical feminist viewpoint, the same processes of identification and differentiation with regard to the Jews in her fiction clearly replicate her male imperialist counterparts. Toward the end of Richardson's *Deadlock* (1921), the racial slipperiness of "the Jew" is made particularly explicit. In an extraordinary encounter in a small London teashop, Miriam Henderson and Michael Shatov, a socialist Zionist, postpone their mutual recriminations about the possibility of women's freedom in relation to what Miriam had earlier called the "mysterious fact of Jewishness" (193). One "deadlock" is replaced by another as Miriam finds herself "frozen ... by the presence of a negro":

Miriam sat frozen, appalled by the presence of a negro. He sat near by, huge, bent, snorting and devouring, with a huge black bottle at his side. Mr Shatov's presence was shorn of its alien quality. He was an Englishman in the fact that he and she could *not* sit eating in the neighbourhood of this marshy jungle. ... Yet the man had hands and needs and feelings. Perhaps he could sing. He was at a disadvantage, an outcast. There was something that ought to be said to him. She could not think what it was. In his oppressive presence it was impossible to think at all. Every time she sipped her bitter tea, it seemed that before she should have replaced her cup, vengence would have sprung from the dark corner. Everything hurried so. There was no *time* to shake off the sense of contamination. It *was* contamination. The man's presence was an outrage on something of which he was not aware. (217).

Miriam's paranoid sense of being "contaminated" and of being frozen into silence by an unexplainable but vengeful animal-like presence is precisely related to the imperial representations of the Jew in her day. By displacing these representations onto a rampantly potent "negro"—"with a huge black bottle at his side"—Miriam is able, as she says, no longer to think of Shatov as a Jewish racial Other or even a threatening male: "Mr Shatov's presence was shorn of its alien quality." Shatov, in his whiteness and assumed Eurocentricity, is finally identical to Miriam in her Englishness but only after his "alien" qualities have been so nakedly displaced onto the "marshy jungle" of Africa. It is the "black form in the corner"—no longer with "hands and needs and feelings"—who is said to "crush" Miriam's "thread of thought" (217). Instead of Shatov, it is now "the negro" who is the potentially "liberating" Other who must be faced before Miriam can speak:

> In the awful presence she had spoken herself out, found and recited her best, most liberating words. . . . Light, pouring from her speech, sent a radiance about the thick black head and its monstrous bronze face. He might have his thoughts, might even look them, from the utmost abyss of crude male life, but he had helped her, and his blind unconscious outlines shared the unknown glory. (219)

The interdependence between the "liberation" of the bourgeois woman and, in this case, the racial exclusion of the black Other connects in part Richardson's *Deadlock* with Charlotte Brontë's *Jane Eyre*.[9] The self-immolation of the Creole woman in Bronte's novel is the prelude to Jane Eyre's own partial freedom in the same way that the "unconscious outline" of "the negro" shares in the "glory" of Miriam's growing sense of separation from Shatov. What is interesting in this context is the blatant arbitrariness of this form of Othering which positions "the negro" in exactly the same role that "the Jew" had occupied only a few pages before. When placed next to "the negro" Shatov is no longer an unEnglish "alien." He has moved from being black to being white and, by extension, from being male to being female. By temporarily resolving her uncertain identification with and differentiation from Shatov, "the negro" makes it possible for Miriam to see the "light" and realize, finally, why she should "liberate" herself from her Jewish admirer.

There is, of course, an important distinction to be made between Richardson's use of an ambivalent racial discourse and that of her male imperial counterparts. The point of *Deadlock* is to show, precisely, how

Miriam's perceptions of Shatov's Jewishness are variable and contingent. The fact that they can be so easily transferred onto another object of fear and desire shows the degree to which such stereotypes are arbitrary and capricious. Richardson's male counterparts, however, in working within fixed racial hierarchies, can only ever view "the Jew"—neither black nor white, neither good nor evil—in futile manichean terms. That "the Jew" cannot be situated easily in relation to rigid colonial "law" should be clear from the writings of Buchan, Haggard, and Kipling. What is more, by questioning the superiority and purity of the Judeo-Christian tradition, these writers themselves undermine one of the supposed bastions of empire. Their inability to contain "the Jew" in relation to the presumed superior history and culture of the West, makes this figure, above all, a fearful and subversive double in their fiction. Such anxious equivocations by the writers of empire contrast starkly with the reductive simplicities of many postcolonial theorists writing today.[10]

2

Charles Dickens' Oliver Twist: *Fagin as a Sign*

JULIET STEYN

Fagin, I fear, admits only of one interpretation; but [while] Charles Dickens lives the author can justify himself or atone for a great wrong on a whole though scattered nation.

So wrote Mrs. Eliza Davies to Charles Dickens in 1863.[1] Her letter, which demonstrated more than unease, castigated Dickens for his particular characterization of the Jew, Fagin, in *Oliver Twist*.[2] She accused him of encouraging "a vile prejudice against the despised Hebrew." Mrs. Davies contrasted Dickens' attitude to the Jews with his well-known position of championing the causes of the oppressed. The anger and anxiety displayed in her letter revealed that she considered the Jews in Britain to be subjugated and generally despised and as such, indeed, more than worthy of Dickens' usual philanthrophic attitude.

As a way of marking his atonement, Mrs. Davies suggested to Dickens that he give his support to a convalescent home for the Jewish poor which was to be a named memorial to Lady Montefiore, wife of the financier and philanthropist Sir Moses. Dickens' reply was to offer a nominal sum of money to the charity. However, he made it plain that this donation was not to be understood as an admission of the validity of her complaint: rather than atone for his depiction of Fagin, Dickens chose instead to justify it: "Fagin in Oliver Twist is a Jew, because it unfortunately was true of the time in which the story refers, that that class of criminal almost invariably was a Jew."[3] Here Dickens unproblematically represents Fagin as a criminal type. He further detailed his reasons for doing so in the Preface to *Oliver Twist*:

> It appeared to me that to draw a knot of such associates in crime as really did exist; to paint them in all their deformity, in all their wretchedness, in all the squalid misery of their lives; to show them as they really were, for ever skulking uneasily through the dirtiest paths of life, with the great black ghastly gallows closing up their prospect, turn them where they might; it appeared to me that to do this, would be to attempt a something which was needed, and which would be a service to society. And I did it as I best could.[4]

"Best" in this context can be understood as the accurate and true depiction of characters. These in themselves were understood as reflections of what actually existed, that is to say, for Dickens, as reflections of reality itself. Evil is rendered specific, as anti-social and criminal behavior—as a socio-logical fact—with all the conviction that Enlightenment science could muster.

Dickens defended his story on the grounds of realism. For many mid-nineteenth-century writers and artists, realism was connected, through a chain of complicities and associations, to scientific materialism, which itself had come to be understood as constituting the truth. Realism promised enlightened understanding and the possibility of social reform. From this point of view, *Oliver Twist* is concerned with the realities posed by the particular time and space of Victorian London and can be understood thus as a critical and moral comment on the harsh and inhumane Poor Laws and their debasing effects on people when treated solely as bodies. Here Dickens the nineteenth-century social reformer speaks: the novel was itself a social commentary, and moral didacticism was for him a social duty. The realistic portrayal of the criminal Fagin, the *Jew*, was a way of articulat-ing a threat to social reform.

By the time Mrs. Davies presented her challenge to Dickens, 25 years after *Oliver Twist* appeared, social Darwinism was providing him with the evidence that each and every Jew could be classified and understood according to the exigencies of the science of race. *Oliver Twist* was written at a moment when scientific investigations were initiating the processes of elaborating empirical and descriptive evidence to define differences between races which were considered essential, that is to say, differences of nature or kind. Human nature, behavior, and language, it was argued, sprang directly from biology. Biology, intelligence, and physical attributes were made central to definitions of racial identity and seen to support the idea of racial hierarchies. Dickens explained to Mrs. Davies, again without equivocation, that Fagin "is called 'The Jew', not because of his religion, but because of his race."[5] Throughout the narrative of *Oliver Twist*, Dickens refers to Fagin as "The Jew." It is only in direct speech that he is given his proper name. If ever he is called "Jew" to his face it is in a derisory manner. Again and again, *Jew* is remarked upon in a language of scorn and loathing. When a young Jew appears in the novel he is figured by and in the image of Fagin and is described as "nearly as vile and repulsive in appearance" as Fagin himself (91). With age, because of his biological inheritance, he would necessarily achieve the vileness of his mentor. If the young Jew replicates Fagin then it is already determined that Jews are heinous: this is their Jewish inheritance, their biological destiny. Dickens uses theories of race to justify to Mrs. Davies his representation of Jews:

> If I were to write a story in which I pursued a Frenchman or a Spaniard as the "Roman Catholic," I should do a very indecent and unjustifiable thing; but I make mention of Fagin as the Jew because he is one of the Jewish people and because it conveys that kind of idea of him, which I should give my readers of a Chinaman by calling him Chinese.[6]

Fagin stands in for all Jewish people, past, present, and future. In *Oliver Twist* Dickens constructs *Jew* through an elaborate synthesis of imagery from the past, made credible in the present and viable for the future, through his application of social and racial theories.

By the 1860's discourses of race had seized the imagination of the European mind and sensibility. So much so that people as "unlike each other as Matthew Arnold, Oscar Wilde, James Frazer, and Marcel Proust" not only agreed with racial categories but actively constructed and used them—as did the enlightened, radical writer Dickens.[7] But his was not the only possible view of the *Jew* in nineteenth-century England. A report, dating from 1831 in the *Edinburgh Review*, on the proceedings of the "Civil Disabilities and Privations affecting Jews in England," suggested that being a Jew was like being born with "red hair" and was as such an accident of birth. The report went on to raise a question:

> If all the red-haired people in Europe had, for centuries, been outraged and oppressed, banished from this place, imprisoned in that, deprived of their money, deprived of their teeth, convicted of the most improbable crimes on the feeblest evidence, dragged at horses' tails, hanged, tortured burned alive . . . what would be the patriotism of gentlemen with red hair?[8]

The point of politics, continued the report, is to make all people—irrespective of their specific histories—into patriotic citizens. Explicit here is the notion that people are socially moulded: they are subject to and subjects of change. In a speech in the House of Commons in 1830, Macaulay, then a Liberal Member of Parliament (later the famous historian Lord Macaulay), also used social and moral arguments to support the extension of citizenship to the Jews. The history of England is, he claimed, "made up of wrongs suffered and injuries endured by them."[9] Dickens in *Oliver Twist*, against such liberal voices, represents Fagin as an irredeemable obstacle to social change and as unchangeable. Sikes declares that being with Fagin reminds him

> of being nabbed by the devil . . . There never was another man with such a face as yours, unless it was your father, and I suppose *he* is singeing his grizzled red beard by this time, unless you came straight from the old 'un without any father at all betwixt you: which I shouldn't wonder at, at bit. (276)

Dickens gives Fagin red hair which, with its demonic references, serves in the novel as a determining feature of Fagin's physical and racial identity: the Jew was born demonic, existing inevitably and always outside the dominion of civilized society. Fagin is presented as a stranger to civility. In an exchange with Nancy, he says, "We must have civil words." Nancy replies "civil words, you villain" (100). For Dickens the Jew cannot be a full member of polite society. He is beyond the Pale of civilized life. The *Jew* is a threat to order and Fagin represents a throwback to earlier, "primitive," preenlightened times.

The philologist Ernest Renan described the Semite as "primitive" and deficient, thus subordinating him to the Indo-European race. It is through the category Semite that *Jew* becomes classified as a race. Futhermore, what the Semitic *Jew* is seen to lack is precisely what defines the Indo-European as superior:

> In all things the Semitic race . . . appears an incomplete race by virtue of its simplicity. The race—if I dare use the analogy—is to the Indo-European Family what a pencil sketch is to a painting; it lacks that variety, that amplitude, that abundance of life which is the condition of perfectibility. Like those individuals who possess so little fecundity that, after a gracious childhood they attain only the most mediocre virility, the Semitic nations . . . have never been able to achieve true maturity.[10]

In this account the male Semite is the child of humankind and ineffectual and weak. The Semite is incomplete: he is intellectually and sexually immature. Fagin too is an embodiment of the primitive. Dickens' description of him is complex and contradictory. Fagin is drawn as ossified (primitive) and shrewd and cunning. Such accounts of the "primitive" marked by denial and disavowal are a register of the complex feelings and fears that the *Jew* aroused.

The figuration of a Jewish type is both a model of and for identity: an identity formed and realized. An identity is assumed between concept and object, between *Jew* (as a regulating idea) and real Jews.[11] The subject, Fagin, is understood as identical with Jew. Jewish identity formation is overdetermined and saturated with meanings. It is subject to endless repetition. What is made to seem repellently alien in *Oliver Twist* was in fact all too familiar: Fagin is a reiteration of the medieval construction of the Jew as demonic (with red hair, a large nose, and a toasting fork), of the Jew as child murderer (seeking rich offal), of the Jew as "avaricious," harking back to Shylock (52, 115, 76). *Jew* in mid-nineteenth-century Britain is a category available and ripe for exploitation, as the novel makes clear. The image of Jew-as-evil possessed a prolific history in popular and literary imagination and was available for Dickens and George Cruikshank, who illustrated *Oliver Twist*, to plunder.[12] Myths about the Jews were powerful enough to be a substitute for reality or indeed to have become reality. Both Dickens and Cruikshank called upon a rich repetoire of signs, attributes, and references through which to identify Fagin and represent and typify the *Jew*. Physiognomy and other external signs such as clothes, language, and social and hygienic codes (odor) were used to mean *Jew*.

The Chapman and Hall edition of *Oliver Twist* carries 24 illustrations which all closely relate to the written text. A particular verbal and visual conjunction is set up in which the relationship between words and pictures is symbiotic: as our gaze strays between the verbal "image" and the illustration, the one informs the other. When *Oliver Twist* was serialized in *Bentley's Miscellany* it was broken into twenty sections for popular reading, which imposed upon its author the need for recognizable threads, compact narrative episodes, and the interplay of powerful textural as well as textual references. Dickens gave Cruikshank quite precise instructions, in an attempt to control the orchestration of the text overall. Writing to Cruikshank about *Mr. Bumble and Mrs. Corney taking tea*, he explained: "I have described a small kettle for one on the fire—a small black teapot on the table with a little tray and so forth—and a two ounce tea cannister. Also a shawl hanging up—and the cat and kittens before the fire."[13] Indeed, the picture includes all those items which are also described, in similar detail, in the narrative on the facing page (141). However, the interplay across the two sites (words and pictures) is contiguous, not homogeneous. Although Dickens tries to defend his text against ambiguity, there can be no guarantees for the "correct" reading. Meanings are adduced, "reality" demonstrated and authenticated, moral truths imparted and learnt in that uncertain space between words and picture (traversing both). Paradoxically, the rich and vivid interplay of verbal and visual imagery works to conflate realism with myths about and fears of the Jews.

Ambivalence is inscribed in the very structure of the novel in which two orders, the real and the fantastic, are connoted. Fantasy is played out in Fagin's psychic and physical domain, a nightmarish, supernatural place. When the supernatural is installed in the novel perhaps it could indicate, as has been argued, that Dickens' concerns were moving away from realism.[14] However, to argue in this way is to miss the point. It was, for Dickens, imperative that the danger of the Jew was perceived as real. Furthermore, it is only through the representation of the extremes, fantasy and reality, that Dickens can present one as that which is not the other. And that which is not the dangerous stinking world of the Jew, is also the real—with all the moral tones that realism carried. Crucially, however, these worlds cannot be kept apart: they permeate each other. Like osmosis each destabalizes the identity of the other, causing dangerous reverberations.

Mr. Bumble and Mrs. Corney taking tea, etching by George Cruikshank

The Jew and Morris Bolter begin to understand each other,
etching by George Cruikshank

Fagin's power is described as pervasive. He is "in-sati-able" (76). His desires are invented as unquenchable. These are made visible by, through, and in the drawing of Fagin's nose. Physiognomy is given as a key to understanding Fagin's character. A large Semitic nose is itself a "representation of the hidden sign of sexual difference."[15] Big nose, with its phallic connotations, denotes *Jew*. Cruikshank, in *The Jew and Morris Bolter begin to understand each other*, highlights Fagin's nose: it is the only illuminated part of his body. And Fagin's nose is not any old large nose. The drawing of it conforms exactly to Eden Warwick's contemporary description of the Jewish nose which is accordingly always "very convex, and preserves its convexity like a bow, throughout the whole length from eyes to the tip. It is thin and sharp."[16] Sharpness, as Gilman reminds us, connotes shrewdness.[17] Indeed, Fagin himself is described as "sharp" by Noah (Morris Bolter), who commends him for recognizing that he and his wife are from the country (263). Fagin is described as striking the side of his nose with his right forefinger. This knowing gesture is frequently invoked by Dickens to signal *Jew*. Noah, wanting to be seen to be as astute as Fagin, tries to mimic his gesture but fails: his own nose, we are told, "not being large enough for the purpose" (263). Fagin's nose is pointed to and pointed out, again and again in pictures, and obliquely referred to in the narrative by contrasting its size with that of other noses. The illustration substantiates the written text which illuminates the picture in a never-ending cycle. The Jewish nose, the ultimate visual sign of difference, is a threat, a lethal concoction of intelligence and potency. It is an ambivalent and dangerous image reminiscent of primal sexuality that is simultaneously loathed and envied.

Dangerous sexuality is signaled in our first introduction to Fagin. The scene is dirty:

> In a frying pan, which was on the fire, and which was secured to the mantelshelf by a string, some sausages were cooking; and standing over them, with a toasting-fork in his hand, was a very old shrivelled Jew, whose villainous-looking and repulsive face was obscured by a quantity of matted red hair. He was dressed in a greasy flannel gown with his throat bare; and seemed to be dividing his attention between the frying pan and the clothes-horse, over which a great number of silk handkerchiefs were hanging. (52)

The squalor and the smell of the setting described by Dickens evoke impurity. The urge to cleanliness, according to Freud, originates in the compulsion to get rid of excreta which are themselves associated with a shameless, unabandoned, animal sexuality.[18] Fagin is dressed in a "greasy flannel gown." Freud points out that a person who is unclean (who does not hide his or her excreta) offends other people by showing no concern for them. Fagin's dirtiness, his bad smell, is both a reminder of the primitive sexuality of the Jew and a threat to sociality or, to follow Freud's argument, to civilization itself.

There is a long history associating the Jew with a particular smell—the *foetor Judaicus*. For medieval anti-Jewish rhetoric, the smell of the Jew was their special distinguishing feature. It was also connected with the sexualized image of the goat; Jews, like the devil, are horned. They share other similarities—a tail and a beard. Bad smells were also associated with the plague, which Jews were blamed for spreading. By the eighteenth century, Jewish smell had been disassociated from the supernatural but became instead an issue of uncleanness. And by the nineteenth century the racialized science of biology labeled the *foetor Judaicus* as one of the natural, inherent signs of Jewish difference.[19]

Throughout *Oliver Twist* bad smells are metonymically evoked. Not only are the subjects that Dickens catalogues redolent of odor but also Cruikshank's illustrations to the text, time and time again, make great play with smoke and other visible vapors. *Oliver introduced to the Respectable Old Gentleman* shows a smoke-filled room. Fumes are emitted from the pipes smoked by the lads, the candle which burns on the table, the sausages being fried in a pan on an open fire, which also smokes. In sum, the Jews's room is shown to be rank, and the walls and ceiling are described, in both pictures and words, as "black with age and dirt" (52).

Oliver introduced to the Respectable Old Gentleman,
etching by George Cruikshank

Dickens employs the sign "bad smell" in his representation of the Jew whose relationship with the world is connoted primarily through smell. Not only is his abode filthy but the very air of Fagin's neighborhood is "impregnated with filthy odors" (51). Fagin is contagious: bad smells emanate from him. Smell is pervasive and beyond rational control. Through smell individuals merge. The self permeates and is permeated by the Other and boundaries dissolve. Bad smells denote the material nature of existence. "Uncivilized" and rotten, they are devices of differentiation and exclusion. The "low" and the "dirty" are placed at the outer limits of civilized life. *Oliver Twist* was written at the time of modernizing the city, where separating the "healthy" from the "contaminated"—"good" from "bad" odors—was a social and medical concern. Through bad smells, Fagin is identified with nature rather than culture. Paradoxically, however, Fagin is situated against nature by being in the city, again confusing the boundaries between nature and culture.

The city, the site of modernity, of progress, and of unassimilable masses, was for Dickens exciting and dreadful: it was a decaying, degenerate, and devouring place. The city is alive, uncontrollable, debasing, and tainting to its inhabitants. Desire for order and intelligibility are in *Oliver Twist* projected onto the country. The text contrasts people who live in the city with country dwellers. People who can see "sky, and hill and plain, and glistening water" are bound, Dickens suggests, "to feel uplifted" and experience "a foretaste of heaven" and "memories . . . not of this world." In the "unnatural" towns, beauty is defiled and people become "pain-worn dwellers in close and noisy places" (195). The country is understood as a haven, a lost paradise, and the city an unyielding hell. The inhabitants of each are determined by the other. These extremes are important; but each seeps into the other, disturbing boundaries yet again. Country people, like the Bolters, are corrupted by the city through their encounter with smelly Fagin—a noxious composite of nature and culture. Fagin is the one who creates havoc and confusion.

Fagin's city is a slimy underworld where "the mud lay thick upon the stones and a black mist hung over the streets; the rain fell sluggishly down, and everything felt wild and clammy to the touch" (115). Clamminess, stickiness is an in-between state. Lacking stability and yet not flowing, clamminess clings. It is an "aberrant fluid or melting solid." As such it is judged as "an ignoble form of existence" that falls outside the basic categories: it is anomalous, hence impure.[20] Impurity is that which departs from the symbolic order. Through identifying Fagin with the filthy city, yet another boundary is drawn—that of the other side. The opposition between order and disorder defines the limits to and boundaries of each as a category of the other. Anything which falls outside order, into the abyss of disorder and uncertainty, is reviled and becomes an object of revulsion.

There, on the other side, the repulsive Jew lurks and creeps about. Fagin only comes alive when others are asleep:

> It was nearly two hours before daybreak; that time which, in the autumn of the year, may be truly called the dead of night; when the streets are silent and deserted; when even sound appears to slumber, and profligacy and riot have staggered home to dream; it was at this still and silent hour. (289)

Fagin is chronicled as an alien estranged from the habits and values of contemporary life. His strangeness, his out-of-placeness, is shown plainly in *Oliver introduced to the Respectable Old Gentleman*, where he is drawn wearing a loose garment reminiscent of a kaftan, which was a relic of medieval middle-class costume: the present is shown as clothed in an outmoded form of life.[21] Enlightenment, which realism desired so fervently, had to bury the relics of the past before it could accomplish its dreams. In the picture of Fagin in prison, *Fagin in the Condemned Cell*, the night before he is to be hanged, his head is covered with a piece of knotted fabric. It resembles a

Fagin in the Condemned Cell, etching by George Cruikshank

kefia. The kaftan and kefia, both with Semitic connotations, give substance to, and again provide the material evidence for, Fagin as out of place in the modern civilized world: as a symbol of the repulsive underbelly of urban experience, he is a ghost which needs to be exorcised.

Thus, as would befit a ghost, it is in the cover of darkness that the Jew skulks

> stealthily along, creeping beneath the shelter of the walls and doorways, the hideous old man seemed like some loathsome reptile, engendered in the slime and darkness through which he moved: crawling forth, by night, in search of some rich offal for a meal. (115)

Popular imagination associated Jews as a whole with participation in magic and bloody rituals, and from this point of view the rich offal touches on the idea of *Jew* as child-murderer.[22] Here Fagin is described as a pre-historic animal, a primitive creature: as such he is an object of loathing ("loathsome reptile," 115) who defies or disobeys the rules of classification. In the hinterland between reality and prehistory, this not-quite-human, the unclassifiable, lurks. Throughout the text Fagin is described variously as "villainous-looking and repusive," "wily" with a "hideous grin," as a body which displays "earnest cunning" and is "infernal" (52, 115, 54, 123, 75). He is "lynx-eyed" or has a "hawk's eye" and an "evil leer" (243, 263, 77). His hand is a "withered old claw" (275). He is a "blackhearted wolf" (277). More, when Fagin "bit his long black nails, he disclosed among his toothless gums a few such fangs as should have been a dog's or rat's" (290). And again, "the Jew sat watching in his old lair, with face so distorted and pale, and eyes so red and bloodshot, that he looked less like a man, than like some hideous phantom, moist from the grave, and worried by an evil spirit" (289). This detailed cataloguing of Fagin's attributes is so excessive that it borders on the hysterical. The Jew is a hallucination. Fagin speaks with "abject humility" (76). He simultaneously "beseeches and pulverizes."[23] He is a figuration of disgust felt for the unknown within the psyche of the Other, a repugnance felt for the Other that also is the self. Fagin presents a desperate image: he is close but cannot be assimilated. The symbolism attached to *Jew* is sinister, dark, dangerous, and strange. The image of the stranger is a vision of disorder:

> The stranger's unredeemable sin, is . . . the incompatibility between his presence and other presences, fundamental to the world order; his simultaneous assault on several crucial oppositions instrumental in the incessant effort of ordering. It is this sin which throughout modern history rebounds in the constitution of the stranger as the bearer and embodiment of *incongruity*; indeed, the stranger is a person afflicted with the incurable sickness of *multiple incongruity*. The stranger is, for this reason, the bane of modernity.[24]

Anything which falls outside the modern order into the abyss of disorder and uncertainty is reviled. It is noncontiguous and disturbs identity. That which does not respect order and system is ambiguous, a composite. This is Fagin.

Fagin is feared and he is fascinating. Through Fagin, Dickens presents a vision of power which does not arouse respect but lets loose various excitements. Fagin is as seductive as he is vile. Both Sikes and Nancy cannot stand the Jew yet they are seduced by him. Bewitched Sikes and Nancy give themselves over to mimetic attraction. Had they not become entangled with Fagin (imitated him), they could have been saved. Imitation and the impossibility of identification lie at the heart of *Jew* loathing. Fagin manipulates others to do his dirty deeds. He leads Nancy "step by step, deeper down into the abyss of crime" (304). Although they themselves are depraved, it is Fagin who must bear the responsibility for their depravity. Yet Fagin inspires loyalty. At first Nancy refuses to betray him: "Devil that he is, and worse than devil as he has been to me, I will never do that," she cries as one

Oliver's reception by Fagin and the boys, etching by George Cruikshank

who is enthralled (286). Fagin can also be very funny. The games he plays at first charmed Oliver and provoked him to "laugh till the tears ran down his face" (57). He seems able to enter the child's world as an immature (primitive) creature might. He is witty and horrifying, desirable and despicable, crafty and intelligent. Fagin summons and repels and is himself hypnotic. Tempting the youth, Oliver, he says: "'Delighted to see you looking so well, my dear'... bowing with mock humility" (97).

Cruikshank's illustration, *Oliver's reception by Fagin and the boys,* cunningly reiterates the humble mien described in the narrative, but here what may have been seen as benign turns sinister under a large dark shadow that dwarfs the image of Fagin. He is the hatred that smiles. Dickens does not merely represent Fagin but projects him. Dickens' desire is disguised as repugnance: desire turns aside and becomes rejection. Fagin is funny, shrewd, and repugnant—in summary, he is charismatic. Fagin's evil is set against equally stylized depictions of other characters. All characterizations in *Oliver Twist* can be seen against this calibration. Sikes and Nancy, although wicked, are redeemable, for their crimes are represented as a con-sequence of social injustice. Fagin, by contrast, is doomed by virtue of his birthright.

The fusion of evil and criminality, specifically identified with the Jew, was itself symptomatic of the fears inspired by the perceived threat of uncontrollable, unassimilable seething masses then gathering in metropolitan centers. The evils attributed to the Jews were prompted by the reorganization of urban life in the nineteenth century. The Jew was seen as the quintessential city dweller and became a body onto which those fears could be projected. Fagin, however, was not simply a criminal but one who preyed on innocent children. His deviancy was an attack on the future as much as it was an anti-social crime of the present. The *Jew* encapsulated fears which themselves anticipated and projected the impossibility of future progress. Fagin filled out and occupied the symbolically important place as Other. Although the category marked by the Other was ambivalent, there was no escape from it. The presence of the *Jew* gave sense to the Other. The Jewish question was part of the general question of social reform and control yet differentiated from it. Nineteenth-century radical liberalism needed exclusions in order to support its workings. *Jew* was installed as a distinctive category in which differences were used to define and maintain social order.

Oliver Twist reveals deep clefts (between progress and regress, the rational and irrational) in Enlightenment thought. The Enlightenment was in part at least a fantasy and spoke in barbed tongues.[25] It is in that very place, lying somewhere between fantasy and reality—a murderous conjunction— that the dialectical tensions of the Enlightenment are reenacted and then resolved through a synthesis in which evil, the criminal (the *Jew*) is annihilated.

Fagin the terrified and terrifying nomad must be exterminated. Even on his last night alive, perhaps parodying Christ in the Garden of Gethsemane, Fagin continues to inspire fear and hatred.[26] He

> started up, every minute, and with gasping mouth and burning skin, hurried to and fro, in such a paroxysm of fear and wrath that even they—used to such sights—recoiled from him with horror. He grew so terrible, at last, in all the tortures of his evil conscience, that one man could not bear to sit there, eyeing him alone; and so the two kept watch together. (330)

Fagin does not repent but curses about his condition. Fagin does not, cannot, atone for his sins. The drawing *Fagin in the Condemned Cell* shows a bible resting unopened upon a shelf in a dark corner of the cell. There is no view through the barred window. A shaft of light illuminates the bench upon which Fagin sits, highlighting the very part unoccupied by him. Untouched by light, he bites his nails, his knees knock together, his eyes bulge white with terror. The *Jew* is irredeemable. In *The Merchant of Venice*, in the figuration of Jessica, Shylock's daughter, Shakespeare indicates that Jews are not doomed by "blood" and can at least be saved by Christianity.[27] Dickens' Englightenment fable does not, cannot countenance even this possibility. In Hannah Arendt's sharp words, "Jews had been able to escape from Judaism into conversion; from Jewishness there was no escape."[28] Liberalism was put into jeopardy by the very existence and form of life of the Jews, since they threw into question (and doubt) the very generality by which liberalism was itself constituted. It was predicated upon the idea of reform or its possibilities, yet Fagin was not reformable. That was his role.

The Jew stood out as the disturbing factor in the projected harmony of the evolving nation. The liberal project offered, as an image of itself, the idea of the unity of man. While it promised radicalism, was predicated upon notions of freedom and equality—seeming to say that all people were welcome to share power—this could only happen if everyone abided by the rules that defined the privileged group which itself constructed its Others. Jews heard enlightenment call, inviting them inside (to become alike), and may have accepted the invitation but were condemned or rejected for doing so. Those on the inside wished to contain the outside and thereby neutralize the power the Others were imagined to possess. By keeping them outside, the fantasy of control and power was preserved. Anti-Semitism revealed the limits of radical liberalism. The racialized sciences perfected the logic of exclusion. *Oliver Twist*—a serialized story read by the man traveling daily from the suburbs into the city on the Clapham omnibus—played a part in rendering such fantasies familiar.

Henri de Toulouse-Lautrec, *Reine de Joie*, poster, 1892

3

Toulouse Lautrec's Illustrations for Victor Joze and Georges Clemenceau and their Relationship to French Anti-Semitism of the 1890's

GALE B. MURRAY

Toulouse-Lautrec's illustrations of Jewish subjects raise very pointedly the question of what is anti-Semitic representation. In the 1890's he designed a poster and a dustjacket for two of Victor Joze's novels about contemporary Jewish mores as well as a set of illustrations for Georges Clemenceau's *Au Pied du Sinaï,* a series of sketches of Jewish life in Eastern Europe. Lautrec presented his art as the product of detached observation, yet his use of caricature and stereotypes to construct the Jew seems to undermine the objectivity of these images.

During the 1890's the Dreyfus Affair became a focal point for anti-Semitic sentiments in France. While many vanguard artists openly took sides, Lautrec's position on the Affair and his attitude toward Jews remain enigmatic. The available evidence presents an ambiguous and seemingly contradictory picture. He customarily did not involve himself with political issues and did not take a public stand on the Dreyfus Affair.[1] Given Lautrec's conservative Roman Catholic and aristocratic background, one might naturally assume him to have held anti-Dreyfus and anti-Semitic sympathies, as did his family and the two artists he most admired, Degas and Forain. Indeed, his name does not appear on the lengthy petition, signed by virtually all of the Dreyfusard artists and intellectuals, in the *Hommage des artiste à Picquart* album, published in 1899.[2] In addition, Joze's novels and Lautrec's illustrations for them appear, to modern eyes at least, to be either implicitly or overtly anti-Semitic.

On the other hand, both Lautrec's art and his lifestyle can be identified with the left-of-center, democratic, anti-bourgeois attitudes taken by other French Realist and Naturalist artists and writers, many of whom, like Zola, eventually became pro-Dreyfus. Lautrec, moreover, was a member of the circle of the ardently pro-Dreyfus and Jewish-owned literary and artistic journal *La Revue Blanche.* He counted among his closest friends the journal's co-director, Thadée Natanson, and the writers Tristan Bernard and Romain

Coolus, all prominent Jews and Dreyfusards. Natanson noted that the Dreyfus Affair presented "A dilemma for Lautrec," who often felt "that he wanted to throw up his hands at the whole mess so that he could continue to live with the people he liked without having to make distinctions."[3]

The fact that Clemenceau, a leading Dreyfusard, chose Lautrec to illustrate *Au Pied du Sinaï*, a book which concludes with a plea for religious tolerance, also seems to suggest that Lautrec held Dreyfusard sympathies. Yet *Au Pied du Sinaï* confounds our expectations. Despite its seemingly sympathetic presentation of Jews, both Clemenceau's text and Lautrec's pictures incorporate, to modern eyes once again, considerable anti-Semitic stereotyping. If Lautrec's illustrations for Joze and Clemenceau seem anti-Semitic by modern standards, one wonders how they were intended and perceived in their own time and just what constituted anti-Semitism in France of the 1890's.

The most aesthetically noteworthy and highly visible of Lautrec's Jewish subjects is his poster of 1892, *Reine de Joie (Queen of Joy)* an advertisement for Victor Joze's novel of the same name.[4] *Reine de Joie* is a critique of the vices and moral corruption of the rich, symbolized by its Jewish protagonist, "Baron de Rozenfeld," a figure loosely modeled on Baron de Rothschild, the Jewish banker and financier. It traces the history of a beautiful Parisian courtesan, Alice Lamy, who has worked her way up in the demi-monde until finally she has the good fortune to become the mistress of the fabulously rich Baron de Rozenfeld. This is the climax of her career, the realization of her dreams, and the ideal liaison. It is a purely mercenary arrangement, in which the baron, an unappealing character both physically and personally, agrees to give her fifty thousand francs monthly and a luxurious mansion on the Avenue du Bois de Boulogne. In exchange she will become his chattel, a beautiful possession to be ostentatiously displayed as an enhancement to his prestige.

What is relevant here is that Joze used a Jew as his archetypal morally corrupt capitalist. In so doing he followed a pattern already well established in French Naturalist novels. Especially after the publication in 1886 of Drumont's anti-Semitic tract *La France juive*, there appeared a spate of novels "developing the image of the rapacious, immoral" Jew, who "insinuated himself into the highest circles of power and prestige." In particular, the type of the Jewish banker-financier, portrayed as "shifty, cosmopolitan, cleverly manipulating . . . single minded [in his] quest for money," was a recurrent character, invariably meant to arouse the reader's revulsion. Even Zola had used this stock figure, in his novel *L'Argent* (1891).[5]

Like Zola, Joze was a leftist, not a reactionary. He announced his socialist sympathies, his abhorrence of the capitalist exploiters, who were "parasites on the social body," and explained his aim of unmasking the "hypocrisy and lies" of bourgeois society in *Mon Album: Les Petites Démascarades* of 1889, a statement of his artistic, political, and social credo.[6] It is likely that his attitudes toward Jews, like Zola's, grew out of the anti-Semitic bias in much of nineteenth-century French leftist ideology. According to Robert Wistrich:

> The socialist tradition of Fourier, Proudhon, and Blanqui appears to have digested the medieval popular feeling against the Jews as usurers into its mainstream, helped, no doubt, by the prominence of the Rothschilds and a number of other Jews (and Protestants) in the French banking oligarchy . . . Indeed, modern antisemitism in France first developed primarily as an offshoot of the early radical attack on the "féodalité financière"—the new financial plutocracy.[7]

The Left played a crucial role in establishing the Jew as a symbol of Capital, "of the grasping financier, the subverter of the social bond," and blaming him for the "excesses of finance capitalism." Moreover, French socialist writers and theorists helped to legitimize "the notion that anti-semitism was a progressive and non-conformist ideology, an ingredient in the revolt against the established order."[8]

This leftist tradition is at the heart of Joze's *Reine de Joie*, which attacks Rozenfeld not so much as a Jew but as a financier. Lautrec followed suit, utilizing the established negative stereotype of the rich Jewish banker and creating a poster with a tone of biting social satire. The purpose of the poster was to boost sales of the novel. No doubt the spectacular success of Lautrec's Moulin Rouge poster of late 1891 made publicity by him an attractive prospect.[9] Joze had chosen a potentially marketable subject, one that combined Naturalist candor, anti-Semitism, and a titillating, soft-core eroticism. In his poster Lautrec played up just those qualities of the novel that would enhance its saleability. He employed strikingly Modernist and Japonist simplifications—flat, unmodeled forms, arresting silhouettes, caricature, and bright colors to create an eye-catching image that brilliantly condensed the novel's message.

We do not know who chose the episode that Lautrec illustrated; it is the culminating one in the plot and, moreover, the one that offered the greatest ironic, prurient, and anti-Semitic possibilities. Lautrec's image of an illicit embrace between the lascivious Jewish banker and the avaricious Gentile courtesan goes beyond Joze's text in exploiting this potential. The moment shown takes place at dinner held in a private room at the Café Anglais, where Baron Rozenfeld and Alice meet to celebrate the successful conclusion of negotiations for their "new liaison," and where the baron displays her to three of his aristocratic male friends. Once seated at the dinner table, Alice unfolds her napkin, and to her delight discovers a million-franc "bill of sale" for the mansion the baron has promised her:

> A million! she cried, joyously. That's nice . . . it's awfully decent of you! . . .
> Starting to rise she wrapped her naked arms around the neck of the baron. And,
> as her lips, in straining toward the mouth of the old man, found an obstacle in
> his large semitic hooked nose, it was there that she planted a kiss.[10]

Lautrec followed the text faithfully; his figures' physical appearances are in keeping with Joze's descriptions, which were succinct enough to leave Lautrec room to elaborate, using caricatural distortion and exaggeration to drive home more effectively all that is implicit in Joze's text. Joze's baron is "an old man, of the semitic type, beardless, with little side-whiskers dyed black, very bald, with the impassive face of a man who knows his own power."[11] Lautrec intensified the old banker's physical repulsiveness to the point of grotesqueness, giving him a caricatured, semitic profile, hooknosed and thick-lipped, a smug expression, a balding head, and a fat, aging body. Although Joze never specified that the baron was fat, Lautrec's figure conforms with the standard literary and artistic image of the corpulent Jewish banker.

Of Alice, Joze tells us only that she is sensual and attractive, has brilliant black hair, large eyes, and "the white teeth of a she-wolf."[12] This suggestion of her predatory nature is what Lautrec seems to embellish in his caricature through the sharp, pointy forms of her face and her literally "grasping" arms, outstretched as she reaches toward the baron to seal their unholy alliance with a kiss. The two figures are, as Richard Thomson has pointed out, an updated version of the traditional ill-matched "old man bargaining for the sexual favors of a young girl."[13] This unnatural and mercenary pairing underlines the poster's tone of moral corruption, decadence, and sexual degeneracy. Discreetly averting his eyes from the distasteful scene is one of the three guests, "the Lord of Bath," a handsome Anglo-Saxon foil for the baron.

The conspicuous eroticism of the poster relates to another anti-Semitic theme underlying Joze's novel, one entwined with the negative association of Jews with the evils of capitalism. This was an identification of Jews with lechery, debauchery, and the promotion of prostitution. A further connection was made between the sexual lust of the Jews and their lust for money, so that Jewish sexuality "was evoked as . . . a facet of the predatory nature of Jews" whose aim was "to seduce, pervert and exploit." At a time of sexual repression, this sexualized concept of the Jew had the power both to attract and repel. And this is evident in Lautrec's Rozenfeld, who exemplifies that "sexual attractiveness of the 'strangely ugly'" and the "horribly sensual" that Jews often stood for.[14]

Lautrec shrewdly used witty visual puns to underscore the erotically charged nature of the image. He pushed his audacious formal abbrevia-

Henri de Toulouse-Lautrec, "Why not . . . once is not a habit," 1893

Henri de Toulouse-Lautrec, *Au Moulin Rouge ou la Promenade—La Goulue et Jane Avril au Fond*, c.1891

tions to the point of ambiguity, teasingly confusing us about whether the baron's right arm (and hand), which is merged into the black silhouette of his evening attire, hangs by his side or slips underneath Alice's décolleté to fondle her.[15] The action is humorously complemented by the slyly suggestive sexual innuendoes made by the forms of the accessories. Lautrec made an analogy between Alice's form and the curving shape of the pitcher—whose open yonic spout inclines toward the distinctly phallic form of the coat-of-arms on the baron's plate—creating a subliminal erotic dialogue which echoes that between the two figures.[16] The result is that the image reads as an off-color joke to be smirked at by the middle-aged bourgeois male viewer (the potential consumer of Joze's novel), to whom it offers a voyeuristic thrill meant to stimulate his sexual fantasy life and hence his desire to purchase the novel.

In several works of the early 1890's, Lautrec similarly presented bourgeois male figures with distinctly semitic features as lascivious voyeurs or consumers of the erotic "products" of Parisian nightlife. For example, in a lithograph of 1893 entitled "Why not . . . once is not a habit," he depicted an encounter between a fat top-hatted bourgeois Jew and two prostitutes, who appear to reject him (they literally turn their noses up in disdain).[17] The title, presumably, is his response to their slight. And Arthur Symons identified the two spectators strolling in the middleground of the painting *Au Moulin Rouge ou la Promenade* (*c.* 1891) as sexual stalkers and "Jews—with visages devoured by degradation and debased cruelty."[18]

There is ample evidence that Lautrec's contemporaries read his *Reine de Joie* poster as socially critical and recognized its Jewish protagonist as a symbol for the corruption and decadence of the rich. Félix Fénéon, writing for the anarchist weekly *Le Père Peinard*, particularly praised Lautrec for the anti-bourgeois aspect of his rendering: "There's nobody like him when it comes to painting capitalists sitting there all gaga with whores on the make, who lick their snouts trying to get them to fork out their cash."[19] Ernest Maindron identified the male protagonist as "a financier of dubious reputation who spends freely to show off his wealth." And Octave Uzanne called him "a typical sad-looking Jewish stockbroker, an old lecher weakened by debauchery, and his dining companion, a cynical whore, provocative in her formidable and triumphant crassness. It conveys the stultifying, moronic effects of a life of pleasure, the stupidity and vulgarity of it all."[20]

The Rothchilds, however, were not amused and attempted to confiscate the poster. On June 18, 1892 *Fin de Siècle* reported:

> It seems that one of our biggest financiers believes he has recognized himself in one of the principal characters of the novel *Reine de Joie*, by M. Victor Joze. The character designated by the name "baron de Rozenfeld" prides himself on being intimately associated with the Prince of Wales. That's why several young stockbrokers, for the last few days, have amused themselves by ripping down the colored posters advertising *Reine de Joie*. But people have gotten wind of it, and sales [of the book] have not suffered.[21]

Lautrec's visual image of the Jew as rich capitalist was no more an isolated one in the 1890's than was Joze's literary one. Lautrec followed a formula commonly employed by caricaturists, who, like the novelists, used "the Jew" as a symbol of lechery, rapaciousness, materialism, and hypocrisy. Such images appeared regularly in the anti-Semitic press, as well as in leftist journals, where they were drawn by artists like Steinlen and Hermann-Paul, both of whom later became Dreyfusards.[22] Significantly, even Pissarro, who was both a leftist and a Jew, used the Jew to represent Capital in his 1889 series of drawings, *Les Turpitudes Sociales* (*Social Turpitudes*). As Linda Nochlin has noted, the Jew was clearly a convenient and readily available stereotype, the most effective visual sign that could be used to "personify capitalist greed and exploitation."[23] Although its use cannot necessarily be taken as a sign of personal anti-Semitism, in accepting and repeating it

Hermann-Paul,
La France Financière, published
in *Le Courrier Français*,
January 6, 1895

Lautrec and others inadvertently may have given tacit support to anti-Semitism.

Joze chose Lautrec to illustrate a Jewish subject on one other occasion, commissioning him in 1897 to design a dustjacket for his novel, *La Tribu d'Isidore*. This was the first in a three-volume series, *Les Rozenfeld: Histoire d'une famille juive sous la Troisième République*, dedicated to demonstrating the negative role played by Jews in modern French society.[24] The ensemble depicted the rise to wealth and power of the Rozenfeld family, that of the baron of *Reine de Joie*. As Joze explained in his preface, they were "a family of modern Israelites in the process of conquering old Europe."[25] He now expanded the brief character sketch of the baron into a more fully realized and extensive study of the Jewish "race," its character, motivations, and modes of operation. With this new project, Joze no doubt hoped to capitalize on the heightened interest in things Jewish and the hostility toward Jews stimulated by the Dreyfus Affair, by now in full swing. And, clearly, his own animosity toward Jews, nascent in *Reine de Joie*, became full-blown and unequivocal in the course of the Affair. He even dedicated the second novel in this series, *La Conquête de Paris* (1904), to Edouard Drumont, whom he addressed as "cher maître:" "You have been the most clairvoyant of all the French. You have called attention to the Jewish peril, the sudden offensive of the semites in the West, at a time when no one in this country was yet willing to believe it. Your *France juive* remains a brilliant beacon for all of those who have the eyes to see."

La Tribu d'Isidore recounts the Rozenfeld's origins in early nineteenth-century Eastern Europe. Its underlying premise, as explained by Joze in his preface, is that "civilized Jew of today, almost always a money-grubber, a shady merchant, usurer or financier, is, at heart, the same as his filthy grandfathers who exploited the peasants on the plains of Poland."[26] Joze none the less disclaims any anti-Semitic intention, maintaining that as a Realist he is merely an objective observer of human behavior:

> First of all, I am an enemy of novels with a thesis, and furthermore I am not an antisemite in the precise sense of the word. I do not belong to any Aryan league, to any anti-Jewish group. I am only a spectator, a passerby who wanders along the highway of life and interests himself in the battles of the human insect.
>
> I observe the diverse manifestations of social evolution as a philosopher, incapable of hating. I do not curse, I record. It's up to others to draw a conclusion from the facts recorded in my writer's notebook.[27]

Despite this profession of objectivity, there is barely a sympathetic Jewish character in the novel. It follows the career of the aptly named Judas Rozenfeld, who around 1840 leaves his home in the Russian-Polish village of Zakroczym to seek his fortune in Warsaw by joining the Russian occupation army. He rapidly rises to become a high-ranking and decorated officer and a spy in the secret police, not through meritorious service and patience, but thanks to his father's lavish bribes to a general, his own nefarious plotting and intrigue, and his conversion to Christianity, a pure expedient, without which he could not become an officer. His insincere conversion is approved and encouraged by his rabbi as a subterfuge to deceive and thereby gain power over the Gentiles. Joze repeatedly hints at the existence of broad and menacing Jewish conspiracies—enabling Jews to infiltrate and move up in the Gentile world by manipulating the army, politics, and finance.

Judas is a thoroughly reprehensible character, corrupt, callous, and unprincipled. Most importantly, he is a betrayer—of his friends and "protectors" as well as his enemies—who is incapable of loyalty or patriotic sentiments. Joze shrewdly chose a timely subject: he probably intended the reader of this study of Jewish treachery, set in a military context in Joze's native Poland, to draw a parallel to Dreyfus's presumed treason in France.

Lautrec's design was printed in a limited edition for collectors, without the text, and issued in April 1897 in a larger bookcover edition with lettering designed by another hand.[28] His lithograph is not a colored image per se, and he did not do it in the strikingly stark and Modernist style he commonly used for publicity images, such as the *Reine de Joie* poster; rather it is a more simple caricatural line drawing, seemingly rapidly sketched, and printed in violet-brown ink against a yellow-beige background. It shows a man, presumably Joze's protagonist Judas, driving a horse-drawn trap, while in the background hover two vaguely sketched heads.

Although Lautrec's image cannot be correlated with any specific incident, it can be reconciled with the general sense of the novel, especially as described by Joze in the preface. Lautrec probably found it difficult to retrieve from Joze's convoluted plot an incident suitable for translation into an illustration that would succinctly convey the book's essence. Turning instead to the preface, Lautrec presented the potential reader with an image of the modern assimilated Jew, Judas, juxtaposed with his forebears, whose heads are rendered in the background. He visualized the latter as types of Eastern European Jews, one shown in full-face, one in profile, with long beards and hooked noses, and suggestions of traditional Jewish attire. The two figures probably can be specifically identified as Judas's ambitious father Isidore on the right (looking forward to the future, as initiator of the family's rise to wealth and power), and his grandfather Abraham, the more spectral disembodied head, with eyes averted, on the left; both are described at the novel's outset, which provides the family's pre-assimilation background and establishes the characteristics which Judas either learned or inherited from his forefathers. Abraham, originally from Vilna, "had been hung in 1809 by Russians who accused him of spying for the Grand-Duchy of Warsaw."[29] Isidore, his son, established himself in Zakroczym in Poland and eventually became a usurer and a middleman in the lucrative grain business, enriching himself by cheating the impoverished Polish peasants.

Since there is no such scene in the book, Lautrec's image of Judas driving a carriage can only be understood in metaphorical terms.[30] He curiously did not depict Judas as a soldier. Perhaps the fact that the image of the Jew as a soldier was not in the current visual vocabulary of Jewish types forced Lautrec to use other signifiers to indicate Jewishness. He resorted to the image of the fat capitalist to personify the Jews, out to conquer "old Europe"—mentioned in Joze's preface—who "at present . . . do nearly everything they wish to in Paris." Lautrec gave his figure the attributes of a wealthy Parisian—the carriage, attire, even the little lap dog, the supercilious expression, and the suggestion that he is in control; he holds the reins. Most importantly, Lautrec created an appropriate sense of the driving force with which his aggressive figure moves forward, a personification of Joze's notion of the Jews' inexorable advance in society, through newly acquired wealth and aristocratic trappings. This sense of momentum is conveyed visually by the diagonal crayon strokes of the reins and on the figure himself, and by the off-center placement of the image, so that the horse and carriage seem to move off the right-hand side of the page.

Lautrec's Judas is difficult to distinguish as foreign, or even Jewish at all, but the presence of the images of his progenitors is a reminder of his connection to them, that he is of the same "tribe." Lautrec thus seems to illustrate Joze's point that under their widely different exterior appearances the Eastern and assimilated Jew are one and the same, that "the civilized Jew of today . . . is, at heart, the same as his filthy grandfathers who exploited the peasants on the plains of Poland." He is a "conquering nomad."[31] Wittingly or unwittingly, Lautrec reiterated visually the tenet of racial anti-Semitism that Joze promoted, the idea that Jews, no matter how well assimilated into modern society, "were none the less indelibly different from non-Jews and fundamentally unchanging."[32]

Lautrec was a dutiful illustrator; he attempted to capture what he recognized as the underlying thesis of Joze's novel. His illustration, once again, gives us no reason to believe he did not share Joze's dislike of Jews. At least he accepted Joze's stereotypical preconceptions about them, if not his more wide-ranging and virulent anti-Semitic ideology. Clearly, Lautrec's image does not have the viciously anti-Semitic tone of either Joze's text or the caricatures of the anti-Semitic press. We can contrast his illustration to the more propagandistic set of caricatures that appeared on July 29, 1893 in Drumont's anti-Semitic journal *La Libre Parole Illustrée*, showing the wealthy Jew as a parvenu. Here the artist counterpointed images of Jews enjoying the pleasures of the French privileged classes (those listed in the "Almanach de Gotha," or social register), such as a box at the opera or rid-

Henri de Toulouse-Lautrec,
La Tribu d'Isidore,
cover design, 1897

Almanach de Go(lgo)tha ("Juifs à l'Opéra, Point de départ, Juifs au Bois") published in
La Libre Parole Illustrée, July 29, 1893

ing in the Bois de Boulogne, with a reminder of their "point of departure,"
an unsavory Jew from the East. However, we are forced to wonder if
Lautrec's message, despite its more subtle and understated delivery, was not
very far removed from that of either *La Libre Parole* or Joze—all three
insinuate that the two types of Jews (Eastern and assimilated) are closer
than surface appearances might imply. Such imagery catered to contemporary fears that the Jews were rising too rapidly in French society, and it
aroused an accompanying distaste and suspicion. In the end Lautrec's
image remains more ambiguous than the images of *La Libre Parole*. It is
obviously more difficult to derive an explicitly anti-Semitic message from
what he pictured. If left to stand independently the illustration appears
innocuous enough. Read in the context of Joze's book, however, its message seems more potent; it becomes a more hostile image.

It is therefore surprising to find Lautrec engaged in a major illustration
project for Georges Clemenceau, a leading Dreyfusard, directly following
the completion of his cover for Joze's *La Tribu d'Isidore*. Clemenceau's *Au
Pied du Sinaï* was published on April 20, 1898 with a cover and ten lithographed illustrations by Lautrec. Four additional lithographs designed by
Lautrec, although rejected by Clemenceau, were included in a small deluxe
edition.[33] This was the height of the Dreyfus Affair, the dramatic and tense-
ly emotional time following the January trial and acquittal of Esterhazy and
publication of Zola's "J'Accuse," when the pro- and anti-Dreyfus camps
solidified. However, both Clemenceau's text and Lautrec's illustrations

were conceived and completed before this critical period. Lautrec wrote several letters that definitively date his work on the project to April and May of 1897.[34] Likewise, the six pieces by Clemenceau in *Au Pied du Sinaï* were all previously published journal articles, dating from 1894 to 1897, most of them following his annual trips to the spa at Carlsbad. He now reissued them virtually unchanged, probably hoping to capitalize on the interest in and saleability of books on Jewish subjects.[35] After the collapse of his promising early political career as a result of his involvement in the Panama scandals of 1892, Clemenceau earned his living as a writer and journalist.

Despite his vigorous support of Dreyfus, Clemenceau, like many others who later became Dreyfusards, appears to have shared the period's widely prevalent dislike of Jews. Numerous slurs on Jews appear throughout his journalistic writings, and those he made in conversation are reported by several contemporaries.[36] Moreover, even though Clemenceau is "often thought of as one of the most important and earliest Dreyfusards," he actually came rather late to the side of Dreyfus. His initial response was to accept Dreyfus's guilt and demand stiffer penalties. He wrote in December 1894 for *La Justice* a scathing attack on Dreyfus, as "Le Traître," and stated privately of Dreyfus's defenders, "Il nous embêtent avec leur Juif" ("They bore us with their Jew"). It was not until November 1897 that he began to voice doubts about Dreyfus's guilt and to call for revision, and he wasn't fully convinced of Dreyfus's innocence until October 1898.[37]

Some have seen his late "conversion" as motivated by the desire to resurrect his political career, but more probably he was moved to support Dreyfus by genuine ideological considerations. These did not, however, include a philo-Semitic sympathy for Jews. Duroselle, Clemenceau's most recent biographer, has noted that "among all the aspects of the Dreyfus Affair, anti-Semitism was certainly the one that least preoccupied Clemenceau." In fact, although anti-Semitism has since been seen as central in the Affair and certainly lent it its "intensity," in retrospect the Affair was more about the struggle between the forces of reaction and progress for control of the French state. In the course of the Affair, many leftists came to see anti-Semitism as a counterrevolutionary weapon of the right, of the enemies of democracy and the Republic, and to distance themselves from it.[38] Thus, Clemenceau began to speak out against anti-Semitism in the winter of 1898. In an article of January 19, he characterized it as "the negation of the power of conscience and the affirmation of privilege, intolerance, and iniquity." In his articles of autumn 1899, he specifically refuted socialist anti-Semitism and the association of Jews with capitalism.[39]

If the Dreyfus Affair made Joze more of an anti-Semite, it clearly made Clemenceau less of one. However, Clemenceau wrote the pieces in *Au Pied* before he developed a consistently strong stand against anti-Semitism. In describing the Jews he encountered in Carlsbad, Cracow, and the provincial villages of Galicia, he tended to utilize, not unlike Joze, a variety of anti-Semitic stereotypes and myths. His descriptions of Jews as dirty and physically repugnant convey a sense of inherent Jewish difference. He repeatedly conjured up the old leftist economic anti-Semitism—using, for instance, the term "semitism" to refer to the rule of money, and referring to Jews as "the deplorable descendants of usurers driven from the temple." And he expressed a belief in the imminence of a Jewish reign, stating that the Jew aims "to fulfil himself by the domination of the earth."[40]

Linda Nochlin has pointed out that Clemenceau's focus on the Jews' otherness is not dissimilar to what one commonly finds in nineteenth-century travel books. To a degree it reflects the "wider phenomenon" of the "late nineteenth-century construction of the Other—Blacks, Indians, Arabs, the Irish."[41] Nevertheless, the fact remains that the particular terms in which Clemenceau constructed his Jews, especially his preoccupation with their supposed craving for money and power, their cunning, and their duplicity, are also strikingly similar to those used in anti-Semitic tracts. The discourse of anti-Semitism consistently flavors the descriptions of Jews in other travel books of the period as well.

A notable case, which goes beyond Clemenceau in its anti-Semitic tone, is *The Jew at Home: Impressions of a Summer and Autumn Spent with Him in Russia and Austria*, published in 1892 by the American artist Joseph Pennell. This too is a compilation of the author's previously published articles; they are accompanied by his own illustrations. Pennell's profession of objectivity, like Joze's, did not prevent him from vilifying the Jews as a detestable race. He employed the usual discourse on otherness regarding the Jewish preference to live in "filth and dirt," and declared that "to civilize the Polish Jew according to our standard is about as difficult a task as to civilize the red Indian." But he also utilized the common anti-Semitic themes about the Jews' "objection to manual work" and singleminded interest in making money, as well as their devious and "calculating" quality, and their solidarity and "clannishness."[42]

Clemenceau's case is by no means so clear-cut. In fact, his book is highly contradictory. Some of his statements show he was not without sympathy for Jews, so that the end effect of his book is much less malignant than Joze's *La Tribu d'Isidore* or Pennell's *Jew at Home*. He praised the Jews' industriousness, energy, and "ability to will and to accomplish."[43] He challenged the anti-Semitic idea of the Jews as a single race, stating they were "far more mixed than they themselves believe and than those pretend who make war upon them." He also questioned the concept that "the Jews shun manual labor," pointing to the existence in Eastern Europe of Jewish farmers and

Henri de Toulouse-Lautrec, *Au Pied du Sinai*, rejected cover, 1897

"artisans of all trades" and asserting that there was no difference between the "wretched Jews of Busk" and "the wretched Christians of Paris." Both were subject to "the heavy yoke with which they are burdened by their big brothers of all races." He even allowed that Jews were the victims of circumstance, although he simultaneously called them "a misfortune which should be remedied." Moreover, he consistently took a stand against violent persecution, and he concluded with an eloquent plea for tolerance. Instead of condemning Jews, "why do we not try, simply and more justly, to frame a more equitable, a more disinterested social code, in which the power of selfish appropriation—be it Jewish or Christian—is rendered less harmful and its tyranny less crushing for the great mass of humanity?"[44]

Ultimately Clemenceau's book remains a hodgepodge of half-baked, ill-digested, and poorly thought-through ideas. His sincerity cannot be doubted; his intention was not to create an anti-Semitic tract. More likely, as A. Coralnik claims in his preface to the English edition, it was to use the Jew as a kind of microcosm "to emphasize his ideas of man and history, of society and its fundamental principles." However, as Poliakov has suggested, Clemenceau's contradictory positions and unexpected prejudices "speak volumes about the climate of the times,"[45] especially about the attitudes toward Jews among the many who were not necessarily declared anti-Semites.

Henri de Toulouse-Lautrec, *Au Pied du Sinai*, cover, 1897

When Lautrec first announced the project to his mother he stated, "I'm working on a book with Clemenceau against the Jews."[46] He may well have been telling her what he assumed she wanted to hear. Unquestionably, however, there is much in Clemenceau's book that would support this impression. In the end, his illustrations present us with some of the same contradictions and ambiguities as the text does. As Nochlin has pointed out, "We don't know quite how to take them: as anti-Semitic caricatures or as misguided but basically well-intentioned vignettes of life in an exotic foreign culture."[47] They lack the satirical edge and ironic bite that give so much of Lautrec's work its distinctive flavor. At the same time they lack the empathy and sensitivity that elevate much of his non-satirical work, such as his representations of prostitutes. He seems to have done these illustrations without strong conviction; as a result, they leave us unsatisfied.

In addition, Lautrec's illustrations for *Au Pied du Sinai* are often seen as undistinguished stylistically. This judgment relates to their replacement of the striking modernistic devices that characterize much of his previous work by a more traditional and old-masterly style, with heavy hatching and emphatic modeling and chiaroscuro. Lautrec occasionally had practiced this more conservative realistic style as an alternative to Modernism earlier in the 1890s, especially when he wanted to probe below the appearances of reality and to create works that were more authentic emotionally than his publicity posters and that often were intended for a more restricted, refined audience.[48] Now, as he began to adopt it as his primary direction, he may well have seen Clemenceau's commission as an opportunity to make works with a more profoundly philosophical and timeless cast. It was just these qualities that a contemporary reviewer discerned:

> M. H. de Toulouse-Lautrec has executed for this book a cover and illustrations "hors-texte" with a great dramatic sense. The mysterious life of the soul bursts forth from these vibrant lithographs with their diffused light. It's not at all caricature, it's not even the depiction of manners, it's the depiction of humanity.[49]

Lautrec may have manifested his initial impression that Clemenceau's book was "against the Jews" in his first attempt at the cover. In somewhat muddled fashion, it appears to allude to a variety of anti-Semitic ideas. The lithograph presents a crudely primitive, long-haired, and bearded Moses, shown in dark silhouette. Having reached the peak of Mount Sinai, he is prostrated, but not before God offering the tablets of the Law: what he reaches toward instead is an image of the resplendent white imperial eagle of Poland.[50] The most immediate implication would seem to be that Moses has discovered his Sinai, and hence the Jew, his promised land, in Poland, and by association that below "at the foot of Sinai" is to be found the mass of idolatrous Jewish humanity described in the Old Testament.

Lautrec cast his Moses in a form which seems to be a curious cross between the devil and the Wandering Jew. Like the Wandering Jew, he appears emaciated, ragged, and exhausted by his endless journey. In the late nineteenth century, with the influx of large numbers of Eastern European Jews into Paris, this was at once the specific French image of the Eastern European Jew and the familiar general personification of the Jewish race, wandering homeless in foreign lands. It also embodied the threat that the Jew posed as a rootless nomad who might overrun and plunder another's land. It was this negative manifestation of the Wandering Jew that was taken up by late nineteenth-century anti-Semites.[51] It is not inconceivable that Lautrec's insinuation here was that the Jew, kneeling before the symbol of imperial power and wealth, was the despoiler of Poland, especially when one considers that Lautrec was fresh from illustrating Joze's *La Tribu d'Isidore*. Significantly, anti-Semites at this time were warning that "France was in danger of becoming another Poland, 'the victim of Jewish usurers and cosmopolitans.'"[52]

Complementing these negative associations is the quasi-demonic character of Lautrec's obscure horned Moses. It may derive from the traditional association of the Wandering Jew, or Jews in general, with the devil.[53] Seen as a satanic figure, venerating an idol of money and power, Moses carries overtones of popular anti-Semitic myths about the Jews' worship of money in place of God. Riva Castleman has associated this image, correctly I think, with the ambiguous final words of Clemenceau's book:

> What the Christians, who are after all still masters of the world, need above anything else, is to better their own ways; then they will not need to fear the Jews who may be reaching out for the crown of opulence, which has ever been coveted by men of all ages and of all countries.[54]

Clemenceau rejected this cover and Lautrec replaced it with a more straightforward illustration of Moses atop Mount Sinai, kneeling before the tablets of the law, with his right hand upraised; at the foot of the mountain is the rubble of the destroyed golden calf, and the plains extending in the distance are illuminated by the light of the rising sun. The new image was succinct, visually effective, and not so vulnerable to anti-Semitic interpretations.

The first two selections in *Au Pied du Sinaï* were fables of Jewish life in Eastern Europe which Clemenceau used to make moralizing points about human nature and the evils of materialism and exploitation of the poor by the rich. To illustrate them Lautrec relied on the manipulation of traditional caricatural stereotypes of Jews. In "Baron Moses," Clemenceau employed the Jew in his standard role as the personification of capitalism. However, the story, and one of Lautrec's illustrations for it, ultimately involves an ironic inversion of that stereotype. Originally published in *L'Illustration*, July 1896,[55] it recounts the tale of Baron Moses von Goldschlammbach, who was "very rich, in fact, too rich"; he was "protagonist of a struggle in which everything serves the abusive power of one individual against the right of all to live." Born into wealth and luxury, he was amoral and heartless, a man unmoved "by the sight of human suffering" and incapable of genuine charity. The baron's spiritual emptiness gradually drove him mad; ironically he became obsessed with the idea of hunger. So that he might experience what it is to be hungry, he rejected all nourishment and starved himself until convulsions of pain impelled him out on the street to beg. Now, in a reversal of fate, he experienced the rich bourgeois's callous indifference to suffering. Finally, recognizing himself in those who rejected his entreaties, he understood "that one must give, give all."[56] But it was too late for redemption, and he tragically collapsed and died before he could put the lesson to use.

Lautrec's pair of illustrations presents a contrast. In the first he showed the bored baron, a standard stereotype of the rich man, "at the opera, seated behind naked shoulders."[57] Here Lautrec recycled one or another of his own scenes of theater loges.[58] In the second, he depicted the climactic scene of the baron begging. He closely followed Clemenceau's text, showing the baron, bent over in the pain of hunger, approaching an impervious

bourgeois, his arm outstretched to tug at the man's sleeve: "unconsciously he imitates the very inflections and attitudes of the mendicants that used to pursue him."[59] In this case, Lautrec simply adapted the stock scene of the beggar spurned by the uncaring, rich, fat bourgeois (often Jewish) that was commonly used in popular leftist and anti-Semitic illustrations. However, he did not employ the unflattering caricatural distortions of the Jewish physiognomy of the more blatantly anti-Semitic caricaturists. And, like Clemenceau, he made a chastening reversal in which the Jew becomes the beggar and is made the victim of his own uncharitableness.

The second of Clemenceau's two fables is "Schlome the Fighter," originally published in August 1895 in *La Dépêche de Toulouse*.[60] It is the story of a poor Jewish tailor who barely eked out a living for his wife and five children

Henri de Toulouse-Lautrec, *Au Pied du Sinaï*, Baron Moses at the Opera, 1897

Henri de Toulouse-Lautrec, *Au Pied du Sinaï*, Baron Moses Begging, 1897

Maximilien Radiguet, *It's necessary that there are some unfortunates, if only to conserve pity in the heart of men*, published in *Le Rire*, March 7, 1896

Henri de Toulouse-Lautrec, *Au Pied du Sinaï*, Schlome Fuss Conscripted, 1897

Henri de Toulouse-Lautrec, *Au Pied du Sinaï*, Schlome Fuss at the Synagogue, 1897

in the eastern Galician village of Busk. To avoid conscription into the Emperor's army, the Jews of that region paid substitutes to take their places. However, in 1848, when no more substitutes could be found, the grand council of "the most pious and wealthiest" Jews of Busk ("that oligarchy of money, which appropriates all it can of the privileges of the less favored classes") decided to draw lots from among the names of the lowliest members of the community, hence choosing Schlome Fuss. The first of Lautrec's two illustrations follows Clemenceau's account of how a "stunned" Schlome was dragged off in the night by the cossacks to serve in the army, while his family was left behind to suffer "the trials of poverty." Lautrec pictured Schlome as a stereotypical Eastern European Jew, with sidelocks and quaint costume, frail and frightened. When the war ended Schlome returned to Busk on leave, having undergone a remarkable metamorphosis. He was no longer recognizable as a Jew, but was a hero and a cossack, "a splendid soldier with braid and gilt and boots, a saber at his side and medals on his chest."[61] The new Schlome appears in Lautrec's second scene, which provides a striking foil to his first. No longer a meek, emasculated, and powerless victim, but an imposingly muscular, virile, and decisive figure, in control of his own destiny, he confronts the townspeople who had betrayed him and "demands justice."[62] On Yom Kippur, he went to the synagogue, "his prayer cloak thrown over the uniform," and as

the Rabbi ascended toward the tabernacle to take the sacred Scroll of the Law ... to the amazement of all, Schlome plunged forward, stepped before the officiating minister and laying an impious hand on his arm, barred the way to the tabernacle.

The indignant crowd of worshipers "rushed toward the blasphemer to punish him for his crime . . . But Schlome dominated the crowd and with saber drawn held back the most daring . . . Standing on the topmost step, the point of his saber against the floor," Schlome spoke, berating them for their cowardice in having "sold me even as Benjamin [sic] was sold by his brothers" and "exposed to abject misery my wife, Leah, and my children."

> I return as avenger. I declare to you today, the day of the Great Atonement, that you will not perform the holy ceremony on which depend life and death of each creature, and that you will not be pardoned, unless you offer me full reparation for your odious crime.[63]

After initial resistance, the villagers acceded to Schlome's demands. His family was granted an indemnity, public apologies were made, and he went off to complete his term of military service. Ironically, once discharged from the army, Schlome grew back his side-curls and reverted "to his previous state of impotence and humility."[64]

Clemenceau used this tale to dramatize his criticism of the exploitation of the poor by the rich. In that sense, it is striking that although the rich Jew continued to play the role of oppressor of the poorer classes, in this case the poor exploited victim was also a Jew. This can be understood in purely anti-Semitic terms, i.e. the rich Jew even sells out his own kind. Alternatively, it may reflect the growing recognition of the existence of an exploited Jewish proletariat, and a new willingness to see the Jew as a victim that developed as a result of "the massive emigration of Eastern European Jewish workers westward from the 1880s on." This was another element that eventually led leftists to "reappraise their assumptions about the socio-economic profile of the Jews" and to distance themselves from an anti-Semitic stance.[65] Here Schlome stands for the ultimate victory of the downtrodden—"He had really fought for his right. He had come out of the fight a victor."[66]

Nochlin has pointed to the other oddity this little story elucidates: the fact that in order for the Jew to take on a positive, heroic image, he must assume the qualities of the non-Jew. It is the point that Lautrec consciously or unconsciously amplified in his contrast between the pitifully passive, helpless, and weak little tailor of his first illustration and the attractive figure of Schlome the cossack, who loomed large, proud, and dominant, in his second:

> This is the only time that a Jew is represented as strong and sympathetic in the series—when the figure is totally unrecognizable as a Jew. We have to discover from the context, rather that this is an anomaly: a Jewish Cossack. This is a token not so much of Lautrec's personal anti-Semitism as it is of the fact that

there was no visual language available with which he might have constructed an image at once identifiably Jewish and at the same time "positive" in terms that would be generally legible. The signifiers that indicated "Jewishness" in the late ninteenth century were too firmly locked into a system of negative connotations: picturesqueness is the closest he could get to a relatively benign representation of Jews who look "Jewish."[67]

It is their potential for "picturesqueness" and the more negative signifiers of Jewishness that Lautrec fell back on in his renderings of Eastern European Jews for the final three selections of *Au Pied du Sinaï*. These are Clemenceau's personal impressions of life in the Jewish ghettos and towns he visited. The first of the three, "En Israël: Carlsbad," was originally published in *Le Journal*, August 1895.[68] It is a colorful description of the orthodox Polish Jews Clemenceau encountered at Carlsbad; its title has the same connotation as that of the book. The newspaper versions of Clemenceau's final two selections, "Impressions of Galicia" (mainly an account of the ghetto at Cracow) and "Busk" (a description of a Jewish village in Galicia), were published as a series of three articles in *La Dépêche de Toulouse* in May 1897.[69] Lautrec's illustrations may also be life studies, based on his own observations of Eastern European Jewish immigrants in Paris. According to Maurice Joyant, to prepare for this project, "Lautrec went into the neighborhoods of La Tournelle, where the milieux of foreign Jews of humble circumstance could be found."[70]

In these travelogue accounts Clemenceau mixed a sense of exotic otherness with philosophizing evaluations of the Jewish character in which sympathetic sentiments are contradicted by overtly anti-Semitic statements. He indulged in considerable negative stereotyping regarding both the physical and character traits of his Jewish subjects, painting them as an alien, foreign race, whose appearance, bodily odors, and behavior evoke feelings of disgust. And he peppered his descriptions with references to the "filthy Jew" and derogatory comments about his deceitful character, "feigned humility," and "obsequiously provocative" nature.[71]

For his part, Lautrec attempted to make his illustrations of these "strange," "squalid creatures" faithful and picturesque counterparts to Clemenceau's verbal descriptions. His somewhat caricatural rendering of the stereotypical Eastern European Jews of Carlsbad, with their "long coats that flap about the heels," towering hats, strong noses, bristly beards, and "greasy" frame of "corkscrew curls that dance and bob to and fro before the ears" is a case in point. The bent posture of the main figure is Lautrec's own addition to the various signs of Jewish difference enumerated by Clemenceau, but it helps to convey the diseased quality the text refers to: "These Jews of Galicia come to Carslbad to be cured of Asiatic ailments

A JEW OF BRODY

aggravated by consanguine marriages."[72] The irony of this could not have been lost on Lautrec, himself the sickly product of a consanguine marriage—but it apparently failed to elicit in him feelings of empathy or an identification with these fellow outcasts.

While Lautrec's image is not flattering, it is not especially hostile. It conjures up, in a milder, less vulgar fashion, the same physically unappealing type of Eastern European Jew frequently found in more overtly anti-Semitic caricatures. It is rather similar to the examples Pennell used to illustrate his less generous characterization of the Eastern European Jew as, "a miserable, weak, consumptive-looking specimen of humanity." Despite Lautrec's (and Clemenceau's) more moderate tone, they ultimately promoted the same notion of the Jews as "a race apart."[73] Given the varying levels of animosity with which this message is conveyed, it is difficult to know where the line was drawn between anti-Semitism and something short of it that was merely character typing.

Lautrec illustrated Clemenceau's description of the religious practices of the Hasidic Jews he encountered at Carlsbad with his "Prayer of the Polish Jews." Clemenceau explained that since this sect "did not accept the ordinary ritual of the Synagogue and met simply among themselves for prayer," he went to observe their Sabbath services "in a small room of a poor restaurant." In this case Lautrec attempted to capture, through a deeply shadowed

Henri de Toulouse-Lautrec,
Au Pied du Sinaï, Polish Jews at
Carlsbad, 1897

Joseph Pennell, *The Jew at Home:
Impressions of a Summer and Autumn
Spent with him in Russia and Austria*,
A Jew of Brody, 1892

Henri de Toulouse-Lautrec,
Au Pied du Sinaï, Prayer of the
Polish Jews, 1897

chiaroscuro rendering, the visual nuances of Clemenceau's quasi-poetic description of the worshipers as mysterious "apparitions" in "those draperies of white, streaked with black . . . Big, white phantoms, their heads under the veil, seemed plunged into the contemplation of the wall, which faced east. The prayer cloak which they receive at the age of thirteen and in which they are buried, must never be washed."[74] Lautrec conveyed the strange spectacle of the rhythmic rocking movement of the prayers, the bowing and rising, the plunging of the heads forward and back, by contrasting a standing figure who inclines forward with seated figures who lean backward. It seems a sympathetic attempt to achieve the Rembrandtesque grandeur and profundity explicitly indicated by Clemenceau in his description: "Beside me is the fine face of an old man, suggesting the gentle philosophers of Rembrandt under the arches of a stairway losing itself in nocturnal darkness, impassive with a discreet little smile."[75]

Lautrec returned to a somewhat less sympathetic stereotyping in his two scenes of Jewish street merchants in Cracow, giving them an almost sinister air and creating images which reinforce negative myths about Jewish business tactics. The first, a densely shadowed portrayal of a vendor crouching in wait for his "prey" in a murky and forbidding back alley shop, recreates the sense of darkness, dirt, and mystery of Clemenceau's text, but avoids reiterating its more directly anti-Semitic overtones:

Henri de Toulouse-Lautrec, *Au Pied du Sinaï*, A Back Room in Cracow, 1897

In the depth of the black little shops, among dress goods, metals, victuals and what not, eyes shine out of the silvery waves of a prophet's beard. Hooked noses, clawlike hands seem to grip obscure objects and refuse to release them unless the tinkling of money is heard.[76]

The second illustration relates to Clemenceau's description of the Cracow cloth market "where Israel is enthroned in all glory." Lautrec captured the aggressiveness of the Jewish merchants as they pursue and assail potential customers. They spy on the passer-by and "plunge upon the innocent" as if "in ambush." "Affectionate hands touch your shoulder or your arm. But do not resist, for the caressing fingers suddenly contract and you are caught."[77] Lautrec followed the old formula of the bourgeois spurning the beggar, but this "beggar" is a nuisance who deserves to be repulsed. He

Henri de Toulouse-Lautrec, *Au Pied du Sinaï*, The Cloth Market at Cracow, 1897

also captured the sense of the crushing crowd, by using a ring of silhouetted heads around the two central figures of the merchant and his prey, the narrator, who attempts to escape his grip.

Modern historians have differentiated between two levels of anti-Semitism. One is "ideological," based on a "structured and intellectualized system of ideas" and "coupled with the emergence of anti-Semitic groups and leagues." This was a relatively new phenomenon in the late nineteenth century, a time when anti-Semitism as a coherent ideology grew in strength. However, it was founded and dependent upon the other, more traditional, vaguer, and more latent, social and cultural anti-Semitism. This was a pervasive dislike of Jews that found expression in "a variety of forms, ranging from hostile beliefs and stereotypes to discriminatory behavior, formal and informal."[78] This more discreet form of anti-Semitism was broadly tolerated and accepted at all social levels and political persuasions, even by Jews, in turn-of-the-century France.

Anti-Semitism was not a clear central motivating force in Lautrec's life and character, but it does seem plausible that he either shared in or condoned the widespread dislike of Jews. The problem of assessing his attitude toward Jews is complicated by the fact that since these works are illustrations of texts by others, we cannot be certain of the extent to which they merely reflect the texts they illustrate as opposed to projecting a personal position. In any case, Lautrec evidently was willing to accept and perpetuate the negative stereotypes of the texts he illustrated and opportunistically to cater to the prejudices of his audience.

Moreover, since we do not necessarily make the same distinctions as did the late nineteenth century, in assessing the relative degrees of anti-Semitism of Lautrec's illustrations and Joze's and Clemenceau's texts the modern observer is confronted by the further problem of where to draw the line between dislike of Jews and anti-Semitism in Joze's "precise sense of the word." In the end, to our eyes, despite the differences in the degree of blatancy between Joze, who verged on outright anti-Semitism, and Clemenceau and Lautrec, who transmitted negative stereotypes, the three have much in common. What is remarkable to us is that even while calling for tolerance, Clemenceau could accuse Jews of the same sins as Joze did, and Lautrec, while accepting Jews as his closest friends, could employ the same derogatory stereotypes.

This was probably not so contradictory and inconsistent a situation in their own time as it seems in retrospect. Clearly the issue of anti-Semitism was seen in different terms in late nineteenth-century France from those of today. The use of racial and religious stereotypes apparently did not have the same offensive connotations as it does to a generation conditioned with the hindsight provided by the Holocaust. Such stereotypes were seen as simply reflecting aspects of reality rather than distorting it, and not as leading to disastrous consequences; obviously one could indulge in negative stereotyping without being identified as an anti-Semite. Clemenceau could perceive the danger of rabid anti-Semitism of professionals like Drumont, yet he was unable to see his own dislike of Jews in the same light. What this study illuminates, then, is the complexity of late nineteenth-century attitudes toward Jews, the difficulty in gaining a perspective on them, and the fact that beyond the easily recognizable anti-Semitism of the fanatic professionals, the situation is not at all clear-cut.

4

John Singer Sargent's Portraits of the Wertheimer Family

KATHLEEN ADLER

Between 1898 and 1908 John Singer Sargent was engaged in a unique project, painting twelve portraits of the London art dealer Asher Wertheimer and his family. He described himself during these years as being in a state of "chronic Wertheimerism."[1] The paintings are all large in size and several were exhibited in the Royal Academy's annual exhibitions. Nine of them are now in the Tate Gallery, London. Although Sargent, like portraitists before him, often painted more than one member of a family, neither he nor his predecessors had ever received a commission on such a scale, particularly not from a middle-class family. The commission represents a challenge to long-established codes for grand-manner portraiture in a variety of ways, not only in its subject and its display, but also in being so overtly a series of representations of "the Jew." The portraits signal the aspirations of a middle-class Jewish family to be regarded in the same light as the aristocracy, and Wertheimer's intention that the majority of them be exhibited in a public space marks a further breach with the conventions surrounding family portraits.

Asher Wertheimer was a well-established art dealer with premises in New Bond Street. He was the son of a bronze maker and art dealer, Samson, who came to Britain from Germany in the 1830's, and the brother of another art dealer, Charles. Samson was one of many dealers in all sorts, not only in art but also in antiques, toys, jewelry, picture frames, and a host of other commodities, who came to London during the Victorian era and who gradually established themselves in English society.[2] Asher specialized in Old Master paintings and *objets d'art*, including oriental porcelain. As a young man, he traveled to St. Petersburg, acquiring paintings there from members of the Russian nobility and selling them in Britain. He repeated this journey several times and also bought works at auctions in Paris and elsewhere in Europe. In the latter part of the nineteenth century, third-generation members of the Rothschild family began to buy art works of all kinds, and Asher was one of the dealers who benefited from this. Other dealers of German Jewish extraction, such as Friedrich Spitzer and the

Goldschmidts, also relied heavily on Rothschild custom, as did Asher's long-established rivals in New Bond Street, Colnaghi's and Agnew's, but Asher was a favorite dealer of the Rothschilds, Baron Ferdinand de Rothschild in particular.[3] He also sold to Sir Richard Wallace, and to collectors throughout Europe. Numerous collections in Europe, the United States, and Britain contain works which passed through his hands.[4]

The year 1898, in which Asher commissioned the first of the portraits from Sargent, was an important one for him: it was the year in which he and his wife Flora, the daughter of an antique dealer, Edward Joseph, celebrated their silver wedding anniversary and it also marked his establishment as a dealer of considerable stature with his purchase of the Francis Hope collection from Lord Francis Clinton-Hope for a total of £121,550. The Hope collection consisted of 83 paintings, among them Vermeers and Rembrandts, some purchased directly from the artists. Wertheimer was part of a syndicate with Otto Gutkunst, representing Colnaghi's.[5]

Sargent's portrait of Asher and his first portrait of Flora were painted to mark their wedding anniversary. The portrait of Flora did not please the couple, but the portrait of Asher was very well received by the family. A second painting of Mrs Wertheimer was completed in 1904, and between 1901 and 1908 Sargent also painted Wertheimer's sons Edward, Alfred, Conway, and Ferdinand and his daughters Helena (known as Ena), Betty, Hylda, Essie, Almina, and Ruby, both on their own and in various combinations. Asher's only regret, it was reported, was that there were not more Wertheimers for Sargent to paint.

By the end of the century, Sargent was the most fashionable and sought-after portraitist in Britain. His portraits cost 1,000 guineas or more, an enormous sum, and his position in British art was one of the greatest prominence. There had always been some critics, however, who regarded him as facile. This view of Sargent culminated in the sustained attack Roger Fry made on him in the *New Statesman* in 1923, when he described Sargent's portraiture, and specifically the Wertheimer portraits, as "art applied to social requirements and social ambitions." Fry continued:

> I see now that this marvellous group of portraits represents a social transaction quite analogous to the transaction between a man and his lawyer. A rich man has need of a lawyer's professional skill to enable him to secure the transmission of his wealth to posterity, and a rich man, if he have the intelligence of Sir [sic] Asher Wertheimer and the luck to meet a Sargent, can, by the latter's professional skill, transmit this skill to posterity.[6]

Fry's view of Sargent, that he enabled the middle classes to attain a position in society, and that he facilitated the aspirations and ambitions of a *parvenu* group, is one with a long afterlife. In 1964, the critic John Russell wrote:

"Quicker than the Home Office, he [Sargent] naturalised those who would otherwise have lingered in the between-world where class, nationality, money, and money's provenance, were matters to be raised without a qualm. For the reassurance-collector, there was no other painter in the country."[7]

Both Fry and Russell manifest their xenophobia in their comments, with which is allied the snobbery of those with aristocratic beliefs toward the upward mobility of the middle classes. In late nineteenth-century and early twentieth-century England, Jews were often those associated with recent wealth and with *arriviste* pretensions, and xenophobia readily combined with anti-Semitism. An extreme but not unrepresentative form of this was expressed by one F. Hugh O'Donnell, who wrote in the *New Witness* in 1913 that London Jews were always prepared to back the eastern Shylocks and that the London community could be increased by any "stuttering alien who paid 60 shillings to become a Citizen of England, an Heir of Magna Carta . . ."[8] Lord Newton, in a debate in the House of Lords on controlling what he called "the tribe of usurers" in 1913, repeatedly referred to Jewish assimilation, to "Blumberg becoming Burton, Cohen becoming Curzon," to what he described as "Moses and Aaron trading as Crewe and Lansdowne."[9]

At the same time, these years between the "Jewish emancipation" of 1870 and the beginning of the First World War have been described as "the Golden Age of the Jewish people in Britain."[10] The circle around the Prince of Wales was known as Edward's "Jewish Court,"[11] so noticeable was his liking for the company of wealthy Jews such as the Sassoons, Ernest Cassel, Baron Maurice de Hirsch, Edward Levy-Lawson, and of course the Rothschilds, especially Barons Lionel and Nathaniel. Both the left- and the right-wing press complained that the Prince of Wales was "practically in the hands of the Jews": his constant need for funds and the readiness of various friends to oblige him ensured that many of his circle were ennobled, and it was possible to say that riches secured readier access to society in aristocratic England than in republican America. Arnold White, author of *The Modern Jew*, published in 1899, commented: "In the art of hypnotizing large communities of shareholders into the belief that something is to be made of nothing, there is no equal to the immigran [sic] Hebrew when he begins to prosper. His success has been imperial."[12] The Rothschilds in particular were seen as being synonymous with the power of money. The historian J. A. Hobson wrote in 1902: "Does anyone seriously suppose that a great war could be undertaken by any European state, or any great State loan subscribed, if the house of Rothschild and its connections set their face against it?"[13] This view of "the Jew" equated all Jews with unprincipled moneylenders and was particularly prevalent during the years of the Boer War, which was widely perceived as being fought to protect Jewish interests. Johannesburg was often described in both the left- and the right-wing press as "Jewburg," with fulminations against the resources in southern Africa passing into the control of "a small group of international financiers, chiefly German in origin and Jewish in race."[14]

The anger that was directed against the controlling interests of rich Jews was also directed against a very different group of Jews, the immigrants from Eastern Europe who were settling in East London. Parts of Bethnal Green were referred to as "Jew's Island," and the Mile End was often described as "Jerusalem" or "a second Palestine." A highly popular tract, Joseph Banister's *England under the Jews*, which appeared in three editions between 1901 and 1907, referred to Jews in a whole range of hate-filled terms, of which "Yiddish money-pigs" and "Yiddish bloodsuckers" are some of the mildest (Banister also speculated whether or not the King was Jewish).[15] The inflammatory nature of much of the writing and the speeches about Jewish immigration led to frequent outbreaks of violence. The 1905 Aliens Act, although it did not specifically mention Jews, was intended to control the influx from Eastern Europe.

The Wertheimers and their circle, secure in Connaught Place in London's West End, were far removed from the open hostility that raged on the streets of Bethnal Green. But no Jew at this period, whether a member of one of the great Anglo-Jewish families, a wealthy art dealer, or a recently arrived immigrant, could ignore the fact that, despite the liberalism which meant that in many ways English Jews were in a happier position than their counterparts in Germany, Austria, or France, the question of Jewish identity was paramount.[16] This was an issue that related not only to how various constituencies of Jews perceived themselves, but also to how they were perceived by others.

Sargent's portraits play a perhaps small but significant part in both these processes. In the year preceding the first of the Wertheimer portraits, his painting *Portrait of Mrs. Carl Meyer and her Children* excited considerable comment when it was shown at the Royal Academy.[17] The reviewer for the *Spectator* said that "even Mr Sargent's skill had not succeeded in making attractive these over-civilized Orientals."[18] Henry James, a close friend of Sargent's, admired the painting, but he too wrote of the children's faces that they were "Jewish to a quaint orientalism, faces to peep out of the lattice or the curtains of closed seraglio or palanquin."[19] This connection between Jews and the otherness of "the orient" was a familiar one with a long history both in England and in France, and is seen to operate here in two ways, in presenting a view of the assimilated English Jews firstly as bearing the marks of civilization to excess—unlike their "English" counterparts who were, of course, regarded as civilized to the appropriate degree—and

John Singer Sargent,
*Portrait of Mrs. Carl Meyer
and her Children*, 1897

secondly as other to the point of being objects of fascination and fantasy
from the world of the harem.

In 1867 Henry James had written that the Americans had the ability to
"deal freely with forms of civilization not our own, [to] pick and choose
and assimilate and in short . . . claim property wherever we find it."[20]
Sargent, who by the late 1890's was becoming known as "the painter of
Jews," had availed himself of this cultural freedom for many years.[21] In the
late 1870's, for instance, he traveled to Capri where he described his main
model as "a magnificent type, about seventeen years of age, her complexion a rich nut-brown, with masses of blue-black hair, very beautiful and of
an Arab type."[22] His Spanish paintings, such as the 1882 Salon painting *El
Jaleo*, reveal the same fascination with exotic "types," and in 1922, near the
end of his life, he showed Martin Birnbaum "an enormous scrap album,
filled for the greater part with photographs and reproductions of aborig-
inal types the world over."[23] Sargent's claim to prefer painting Jewish
women because they had more "life and movement"[24] than English women
is part of both his continuing fascination with the other and, perhaps, his
identification with this otherness. Despite his eminence as a painter,
Sargent was himself something of an outsider: as Trevor Fairbrother has

recently suggested, he was almost certainly homosexual,[25] and he was an American born in Italy, who grew up in Europe without ever living in the United States. Henry James asked "But *is* a painter an American . . . after he has become an RA, especially a painter born, like Mr. Sargent, beside the Arno and with 40 years of Europe on his conscience?"[26] Sargent painted the cream of British, French, and American society without ever feeling at ease in their company, saying that every new portrait made him at least one enemy. The savaging he received at the hands of critics like Fry reminds one that the most apparently accepted of figures can easily become a pariah to a group with different values.

Sargent's paintings served as statements of wealth and success, both in their nature as objects, grand society portraits intended to hang first on the walls of the Royal Academy and then in wealthy dwellings, and as testaments to what his sitters had achieved in being able to commission a painting from him. Wertheimer must have intended the initial portraits of himself and his wife to function in this way, and his own portrait to attest to his stature in the world of art dealing. When it was exhibited at the Royal Academy, it was generally very favorably received. The critic of *The Times* began his two-part review:

> We speak of genius; nobody that was present at the private view yesterday . . .
> will require to be told that we speak of Mr. Sargent. . . . his "Mr. Wertheimer" is
> nothing short of amazing. Assuredly Mr. Sargent is such a painter as Cromwell
> would have loved . . . He has sometimes been charged with a tendency, if not to

John Singer Sargent,
Colonel Ian Hamilton, 1898

John Singer Sargent,
Asher Wertheimer, 1898

caricature, at least to dwell upon some marked characteristic of a face, or some habitual attitude of his sitter, a little too exclusively . . . But in the portrait of which we are speaking there is no dwelling upon any one feature at the expense of the rest, because everything here is characteristic and everything has been put in its place by the painter with the most astonishing realism. It would be very hard to name any other modern painter that we could rank with this for sheer power of expression.[27]

Next to one of Sargent's more conventional society portraits, such as that exactly contemporary of Colonel Ian Hamilton, the portrait of Asher Wertheimer may, despite the *Times* critic's views, be seen to come perilously close to caricature. While the portrait of the Colonel focuses on his digni-fied stance and profile, and particularly on the details of his uniform, the portrait of Asher—"the Jew"—incorporates many of the elements beloved of anti-Semitic caricature. Wertheimer has the hooded eyes, large nose, and above all, the fleshy lips that are seen to characterize the "race."[28] His cigar indicates not only wealth but also vulgarity and sexuality. The notion of the excessive sexuality of the Jew is here displaced onto the dog in the extreme foreground. A favorite family pet, who appears in other portraits, this large poodle called Noble is an animal controlled and constrained not only by its pedigree breeding but also by the artifice of its clipping. But its animal nature is made manifest in the slavering tongue, a shocking pink accent in the foreground, startling against the dark tones of the painting and suggestive of passion and sexuality in a way quite unknown in, for instance, the portrait of Colonel Hamilton. Another aspect of "the Jew" is suggested in the pose: Wertheimer is represented looking slightly off to the side, in a manner which hints at furtiveness. This portrait could be, and indeed often was, regarded as the very image of the stereotype of the rich Jew, excessively flashy and, since art dealing was viewed as only slightly above money lending, probably of somewhat dubious honesty. From its first exhibition, despite the high praise often afforded the work of Sargent, the portrait of Asher was also always thought to reveal the characteristics of Wertheimer's "race." Henry Adams wrote of it: "Sargent has just completed another Jew. Wertheimer, a worse crucifixion than history tells us of."[29]

But the portrait of Asher is not just a caricature, despite its caricatural elements, nor is it simply anti-Semitic despite its anti-Semitic elements. It represents Wertheimer as a benevolent but humorous patriach, and it was hung in the dining room of the family home in such a way that it looked down on the family. Wertheimer and his family liked both the portrait and the artist, and Sargent had considerable affection for the Wertheimers. In later years, he referred to the family dining room with its display of eight of the portraits as "Sargent's mess" and the Wertheimers' home was apparently something of a refuge for him from less enjoyable social obligations.[30] The portrait therefore served both as a likeness which satisfied the family and as an image which proclaimed the sitter's identity as a Jew—a Jew of a particular class, distinguished by his wealth. The painting may today seem obscure, both because the sitter is no longer well known and because Sargent has been so marginalized in accounts of twentieth-century art, but it was not marginal or obscure at the time of its first showing, or at its later showings in New York in December 1898 and at the American section of the Exposition Universelle in 1900. Robert Ross, writing in *The Art Journal* in January 1911, described it as "one of the great portraits of the world, the only modern picture which challenges the Doria Velazquez [the portrait of Innocent X] at Rome."[31]

Sargent's approach to portraiture *was* in many ways caricatural—he liked to seize on the essential physical characteristics of his sitters, and heighten them. Unlike a caricaturist, however, he worked within the bounds of the conventions for society portraiture, and could not afford to offend his patrons. The Wertheimers, in particular Asher and his daughters, appear to have appealed to him because of their vitality and their confidence, and in these portraits, he trod a fine line between the necessary strictures of grand portraiture, his interest in their otherness as physical types, and his friendship with the family. The painter and critic Jacques-Emile Blanche, who knew both Sargent and the Wertheimers, wrote:

> He [Sargent] found the Jewish type . . . more inspiring than aristocratic sitters. He was excited when he did the Wertheimer family, the father whom Rembrandt would have painted with a turban, the daughters with their gipsy complexion; just as Carmencita had once moved him. Here was something that did not intimidate him, they appealed to him because they were more human in their eagerness, their simple confidence in their superiority, and this he made clear in their expressions. English Jews lose their characteristics of hunted wanderers, for they know how to blend into a liberal and practical society which has a sense of values and rewards them, knowing how to extract a profit from the services they render.[32]

Even more problematic than the representation of the Jew was the representation of the Jewess, and I want to consider three of Sargent's portraits of Wertheimer's daughters. Also hung in the Wertheimer dining room was the double portrait of Ena and Betty, exhibited at the Royal Academy in 1901. The critic of *The Times* praised it as "instinct with life," and it is indeed the vivacity of pose which is striking, particularly in contrast to many of Sargent's portraits of society women.[33] The poses of the two sitters, especially their physical closeness, emphasized by the position of Ena's arm around the waist of Betty, stress their physicality. Ena (in white) and Betty (in red) are very daringly dressed.[34] Contemporary fashion was generally far more covered up than this and although white was very fashionable, trimmings were all the rage at this date. The dresses suggest that the sitters were audacious young women who risked contravening the codes of society. They also invoke one of Sargent's most notorious portraits, that of *Madame X* (Madame Gautreau), shown at the Paris Salon in 1884. In that painting, Sargent was required to add shoulder straps to the dress to conform with standards of decency. Recent cleaning of the Ena and Betty portrait at the Tate Gallery has revealed that the strap of the red dress worn by Betty was originally painted as if it had slipped off the shoulder, suggesting even more than in the present state of the painting that these women were not only "vivacious" but also verged on the immodest.[35] As in the portrait of their father, Sargent alludes to their sexuality—the sexuality not only of these specific women, but the fantasy of the sexual Jewess, the other to the modest Christian maiden.

In 1905 Sargent painted Ena on her own in a portrait which is known by the French title of *A Vele gonfie* ("In full sail"). Exhibited at the Royal

John Singer Sargent,
Ena and Betty Wertheimer, 1901

Academy in the same year as the ambitious *Marlborough Family*, this painting is a total contrast to that exercise in formal grand portraiture. Described by the critic of *The Times* as a "dashing young lady in fancy costume," the painting represents Ena as she apparently swept into Sargent's studio one day, full of impatience at the length of time he was taking to paint her.[36] Her cloak billowed about her, and Sargent asked her to move it about to keep it that way. According to the family, Ena took a broomstick and stuck it through the cloak—the broomstick is visible at the right of the canvas. She is wearing a male military uniform and a cavalier's hat. Since the painting was executed in Sargent's Tite Street studio, the uniform was presumably one of Sargent's props. The painting was given to Ena by her father on the occasion of her marriage to Robert Mathias. A painting of a bride in male military dress uniform makes this a very unconventional wedding picture. As Marjorie Garber has pointed out, "*transvestism is a space of possibility structuring and confounding culture* [her italics]: the disruptive element that intervenes, not just a category crisis of male and female, but the crisis of category itself."[37] The category "the Jewess" is itself one of a crisis of definition, and here this crisis is made explicit. The painting subverts the functions of categorization in its defiance of firm boundaries. Ena's appearance was totally at odds with conventional constructions of femininity and "daintiness": she was over six feet tall, with high coloring. The broomstick carries

John Singer Sargent,
Almina Wertheimer, 1908

inevitable associations with witches—"the Jewess" has long been associated with the powers of darkness and sorcery. Yet, at the same time, the word
"dashing," so opposed to any idea of the occult, is appropriate for the air of
vivacity and energy conveyed in this portrait. But "dashing" is an adjective
more often used for men—particularly young army officers—than for
women, especially for young Edwardian women. The wearing of a dress
uniform is an act of defiance, but it is carried off with an air of mischief
and delight. The portrait is very different from many of Sargent's more
conventional portraits of rather vacuous and dull young women. It is a portrait of a person of whom Sargent was clearly fond, and a representation
which conveys a sense of "the Jewess" as a force of nature, blown by the
wind. The portrait suggests an enjoyment on the part of the artist and his
sitter in exploding the conventional expectations of society portraiture.

In the last portrait of the series, that of Almina, the fifth surviving
Wertheimer daughter, born in 1886 and painted by Sargent in 1908 when
she was twenty-two, explicit reference is made to a tradition of the oriental
princess. This painting was not exhibited at the Royal Academy and was
hung in the Wertheimer morning room adjoining the dining room. Almina
is represented wearing a Persian costume and holding an instrument called
a *sarod* from north India (she is not shown playing it—it had to be held ver-
tically to be played). The portrait is in many respects a parody, a play on the

stereotype of the Jewish (or oriental) princess. Like Ena in *A Vele gonfie*, Almina in her extravagent costume plays to notions of excess and deviance (for it is a man's costume she wears). She is shown as an exotic object of desire; the still life of slices of melon in the foreground underscores both the exoticism and the "ripeness" and sexuality of the sitter. This portrait embraces the stereotype of "the beautiful Jewess" and acknowledges how that stereotype, as Carol Ockman has shown, lumps together Jewish women with Turkish, Greek, and Spanish women—but never, of course, with "English" women.[38]

In these portraits of the Wertheimer daughters, the issue of identity is very much to the fore. The sitters' identity as "Jewesses" was never in doubt to viewers and, especially in the portrait of Almina, it is explored in relation to the notion of the orient.[39] In the other two portraits, there is a marked sense of deviance from conventional expectation, and a characterization of "the Jewess" as daring to the point of excess. As in the portrait of Asher, these portraits are not simply caricatural, nor do they simply subscribe to anti-Semitic stereotype. Often the broad-brush approach was all that Sargent deemed necessary: in the portrait of Colonel Hamilton almost nothing is indicated about the sitter as an individual; his uniform almost entirely constitutes his persona. But in the portraits of the Wertheimers, Sargent's knowledge of and affection for the family works to counter the stereotype, and his sitters, particularly Ena and Almina, appear to have delighted in the opportunity to strike exaggerated poses and wear fancy dress.

The portraits of the Wertheimers were widely exhibited. Many of them received their first showings at the Royal Academy, and several, including the portrait of Asher, were shown in other venues. But controversy about the group of portraits entered the public domain in 1916 when Wertheimer declared his intention to leave them for "the benefit of the nation." His death two years later, in August 1918, occurred at the height of violent anti-German feeling in Britain, and his obituary in *The Times* demonstrated the importance of issues of identity in its stress, not on his Jewishness, but on the fact that, despite his German name, he was "British" through and through: "For Germany and the Germans he always had the most undisguised hatred and contempt, professional and personal, and after the war broke out he invested large sums in British war stock."[40] This fluidity in the transfer of anxiety from one group to another is one of the characteristics of stereotyping.[41] Often regarded as the epitome of "the Jew," Wertheimer is here retrieved from one otherness more feared at that time than "the Jew"—the German. Hostility toward Germans or perceived Germans was so strong that Asher's two surviving sons, Conway and Ferdinand, both changed their names at this period, adopting Conway as a family name and becoming known as Conway Conway and Bob Conway.

The paintings were left to Mrs Wertheimer during her lifetime and continued to be hung in the family home, but soon after her death in 1922 nine of them entered the National Gallery. Four years later, in 1926, they were moved to the newly created "Sargent Room" of the Tate Gallery, then the National Gallery of British Art, an adjunct to the National Gallery. It was at this time that the perception of the group of paintings as excessive and as embodying what were seen as characteristics of the Jewish "race" surfaces most vividly. In a parliamentary question session about the bequest, reported in *Hansard* on March 8, 1923, the Member of Parliament for Oxford University and Chichele Professor of Modern History, Sir Charles William Chadwick Oman said: "Can the right hon. Gentleman [the Chancellor of the Exchequer, Stanley Baldwin] manage that these clever, but extremely repulsive pictures should be placed in a special chamber of horrors, and not between the brilliant examples of the art of Turner?" This vividly conveys the sense of disquiet, even revulsion, and above all the sense of otherness which was evoked by Sargent's paintings. These paintings, in this view, partook of the characteristics of a freak show. The reference to Turner indicates the extent to which the Wertheimer portraits, rather than the works of the American Sargent in general, were perceived as alien to understood notions of Britishness and British art.

This is due to two factors: first, the fact that the portraits were so clearly identified as representations of "Jews," in a range of critical comment from their first exhibition through to their display as a group, first at the National Gallery and then at the Tate; and second, because the idea that a single family, without aristocratic claims or pretensions, could presume to have twelve portraits of its members, all large in size, was regarded as excessive. And it is excess that most characterizes criticism of "the Jew" in Britain at this period. In the early years of the century, wealthy Jews, like the members of King Edward VII's circle, were viewed as excessively wealthy and excessively powerful, controlling too many business and even military interests. Poor Jews in the East End were, in different ways, also regarded as excessive: they were seen to pose a threat to long-time local residents because they took their jobs and their housing, were dirty, looked peculiar, spoke a peculiar language, did not mix with others, and by having large families threatened to gain dominance. In the years leading up to the passing of the Aliens Act, the language of excess echoes through the debates and disputes about immigration to the East End. After the First World War, when the Wertheimer portraits were exhibited as a group, another form of excess was perceived. One Wertheimer portrait a year in the Royal Academy was acceptable, even interesting, but the whole group together was simply too much. Although the debate tended to be couched in terms such as whether it was acceptable for works by a living artist to enter the National Gallery, the Wertheimer gift was regarded as an attempt to storm the hallowed halls of the galleries.[42] In 1924, the Keeper of the National Gallery, Henry Collins Baker, wrote to Conway Conway that the "very exceptional procedure" of devoting one room to the series of portraits had "given rise to a considerable amount of antagonistic feeling and criticism in certain artistic circles."[43] The challenge the group posed to grand-manner portraiture of the eighteenth century was heightened by the fact that the Wertheimer portraits were exhibited between portraits by Reynolds, Lawrence, and Opie, and a huge amount of press publicity ensured that they received wide public attention.[44] In 1926 the group was displayed, together with other Sargent paintings including the portrait of the Hunter sisters and *Carnation, Lily, Lily, Rose* in the newly constructed "Sargent Room," part of the gift of Sir Joseph Duveen to the Tate Gallery. But very quickly, despite the protests of Conway Conway that his father had always intended the portraits to be shown as a whole, the group was dispersed, and the portraits have not been displayed together for many years.

A quarter of a century elapsed between Wertheimer's first commission to Sargent and the public display of the paintings. Sargent's reputation, at its peak during the years the portraits were painted, had ebbed. He refused to have anything to do with modern art, saying in 1914 to Paul Helleu: "Ingres, Raphael and El Greco, these are now my admirations, these are what I like."[45] Although his work was still praised, criticisms like those of the artist Forbes Watson and the photographer Paul Strand because increasingly common. Watson argued in 1917 that Sargent and his supporters constituted an aging generation ignorant of the "vital art" that flourished in Paris in the 1890's,[46] while Strand dismissed Sargent's watercolors as "a record of something that has been seen rather than life that has been felt."[47] The gift to the National Gallery reinforced the sense, even before his death in 1925, that he belonged to the great tradition of British portraiture, the heir to eighteenth-century portraitists like Reynolds and Gainsborough. He was no longer seen as the brilliant chronicler of the contemporary he had appeared to be at the turn of the century.

The reception the group of paintings was accorded was also affected by changing attitudes to British Jewry from the First World War on. During the Russian Revolution Jews were widely believed to have been the one group who gained from events in Russia. The publication in English in 1920 and the widespread discussion of the *Protocols of the Elders of Zion* fostered this climate of distrust of the intentions of Jews.[48] While sinister motives were not overtly ascribed to the Wertheimer gift, the portraits were viewed as a manifestation of an attempt by a Jewish family to infiltrate a British institution and to challenge its conventions of acceptability and propriety.

5

Salome, Syphilis, Sarah Bernhardt, and the Modern Jewess

SANDER L. GILMAN

A Problem in the Gendering of Stereotypes

One of the most fascinating problems in tracing the stereotype of the Jew in turn-of-the-century German culture is the evident difference which gender makes in the visibility of the Jew. Among Jewish and non-Jewish writers representations of Jewish men are immediately and always identifiable. In the stereotypical representation, the male Jew may try to hide or disguise his identity, but eventually he is revealed. In this German fantasy of difference, whether positive or negative, the Jewish male body is indelibly marked and is therefore always recognizable.[1] And it seems to make little difference whether the authors employing these stereotypes are male or female, Jewish or non-Jewish.

When Jewish women are represented, the qualities ascribed to the Jew and to the woman seem to exist simultaneously and yet seem mutually exclusive—much as in M. C. Escher's merging and emerging image of fish and birds.[2] When we focus on the one, the other seems to vanish. It is clear that neither the qualities ascribed to sexuality nor those ascribed to race are primary: rather, qualities from each reinforce those ascribed to the other. Central to the arbitrary but powerful differentiation between the stereotype of the Jewish man and of the Jewish woman is the different meaning of male and female sexuality at the *fin de siècle*.

What will be illustrated is the construction of antithetical images of the male and the female Jew at the turn of the century in German culture. Each image is constructed to influence aspects of a world understood as out of control. The feminine is primarily an "inclusionary stereotype": woman is not the opposite of man but is reduced to his complement. For, in the eye of the male, there can be no reproduction without woman; thus, woman must be in many ways protected. The stereotype is that women are weak, while men are strong; intuitive rather than intelligent, and so on. It is only in the work of a very few individuals of the time, such as Arthur Schopenhauer or P. G. Möbius, who either did not wish to, or could not, sustain relationships with women, that the woman becomes totally expendable.

By the end of the nineteenth century, the relationship of the empowered male to the stereotype of the woman had become strained by what the male regarded as threats. The female was consequently marginalized. Thus, the intellectual woman, seen as the antithesis of reproductive, is viewed as sterile; the prostitute, seen as a threat because of the male's anxiety about spreading sexually transmitted disease, is viewed as destructive, as criminal. But these conceptual categories—the extension of the image of the "bad" Other—are always linked to the image of the "good" (m)Other. Here is where the inclusionary image of the woman is most powerful.

Jews had been classified as an inclusionary category with a status analogous to that of the woman. (The Jew is always defined as masculine.) As long as Christians viewed themselves as the extension and fulfillment of the Jew, they still needed the Jew. The "Synagogue" was thus old, while the "Church" was young. But even this theological model always proposed the female Jew as inherently different from male Jews, yet also different from the ideal feminine. Chateaubriand in *Essay on English Literature* (1825) wrote that "Jewesses have escaped from the curse of their race. None of them were to be found in the crowd that insulted the Son of Man ... The reflection of some beautiful ray will have rested on the forehead of Jewesses."[3] "I hate Jews because they crucified Christ," said the anti-Dreyfusard Paul

MR. JEREMIAH BUILDER : " Rachel ! ven that boy vas ter-venty-vun, I take him into partnership ! "

The Jewish child, with his "Darwin's ears," represents the "superior degenerate" offspring of the Jewish male and Jewish female, whose physiognomies are virtually interchangeable. From *The Butterfly*, May–October, 1893.

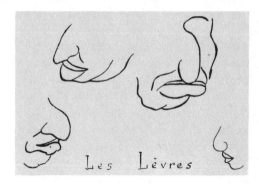

Les Lèvres

The lips of the Jew are seen as a sign of the difference and ugliness of the Jew. From the anti-Semitic physiological study of the Jew's body by "Docteur Celticus," *Les 19 Tares corporelles visibles pour reconnaître un Juif,* 1903.

The Jewishness of the "beautiful" Jewish woman is stressed in terms of her physiognomy. From *The Butterfly,* May–October, 1893.

The interchangeability and immutability of the physiognomy of the male and female Jew. From *The Butterfly,* May–October, 1893.

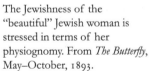

Bourget at the end of the nineteenth century, "I adore Jewesses because they wept for him."[4]

However, with the secularization of the image of the (male) Jew there is no longer any need for the parallelism of the Jew to the Christian. The Jew thus becomes "exclusionary," defining what the constructed image of the Aryan is *not*. The Jew becomes the projection of all the anxieties about control present within the Aryan. There is no need to "protect" aspects of this image, since there is no such necessary link between the male Jew and the male Aryan as remained between the male and the female.

The circumcised Jew becomes the representative of the anxiety-provoking masculine (an image tied closely to the anxiety about syphilis, for circumcision was understood as a prophylactic against sexually transmitted diseases).[5] He thus becomes inherently "bad" and as a result, the difference of the Jewish male body and mind from those of the Aryan becomes absolute within the Western tradition. One can observe how the very body of the male Jew becomes the image of the anxiety generated by the sense of the loss of control.

The Jew's compromised masculinity, his "femininity," is one of his defining qualities. He is not quite a man and yet certainly not a woman (that is, a protected potential mother). He is constructed as a "third sex," thus separated from the representation of masculinity and femininity. And, indeed, when we examine Jewish self-representations of masculinity at the turn of the century, self-questioning seems always to be present. Yet the femininity of the Jewish woman seems to be accentuated, as in the German proverb: "God created the Jew in anger, the Jewess in wrath (i.e. the Jewess is even worse than the Jew)."[6] Anti-Semites such as H. G. Nordmann could write in 1883, that "the Jewish nature of a woman is even more repellent than that in a man [*Mann*], it is even more unfeminine as it is inhumane [*unmenschlich*]."[7]

What I intend to examine is the construction of the Jewish woman and to ask when does her "Jewishness" and when does her "femininity" become her defining moment. To do so I reconstruct specific moments in one of the master narratives of this stereotype at the *fin de siècle*, the story of Salome. How is the exclusionary stereotype of Jewishness, with its evocation of the "third sex," transmuted into an image of the feminine? I shall examine how anti-Semitic non-Jewish male authors construct Salome as the essential "woman" and simultaneously evoke this image in representing the essential "Jew." And how was such a conflation of images dealt with by a Jewish woman writer of the time in her construction of the "Modern Jewess?" These alterations and transmutations are constant and interrelated markers of difference in *fin-de-siècle* German and Austrian thought—the nature of the Jew's language and its function as a marker of Jewish sexuality—and they serve to mask and highlight the difference in the gendering of the stereotypes.

Salome and Syphilis

In 1930, Hans F. K. Günther, one of the leading anthropologists of the Weimar academy, published his full-scale *Anthropology of the Jews*.[8] Günther had begun work on this topic in an appendix to a work on general anthropology (published in 1922), seeing the Jews as a specific subset of the human race deserving or requiring special consideration. Much attention had been given to the anthropology of the Jew in both Jewish and non-Jewish as well as anti-Semitic writing at the *fin de siècle*, but Günther's work came to be seen as the standard work on the anthropology of the Jews, especially in the Third Reich. It consisted of a survey of the history and culture of the Jews and a detailed presentation of the physical anthropology of the Jew. As with most nineteenth- and early twentieth-century anthropologists, Günther focused on those qualities of all Jews, both male and female, that separate the Jew from all other human beings. Thus, in his chapter on the special nature of the Jewish voice, Günther observed that the Jew's speech is set apart from that of all other peoples. For Günther, there is no gender difference in terms of the signification of the Jew's voice. The *Mauscheln* of the Jews, according to a standard German dictionary cited by him, is the "presence in language of unique Jewish elements."[9] In the same paragraph Günther called upon the theologian Johann Jakob Schudt, the late seventeenth-century orientalist who was the authority on the nature of the difference of the Jews, who saw *Mauscheln* as the "unique accent of pronunciation and elocution of language which betrays a Jew the moment he opens his mouth."[10]

The most important authority for Günther's proof of Jewish difference is Richard Wagner, who said the special language of the Jews was to be found in the song, "as the song is the language spoken in the most extreme passions."[11] German high culture was seen as the least accessible sphere of society open to Jews. Wagner explains *Mauscheln*, especially in musical form, as the sign that all Jews, male and female, no matter how long they have lived in a land, will always speak its language as an outsider. For Günther, the specific nature of Jewish speech reveals itself especially in the sung voice, the example not only of Jewish difference but also of its difference in the arts world, to which the Jews cannot belong. Günther finds the clearest representation of Wagner's theoretical statement in a later musical text. It is Richard Strauss's opera *Salome* (1905) and, specifically, the "contested conversation among the five Jews, which is an attempt to represent the *Mauscheln* of excited Jews in artistic form" (p. 255).

Günther's view was not only that all Jews spoke differently because of the "alien" world of European high culture in which they could not truly function, but also, according to a medical authority of the day, that Jews speak differently because the "muscles, which are used for speaking and laughing, are used inherently differently from those of Christians, and this use can be traced . . . to the great difference in their nose and chin."[12] The difference of the language of the Jew is reflected in the difference of the Jew's body—a major factor in the structuring of Günther's argument. Language use, especially language use as it relates to high culture, reveals (because of the very truth value of high culture) the essential nature of all Jews, at least according to the neoclassical aesthetics to which much of *fin-de-siècle* German conservative society subscribed. Thus, the language of the Jew is a marker of the Jew's difference from the male Aryan (Günther himself) who clearly, in the writing of his scholarly monograph, has control of the discourse of science and culture.

Before I knew Günther's argument, I independently reconstructed the image of the corrosive, contentious, debating male Jew in Strauss's *Salome*.[13] But there is a corollary question which stems from Günther's reading (and my reconstruction of its context): why are only the males, the five argumentative Jews and King Herod, seen to be the racial representatives of the world of the Jews in Strauss's opera? Or rather, why are the other members of the royal family on stage, Herodias and Salome—Jews by inheritance and ritual within the legend—not represented or understood by Strauss's German contemporaries as Jews?[14] The claim that it is the voice of all Jews which marks the Jew as different should include Salome and Herodias. This exemption of the female members of the court from consideration as prototypical, stereotyped Jews clearly reflects an early twentieth-century German reading of Strauss's *Salome*. It is remarkably different from the American reception. Richard Aldrich, the *New York Times* reviewer, commented that all of *Salome* was "a picture set in the time of Jewish decadence and the Roman domination."[15]

The German reading of Oscar Wilde's play *Salome* does contain a stereotypical image of Salome and Herodias as Jewish women. Yet that reading is so closely linked to the general qualities ascribed to the "feminine" at the time that later writers such as Hans Günther could not see the specially Jewish aspects of the figures.[16] Here we have a classic case of the simultaneous yet exclusionary existence of two related images of difference—the *femme fatale* and the *belle juive*—which usually function in two different contexts, the former misogynist, the latter anti-Semitic. Yet, from the reception of Strauss's opera in the German-speaking world, it is clear that the dangerousness of the Jewish woman is ascribed to the destructive feminine within the world of culture, in order to construct another exclusionary category

The language of the Jew reveals the Jew's hidden character, no matter what language the Jew tries to speak. From *The Butterfly*, May–October, 1893.

FROM THROGMORTON STREET

FINKELSTEIN (emphatically): "I don'd care vot yer say, yer tief; yer robbed me, I dell yer! yer a liar und a placguard, und a schwindler und a schweinpig: und dot's plain English!"

analogous to that of the bluestocking and the prostitute. In Strauss's and Günther's reading of Wilde's drama, what dominates the representation of the women is their femininity. Prior to Strauss's setting of his edited version of a translation of Wilde's play, there was a widely read drama, Oskar Panizza's *The Council of Love* (1895), in which the figure of Salome was introduced as part of an image of female corruption closely associated with but contrasted to that of the image of the Jewish male. It is in this text that the implied qualities of the "woman" and "Jew" present in Strauss's reading of Wilde can be examined.

The Salome legend as the representation of the Jew and the woman is at the center of one of the central tropes of Panizza's *The Counil of Love*, perhaps the most scandalous text of the German *fin de siècle*. In 1895, the publication of his play led Panizza to be sentenced in Munich to a year in prison for blasphemy. The trial became one of the most notorious scandals in the literary world and made the text an underground bestseller, at least among the intellectual avant-garde. The work, according to the author, is a satire on religious belief.[17] Set in the Renaissance, it represents the introduction of syphilis into the world through the agency of Salome who is the chosen vehicle by which the Devil corrupts the flesh. While ostensibly attacking all religious belief, Panizza used many of the contemporary images of the Jews to characterize even Christian icons such as God the Father and Jesus. (This was very much in line with Nietzsche's attempt to see Christianity simply as an extension of Rabbinic Judaism.)

Panizza, trained as a physician at the University of Munich, was, like so many males at the turn of the century, syphilophobic.[18] Employing the exclusionary stereotype of the Jewish male, he constructed an even more repellent fantasy of the diseased male Jewish body. In his drama, the Devil, the eventual seducer of Salome, is visible as a Jewish male whose corruption is written on his body. "The Devil stands before them, leaning on one foot and supporting the other with his hands. He wears a black, close-fitting costume, is very slender, close-shaven with a fine-cut face, but his features wear an expression that is decadent, worn, embittered. He has a yellowish complexion. His manners recall those of a Jew of high breeding. He leans on one foot, the other is drawn up."[19] The "yellowish" skin color, the limping leg, the degeneracy of the Jew form Panizza's image of the seducer of humankind.

The Jew's "yellowish" skin is part of the standard image of the diseased Jew. Johann Jakob Schudt cited the male Jews' physical form as diseased; "among several hundred of their kind he had not encountered a single person without a blemish or other repulsive feature: for they are either pale and yellow or swarthy . . ."[20] Schudt's view saw the diseases of the Jews as a reflex of their "Jewishness," of their stubborn refusal to acknowledge the truth of Christianity. But it reappears two centuries later as a sign of the ill Jewish male. This yellow skin later marks the bearded "friend in Russia" in Franz Kafka's tale of the "Judgment" (1913) where "the jaundiced color his skin had begun to take on seemed to signal the onset of some disease."[21] The male friend from Russia bears the qualities of illness associated with the diseased Jew, including his skin color.

The limping Jew, as I have argued elsewhere, is a sign of the exclusion of the Jewish male from qualities associated with the masculine at the *fin de siècle*.[22] Panizza's Devil as Jew as Devil clearly limps:

> The Devil turns on his right heel, smiles sardonically, and shrugs his shoulders. He feigns regret. Very much the Jewish merchant. A painful moment. . . .
>
> Mary: By the way how is your foot?
>
> The Devil: Oh, so-so! No better! But no worse, actually! Oh, god! (Hitting his shorter leg a blow.) There's no change any more! Blasted thing!
>
> Mary (in a lower voice): Your fall did that?

(The Devil, not reacting, is silent for a while; then he nods gravely.) (91–92)

The trope of the limping Devil and the limping Jew are interchangeable at the turn of the century and are here set within a secularized (and anti-Christian) theological model of the Jewish disavowal of God/Christ. At the *fin de siècle*, it is the syphilitic who limps, as the Parisian neurologist Joseph Babinski was to show in 1896, when he proved that a diminished plantar reflex was a sign of neurosyphilis. But within the related images of the lame Jew and the limping Devil, the association with the gait of the syphilitic was already well established in the culture of that time.

Panizza's image of the limping Devil reveals him to be a syphilitic Jew. The male Devil is thus a prefiguration of the central theme of the play—the introduction of syphilis into the world of the Renaissance. He is already infected with his "disease," his Jewishness, and he will spread it in society at large through the creation of an appropriate medium. Syphilis, which was actually understood as a Jewish disease as early as its first modern outbreak in the fifteenth century, is introduced into Panizza's debauched world of Renaissance Rome and the history of the West by the Jews, in this case, the Jewish male Devil.[23]

Syphilis is written on the male Jew's body, revealing his corrupt soul. But it is not just the Devil who is a corrupt Jewish male, but all of the figures of the "Jewish" Bible, in both the "Old" and "New Testament." Panizza's image of all of the male figures in the pantheon of the gods stresses their visible deformities. God the Father is the limping, syphilitic Jew whose tubercular son, Jesus Christ, has inherited his disease and shows symptoms of locomotor ataxia and mental deficiency, employing much of the vocabulary which comes to categorize the hidden nature of the Jew in the contemporary medical science. God "has a backward curvature of the spine. ... He coughs. His throat rattles. He gropes His way awkwardly, leaning forward, dragging His feet" (19). Just as the Jew is immediately recognizable, so, too, will be the syphilitic, who as of this moment in the play exists only within the vocabulary of images which its author used to characterize the "Jewish male." Mary, therefore, is spared any overt pathological physical characterization.

For Panizza, the new disease of syphilis, too, will be written on everyone's body as men are seduced and infected and in turn infect women. It will be a visible sign of their corruption, of their "Jewification" (to use one of Adolf Hitler's favorite words):

The Devil (sneering): In a matter of six weeks they won't recognize their own bodies! Their hair will fall out! Their eyelashes will fall out! Their teeth will fall out! They won't be able to chew, and their joints will be sprung! Inside of three months their entire body surface will look like a sieve and they'll go window-shopping to see the new styles in human skins! And I don't think that the fear will remain only inside their hearts! The stench of it will seep out through their noses, and their friends will exchange glances, and the ones that are in the first phase of the disease will laugh at those in the third or fourth! A year later their noses will fall off into their soup, and then it'll be the rubber-goods department for a new one! (128–29)

The traditional evil smell of the Jews, the *foetor judaicus*, and the Jew's nose are all echoed in the Devil's construction of this new disease, which will expose the inner corruption of each human being for all the world to see.

The vehicle of this destruction of Western society through syphilis, according to Panizza's construction, must be a woman. The Jewish Devil is made to seek the perfect "mother" for this disease. He calls the role of the women he finds in Hell, and all of them have one thing in common—they are mute. Helen of Troy will not do. She is a "poor simple thing" (106) who does not think. Héloïse had indeed "seduced her teacher" but "out of love," and is therefore eliminated (108f.). Agrippina is a plotter and murderess but has no "artistic drive," no "authentic naïvité" but merely "limitless ambition" (111). It is only Salome, the Jewish Princess, who fulfills the Devil's every need. His exchange with her is of sufficient interest to be reproduced in its entirety:

Tell me, pretty child, you were at Herod's banquet?
(She nods affirmatively.)
You danced, didn't you?
(She nods.)
Why?
(She doesn't know.)
Was it because pretty young girls always like to dance? And because you had taken dancing lessons?
(She nods.)
Everyone applauded?
(She nods.)
And so Herod said you could name your own gift?
(She nods.)
So you said you wanted a head?
(She nods.)
A man's head?
(She nods.)
A real man's head that was still alive?
(She nods.)
Why?

(She doesn't know.)

For a toy?

(She hesitates and finally nods affirmatively.)

So Herod sent you into the prison with the hangman and there he cut you a head?

(She nods.)

It happened to be the head of John the Baptist?

(She nods indifferently.)

They laid it on a platter and you brought it back into the banquet room?

(She nods.)

The blood ran into the platter until the platter was full?

(She nods.)

You got your fingers wet?

(She nods vigorously.)

Did you like that or didn't you?

(She nods yes.)

What do you mean, yes? Did you like it or didn't you?

(She rubs her hands together.)

You mean you got a kick out of it?

(Her affirmation is very clear.)

You must have very sensitive fingers!

(No answer.)

And then, then you gave the head to your mother as a gift?

(She nods.)

Why?

(She shrugs.)

It was already dead?

(She nods sadly.)

Yes, amputated heads don't last very long! Now, tell me, did you care about any of the people? Was there any one that you loved?

(She doesn't know what to say and finally shakes her head no.)

Did you love Herod?

(No.)

Saint John?

(No.)

Your mother?

(She shrugs, then shakes her head no.)

But you did like your sliced-off head?

(She nods very definitely. The Devil suddenly jumps up.)

You're it my child . . . We have great things to do together, you and I! You will be the mother of a magnificent race which no aristocracy will ever equal. Your children won't have blue blood or red blood in their veins. It will be a far more remarkable kind of blood! You're the only one of your kind in my whole, huge realm! (111–15)

All of the rhetoric which Panizza places into the mouth of the Devil is racial rhetoric. It evokes the debate about the special status of the Jewish sexuality at the *fin de siècle*, specifically the sexual selection ("inbreeding") and its pathological results. The daughter born of the pairing of the Devil and Salome is syphilis incarnate. She is called simply "The Woman"—"a young blooming creature with black hair and deep black eyes in which a smouldering sensuality, as yet only half awakened, is apparent" (121). If indeed the body of the Jewish male is marked and made visible by the signs of his pathology, the woman's beauty is a visible sign of her danger to all human beings.

She begins to spread her disease with her seduction of the pope and then "to the rest of the human pack" (140). It is vital to note that, while Salome is in no way to be distinguished by her language or gestures from the other women in Hell, her daughter—the daughter of two Jews—seems to bear visible signs of her difference. And her visibility seems to stamp her as a corrupted and corrupting Jew. Her physiognomy is overtly that of the *belle juive*—the dark hair and black eyes are the salient markers of the beautiful Jewess in European, but especially nineteenth-century German-language, drama. One thinks immediately of the physiognomy of the seductive Rahel in Grillparzer's *Die Jüdin von Toledo*. Or, indeed, of Merimée's if not Bizet's Carmen—whom the narrator first takes for a Jew. Yet this visibility is in no way signposted for the reader/audience by Panizza. Unlike his representation of the Devil, whose Jewish identity is manifest, Panizza never overtly characterizes either Salome or "The Woman" as a Jewish woman.

The image of the "dark" woman, while echoing the Western trope of the "blackness" of the Jews, is at the same time a sign of the *femme fatale*. (Thus, Bizet's representation of Carmen is clearly as a "Gypsy" and not as a Jew.) It is not an exclusionary sign of the ugly and the pathological, but rather an inclusionary sign—for even the "dark" woman here is an object of desire, unlike the yellow, limping Jewish Devil. Otherwise, it would be counterproductive, as her inclusionary "feminine" qualities are needed to make "the Woman" an object of desire, an object which the Jew cannot be. (One can speak here of the attractiveness of difference, but "The Woman's" difference is clearly distinguished from that of the male.) The inclusionary stereotype enables the seduction of all the men in the papal court to take place. Salome and "The Woman" must be attractive to the males they are to seduce. And yet, the selection of a Jewish mother and a Jewish father produces a Jewish daughter, which the reader/audience intuitively knows and yet represses. Her Jewishness (read: her pathology) is represented by her visibility as a woman, a visibility very different from that of her "father," the Devil, and very similar to that of her mother, Salome. The inheritance of Jewish identity through the mother is here suppressed, it is the feminine which is her maternal inheritance. Her visibility to the audience as "The Woman" triggers the male (or at least Panizza's) anxiety about syphilis, about this hidden, dangerous aspect of the stereotypical feminine. Here, the Escher-like image of the Jewish woman is evoked: is she primarily a woman or primarily a Jew? Both images are present, yet they are so constructed that one must function as an inclusionary stereotype (the woman) while the other (the Jew) signals this as an impossibility.

A counterimage can highlight how highly contextualized Panizza's (and Strauss's) images of Salome are in the *fin-de-siècle* anti-Semitic discourse of difference. No such hint of this double image of the Jewish woman appears in a contemporary "Jewish" version of the Salome legend. The Viennese poet Ignatz Kohn's "Salome" (1902) appeared in the leading secular Jewish periodical *East and West*:

> Jochanan, I love you,
> My soul longs for you,
> Pain-bringing pain redeemer
> Jochanan, I love you.
>
> Deep in my soul there is a yearning.
> Look! I am beautiful and young . . . so young!
> Dreams go through my soul,
> That let me sense what is.
>
> Before me life extends blooming.
> Look! I am beautiful and young . . . so young!
> Before me I see a life of pleasure,
> But I thirst for pain and suffering.
>
> Pain, I greet you! I want to kiss you!
> My soul wants to sip on pain,
> Jochanan my soul loves you,
> Jochanan, I want your life.
>
> I don't care if people curse me!
> I want to see God bleeding in you,
> My soul cramps and cries,
> My soul jubilates in pain.
>
> Jochanan, I love you,
> My soul longs for you,

Pain-bringing pain redeemer
Jochanan, I love you.

(Jochanan, ich liebe dich,
Meine Seele trägt nach dir Verlangen,
Schmerzenbringender Schmerzerlöser,
Jochanan, ich liebe dich.

Tief in der Seele lebt mir eine Sehnen,
Sieh'! ich bin schön und jung . . . so jung!
Über die Seele gehen mir Träume,
Ahnen lassen sie mich: was ist.

Vor mir weitet sich blühend das Leben.
Sieh! ich bin schön und jung . . . so jung!
Vor mir seh' ich ein Leben voll Freude,
Aber ich lechze nach Leid und Schmerz.

Schmerz, dich grüss' ich! dich will ich küssen!
Schlürfen will meine Seele am Leid,
Jochanan dich liebt meine Seele,
Jochanan, dein Leben will ich.

Kümmert es mich, wenn die Menschen mir fluchen!
Gott will ich seh'n, verbluten in dir,
Meine Seele krampft sich und weinet,
Meine Seele jauchzet vor Schmerz.

Jochanan, ich liebe dich,
Meine Seele trägt nach dir Verlangen,
Schmerzbringender Schmerzlöser,
Jochanan, ich liebe dich.[24])

For Kohn, Salome is purely the feminine. No Jewish overtones are permitted in her representation—she is "beautiful and young . . . so young"—and her monologue (echoing Wilde's last monologue for Salome) is an outpouring of her destructive adoration for the body of John the Baptist. The poem was accompanied by an engraving of Rubens' fulsome image of Salome bearing the severed head of John the Baptist. While dark-haired and dark-eyed, Rubens' image, like that of Kohn, evokes the feminine and excludes any image of the Jew. As a Jew himself, he permits Salome to represent only the destructive feminine.

Sarah Bernhardt and the Disease of the Jew

The contradictory image of the Jewish woman found in Panizza's drama draws on the contemporary general image of the *belle juive*. Yet there was also a real "Jewish" woman of the time who, more than anyone else, came to represent the embodiment of this destructive stereotype. That woman was Sarah Bernhardt (1844–1923), Wilde's original Salome. This association of the image of Sarah Bernhardt with the Salome tradition is to be found when it reached the level of a public scandal almost as notorious as the scandal surrounding Panizza's arrest for blasphemy. In June of 1892, Bernhardt had begun rehearsals for Wilde's drama at the Palace Theatre in London.[25] Within the month, the Examiner of Plays for the Lord Chamberlain denied his approval for its performance, as it represented biblical figures on the stage. Wilde's anger at this was extreme; indeed, he threatened to renounce his British citizenship and become a citizen of France. And for a moment, this British theatrical scandal linked the figures of Salome and Sarah Bernhardt. In fact, one of the original reviewers (in *The Times*, February 23, 1893) erroneously implied the drama had been written for Sarah Bernhardt. Even though Wilde had not written Salome for *La Divine Sarah*, she truly seemed to be the role's ideal embodiment.

The image of Sarah Bernhardt was a most complex and diffuse one— and one powerful aspect of it, in Germany as well as in France, was its anti-Semitic overtones.[26] In France, Marie Colombier had published *Les Mémoires de Sarah Barnum* (1883), which depicted Sarah Bernhardt as an ugly, money-hungry, sexually promiscuous, and destructive Jewish woman. She was also understood as the exemplary tubercular Jew. For the historian Anatole Leroy-Beaulieu, in 1893, saw in the face of all Jews "those lean actresses, the *Rachels* and *Sarahs*, who spit blood, and seem to have but the spark of life left, and yet who, when they have stepped upon the stage, put forth indomitable strength and energy. Life, with them, has hidden springs."[27] It is Sarah Bernhardt and Rachel Félix (1820–58) who represent the face of the sick Jew. At about the same date, the anonymous *Sarah's Travel Letters from Three Continents (America, Europe, and Skobolessia)* appeared in German.[28] For Germany, this text (which seems to be completely independent of the Colombier volume) presents a specific voice and image of Sarah Bernhardt which can lead us to a deeper understanding of the cultural discourse about the repression of the Jewish element of Salome. Written by the minor Viennese playwright and editor Ottokar Franz Ebersberg, it purports to be a series of letters from Sarah Bernhardt to her admirers (especially to Benjamin Disraeli) and from them to her.[29] Given the convention of the time, discourses among Jews overheard by non-Jews are assumed to reveal the Jew's hidden nature. Here, Günther's image of a specifically Jewish language is linked to the character of the Jews: Jews lie to non-Jews but tell the truth among themselves. According to these letters, Sarah Bernhardt is the "most notable embodiment of the Semite" (133) and represents all Jewish "racial qualities" (20). Sarah Bernhardt's language in her letters reveals her true nature. Her language is a Jewish language, unlike the mute discourse of Panizza's Salome, which is identical in form if not in content to all of the other women that the Devil evokes.

In the sixth letter to Disraeli, dated from Indianapolis, February 26, 1881, "Sarah Bernhardt" presents her insight into the nature of the Jewish woman and the tradition into which she sees herself fitting, to her Jewish correspondent Disraeli. She recounts that she had been studying the accounts of the Wandering Jew, but truly to understand her people she had to turn to "her own sex: to the Misses Esther and Herodias 'of the Persian and Jewish ballet,' to the beloved of the Polish king Casimir and the 'Little Dove' of the Nordic Kings—was it not Jewesses who accomplished everything and forced themselves into the text of the enemy, and if flattery did not succeed, killed them as Judith did the stupid Holofernes" (60). She follows this with an account of Jewish women who were prominent (or rather infamous) in her own time, such as Anna Kaulla, the friend of Heine, or Madame Friedman Persigny, the daughter of Prince Persigny of Paris, who was accused with her father of embezzlement. Indeed, even women whom

The masculinized body of the tubercular Sarah Bernhardt playing Hamlet at the Adelphi Theatre in London, June 12, 1889.

The tubercular body of Sarah Bernhardt as the tubercular "Dame aux Camélias."

the author does not believe to be Jewish, such as Sophie Arendt, the author of a widely discussed book on the loves of the Jewish Socialist Ferdinand Lassalle, acquire Jewish characteristics by their very association with Jews. Being a seductress is contagious and marks one as a Jewess. And such seductresses are dangerous—they kill non-Jewish men like Holofernes. (The confusion between Judith's beheading of Holofernes and Salome's demand for John the Baptist's head is a set topos of the *fin de siècle*.[30]) Sarah Bernhardt's catalogue begins with Esther and Herodias, the mother of Salome, who are described as dancing girls, a euphemism of the late nineteenth century for prostitute. (In the Salome legend, the dance of Salome is often attributed to Herodias.) The catalogue ends, however, with the actual killing of a non-Jewish male. Non-Jewish males are at risk when they are exposed to Jewish women. Thus, the association of Sarah Bernhardt with the Salome legend is fixed as the history of the Jewess as sexual seductress. She is as dangerous as she is seductive—she is the essential *belle juive*.

The association of Bernhardt with the image of Salome does not rest on this rather oblique single entry in her catalogue of *belles juives*. Rather, the volume concludes with the twenty-second letter written by her to the famous Viennese artist Hans Makart. He is accused by her of having withdrawn his portrait of Sarah Bernhardt from the major art exhibition of the year. He is not Jewish, so her letter to him is both duplicitous and contains intended multiple meanings. *La Divine Sarah* condemns him for having withdrawn the painting, noting that he himself had praised the picture as having been painted in "a true passion." She believes that he withdrew the portrait because some "high personage" commented to him: "You are now painting trash" (176).

But the prime reason it was withdrawn seems to have been the portrait's color. The image itself was jaundiced. The accusation that the picture was *too yellow* evokes all of the images of decay and degeneration evoked in general by yellow at the turn of the century, but also the parallel image of the diseased and "yellow" Jew. (One need only remember *The Yellow Book* whose color evoked the very spirit of *fin-de-siècle* self-conscious degeneracy.) And Sarah Bernhardt observes: "Yellow on yellow was the color of Henri Regnault, the late master from Paris, when he painted his Salome— shouldn't the famed Sarah not also be permitted to be yellow? . . . Yes, Mr. Markart, even though my statue has been rescued from the Ring Theater fire, my portrait must now be driven away. And yet my head and arms are so beautifully made up, the gown, the table cloth, the embroidery, the palm fan, everything is so beautifully yellow. Take assurance that I, too, have become truly yellow from gall, because you, whom I held to be my friend, betrayed me, after you painted me yellow" (177). Thus the volume ends—a banal ending perhaps, yet it ties the image of Sarah Bernhardt to Makart's *fin-de-siècle* "modern" excesses and to the image of a Salome painted in the corrosive colors of the degenerate. (Makart is now associated with the full-blown academic, historical painting of *fin-de-siècle* Vienna; yet in the 1880's, he was considered the most "modern" of painters.) The disease of the male Jew is literarily marked on her yellow skin as on the skin of the male Jew and is reflected in her ventriloquized Jewish voice in these letters.

It is clear that the image of Sarah Bernhardt in this text generates a further exclusionary category of the female. And it is made exclusionary through its association with the image of the Jewish male. Bernhardt as the exemplary Jewish woman is represented as the diseased Salome, the destructive seducer, but also has some of the overtones associated with the "bluestocking." Her image in this text is "mannish" in her demand for control over the world—but this is also Jewish. She represents herself as the embodiment of the modern woman, whom the minister at her wedding believes to be really a boy in disguise. He refuses to marry them because there is not to be any "confusion about the sex of those about to be married" (174).[31] According to her own account in the text, she does not "withdraw with the other woman when the gentlemen begin to smoke and drink their sherry" (3). She represents precisely the anxiety about "modern woman" that is associated, as early as 1849, with the emancipation of women. The conservative German author Louise Otto-Peters wrote at mid-century that "emancipated women are the sexually ambiguous type [*Zwitterwesen*] such as George Sand or Louise Aston, dressed like men, smoking cigars, hair cut short, praising free love. This is imported from France by the Young Germans who praise the 'emancipation of the flesh'."[32] It replicates almost verbatim the image of Bernhardt presented in this text. Bernhardt's seemingly "feminine" nature masks a masculine one, that of the *fin-de-siècle* image of the lesbian as crypto-male.

The Jewishness of Bernhardt provides an ambiguous masculinity—making her a "third sex." And this is associated in a direct manner with her "modern" image as Salome, the Jewish princess whose visibly yellow skin reveals her diseased, corrupt nature as a Jew. Bernhardt is Salome, and Salome is diseased in more than one way. The visibility of Salome and Bernhardt reflect a specific debate about the sexuality of the Jew. For the Jewish female becomes the destructive seducer—the parallel image of the Jewish male (as in Panizza's image of the Devil). And this primacy of the stereotype of the Jew is reflected in her represented language. *La Divine Sarah* is the embodiment of the sexuality of the Jew and, therefore, of the modernity which this sexuality comes to represent. It is this which her image evoked. Imaging Bernhardt playing Salome on the London stage was the perfect meshing of the role and the performer. For in this match of the emancipated Jewish actress and the destructive biblical Jewess, the nature of the Jew as the corrupter of the non-Jewish world was embodied.

The "Modern Jewess" as seen by a Modern Jewess

After the turn of the century, the discourse about the destructive Jewish female as the epitome of the modern woman becomes a commonplace. So much so, in fact, that "modern" Jewish women were constrained to explore the meaning of this stereotype in terms of their own self-representation. From the externalization of these stereotypes of the Jew and the woman in action, we can turn to the programmatic presentation of the "modern Jewess" by Else Croner, published in 1913, which offers a summary of the discourse about modernity and the Jewish woman.[33] (Croner used the term "modern Jewess" and I shall use it when referring to her construction.)

Sarah Bernhardt was represented as the quintessential "modern" woman in the stereotypical discourse of the late nineteenth century. Croner's account of the "modern" Jewish woman focused on two aspects of the representation of Bernhardt in Ebersberg's text—the sexuality of the Jewess and its relationship to the representation of the special language of the Jewess as the sign of the modern. Croner's text presents a post-1900 attempt on the part of a self-identified Jewish woman to construct and thus rescue the image of the Jewish woman as different from both the anti-Semitic image of the male Jew and from the misogynist image of the woman. She wishes to construct an image in which both feminine and Jewish qualities are visible simultaneously. Her construction of an independent image of the Jewess is an act of resistance, given the invisibility of the Jewess in contemporary culture, as in the popular German reception of Strauss's opera.

If there is something masculine and destructive in the stereotype of the Jewish woman at the *fin de siècle*, Croner provides a countertype. She constructs an image, as she herself says, of the "modern Jewess" who is defined by her heterosexuality. In this regard, she is the "most feminine of all women." The shift between the older reality of the Jewess in the ghetto and that of the "modern" Jewess is marked by the abandonment of early marriage as a means of channeling her sexuality. She "matures earlier" than all other women. In the ghetto, this maturity was recognized and controlled through the institution of early marriage. She has a "greater hot-bloodedness, liveliness, and sensibility" which "is the result of [her] early development." And this is because she is constituted as biologically different. She is an "oriental" (74). These images reevaluate positively precisely those negative qualities traditionally associated with the image of the "modern" woman (more intensive sexuality) and the Jew (destructive sexuality).

By the time the Jewess entered into sexual maturity, she was already married, and this early marriage "allow[ed] her to avoid side steps and mistakes but also robbed her of the individual choice and an erotic life full of play and pleasure." (72) And one might add to this, as one constantly finds in the medical literature of the period, that such an early marriage enabled her to avoid syphilis and its consequences. Thus, the Jewess in the ghetto, according to Croner, was sexually less liberated, yet sexually more fulfilled, than her non-Jewish contemporaries. And she was less at risk for disease. Croner thus answers the long association of Jews with sexually transmitted disease by evoking the sexual practices of the Jews, practices which are often associated with the very image of the pathology of the Jews.

According to Croner, with civil emancipation and the introduction of "Western norms" of sexual behavior, the Jewish woman began to marry later and later. She became more and more like her non-Jewish counterpart, who married on or after the end of her second decade. Yet unlike her "occidental" counterpart, all of her "oriental" being is sensual and sexual. For the Jewish woman, there is no rejection of the flesh. "'To marry is good, not to marry is better' is a New Testamentary idea unknown in torah and Talmud" (74). Her desire is to "marry and reproduce." Her drives are purely biological. She is an "individual of reproduction and completely intuitively desires the preservation of her species" (76). Thus, Croner refutes the charges made by a number of her contemporaries, such as Otto Weininger, that central to all women is the biological imperative to reproduce. Here, however, it is linked to the sexual selectivity of the Jews.

According to Croner, the modern, emancipated Jewess had the potential to develop in two radically different directions. At this juncture, the German/Jewish author projects all of the negative images of the Jew and the woman outside herself. She has begun to construct the image of the Western Jew as the romantic reversal of the standard stereotypes of the woman and the Jew. She now places the originally negative images outside of her own self-definition. She places it in the East among the Eastern Jewish women. The Russian Jewess is the destructive seductress. She traps her object—whether Jew or non-Jew—without "shame or propriety, she masters and tortures him, drains him of the very marrow from his bones and eventually drives him 'through her life' to death" (76–7). The Russian Jewess, unlike the German Jewess, once she abandons the confines of the ghetto, is given no alternative in her culture but to revert to a more primitive and intuitive sexuality.

The German Jewess, even with her "greater sensuality," is in general quite different. She, too, abandons the religious strictures of the ghetto, but she replaces the rules of religion with the "intellect" which governs her sexual life. There is no intuitive sexuality among German Jewesses. "The Jewess is not 'Gretchen' and 'Klärchen.' She is always the queen of love; she and not the man grants, makes happy, heightens. Here, her character is close to that of the American woman. An American Käthchen of Heilbronn is as unthinkable as a Jewish 'Klärchen' (78). The passive, dependant image of the woman is foreign to the Jewish woman in the West ("America"). Her heterosexuality is controlled by her rationality at all times. It is less passionate and, therefore, more controlling of the male. Croner's dichotomy between destructive and acceptable independence becomes the difference in the image of the Eastern and the Western Jewess. The destruction and corrosion associated with the sexuality of the Jewish woman at the *fin de siècle*, with Sarah Bernhardt and Salome, is projected onto a construction of the Eastern Jewish woman. Here, the position of the acculturated Jewish woman becomes the antithesis of the universalizing image of the female in thinkers such as Weininger, whose image of the female is, in fact, identical with that of Croner's "Eastern Jewess."

Croner's need to split this stereotype is further reflected in her attempt to adapt the stereotypical image of the language of the Jews as a sign of the "modern Jewess." If the representation of female sexuality is restructured, so too is the universal stereotypical attribute of the Jew's language. The language of the Jewish woman becomes the focus of the anxiety about the sort of control attributed to the sexuality of the Western "modern Jewess"—cold and controlling. The language of the "modern Jewess" is "elastic to the point of disconnectedness, sensible to the point of nervousness, and elegant to the point of glossiness" (91). Here, the anxiety about pathology ("nervousness") is articulated in the context of the heightened risk for mental illness on the part of Jews, a commonplace among Jews of the *fin de siècle*. This nervousness was understood as a sign of her moving into the competitive world of "modernity." Her ghetto ancestry, where her ancestors spoke "a bad, clumsy German," is behind her. Indeed, she is, at least in her writing, the new ruler of the language and "exceeds many German women in glossiness and grace of style" (92). But there still remain clear signs of her racial difference in her biology, her intonation, and her choice of words. Her larynx has been practiced in pronouncing hard, guttural sounds for a thousand years and their echo is still to be heard in her pronunciation of German. Her "Hebrew larynx unintentionally transfers these sounds into German" (92). Her pronunciation is "jumpy, disjointed; her sentences remain often incomplete, entire words and syllables are swallowed, the concluding syllables are only hinted at, and the intonation only marginally sketched in" (93). Here, the counterdiscourse is repressed and projected by Croner: that it is the sexuality of the Jew which (in terms of racial-biological argument) is inherently different. This image, tied to the image of the circumcised male Jew, is displaced onto the voice of the "modern Jewess" who comes to be vacuous in her modernity. Her choice of words becomes banal. She calls everything "neat" (*großartig*). Needless to say, this description of the slangy, hyper-anxious, visible (or rather, audible) language is tied to the prototypical "Jewish Princess"—the class-bound image of the Jewish woman as parvenu, which reappears in the United States after the Second World War.[34] But it is a language written on the body. It is a gendering of the Jewish voice which is understood by Günther and the physical anthropologists to be a universal sign of the "Jew." It is the antithesis of the controlled, incisive, and academic language which Croner herself employs in her own writing. Here the question of the nature of the Jew's body and the Jew's language are linked in the representation and projection of the "modern Jewess" as an object beyond the text, an object of investigation and a category which excludes the author.

While there is only a little trace of *Mauscheln*, there are still some remnants of the language of the ghetto in her language, such as the use of "German-Jewish" words which give an "intimate but not always proper and resonantly beautiful tone" (94–5). Here, the sexual difference of the

Jewish woman, her improper intimacy, is displaced by Croner onto her larynx, to be articulated in the description of her language. But Croner further distinguishes the language of the "Western modern Jewess" from that of the "Eastern Jewess." What clearly remains different and visible are the former's gestures. She has a "greater power and rapidity of gesture." Among the German Jewesses (not as "oriental" as the Eastern Jewesses), gestural language is a sign of the oppression of the Jews in the West. (According to Croner, true "orientals" use minimal gestures.) She had to "catch the ear of her oppressor" (95). The inherited characteristics of oppression continue to shape the language of the emancipated Jewish woman. The image of the Jewish woman and her gestural language seems fixed. When the Nazi-Germanist Wilhelm Stapel imagines Heinrich Heine's "Lorelei," he "feels immediately the words flowing into his arms, a compulsive shrugging of the shoulders as the hands move apart: a typical Jewish gesture."[35] The stereotype of the Jew is articulated through visibility: Jewish women become visible through their language and Jewish men are visible through their deformities. Croner now returns to the argument against this difference being the result of biological predisposition. She evokes the history of the oppression of the Jews as an explanation for their difference and thus recapitulates the liberal promise of the Enlightenment—become like us and we will treat you as we ourselves wish to be treated. Croner's construction of the "modern Jewess" is an attempt to come to terms with the qualities which embodied the double image of Jew and woman at the *fin de siècle.*

An analogy to Croner's argument can be found in the controversial 1930 essay on female masochism by Sigmund Freud's Jewish analysand Helene Deutsch.[36] Deutsch, building on work by Freud and Karl Abraham, accepted the view that female masochism was the psychological reflex of the reproductive biology of the female. Her essay concludes, however, with an analysis of the historical shift in the meaning of the woman's body at the turn of the century. Women of the nineteenth century were able to repress their anxiety about their bodies in a denial of the sexual: "If questioned about the nature of their experience in coitus, they give answers which show that the conception of orgasm as something to be experienced by themselves is really and truly foreign to them." These women receive pleasure only in giving pleasure to the man as "they are convinced that coitus as a sexual act is of importance only for the man. In it, as in other relations, the woman finds happiness in tender, maternal giving." But this stage has now been replaced by that of the "modern woman" whose sublimations "are further removed from instinct." This is the result of "social developments and that is accompanied by an increasing tendency of women toward masculinity." This echo of the earlier attack on the masculinization of the "bluestocking" points toward the gradual sublimation of the masochistic aspect of the female psyche. She and her heirs demand to be freed of the pain associated with reproductive sexuality: "Perhaps women of the next generation will no longer submit to defloration in the normal way and will give birth to children only on condition of freedom from pain." Anesthesia becomes the answer to the biology of pain which, according to Deutsch, is the condition of all women. At this point in her argument Deutsch makes a move into the future, in which women will have to generate symbols to compensate for the absence of those painful experiences which represent the masochistic nature of the feminine: "And then in after-generations they may resort to infibulation and to refinements in the way of pain—ceremonials in connection with parturition." Female circumcision and birthing ceremonies are the counterimage of the male Jewish symbolic world with its stress on male circumcision and the ritual of manhood, the *bar mitzvah*. But they also extend the idea of the act of circumcision as a magical prophylaxis against sexually transmitted diseases. "Infibulation" becomes a symbolic extension of the marking of the body as a sign of health.

Deutsch reverses Croner's reading. She moves from the universal biological quality of masochism in all women ("the most elementary force in feminine mental life") and shows this to be an encoded reading of the female Jewish body and the female Jewish mind and psyche, suffering from the social repression of the Jews in Western culture. This is a parallel but opposite movement to that of Croner. Deutsch, having assumed a biological universality of all women, comes to read the body of the woman as the body of the Jew; Croner departs from "culture" as the formative force in the "modern Jewish woman" and is shipwrecked on the reef of "nature."

In fantasy, I imagine how Else Croner would have read Salome. She would have been seen as a "modern" woman—on the one hand, as an "Eastern Jewess" stripped of her racial identity and reduced to the elemental forces of the feminine; on the other, as a "Western Jewess" attempting to capture the eye of her oppressor through the gestural language of her dance. Thus Croner constructs her image of the "modern Jewess" as a representation of the woman as Jew within the discourse of an age which could focus on either Jews or women. As a German Jewish woman, she still was constrained to separate this image from her own image as a Jew and a woman. Here is where Salome lurks in her perspective—as a Jewish woman in the East, but only from the Jewish female perspective. The "oriental," gesticulating, sexually destructive image of Panizza's Salome, associated with the contemporary anti-Semitic discourse, is subsumed under Croner's image of the modern Jewish woman, but distanced in every way from herself. Here, to construct and externalize stereotypes in culture becomes a means to measure the limits of this "double vision" that constructs the image of the Jewish woman, but rarely permits it to be seen in its totality.

6

When is a Jewish Star Just a Star?
Interpreting Images of Sarah Bernhardt

CAROL OCKMAN

The multiplicity of Sarah Bernhardt's identities is staggering. Any list of her occupations would have to include actress, theater impresario, sculptor, painter, playwright, author, and model for health and beauty aids. Such a list entirely omits the extraordinary success of these endeavors and the symbiosis between the endless public fascination with Bernhardt and her continuous self-fashioning. It also excludes the well-known facts of a scandalous private life, including a mother who was a courtesan, an illegitimate son, Bernhardt's own recourse to prostitution early in her acting career, and a reputed promiscuity that encompassed liaisons with numerous men and probably women.

Bernhardt's reported eccentricities ensured that she was constantly in the public eye. She flaunted her thinness, which was mercilessly caricatured in the press, by wearing form-fitting dresses with long trains that became the height of fashion. She made a splash as an intrepid balloonist and capitalized on the experience by writing a book entitled *Dans les Nuages*. She had an indomitable passion for animals and claimed to have had an exhibition of her sculpture in London for the sole purpose of expanding her domestic menagerie, which at one time included three dogs, one parrot, a monkey, a cheetah, a wolfhound, and six boggle-eyed chameleons.[1] It is not only that Bernhardt violated the codes of accepted femininity but also the sheer bravado with which she did so that is arresting.

Contemporaries had complex responses to Bernhardt's behavior. Her idiosyncracies are so often remarked upon that it is virtually impossible to distinguish the facts of the life from representations of them. Even more conspicuous is Bernhardt's role in fabricating her own myth. By cultivating the image of her own unconventionality, she, more than anyone, compounded the confusion between life and performance. To the list of identities we have already assembled, we might add the fact that Bernhardt was a Jew. Faced with a life already distinguished by an astonishing excess of oddities, we might well wonder what it meant for Sarah Bernhardt to be Jewish in the late nineteenth century.

Even to say that Bernhardt was a Jew is a complicated affair. She was baptised and sent to a convent school near Versailles. Based on her own account, we might argue that she wasn't Jewish at all. Her memoirs only recount her life through the year 1881, so do not tell the full story. For instance, she is known to have been later a Dreyfusard and it is even thought that she may have stimulated Zola to write "J'Accuse" (1898).[2] Popular accounts often mention the fact that Bernhardt's mother was Jewish but equally important is the allusion to the actress's mysterious paternity and the less than veiled suggestion that her mother was a courtesan. In addition to references to Bernhardt's Jewishness in standard biographical profiles published during her lifetime, the fact that she was often compared to the actress Rachel (Elisa-Rachel Félix) might be taken as a gauge of contemporary awareness that she was a Jew.

In discussions of Rachel, who was credited with singlehandedly reviving the moribund art of tragedy in France, Jewishness was not only remarked but perceived as remarkable. On the occasion of her debut, the American actor Edwin Forrest described the thirteen-year-old Rachel as "that Jewish-looking girl, that little bag of bones with the marble face and the flaming eyes—there is demoniacal power in her. If she lives and does not burn out too soon, she will become something wonderful." The British writer George Henry Lewes was equally enthusiastic: "It will ever remain a curious problem how this little Jewess, this *enfant du peuple*, should, from the first moments of her appearance on the stage, have adopted—or rather let us say exhibited—the imperial grace and majesty which no one but herself could reach."[3]

Rachel's stereotypical Jewish origins seem to account, at least in part, for the prominence Jewishness achieved in contemporary descriptions. Born in 1821, the second daughter of itinerant Jewish peddlers, she was discovered by a schoolteacher from Paris on the streets of Lyons, where she and her sister Sarah were singing. The actress's matter-of-fact identification of herself as a Jew, well expressed in her declarative "Don't think it's so easy to bury people of my race and merit," may help to explain the freedom with which her contemporaries invoked her Jewishness.[4] Although Bernhardt's self-identification was less straightforward, it is clear that contemporaries were conscious of her Jewish origins. It is equally true that the perception of her Jewishness was often conflated with other discourses.

What I will explore in this article are the ways in which Jewishness is represented in contemporary texts and, particularly, in visual images of Sarah Bernhardt. Let me begin with a caveat. The very idea of looking for Jewishness poses a problem. On the one hand, looking for Jewishness seems to exemplify those strategies that reduce people to pared-down, usually stereotyped essentials: Jewishness is visible, it can be detailed in any number of legible signs or symbols. As such, it works against assimilationist

Cham [Amédé de Noé], *Andromache Abandoning Pyrrhus to Follow Barnum*

strategies. On the other, there is the possibility that Jewishness cannot be identified, is not recognizable. Inasmuch as assimilationist success entails the disappearance of Jewish or any other alternate identity, it too poses problems. Of course, this presumes that assimilation works. Looking at the case of Bernhardt, and to a limited extent, that of Rachel, it seems clear that Jewishness can always be known and deployed. How else do we explain the need to publish Bernhardt's baptismal record in a newspaper?[5] For the Jewish-identified Rachel, Jewishness might be seen as the necessary rigging in the construction of her extraordinary success. The tendency to emphasize the unlikelihood of that success reinforces the belief that it was rare for Jews in nineteenth-century French theater to achieve eminence and the assumptions—that Jews have been excluded, are incapable of success—which lie at its heart. At the other extreme is the argument that everyone in the theater was a Jew.[6] Underpinning both positions lies the type of regulationist discourse often used in discussions of prostitution.

Actress and prostitute were often considered synonymous and the theater, hardly an elevated calling in the nineteenth century, was a logical profession for those consigned by class or race to the lower echelons of society. In this context, it becomes difficult to separate the perception that Rachel and Bernhardt were promiscuous from the perception that they were Jews. Their sexual freedom was as much a part of their renown as their enormous success on the stage. Bernhardt's history, in particular,

Marcelin [Emile Planat], *The Great Tragedienne Begins Her 190th Season*, published in *Journal pour rire*, November 20, 1852

Sahib [Louis-Ernest Lesage], *Théodora Puff*, published in *La Vie Parisienne*, November 20, 1884

including a mother and aunt who made their living as courtesans, might be said to embody one of the major tropes about her own metier. Rachel's and Bernhardt's perceived impropriety was often expressed as unwomanliness or mannishness. In Bernhardt's case, the perception was magnified because, in addition to acting, she also had careers as a painter and sculptor. The fact that she and Rachel were both wildly successful performers, who refused to limit themselves to the theater where they had established their reputation, seems to be integral to a discourse of greediness more commonly associated with male Jews. When we consider how Jewishness is represented in their visual lexicons, it becomes clear that Rachel and Bernhardt were as often associated with stereotypes generally reserved for male as female Jews.

Among the images which best exemplify this kind of genderbending are the most unequivocally anti-Semitic ones—those representing Rachel's and Bernhardt's putative lust for money. Questionable monetary morals are the subject of Cham's *Andromache Abandoning Pyrrhus to Follow Barnum*. A desperate Pyrrhus, racing to the balcony of the Théâtre Français, gesticulates histrionically toward the classically garbed Rachel. Oblivious, she strolls away from the theater on the arm of P. T. Barnum, dressed in frock coat and top hat, a sack of money prominently displayed in his right hand. Marcelin's *The Great Tragedienne Begins Her 190th Season* (1852) refers both to the enormous popularity and sizeable revenues derived from Rachel's performances at the Odéon. Rachel appears in a chariot in front of the Théâtre Français. Frail yet regal, she holds the reins in one hand while the

other dangles visibly alongside the large cashbox upon which she sits. A charioteer less than half her size stands before her sounding her arrival on cymbals and drum. In a way quite distinct from Cham, Marcelin appears to underline the specifically racial character of the entrepreneurial, grasping spirit equated with Jews by showing Rachel and her herald with distinct hooked noses, protruding fleshy lips, and convex brows.

In a much less noble setting, a similar indictment of materialist showmanship is caricatured by Sahib in *Théodora Puff* (1884). Victorien Sardou, the dramatist who created Théodora and a number of other popular roles for Bernhardt, is seen at the left, wearing a fur-trimmed coat, top hat, and, it would appear, a dress. He too beats a drum and sounds cymbals while next to him Bernhardt, clad in a gown resembling some of the elaborate confections from her theater roles, and a drum major's hat, blows on a trombone. Here the qualifier *Puff* is used to link Bernhardt's theatrical enterprise to charlatanism. Defined as "publicity brought to perfection," *le puff* "is the art of duping naive people through exaggerated claims." Suggestions of charlatanism and the very concept of *puff* inevitably evoke P. T. Barnum who, in the nineteenth-century imagination, was thought to have raised *le puff* to an art.[7]

Bernhardt's prominent pointed nose and the handwritten advertisements plastering the makeshift music hall are both featured in the accompanying text. The joke about the nose revolves around Bernhardt's putative illness when rehearsals for *Théodora* are scheduled to begin: "The great tragedienne is ill. It's clear that something is wrong with her nose. M. Victorien Sardou hastened to reply by telegram: 'Blow it.'" The saga of Bernhardt's illness is interrupted by advertisements for products like *Théodora* chocolates, touted as ideal for travel because they don't melt in your pocket, and available everywhere. Eventually the reader is returned to the fate of Bernhardt's nasal ailment:

> Following a meticulous and expert examination, the skilled academician [Sardou] removed, by means of an extractor, the foreign body swelling the nasal appendix of the intended Théodora ...
>
> This specimen was sent immediately to the Cluny Museum ...
>
> M. Victorien Sardou donated his apple-corer to the artillery museum ...

The text concludes with a series of advertisements:

> Plus de Coryza,
> Bonnets préservatifs Sardou
> Dans tous les passages.
>
> Les dents repoussent!
> Avec le dentifrice Théodora.
>
> La Vie sans douleurs
> par le Laxatif dulcifiant Théodora.
>
> Plus de cadavres!
> Incinérateur Théodora.
>
> (No more Coryza,
> Sardou condoms
> In all the arcades.
>
> Teeth grow back!
> With Théodora toothpaste.
>
> Life without pain
> Use soothing Théodora laxative.
>
> No more corpses!
> Théodora Incinerators.)[8]

Despite its humor, this satire of entrepreneurship, with its crescendo of sexual, eschatological, and morbid advertisements is also chilling, no less so when we see that the performance attracts a bourgeois audience containing several stereotypically male Semitic faces. Jewishness is here invoked as an almost programmatic illustration of the common equation between capitalism and Jewish finance made across the political spectrum at this time.[9] Furthermore, in the light of Sardou's costume, this kind of shameless self-promotion might be said to be strangely feminized. The allusion to P. T. Barnum, which we have already seen in Cham's caricature of Rachel, emphasizes the depraved character of the actress's love of gain. In the fictionalized biography entitled *Les Mémoires de Sarah Barnum*, this trait is unambiguously depicted as a natural feature of Bernhardt's Jewishness.

When the title character in Marie Colombier's *Les Mémoires de Sarah Barnum* first appears, she is about to compete for the annual prize in Comedy.[10] Colombier presents us with a personnage who "in spite of her Jewishness" has the good fortune to possess the "classic physiognomy of a Catholic Virgin." With "her pure features, her oriental eyes ... especially the serpentine contours of her body . . . the firm globes of her breasts and hips" (5), Barnum evinces the pleasing combination of seductiveness and classic beauty so often elaborated in descriptions of *la belle juive*.[11] First published in 1883 and reprinted in 1884, *Les Mémoires de Sarah Barnum* describes the rise and fall of a barely veiled Bernhardt with such gutter tactics as to have provoked a law suit and a flood of outrage on Bernhardt's behalf, even from people who normally disliked her.[12] Colombier, a fellow actress and close friend until they quarreled over the terms of her contract on Bernhardt's first American tour, was privy to all the details of the life of her more famous colleague. Family members, lovers, friends, and associates have pseudonyms recognizable to anyone with even a modest knowledge of the actress's life: her son Maurice appears as Loris; his putative father, the prince de Ligne, is the prince de Dygne; Rilly and de Chesnel, the directors of the Parthénon, are Chilly and Duquesnel of the Odéon; the actress Hagal is Hagar; the actor Jacques Damala, whom Bernhardt marries, is Jack Madaly; her frequent co-star Mounet-Sully is Money; the sculptor Gustave Doré, Gustave Dargent. Bernhardt's mother is alternately "la Juive" or Esther; and Marthe Pigeonnier is Colombier herself.

Among the tropes which Colombier rehearses in her text, many fuse stereotypes of Jewishness with well-known details of Bernhardt's appearance and life story. Perhaps the most salient Jewish characteristic of "la Barnum" is what Colombier at one point describes as "the commercial intelligence inherent to her race" (27), at others "the lust for profit" (57), "the instincts of a daughter of Israel" (85), "the absence of morals characteristic of all the Barnums" (142). Repeatedly she is represented as "parched for publicity" (139), "Publicity—her one true love" (169). Greed, immorality, and self-promotion are linked to other character traits that

Colombier sees as specific to Jews: ostentation or bad taste ("when she moved her right hand, a huge number of bracelets, whose varying forms were too eye-catching, tinkled at her wrist" [6]; "it [the apartment] resembled . . . a curiosity-shop" [65]); vulgarity ("brand-new furniture jostling against threadbare pieces, the general effect vulgar" [10]); slovenliness ("here and there irrefutable signs of disorder, of filth even . . . grease spots everywhere; the carpets, the curtains, all stained" [10]; "for, la Barnum, a true daughter of Israel, was dirty" [66]).

Many of these characteristics double as orientalist tropes: Colombier refers, for example, to Barnum's "disorder and her oriental laizzez-faire" (66), a doubling intensified by Colombier's constant equation of Barnum and her family with prostitution. When she describes the salon of Barnum's mother as "this cacophony of disparate objects," what she finds there is not only stereotypically Jewish but "peculiar to courtesans." We are told how "La Juive" encouraged her daughter Sarah and then the younger ones to flirt with men for money. Not only does the author suggest that Barnum's son Loris was illegitimate but that the paternity of the prince de Dygne, whom Barnum met on a park bench in the Tuileries, could not be proved: "she used to visit certain sisters of charity whose white-haired women . . . paid her to spend several hours. Wasn't it in one of these discreet sanctuaries that she contracted her present infirmity?" (43–45) In addition to this insinuation that Bernhardt worked in houses of prostitution, Colombier also recounts that "to kill time, she would visit the fashionable courtesans. One used to see her, for example, at Cora Pearl's." (73)

Barnum's need for money, fostered by her mother, was insatiable. She was not only greedy but a spendthrift. Her desperate pursuit of funds was inseparable from a voracious desire for publicity: "in the Barnum family, you couldn't take a spoon of castor-oil without recounting it to the press and public." (296) Barnum's ceaseless and unscrupulous attempts to attract attention are a leitmotif of the book, among them: simulated attacks of advanced tuberculosis à la Marguerite Gauthier (145–6); an attempt to poison herself to win back a disenchanted, rich protector (119–20); the sudden taste for skulls, with which she decorated her bedroom (184); a coffin in which she occasionally slept and in which she kept vigil while her sister was dying in the nearby bed (184–7). Less macabre but equally powerful, "she launched her own house of fashion, whose silky nervousness, if you'll pardon the metaphor . . . ultra-Parisian *chic* and elegance at affordable prices didn't take long to revolutionize not only female dress but genre painting" (125). Not content with multiple achievements, she wanted more: "For this insatiable collector of vocations, it wasn't enough to be an actress, a sculptor, a painter and a balloonist. Inasmuch as it was the best means of publicity, writing tempted her as well" (201).

Barnum's desire for ever greater renown was the illusory compensation for the greatest tragedy of her life: her inability to love: "Fame was fine; profits were better, but she would have given her name, her success, and her money in the cashbox for a kiss that would make her tremble, for love's frisson." (319) In short, Barnum's only failure was as a woman; she had achieved all her dreams "except that of being a woman, of feeling herself shiver in the arms of a loved one!" (296) Colombier insists on Barnum's unwomanliness, describing her variously as an "analytic woman with sangfroid" (189) or "an eternal female Don Juan." (169) It is thwarted womanhood, as Colombier conceives it, that leads ultimately to Barnum's death, detailed in a manner all too reminiscent of the grizzly demise of a similar character, the actress and courtesan Nana in Zola's eponymous novel (1880).

Few journalists deigned to dignify Colombier's mud-slinging by writing about the book. Even so, the attempts to explain away the attack by labelling it "une affaire de femme" seem to tell only part of the story.[13] For Colombier, writing in the same decade in which the Dreyfus Affair began, stereotypes of Jewishness present themselves as among the most effective ways to launch a slander. As if the distinctive mixture of *belle juive*, whore, and megalomanic publicity seeker of the protagonist were not enough, Barnum's story is punctuated by other stereotypical Jewish characters—her sister Reine, conceived as a more heart-stopping version of *la belle juive*, and a cast of Jewish lovers, including Schremer, alternately described as the "old jeweler as rich as he is stingy" (84) and "this de Sade of jewelry" (85), and Marasky, "one of the very richest bankers from Odessa" (119).

This anti-Semitic content is never mentioned by Octave Mirbeau, one of the few journalists to discuss *Les Mémoires de Sarah Barnum*. As others have done since, he attributed the book to the man who wrote its preface, Paul Bonnetain, author of *Charlot s'amuse*, whose themes, according to Mirbeau, are masturbation, homosexuality, and nymphomania. In an essay entitled "Un Crime de Librairie," published in *Les Grimaces* in 1883, Mirbeau found the book so obscene as to wonder why its authors, putative and real, had not been arrested. He concludes with an exhortation to Sarah Bernhardt's son: "If I were M. Maurice Bernhardt . . . I'd take a hammer and crack the skull of M. Bonnetain; then I would drag Mlle Colombier to a public place, turn up her skirt and show her old wrinkled behind to the crowd." In fact, the publication of the book did spawn a duel in which Mirbeau, among others, participated.[14]

The front cover of *Les Mémoires* shows a Barnum that is unmistakably Bernhardt. Her thin, nervous form coiled for momentum, she charges forward with the force of a projectile. Given the blatant anti-Semitic content of the book, Léon-Adolphe Willette's exaggerated treatment of

Willette, cover of Marie Colombier's *Les Mémoires de Sarah Barnum*, 1883

Bernhardt's nose and hair might also be taken as evidence of her Jewishness, along with the six-pointed star which hovers just above her head.

When I began looking for Jewishness in images of Sarah Bernhardt, it was the six-pointed star in Willette's caricature, not the enlarged nose or the frizzy hair, which seemed to me an incontrovertible symbol of Jewishness. Unlike the star, the physical traits gave me pause as stereotypes of Jewishness. Virtually every image I had seen of Bernhardt, every account I had read, including Bernhardt's own, suggested that she did have unruly hair. It appears even in her most formal portraits, like the one by Jules Bastien-Lepage exhibited at the Salon of 1879.[15]

Inasmuch as the modus operandi of stereotypes is the exaggeration of physical traits, it can be very difficult to distinguish between caricature and anti-Semitic caricature. To disabuse myself of the knee-jerk equation between overlarge noses and Jews, I spent one afternoon in the Bibliothèque Nationale looking at caricatures in which the subject's salient feature was a big nose. In six months of *Trombinoscope*, with caricatures by Moloch, the list included Napoleon III, the dramatist François-Jules-Edmond Got, and the writer Louis Veuillot. Thinking about the complicated relationship between stereotype and resemblance, I paused to consider whether the French often have prominent noses. I told myself that Edouard Drumont's *La France juive*, considered the *urtext* in presenting Jewishness as a race, did not appear until 1886. Were the nose and hair in Willette's caricature signs of Jewishness too? I thought about the description of Bernhardt's nose in the text of *Les Mémoires*: "her Jewish profile softened by the swelling of the cheeks." (5) Certainly the nose is part of those classic features so often catalogued in descriptions of *la belle juive* to evoke the seductive beauty that is a common stereotype in representations

Alfred Le Petit, *La Poule aux oeufs d'or*, published in *Le Grélot*, December 31, 1882

of female Jews. And then there is Sahib's caricature of Bernhardt and Sardou with the accompanying text featuring the actress's nose. A caricature by Alfred Le Petit (*Les Contemporains*, no. 28, 1880–81) showing Bernhardt as a bird included not only a human face with a prominent nose but also a cluster of money bags hanging from her neck. The caption appears to refer to her ample revenues at the end of the dramatic season:

> Sarah, comme les hirondelles,
> Avec mai, vient à tire-d'elles.
> La divine, malgré les ans,
> Enchaîne jeunesse et printemps.
>
> (Sarah, like the swallow
> Come May, flies off at full speed.
> The Divine, in spite of the years,
> Holds captive youth and springtime.)

I added to this mix another caricature by Le Petit of 1882 purporting to show Bernhardt in the play *La Poule aux oeufs d'or*. Under the watchful eyes

of Sardou and the caricaturist himself, Berhardt, her serpentine form twisted into the outline of a hen, her spindly arms and legs metamorphosed into
fowl's wings and feet, adds two more golden eggs to the bounteous trove
displayed behind her. Thérésa (Emma Valadon, not to my knowledge a
Jew) had also been caricatured in the role by Gill (*L'Eclipse*, March 30, 1873).
Like Bernhardt, she is shown none too flatteringly—as a ludicrously stunt-
ed hen above a pot of money. But Bernhardt's huge pointed nose is entirely
different from the fleshy one sported by Thérésa's hen. In fact, it is very
much like that found in Sahib's *Théodora Puff*. Leafing through the journal in
which the caricature of Bernhardt in *La Poule* appears, I couldn't help noticing that several issues earlier there is another caricature, also by Le Petit,
showing a man with a lengthy beard wearing a long coat and top hat. He is
chained by 100-franc pieces to a doglike creature whose collar identifies
him as Léon Say, the former finance minister of France. Say holds a musical
instrument with a score attached entitled "Financial muddles." His companion, the man with the long beard, has a huge beaked nose under which
protrudes a large bowl, containing three coins. On its rim is written: "Have
pity on Rothschild."[16] At the very least this group of caricatures suggests
that when a person is known to be Jewish, a stereotypical Jewish nose is
always deployed in scenes involving obsessive money-making or money-
earning. With regard to anti-Jewish sentiment, this appears to be more a
case of business as usual than evidence of a more generalized escalation.
Nonetheless, it seems significant that a number of Bernhardt's caricaturists
including Willette and Le Petit, whose works I discuss here, went on to
make explicit anti-Semitic works during the Dreyfus Affair.[17]

If overlarge noses originally gave me pause (as indeed, in retrospect it
seems that the notion of any fixed sign should), I had no such hesitation
about the six-pointed star. From the outset I had understood it to be a clear
index of Jewishness. In Cabriol's caricature, *L'Hydropathe Sarah Bernhardt*, its
use as a bold framing device for the diminutive figure of the actress underlines other disturbing aspects of the image: the way she is sitting, splay-
legged on a turned-around chair, the elongated face with its regular, and
unmistakably, Semitic features, the topheaviness of the image, produced by
the large head and the outsize frilly collar countering the thin but forcefully
positioned legs. The collar, pants, and beribboned shoes refer to the outfit
Bernhardt wore in her studio and are a frequent focus of the caricatures
made after she achieved recognition as a sculptor in the late 1870's.[18] The
attributes of her various careers, palette, mallet and calipers, lyre and
plume, tragic mask and brush, often appear in these images and in at least
one instance—the caricature by Coll-Toc—they are joined by money. The
death's head smoking a cigarette lends a sinister quality to this image, yet it
is benign when placed next to Gill's. In addition to the attributes of her

1ʳᵉ ANNÉE — N° 6.   Prix : 10 centimes.   Le 5 Avril 1879

LES HYDROPATHES

JOURNAL LITTERAIRE ILLUSTRÉ
Rédacteur en chef : Émile GOUDEAU

Directeur-Administrateur : Paul VIVIEN | ABONNEMENTS : | Secrétaire de la Rédaction : J. JOUY

BUREAUX | Paris. — Province. — Étranger | BUREAUX DE VENTE
50, Rue des Écoles, 50 | Un an : 3 francs | 13, Rue Monge, 13.

L'hydropathe SARAH BERNHARDT

Cabriol [Georges Lorin],
L'Hydropathe Sarah Bernhardt,
published in *Les Hydropathes*,
April 5, 1879

Coll-Toc, *Sarah Bernhardt*,
published in *Les Femmes du jour*,
April 1886

Gill, *Sarah Bernhardt*

Gill, *Sarah Bernhardt*, published in *Les Hommes d'aujourd'hui*, October 25, 1878

Coll-Toc, *Marie Desclauzas*, published in *Les Femmes du jour*, April 1886

professions, Gill endows the figure with a prominent hooked nose and a serpentine form whose cloven hooves and tail suggest the sphinx. More baldly than any other, his caricature makes a malevolent equation between Bernhardt's multiple occupations, Jewishness, and destructive sexual power. But even in an image like Coll-Toc's, in which Bernhardt's prominent nose is neither hooked nor bumpy, her profile and frizzy hair would have been understood as Semitic.

A caricature by Gill in *Les Hommes d'aujourd'hui* of 1878 shows Bernhardt in profile with a star above her head. Although it predates Willette's image, it is not unlike his caricature on the cover of *Les Mémoires de Sarah Barnum*. The article by Félicien Champsaur accompanying Gill's print makes much of Bernhardt's eccentricities: studio clothes that make the critic liken her to a "joli garçon," attempts to poison herself, the coffin, balloon ascensions, pets of all races and sizes. At first, Champsaur appears to see these as the license of artists: he finds a pedigree for Bernhardt's work in that of George Sand, perhaps the most renowned amazon of the nineteenth century, as well as in Frédéric Lemaître's sartorial antics. But as the list of oddities swells, it becomes increasingly clear how they are interlaced or explained by stereotypes of Jewishness. After mentioning the pets,

Champsaur describes how Bernhardt recounted to the concierge at the Comédie Française one evening that she had killed a small, black dog that she used to like. Questioned about the motive, she replied "No reason." But the real reasons are revealed two lines later: "She has Jewish, nomadic blood in her veins. What's more, she's a woman." Champsaur's text recommends in closing that anyone desiring further confirmation should contact two rivals for her affection. The lewd sexual innuendo clearly reveals how the fusion of Jewishness and femaleness elicits stereotypes of sexual impropriety.

Cabriol's caricature emphasizes the masculine aspects of Bernhardt's studio attire, perhaps in keeping with the fact that, until Bernhardt's nomination, the honorific distinction of *hydropathe* had been conferred solely upon men. Although she is also the first woman to appear among *Les Hommes d'aujourd'hui*, Gill's caricature seems to emphasize the femaleness which Champsaur asserts to be her true nature. Instead of her studio pants, Gill shows Bernhardt wearing the long skirt and train for which she introduced the fashion. While the text, in noticing her exquisite voice, describes the actress as a bird, in Gill's image she sports prominent butterfly wings, echoing both her collar and the bows ("noeuds de papillons") on her shoes. Even with the offensive Jewish stereotypes in Champsaur's text, the five-pointed star above Bernhardt's head is not a Jewish star. Neither, it would seem, is the six-pointed one in Willette's or Cabriol's caricatures. For if seeing is believing, my initial conviction that a hexagram is a more stable index of Jewishness than a huge nose or unruly hair would have produced a host of Jewish popular entertainers, among them Thérésa, the famous chanteuse, and others less well-known today—Céline Chaumont, Sirius (Canicule Mathilde-Frédégonde), Marie Desclauzas, and undoubtedly others—who were not Jewish. While I knew that the notion of a star, "la grande étoile," certainly existed before the 1880's, I never thought that in addition to the five-pointed star, it could be symbolized by what I had always known as the Jewish star.

My brief excursus into the history of the six-pointed star suggests that it was surprisingly ecumenical. Scholarly accounts of the symbol's use in the nineteenth century are sparse and contradictory.[19] My concern, of course, is with whether a nineteenth-century audience would have perceived it as a symbol of Jewishness. Given what appears to be a widespread awareness that Bernhardt was Jewish, at least among the nineteenth-century critics and chroniclers of her life whose works we have examined, I am inclined to think that the hexagram in images of Bernhardt, much like the nose, would have functioned as a sign of Jewishness. As I have already suggested, however, invoking the actress's Jewishness was only one of many strategies used to convey her inappropriate behavior.

Caricature after Clairin, published in
Le Type, May 21, 1876

Georges Clairin, *Portrait of Sarah
Bernhardt*, Salon of 1876

The sheer number and variety of representations of Bernhardt make them extraordinarily complex. Although Bernhardt's reputation rests in large part on her achievements as a classical actress, her identity as a tragedienne is not paramount in paintings and caricatures in the way it is for Rachel. The metier of classical muse is only part of Bernhardt's long and varied career. After leaving the Comédie Française in 1880, she purchased and performed in her own theaters, supplementing her classical repertory with more popular melodramas written especially for her by Sardou and others. Late in her career, she did four vaudeville tours in the U.S.A., sharing a bill with the young Jack Benny at the Majestic in Chicago and a blackface act at Keith's Hippodrome in Cleveland.[20] In bridging highbrow and more popular entertainment, Bernhardt ineluctably stimulated gossip, never in short supply, about her impropriety. She posed a further challenge to conventional notions of womanhood by having metiers as an exhibited sculptor and painter, and published author. Inasmuch as Bernhardt's career spanned the entire Third Republic until her death in 1923, it saw the birth of the commercial entertainment industry and a notion of mass culture entirely different from the Restoration and July Monarchy years in which Rachel lived and performed. Unlike Rachel's, Bernhardt's visual lexicon has to include advertisements ranging from Pear's Soap to throat lozenges.

Any complete investigation of Jewishness in representations of Rachel and Bernhardt would have to take into account the repetitive use of their distinctive physical traits. In images of Rachel, much attention was paid to her expansive brow, identified both admiringly and critically as the site of her great cerebral powers. Bernhardt's uncontrollable hair, accused of breaking combs and likened to "negro's wool," was a common visual metaphor. Thinness was perhaps the salient feature most commonly evoked for both actresses, although their physical presences were perceived in diametrically opposed ways. Rachel was frequently likened to a classical column and her ramrod stance is echoed in many paintings, caricatures, and photographs. Conversely, Bernhardt is most often remembered in a serpentine, spiralling pose, indelibly embodied in her most famous painted portrait by Georges Clairin (exhibited in 1876) and also in countless caricatures.[21] These differing modes not only bespeak differing styles of declaiming, they are also evidence of transformations in the theater itself: by the time Bernhardt was performing, it was impossible to think of a classical theater in the sense in which it existed when Rachel was perceived to have brought it back to life. All these images are informed, at least in part, by the subtext of womanhood gone awry, either in the sexual arena through promiscuity or in the creative one through mannishness. Jewishness frequently intersects with stereotypes of unnatural femininity in both these realms.

To the examples we have already examined—money-grubbing and publicity-seeking, on the one hand, and too much creative endeavor, on the other—we might add the oversexualized woman. This, I would suggest, can take many forms. In Clairin's portrait of Bernhardt and the caricature of 1876 based on it, the close relation to legions of odalisques, of which the most notorious in recent memory would have been Manet's *Olympia* (exhibited 1865), suggests an identification with sexuality that not only speaks to Bernhardt's own past but, it seems, to a certain brazen assumption of that sexuality that is highly reminiscent of its notorious prototype. Upon initial consideration, Rachel's typical columnar stance and frequent representation as the personification of tragedy would seem to banish any suggestion of a sexual persona. But the loose, flowing drapery and exaggerated contrapposto we find in the most famous painted portraits by Gérôme and Ingres's student Amaury-Duval sensualize her form even as they liken it to classical architecture and sculpture. What I am suggesting is that even the noble classical persona that is integral to representations of Rachel may have a sexual dimension that is as much a part of stereotypes of Jewesses as it is of actresses.[22]

In this context, what is striking about representations of Bernhardt is their very unruliness. Neither the fact that she was Jewish nor the fact that she was a woman can begin to account for how she is depicted. The insistence on multiple stereotypes in representations of Bernhardt is itself distinctive. Colombier's *Mémoires*, Champsaur's account accompanying the caricature by Gill, and other caricatures depicting Bernhardt's various professions contain so many indexes of the aberrant that it is virtually impossible to configure them into a coherent whole. Bernhardt herself had much to do with this. The perfect exponent of mass culture, the personae she constructed for herself were both so numerous and so rich as to resist attempts to attack any one aspect of her identity.

Bernhardt also actively manipulated stereotypes. To the perception that she was emaciated, sick, skeletal, Bernhardt responded in kind. She modeled sculptures of death's heads, had herself photographed in a coffin, and marketed the pictures. She made her thinness fashionable. It is impossible to think about Clairin's portrait or any of the other images emphasizing her serpentine form without thinking about her role in dress reform.[23] The dresses she wore featured high necks and curling trains and were molded tightly to the body in a way which eliminated the corset. In Clairin's portrait, as well as in numerous other non-satirical images, she is shown wearing just such a confection, whose serpentine form is prolonged by the addition of the greyhound at her feet. Furthermore, there are instances in which Bernhardt herself speaks about her thinness or her illnesses, and others in which she chides her public for its implacable insistence on them.[24] As a woman who had several careers, who was perceived as a fashion-setter, who advertised health and beauty products, who was the first actress to play both Hamlet and Ophelia (if not in the same performance), who acted for the last years of her life with a wooden leg, Bernhardt's visibility and seeming omnipresence in the public world might well have elicited the charge of publicity monger. But in keeping herself so relentlessly, and under so many guises, before the public eye, she also ensured continual curiosity and recognition.

To an increasingly anti-Semitic world, her Jewishness could be evoked to stigmatize a woman whose capacities for myriad successes in the public realm would consistently be the target of ridicule and envy. If we keep in mind Colombier's epithets condemning Barnum as "an analytic woman with sangfroid" and "an eternal female Don Juan," it is clear that stereotypes of Jewishness were inseparable from the terror of woman's power. In a time of feminist gains and nascent malaise about mass culture, it should come as no surprise that attempts to stereotype Bernhardt are evidence of larger cultural and political anxieties. It is even possible that the caricatures of Bernhardt we have examined played a role in codifying for a large public the anti-Semitic signs that would be elaborated with ever increasing brutality in the next decades. If primal fear mobilized the filthiest accusations of dog murder, nymphomania, and insatiable greed, representations of Bernhardt were equally fueled by consuming envy or a more than grudging admiration of their indomitable subject. For this was a life so exceptional as to be fully as outrageous as any of the representations of it.

7
Proust: In Search of Identity

JULIA KRISTEVA

Subjectively, the issue of "national" identity is that indistinct domain of psychic and historical experience which transforms identity into belonging: "I am" becomes "I am one of them", "to be" becomes "to belong." Many are pleased with this reduction in the scope of existence; they seek either an optimal version of it, or use it to support fundamentalist beliefs. Proust is perhaps the first modern French writer to portray, albeit in an ambiguous and fiercely ironic way, the sadomasochistic dynamic of "belonging" (to a nation, religion, and any, but especially a gendered, group). He contrasts this with what he considers to be the "truth of Being," that is, the "incorporated time" of writing.

To illustrate Proust's ambiguity about the question of belonging, I start with two examples. On July 29, 1916, Proust wrote in a letter to an acquaintance that he had discovered a "certificate" of his christening and his first communion while searching through his father's papers. Although the christening can be vouched for, no "certificate" of first communion is officially issued (unless specifically requested), and none can be found in the records of Saint Louis d'Antin, the church where he was christened, or in Proust's own papers. The peremptory tone of the letter, which mentions an "archbishop of Saint Louis d'Antin," implies that the "certificate" is an exaggeration intended to convince the recipient of Proust's successful assimilation.

In contrast to this, at the end of *Le Temps retrouvé* (*Time Regained*, 1927), the last part of *A la Recherche du temps perdu* (*Remembrance of Things Past*), Mme. Verdurin, who identifies herself with France by speaking of "we" when speaking of diplomacy or of France's military policies, denies the baron de Charlus (one of the narrator's potential alter egos) the status of belonging to the French community: "'What is his nationality exactly, isn't he an Austrian?' . . . No, he is Prussian, she would say."[1] Of course, the baron, whose mother was a Bavarian duchess, could be of the "French body" just as easily as of the "German body." But is it a question of the body that is the basis for the narrator's cultivation of ambiguity? At the end of the novel, after having transexualized sex, Proust seems to enjoy disintegrating the nation. Proust admits that he, personally, is attached not to the "body

France" but to the "actor France" (3:798–9). And if we acknowledge that the "social kaleidoscope" that is *A la Recherche du temps perdu* was the first description of a "society of the spectacle," written by a man whose polyphonic identity was described by the admiring Jacques Rivière as an "atomic fission,"[2] how could he but be attached to the latter rather than the former? So what is identity for Proust, and how is it manifested in his writings?

Since a writer is, basically, someone who writes, we will consider Proustian identity—and from this his relationship to national, religious, and social belonging—within the logic of his writing. With its plethoric metaphors, excessive syntax, and imposing but indistinct characters, critics keep losing their way in Proust's meandering text. For clarity, we shall focus on the characters, and through their enigmatic identity will consider the history in which they, and both the narrator and Proust himself, were implicated—the history of the Dreyfus Affair.

The Attraction of the Classical

The realist novel and its characters make it difficult for contemporary readers to grasp the long and complex development of character in Western narrative. It may be useful briefly to chart this evolution as, beyond realism, Proust's search for the "actor France" is nothing other than the search for a French history of the classical tradition of rhetoric.

The Greeks did not conceive of characters as such. According to Aristotle's *Poetics*, narrative is constructed of "actants" (*prattontes*). Whether models or copies, real beings or fictional ones, the "actants" are nonetheless attributed with ethical characteristics (such as baseness or nobility). What is a character, what is "ethos?"[3] It is that which reveals personal choice, the kinds of things a person chooses or rejects. Thus a speech in which a character demonstrates no preferences or aversions, is not a revelation of character.

Hence, the character who is born of the world and molded by the plot, makes deliberate choices which tell us as much about himself or herself as about the author and his or her beliefs, politics, and rhetoric. Far from being a self-contained entity or "subject," the character—in classical antiquity the ethos—appears and disappears according to the needs of the story, with actions and speech as one.

Later, the term "character" was substituted for the word "ethos." In order for "character" to be stripped of the moral choice inherent in the concept of "ethos," and in order to incarnate a body inhabited by the soul, there had to have been the impact of the individualism of Christianity, with its passionate imagery and its synthesis of the subjective and the universal in the figure of Christ, the "absolute subject." The Greek word for "character," which refers to a mark, imprint, sign, or coin, connotes an incision that cuts and forms. This notion of character was later subjected to Latin, biblical, evangelical, and medieval narratives before becoming the "figure"—before "moral" was transformed into "representation."

As we cannot recapitulate the entire development here we shall simply note that it culminates in the work of the sixteenth-century writer Jules-César Scaliger. His *Poetices* emphasizes the representation of action through characters who make it visible.[4] He thus avoids the psychological and ideological values that the nineteenth century attributed to the concept of character, and allows us to situate the often disconcerting specificity of Proust's characters, as well as those of other modern writers, in relation to the tradition of classical rhetoric. This classical lineage, far from being paradoxical or merely snobbish, means that we find the same subjection of the "figure" to expression (*dictio*) in, for example, La Bruyère and a modern writer.

According to Scaliger, the character, like a statue, is founded in expression: "Just as a statue of Caesar is an image of Caesar, the poem is an image of what it describes." In other words, if the poem is an image, this should be seen as a statue. Phonic material is therefore plastic, it can be carved or modeled in order to shape something not *per via di porre* as in painting, but *per via di levare* as in sculpture.

The person who used the expressions *per via di porre* and *per via di levare* was not Scaliger but Freud. From within his Viennese study Freud borrowed these terms from another Renaissance Man, Leonardo da Vinci, to describe psychoanalytic representation, which he roughly equated to sculpture. Style and phrasing are simply tools that serve to convey this representation—the interpretation is the only thing that matters; style and phrasing are used in the service of a vision, an apparition in real volume, of a character appropriate to his or her *res*. Proust wrote: "Style . . . is . . . a vision" (3:931), thereby linking his desire for both precision (mastery of ideas) and ecstasy (going beyond technical appearances to perceived aberrations).

Reviving a mythical, Egyptian, and Greek memory, Proust endeavors to derive the main effects of his characters from the synthesis of the character as monument and the song-style of their creator. In 27 BCE a colossal classical statue breaks into song, as if suffused with poesis: "and I sing: for the poet is like the statue of Memnon; a ray of morning sunshine is enough to make him sing." In Proust's 1908 Notebook, which contains the earliest drafts of the novel, the singing statue is already included: "happiness is but a special sonority of strings that vibrate at the slightest movement and are brought to song by a beam of light. A happy man is like Memnon's statue: a ray of sunshine is enough to make him sing."[5] Statuesque and colossal, these giants reappear at the end of *A la Recherche* as monsters stranded on the plinth of incorporated memory, filling a space prolonged in time (3:1107). Clearly, Memnon's statue serves as a framing device for *A la*

Recherche at its beginning and close, a bridge between Aristotle and Scaliger, and the polyphony of modern characters.

The statuary fate of the character, which in the Middle Ages and the Renaissance embodies the Greek *ethos*, becomes increasingly flexible with time. It eventually loses its rigidity, and is rendered more fluid by the dynamic and logical pleasure of the *dictio*, which culminates in the neoclassical *Caractères* of La Bruyère (1688). La Bruyère, Madame de Sévigné, and Saint-Simon were the other primary classical bases upon which Proust sculpted his own monumental characters. Although we cannot fully explore Proust's debt to classical concepts of character and rhetoric, I shall suggest that as embodiments of the author's style, Proust's characters are simultaneously statue and point of view. The characters of La Bruyère, Sévigné, and Saint-Simon belong to the court (the external world) and are also metaphors in discourse. It is this ambiguity between the classical and the realist or naturalist character which was significant for Proust.

Proust rediscovered the major elements of classical rhetoric (the conversation, the letter, and the memoir) without going back to the Latin texts of his erudite antecedents. Instead he turned to the formulaic expression of character-portraits by La Bruyère, Sévigné, and Saint-Simon. Proust searches passionately for social equivalents of their characters in the ridiculous yet attractive vestiges of "nobility" that the nineteenth century tried to perpetuate in its prestigious salons, literary societies, and clubs, vestiges from the Restoration, through the Second Empire to the Third Republic. In the text, the aristocracy, as the summit of society, was then irradiated by its racial other, the Jew, and its sexual other, the homosexual.

Characters in this textual dynamic are dramatically transformed, crystallized within the limits of speech: they become contagious, confused, blurred. Is Swann a character? Does he have character? And what about Odette? Or Albertine? The unifying features of these characters are fragmented into a multiplicity of attributes. These characteristics are unified only within the febrile discourse of the enamored narrator: "Unique, we suppose? She is innumerable."

Mere comedy? A return to Aristophanes, to Molière? No, the outline itself disappears, the imprint leaves no trace, and the substance of the statue becomes alchemical, suffused with both life and death. Is it a transubstantiation then (a term Proust uses with evident pleasure, and a term also loved by Joyce)? Perhaps so, but only the narrator is capable of transcendence. The others, in the rare moments when the heart reaches them, are characters. But what exactly might this mean?

On the one hand, formed as they are by sadomasochism and inscribed within a metaphoric circle that maps the present onto the past, their multiple "looks" recall the individuation of Scaliger, La Bruyère, or even

Sévigné's characters. On the other hand, released from this grip of metaphor and passion, these creatures recover their hypnotic scintillation, their roles, and their Saint-Simonian masks. Proust's characters step out of the seventeenth century and are ready to enter the television screen.

The passion that transcends, cuts through, and reconstructs these characters (reuniting Charlus and Morel, Albertine and the narrator, Odette and Swann) continues to give substance to the figures at the very moment when their psychological and social dimensions break down. Faced with passion and its secret inversion, spite is unremitting but, emerging as irony, it becomes a new and devastating ethos: the annihilation of love, rendering jealousy insignificant. The most passionate of the passions is that of death, which comes to us all. Is it a fatal cruelty? No, it is only the supremacy of inconsistency.

Although Proust's characters retain the statuary aspect of seventeenth-century texts, they are primarily located within the speech of the narrator, sent from place to place, their resistance overridden, and their openness ridiculed, more emphatically than in the texts of any of his precursors. Imagination fragments and isolates; it makes distinctions and thus colludes with snobbery; imagination is snobbish. At the same time, it necessarily connects, at the heart of this coexistence of styles, the verbal treasure sounding the narrator's disillusioned memory. Strengthened by this transitivity, imagination carves out the tragic or comic traces of character. Through the immediacy of detail, Proust's portraits take on both the stability of realism and the flowing grace and lively inconsistency of subjective creatures—like spirits or ghosts projected by the narrator's memories.

Their statuary aspect does not disappear; it is inflected and derealized. The statues cannot share, without communication; sharing they remain solitary. Through the narrator's skill they are placed in a range of social environments; he sets them on a myriad of stages of his own sensitivity and speech. Because of this transitivity, the imprints of the statues multiply and contradict one another. It is pointless to search for their equivalents in the novel's contemporary social context, for the narrator tells us that "These shifting and confused gusts of memory never lasted for more than a few seconds; it often happened that, in my brief spell of uncertainty as to where I was, I did not distinguish the various suppositons of which it was composed any more than, when we watch a horse running, we isolate the successive positions of its body as they appear upon a bioscope" (1:7). Superimposition of memories (and therefore true), yet rendered in discourse (and thus overdetermined). Not the realities or "keys" and especially not the voice of an identity or an ideology, Proust's characters require a politics of the novel—a politics of identity and belonging.

The greatest concerns of the realist novel are to integrate with or to escape from a social "milieu," while its stylistic skill is limited to what can be defined within linguistic identity. Moreover, a novel's success, which is increasingly a matter of the media, is only possible if readers can discover their "own" world within it. Bestsellers are always "local," they bring me back to "my poor rural childhood," "my homosexuality," "my feminism," "my suburb," and so on.

As soon as a character departs from the territory, whether because of the many forms of language s/he uses or because of the diverse vicissitudes engineered by the narrator's rhetorical moves, s/he loses the sculptural realist dimension. S/he is then no longer considered to be real, but rather a verbal, abstract, and intellectual creation. Then readers of the realist novel are disappointed, and deprived of their "right" to illusion. The French Nouveau Roman exasperated the bourgeoisie by baring every last thread of the stuff of narrative device. For those who are not so naive as to seek a return to statuary form Proust's work remains as stimulating as it is enigmatic. For Proust synthesizes the fixity of social milieus without a narcissistic desire to be part of them and illuminates the absurdity of such vice. From Memnon to Golo, from the statue to the spectacle, to the magic lantern projecting the character, from the "body France" to the "actor France," the paradox of Proust's characters points us to the heart of the narrator's untenable identity, that is to writing itself.

What is the origin of this paradoxical link between the outside and the inside? What is the origin of this pivotal position which steadfastly belongs to both sides (the *côté Méséglise* and the *côté Guermantes?*), and yet fervently chooses to favor neither, placed as it is in the "pure time" of the work. The specificity of this paradox, which is that of contemporary aesthetics, certainly cannot be reduced to Proust's social status, although, as the novel's themes indicate, social status plays a large part. From a political and ideological standpoint the question might be: to which side does the narrator belong, when he can clearly see all the sides, when he knows them fully, when he loves them deeply, and when he is in full flight from them? To all the sides? To none of them? In other words, or more bluntly, how was it possible to be both Jewish and French during and after the Dreyfus Affair?

The Dreyfus Affair, or, the Elusive Truth: The Centre and the Periphery

Proust, a delicate child, was born to a Jewish mother and a Catholic father on July 10, 1871 and was christened on August 5 in the church of Saint Louis d'Antin, Paris. Both Jewish and Catholic, neither one nor the other, or perhaps both simultaneously, Proust was destined to live through the historical events that overwhelmed the turn of the century—the Dreyfus Affair and the First World War.

The Third Republic was a strange society in which a descending aristocracy played at being a bogus Versailles, and allowed a few rich, idle, or "French" Jews to join in their infantile games—a Rothschild, an Arthur Meyer, a Haas. In May 1885, the princesse de Sagan threw an animal masquerade ball in her Persian Villa at Trouville. *Le Gaulois* described it as one of those masterpieces of bucolic impertinence where the "beautiful people," dressed as a phantasmagoric menagerie of bees, giraffes, and birds of paradise, basked in a choreography of exquisite nostalgia which might have been simply amusing were it not so provocative, and therefore so grotesque and morbidly stupid. Edouard Drumont, a well-known French anti-Semitic writer, remembered it thus: "All the Jews are there, naturally, laughing at the degradation of this miserable aristocracy . . . Here's what the Christians did, in the month of May 1885, to celebrate the profanation of the church of Sainte Geneviève! and all that to get a mention in Arthur Meyer's newspaper!"

Drumont was lying by omission. The Jews were far from simply "laughing." Those "French" and idle Jews were certainly flattered to belong. But what was even more amusing, because more radical, was the reaction they produced in the aristocrats, who lacked the courage to recognize either their demise or their perversity. To be depraved in the company of these Jews would be even more strange, more piquant. "Smarter," Odette would say, but she was vulgar; the others said nothing. In any case, with these Jews it was altogether a different matter. After all, theirs was not simply an ephemeral nobility threatened with obliteration by a bit of a Republic. After all, with these Jews one might have, who knows, a new order, a future almost, why not a project? Alas, the Jews adapted to a world that, as each knew, was not meant for them. But another way, a good way, "Guermantes way," benefited from this adaptation, by transforming its own weaknesses into vice, into hope, into a tomorrow.

This unconscious calculation was not completely without sympathy. But it could not take into account Catholic conservatism, which continued to consider Jews as criminals, responsible for the death of Christ. And there was popular violence which scapegoated Jewish capital for causing the poverty actually brought about by the industrial expansion based on speculation.[6] Affair followed upon affair (Panama, Reinach), and then came *the* affair.

In 1894, nine years after the princesse de Sagan's masquerade ball, Alfred Dreyfus, a Jewish officer in the French armed forces, was condemned for spying for the Germans. The young Proust was one of the first militant Dreyfusards. Deeply committed to the Affair, he nevertheless remained on the periphery. Although he was never committed to any collective solution to any problem, he never ceased to be tortured by religious, sexual, and stylistic ambiguity. Indeed, with his friends Jacques Bizet, Robert de Flers, Léon Yeatman, Louis de la Salle, and the two brothers Halévy, Proust organized the *Manifeste des cent quatre*, which in one month accumulated 13,000 signatories in support of Dreyfus.

And yet at the end of *Le Temps retrouvé* the narrator classifies the Dreyfus Affair, as well as the First World War, among the unimportant events which "distract" the writer from the "interior book of unknown symbols . . . every public event, be it the Dreyfus case, be it the war, furnishes the writer with a fresh excuse for *not* attempting to decipher this book: he wants to ensure the triumph of justice, *he wants to restore the moral unity of the nation*, he has no time to think of literature." Beyond the well-known indictment of "notational literature," this sentence shows Proust's disillusionment with social and political life, and more particularly with the dogmatism inevitably brought about by commitment. In this case, Proust, although initially a Dreyfusard, was revolted by the anti-clericalism and political cynicism expressed by some of his own side. In *Le Côté de Guermantes* Bloch, who was naive, believed that "truth . . . resided permanently, beyond the reach of argument and in a material form, in the secret files of the President of the Republic and the Prime Minister, who imparted it to the Cabinet" (2:248–9). By contrast, the narrator, along with Proust, becomes convinced of the opposite view. As the Affair progressed, although it was never really recognized, Dreyfus's innocence became obvious. And it is evident that partisan interests appropriated the truth in order to exploit it for personal or ideological ends. The narrator's attitude thus changes through the course of the book. While at first he identifies with the fate of the condemned and exiled Jewish colonel, he eventually comes to see society as mesmerized, subjugated by corruption and the abuse of power, incapable of truth. In this particular case, Combes's anti-clericalism and Marxist anti-patriotism could hardly appeal to Proust.[7] When all is said and done, whatever one may initially or naively have believed, everything can be used for manipulation and corruption. The "inner book" then provides an escape. The exploitation of the affair by the Dreyfusards, as well as the subsequent death of Proust's mother, combined to convince Proust that that social commitment was pointless. The novel alone was to become the "authentic" setting for "real life."

Indeed, who was to be trusted? "The social kaleidoscope was in the act of turning and . . . the Dreyfus case was shortly to relegate the Jews to the lowest rung of the social ladder." A "storm" and "cyclone," the event only served to crystallize tendencies inherent in French society: although Bloch still passes unnoticed, "leading Jews who were representative of their side were already threatened" (2:194). The French salon cultivated its Jews as an eccentricity, an "orientalism," an "aesthetic curiosity," or as "local color," unless ennobled by "English or Spanish descent."

In this kaleidoscopic turmoil it is Swann, as often, who most closely represents the narrator's sympathies and reservations. A Dreyfusard from the start, Swann too is described as "comically blind." He recovers a certain admiration for Clemenceau, whom he had previously considered to be a spy for the English. And more seriously still, "the wave overturned Swann's literary judgments too, down to his way of expressing them. Barrès was now completely devoid of talent, and even his early works were feeble, could scarcely bear rereading" (2:605). Initially identified in the Dreyfusards, this fundamentalism (before the term existed) allowed Proust to level a similar accusation—and he must have thought it clever—at the anti-Dreyfusards.

The attempt to close down the churches was bound to provoke Proust's indignation, and this certainly accounts for the writer's defence of men who were as hostile to Dreyfus as the members of Action Française. *Le Côté des Guermantes* is dedicated to an admirer of Drumont and cofounder of the associated paper *L'Action française*, Léon Daudet, whom Proust ultimately considered to be the incarnation of the French mind with a lineage stretching back to Saint-Simon—something the narrator had always wished to possess, during, despite, and eventually without Dreyfus. To transcend the Jewish suffering of Dreyfus, and of Marcel himself, in order to achieve the literary style of Saint-Simon was his great personal and literary ambition, which predated the Dreyfus Affair and which no doubt sharpened the disillusionment that followed in its wake. "Since I can now only read one newspaper I read, instead of the ones I used to read, *L'Action française*. I can say that, in this matter I am not without merit." Exactly! "The thought of what a man could suffer, in the past made me a Dreyfusard and you can imagine that reading a paper that is infinitely more cruel than *Le Figaro* or *Les Débats* (which used to satisfy me) often gives me what feels like the beginning of heart failure." Proust's frankness is not without its own cruelty toward the paper. But disillusionment does not stop him: he adds "which other newspaper has a portico decorated by a fresco by Saint-Simon himself, as Léon Daudet tells me? . . . the false heroism of Colonel Henry (whom I do not find heroic at all, since I have become estranged from all the affluent Dreyfusards who are trying to assimilate into the [elite] Faubourg Saint-Germain)."[8] Proust was yet to make a place for himself in the Saint-Simonian pantheon of letters. This was to be another affair, the Proust Affair.

Red and White

Several references to Judaism in Proust's text reveal its influence on him and how he chooses to represent this.[9] Proust frequently quotes from the Bible, as well as from the Gospels. These citations give emphasis to the essential moment of a sentence or a thought, referring to the canonical meaning of the sacred text while endowing it with an emotional or comical personal aspect.[10] Such biblical evocations are a part of Proust's general cultural heritage, but he uses them with an idiomatic intensity and frequency. It seems that he was also interested in both the esoteric currents of Judaism and their consonance in Christian culture. Through Ruskin and the cult of Venice, it was ecclesiastical architecture that filled Proust with wonder and offered the narrator a privileged example of the embodiment of the sacred that was the aim of the *temps retrouvé*. The Jewish tradition merges imperceptibly into the splendor of this Christian art. It imbues it with a mysterious ambiguity that moves the narrator's aesthetic to the abstract purity of wisdom (the Zohar), but also to the recognition of the permanence of vice (Sodom and Gomorrah). The link between Judaism and Venice is already suggested, enigmatically, in *Jean Santeuil* (written 1895–1900) when the young man breaks a Venetian glass and dreads that his mother's anger might be followed by a paternal reprimand. The young man receives nothing but the following explanation, which is strange coming from a Catholic mother: "He thought that she would scold him and call his father. But she sweetly kissed him and said, 'It will be like in the temple, the symbol of an indestructible union.'"[11] On the other hand, in the drafts of *Contre Sainte-Beuve*, written toward the end of 1908, the narrator's mother assumes some pronounced stereotypically Jewish characteristics.[12]

Ambiguous and diffuse, Proustian Judaism turns up when least expected. In Roussainville Proust curiously adds a Saturday rite to that of the Dominican Mass. On Saturday they eat earlier because Françoise has to go to the Roussainville market. Also, in *Cahier 9* the servant is represented as a follower of the "ancient Jewish Law." These details have disappeared from the final version and Françoise eventually finds herself cleansed of her Judaism. Elsewhere, red and pink are systematically associated with Judaism. The Jewish redness of Gilberte, which she inherits from her father, joins the pink so enjoyed by Proust: Odette the woman in pink; the red dress and shoes of Oriane; the hawthorns, initially pink or white, which from the point of Gilberte's first appearance in the story polarize this part of the story into two series—the Catholic virginal white versus the sexual Jewish pink. Pink often has maternal connotations, but it can also suggest the secret attractiveness of paternal authority, when it is imagined to be Jewish. The conjunction of sexuality and Judaism is also colored pink through references to Albertine: she is simply a pinkness for Marcel. Finally, a spectrum of Jewish literary references runs through *A la Recherche du temps perdu*, including Racine's two Jewish tragedies *Esther* and *Athalie*.

Proust's irony, the manifest inverse of his guilt, combines the dual singularities of Judaism and homosexuality through a relentless pursuit of their conjunction. Sodom and Zion become fused and contaminate one another. The fusion is also unbearably ambivalent, and some of Charlus's flights of oratory prefigure the horrors of modern events, of which Proust was unaware: "But then a ghetto is all the more beautiful when it is even more homogeneous and more crowded."[13] But ultimately, it is always Proust's irony, the other side of his uneasiness and loneliness, that motivates him. Far from erasing differences, the ironic superimposition of codes reinforces the polysemy and overdetermination of Proust's characters. They appear as ambiguous, unattainable, like the reverberation of a bioscopic image.

It is not a question of describing the sociological reality or the community of the Jew, or of mastering the psychological reality of the homosexual. By superimposing the two marginalities, by juxtaposing the hostility and denigration in which each are held in "society," Proust inverts the calumny. By dissipating this persecution he simultaneously undermines the need to identify the denigrated. He takes them from their sociological or psychological pedestals and reduces them to particular characters. In the end, only the involutions and outbursts of his own character, his own most secret differences, regrets, and pleasures remain.

In the double reference to the Hebrew towns of Sodom and Gomorrah, and to the book of Daniel, the fates of Judaism and homosexuality are intertwined. Biblical judgment condemned the two cities for their sexual vices and greed. The opening of *Sodome et Gomorrhe* (part four of *A la Recherche*, which inverts the condemnation of homosexuality that Proust published with the title "La Race Maudite" in *Contre Sainte-Beuve*) considers the homosexual an "extraordinary creature" destined for exile and redemption. The "transmutation" of Charlus into a woman is described in a long digression that explicitly cites the language of Daniel.

The Zoharic tradition, particularly Daniel, knew how to look into a face and decipher the signs of another soul with which it is coupled. Similarly, Proust looks into the homosexual's face and deciphers the presence of maternal traits. In doing so he draws on the mystical tradition without abandoning his tendency to treat homosexuality and esotericism with irony. (Proust conceives of homosexual experience as a mere esoteric experience.) However, this polysemy leaves open the idea of a promise of salvation.

At this point one should try to understand how the narrator was able to assimilate the Jew and the homosexual—the two singularities which excite his tender irony and cruel sarcasm, but which must be surpassed by the singularity of art. All groups, amassings, kinships of these singularities provoke the narrator's distrust and rejection. "Let us ignore for the moment, those who . . . wish to share their taste . . . with apostolic zeal, just as others preach Zionism, conscientious objection, Saint-Simonianism, vegetarianism or anarchy . . . but I have thought it as well to utter here a provisional warning against the lamentable error of proposing (just as people have encouraged a Zionist movement) to create a Sodomist movement and to rebuild Sodom" (2:643,655–6). Militant and exemplary vice, and even anarchy, creates uniformity and thus destroys singular experience.

For Proust, against the group but sharing in its fate, it was a question of avoiding the group instinct and of constructing simple "fugues": surprising, cruel, and ridiculous impressions. The positions that Proust took up during the unraveling of the Dreyfus Affair stemmed from this position; while the Affair in other respects had to consolidate group identity. But is a fugue, in its musical sense, what one would call a true "position?"

From Vice to Infinity

In her work "Anti-Semitism," largely inspired by the legacy of the Jewish image in Proust's writings, Hannah Arendt emphasizes the role played by Jewish assimilation in the catastrophic destiny of the twentieth century, a century despicable enough to conceive of a "final solution." As a result of their acceptance of the ideals of the bourgeois revolution, Jewish adaptation to the management of capital and industry (and simultaneously to politics, the press, and the army) was limited to the upper classes. More treacherously, Jewish origin, when removed from its religious and political meaning, became a psychological quality, was transformed into "Jewishness," and from then on could be conceived of only in terms of virtue or vice. For some it was "interesting" vice, for others it became a criminality which had to be exterminated, especially when political and economic conditions produced the need for a scapegoat: "such perversion was made possible by those Jews who considered it an innate virtue."[14]

Arendt stresses this reduction of Judaism to a difference and singularity, if not a psychic or moral curiosity. (She does not explore the sexual connotations of this, but as a reader of Proust it can be assumed that she was sensitive to this aspect.) She implies that this is why the Jews confined themselves, and allowed themselves to be confined, to an elite capable of humility as well as arrogance. Abandoning Judaism as a religious sign, Jewishness came to signify a closed clan. Some in *A la Recherche* joined them and were often flattered to be attributed with eccentricity and distinctive perversity.[15] Some, for example, declared themselves Dreyfusards through snobbery, such as the Verdurins and even the duc de Guermantes, who was happy to express sympathy for the Jewish colonel if only to impress the Italian ladies he met at the spas.

But once declared innocent, Dreyfus ceased to signify vice and therefore became uninteresting. Poverty expresses itself in base instincts, and the poverty-ridden populace, and with it that part of society that "showed itself willing to incorporate crime in the form of vice, was soon ready to purge itself of its viciousness by openly accepting criminals and publicly committing crimes."[16] Arendt identifies the treacherous sociological, religious, and psychological conditions that caused the Dreyfus Affair, and sees their culmination in the extermination camps and the Holocaust. The assimilation of Judaism as Jewishness, which was desired or tolerated, is seen as one of the conditions for the unprecedented massacre; and only the Zionist courage to restore origins is seen as an alternative or safeguard. Crossing the Proustian Way, of Jewishness as vice, and recognizing Proust's diagnosis as true, the philosopher turns away from it in order to seek a political solution.

The writer Proust's obsession is something else. Consider Swann, a central character. In the initial draft of the novel he was to be the main character, before Marcel and the narrator made him an alter ego. In the final version he remains inspirational to the work. Consider also Bloch's expressive, cathartic presence as the unadaptable, blundering fool. Recall the numerous debates about the Affair, the anti-Semitic comments made by Charlus and Norpois, and the expiatory violence of the narrator himself, who relentlessly pursues his alter egos as if to purge himself of his own "stench."[17] It is clear that the Jewish problem is the open secret of *A la Recherche du temps perdu*, like "Swann's punchinello nose."[18]

But where is the narrator? At the center and at the periphery. Swann's elegant idleness, and his mistaken belief that life is a novel, can easily be assimilated into the elite of the Faubourg Saint-Germain. The Faubourg rejects Bloch's boorishness but it is eventually assimilated into him. For the Jews, that singular people, are like a mirror reflecting the group's singularities and the singularity of clannishness. Whether aristocrats or homosexuals, the Chosen ones of blood or the Chosen ones of sex, they recognize their difference within that mirror. The group's boundaries begin to shift, the barriers are no longer impenetrable. The group becomes nervous, it allows itself to be seduced, penetrated, contaminated. Of course the hierarchies are maintained, but how long will they last?

There is a common logic uniting all these differences, one which Arendt names "vice," and which Proust dramatizes. Every group, of course, congregates around one figure who is considered to be unlike the others, and the group exists with him and against him, in a sadomasochistic dynamic. The logic of sadomasochism is a hatred of love, a love of hatred, persecution, humiliation, delightful grief. There is no social exit from this dynamic. Every aspect of the social is incorporated into it. "It is the *soul* . . . of the ancient Hebrews, torn from a life at once *insignificant and transcendental* . . . so disturbing because it does not appear to emanate from humanity, so deceptive because it nonetheless resembles humanity all too closely . . . that gives us a sense of the supernatural, in our poor everyday world where even a man of genius from whom, gathered around a table at a seance, we expect to learn the secret of the infinite" (2:195–6). The insignificant yet transcendental soul of the genius, or of the Jew deracinated from the past, radiates the "secret of the infinite" onto our poor world, gathered, as if around a seance table. The narrator and Jews such as Swann and homosexuals such as Charlus hold the secret of society, even the most refined society such as that of Saint-Germain. They hold its key, they are killed by it, but die with the truth.

"To belong or not to belong": the unavoidable predicament. It is unimaginable that a new territory, separate or innocent clan or sect, could be created. The same logic assails you, the vertigo of being one of them or not being one of them. Sadomasochism plays it part: I belong to them—they love me; I don't belong to them—they are killing me. Being becomes a question of love; that is, of belonging, identification . . . and regret.

Dear Hannah Arendt, vice is not a historical accident. Vice is latent, it is the other face of society, it is infinite. Proust seems to have realized this as well as Freud did, and without his help either. There is simply no way not to be part of it—a part of society and thus of perversion. Except perhaps to describe it; to deconstruct, reconstruct, reinvent. Writing does not efface vice, it absolves it. To the realism it sustains, the novel adds a metaphysics in which vice is at once approved and reproved. In the final analysis vice is exhibited in order to be evacuated.

In fact Arendt is mistaken: according to Proust, Jewishness is not a vice. "Assimilated," inserted into another religion (here Catholicism), as a fascinating and abject foreign body, Jewishness manifests the sadomasochism inherent in the dark heart of every society. Jewishness is the index of truth when it focuses social groups. By being removed from those groups in order to consolidate the purity of Judaism, it is protected, but at the risk of perpetuating ethnic, clan, and national warfare. Such is the logic of history, and Arendt seeks a tolerable outcome of history. By contrast, when it reveals a truth intrinsic to unified groups, Jewishness bears witness to the infinite reversibility of passions—love, jealousy, and death. It offers simply beauty, and no historical solution. If Judaism has its history, Jewishness inspires art. Beneath passing time, which is necessarily lost, remains time regained. This is Proust's Way: the incorporation of pure time.

This incorporation is violent: it is the price of true beauty. Proust relentlessly pursues Swann—his nose, his odor, his uneasiness—just as he relentlessly pursues the senile and impotent old Charlus. One recalls Françoise who, having learnt to understand literary work, through living the narrator's life adores slaughtering chickens: "looking at her enemy's cadaver," she cannot help but shout "filthy beast! filthy beast!" In the same way and in order to cook a character, Proust the chef empties his prey of some of its substance in order to stuff it with his own, his body and soul dying and being resuscitated in the superb preparation. Thus, his projections are made flesh.

From this sadistic, borderline position, writing inflicts marks on the characters that, being potentially those of the narrator, make them engaging, credible, and at the same time elusive. Gone are the statues à la Balzac, but in their place are projections—Proust's, mine, yours. Who's who? Swann or Haas, Swann or Charlus, Charlus or the narrator? The narrator always and indefinitely? Let us take Swann, sublime, Wagnerian, Botticellian aesthete: "Swann's punchinello nose, absorbed for years within a pleasant face, now seemed enormous, tumid, crimson, the nose of an old Hebrew" (2:715); "a prophet's beard beneath a huge nose which dilates to inhale its last breath" (2:730). Very much like the dying Proust, if only he could have known. "Swann, with his ostentation, his loud, desperate name dropping, was a vulgar show off whom the Marquis de Norpois found, to use his own epithet, 'puant.'" Fortunately, it is Norpois who says it, for if it had been the narrator the word would have been rather catty. But against whom is such nastiness aimed? Since Swann is the main subject of the book it is he, and hence the narrator himself. . . .

To sum up, in order to create characters one must know how to be one (of them) and not to be one (of them). To know how to be Swann, to love him and also be detached from him, to be no longer part of him. To do both simultaneously, before once again finding that strange osmosis of the projectionist and the shadow: "And yet, my dear Charles [Haas], whom I used to know when I was so young and you were nearing your grave, it is because he whom you have regarded as a young idiot has made you the hero of one of his novels that people are beginning to speak of you again, and that your name will perhaps live" (3:199). Who will live? Who is the character? Haas, the prototype? Swann? Proust?

Inside and out, at the center of the clan, and at its periphery, this is how to carve—into other people's flesh and into one's own, sadistically, with precision.

Proustophiles and aesthetes note: no sooner are clans or groups formed than vice is created. They enjoy possessing their "other." They close in on him or her, sadomasochism takes hold again, they are capable of anything. Proust sounded the depths of the effects of clans and groups in order to measure the enjoyment as well as the impossibility of them, and the desire to leave. Let us not enclose him.

Contemporary intellectual life in France and especially literary life has inherited the classification which nurtured La Bruyère and Proust. Intellectual life cultivates and petrifies, excluding newcomers, rejecting intruders, cherishing the favorites, those of the harem. Recognition and adoption can be in terms of class, sex, taste (which turns out to be aesthetic or ideological indulgence). The vice still tightens, and the French version of Hamlet's question remains "To belong or not to belong." A rejected writer's strange style can be qualified as "Franco-Yiddish" (Céline, the anarchist, made himself the curator of the rhetorical sanctuary, displacing Proust). From a different viewpoint, one can imagine that this impenetrable clannishness of the French literary world is the product of a "Jewish" intelligentsia, which has become hostile to pure and "old stock" French (from Drumont to Bernanos and Le Pen, this specter of nationalism haunts the nevertheless quite real milieus of French literature and journalism). What was once a source of linguistic identity, inviting stylistic transgressions, clannishness, like nationalism, seems today not only to be antiquated but also a mere institutional defence without ethical or aesthetic project, blocking the evolution of the French novel.

Within these conditions, Proust's twofold project of unraveling nationalism and clannishness through Jewishness (itself disposessed of a "proper" identity) and of revealing the sadomasochistic dynamic of these boundaries, is one of unrivaled sociological and metaphysical ambition. Proust dangerously regionalizes the literature that succeedes him, by locating it in politics (when that literature aspires to universality, as with Malraux and Sartre) or in aesthetics (when it feigns textual subversion, only to be better accepted as belonging, as in the French Nouveau Roman or Postmodern minimalism). Neither of one side nor the other, and constantly beyond both, Proust never ceases to disturb all those who wish to belong.

Translated by Claire Pajaczkowska

8

From Fin de Siècle to Vichy: The Cultural Hygienics of Camille (Faust) Mauclair

ROMY GOLAN

In 1944 Camille Mauclair—a novelist, poet, essayist, playwright, journalist, pamphleteer, critic, writer of travelogues, and the author of some one hundred books and over a thousand articles—wrote a thirty-page booklet entitled *La Crise de l'art moderne*. It begins thus:

> There have been great poets, great scientists, and great Jewish philosophers, but few or no Jewish painters. The visual arts have never been the strong point of Jews. Yet since art is both a creation of the spirit and a material object whose sale feeds its author, the Jews, for whom everything is reduced to commerce, have turned their attention to this field of activity. The profession of art dealer is a legitimate one. . . . Jews can be reproached for having introduced to the commerce of painting strategies of dishonesty and corruption. Writers such as Balzac and Zola had already denounced this in the previous century. But it is in the course of the last fifty years that the Jewish influence in the fine arts has assumed an ever larger and nefarious role.[1]

In his bitter account of the fifty-year saga of the Jew in modern art, Mauclair retraced, ironically enough, his own life story. Ignoring for a moment the text's malevolent tone—that is, focusing on the text as history rather than discourse—one has to recognize that many of the facts reported in his booklet are actually correct. So let us find out more about Mauclair's context from his own text:

> 1891 marks the first intervention of Jews in defense of avant-garde art in *La Revue Blanche*, where everybody was Jewish, starting with the three Natanson brothers. . . . and where anarchism, anti-militarism, trendy scepticism were cultivated and where modern painting was defended in tandem with the dealers. The house critic [Félix Fénéon] became a salesman in a Jewish gallery. . . . The system outlined at this time solidified around 1900. The result was a consortium of major Jewish dealers such as Wildenstein, Bernheim frères, Hessel, and Rosenberg. . . . Until then the great writers, thinkers, and intellectuals were outsiders to the gallery world. The new consortium led, instead, to the surge of

pseudo-critics, total unknowns, appointed by dealers, into the magazines. Let us mention first of all the Jews: Meyer, known as Louis Vauxcelles; Claude Roger-Marx, Florent Fels (a shady personality now sold to North African dissidence); Waldemar George, a Jewish Pole manager of the half-Jew Picasso; Adolphe Basler, an Austrian Jew. Then come the non-Jewish anarchists and communists: the Belgian Fierens, the communist mason Jean Cassou, Jean Cocteau, Charensol, Guenne, Warnod, etc. . . . all second-rate and now forgotten. . . . The ministry of Fine Arts fell under the directorship of the Jew Paul Léon, followed by the Jew Huysmans, supported, during the years of the Popular Front by the Jewish minister Jean Jay and of course Léon Blum, who signaled the triumph of all things Jewish until 1940. . . . This Jewing [*enjuivement*], which began in France, soon spread to other nations, namely the U.S.A. and central Europe. In Weimar Germany, Fauvism, under the name "expressionism" was propagated by the Jew Cassirer in liaison with the Parisian Mafia, and the Jewish critic Meier-Graefe, Duveen in London, Knoedler in New York. . . . All Jewish galleries are finally closed! All the Jewish critics excluded from the newspapers. All of this is excellent! Yet the purge is far from over. The Jewish poison will only dissolve itself slowly. (10)

In the context of Vichy, one could argue that there is nothing particularly remarkable about Mauclair's vilifying prose. Four years into the Vichy regime, even the most distracted reader would have been able to read between the lines, fill in the gaps, and make sense, for instance, of Mauclair's inclusion of the Catholic (yet avant-gardist) Picasso and the equally Catholic (yet homosexual) Cocteau in his list of Jews/undesirables/others. And blacklisting aside, by the time Mauclair wrote his booklet, the great "cleaning up" of the "real" Jews in the French art world (and elsewhere) had already been accomplished, in part thanks to his own writings.[2] Nor was Mauclair's ideological trajectory from *fin-de-siècle* anarcho-Symbolist to Vichy hygienist unique. He belonged, after all, to the generation of French arch-nationalists that included the royalist Charles Maurras and, more to the point, the anarchist-turned-*revanchiste* Maurice Barrès, who although dead since 1925 was never more alive than in the early 1940's. To these one may add a slew of other late nineteenth-century socialists and anti-materialists turned Fascists by the 1930's, from Jean Sorel to Marcel Déat.[3] What is significant, as will be contended in this essay, is that in belonging to the realm of cultural politics rather than of politics proper, Mauclair's critical itinerary and discourse evolved not in some protected outpost of French refinement and decorum, but in the sector that became most vulnerable to the waves of nationalism and xenophobia that had come to affect French social and political life. And this not so much during the infamous years of the Dreyfus trials in the 1890's as during the 1920's, a decade that has often been viewed by historians as a moment of relative serenity for Jews in France, lodged as it were between the trauma of the Affair and the rising specter of Fascism in the 1930's.

Indeed, there is little to detect of the future anti-Semite in Mauclair's early career.[4] In 1891, at the age of eighteen, and conveniently eliding his uneasy middle name of Faust, young Camille set out to write for no less than six small magazines that proliferated in France during the years of Symbolism: *La Conque, Chimère, La Revue Indépendante, La Revue Anarchiste, L'Endehors*, and the Natanson brothers' *La Revue Blanche*. A year later, he joined the staff of what was to become one of France's best and long-lived literary magazines, *Le Mercure de France*.

A fervent and often inspired supporter of Symbolism, Mauclair believed in such vintage fin-de-siècle concepts as art for art's sake, the quasi-religious function of art, and the image of the artist genius sheltered in an ivory tower. The epitome of such purifying and redeeming functions was encapsulated for him in the ethereal poetry of Stéphane Mallarmé, on whom he would write some moving pages in the late 1890's.[5] The key to Mauclair's cult of artistic individuality mixed with anarchist leanings was Barrès's "culte du moi," as evidenced in his first novel, *Le Jardin de Bérénice* (1892), and his "Notes éparses sur le Barrèsisme" published in *La Revue Indépendante* that same year.

For all of his seduction by Barrèsian rhetoric, however, the Mauclair of the 1890's was a convinced internationalist. He was one of the greatest French champions of Belgian, British, and Scandinavian Symbolist painting and theater, and while he mostly kept at arm's length from Germany, he saw Belgium as an important intermediary between French and German culture. As a main supporter of Lugné-Poe's avant-garde Théâtre de l'Oeuvre at its founding in 1893, Mauclair was closely involved with a theater where eight of the twelve plays comprising the first season were by non-French playwrights such as the Belgian Maurice Maeterlinck, the Norwegian Henrik Ibsen, the Swede August Strindberg, and lesser known names like the Dutch Herman Bang and the German Gerhardt Hauptmann.

This did not prevent Mauclair from being among those anarcho-Symbolists who in 1894 immediately assumed that Captain Dreyfus was guilty of high treason to the German foe. Yet by the time the case was a *cause célèbre*, he had changed sides, joining the staff of Georges Clemenceau's *Aurore*, the daily that was to publish Emile Zola's "J'accuse" in 1898. Mauclair was now convinced that it was the petty bourgeoisie he had always despised who had wrongly accused Dreyfus. As the scholar Charles Clark William has convincingly shown in *Camille Mauclair and the Religion of Art* (1976), this shift in alliance can be linked to a larger change in

Mauclair's aesthetic beliefs. Turning against the obscurantism of Symbolism he now envisioned the possibility of bringing art to the masses.[6] Personal as it may have been, although we are given little insight into that aspect of Mauclair's mind, this attitude was in sync with the politics of the time. For one finds that, under the doctrine of "solidarism," the Third Republic was striving to accommodate—probably as much out of conviction as in order to absorb the worrisome rise of Socialism, Syndicalism, and Anarchism—stronger social concerns by the turn of the century.[7] Mauclair's position was now an eclectic and, indeed, even a progressive one. He could praise everything from the rosy Realism of the pious peasant paintings of Millet, Bastien-Lepage, and Roll, all the way to the work of Pissarro, Daumier, Manet, and even Courbet. In 1896, as one of several art critics to focus new attention on the fate of the French decorative arts, Mauclair gave large and positive coverage in *Le Mercure de France* to Samuel Bing's new store L'Art Nouveau. This was in notable contrast to conservative critics like Arsène Alexandre who, reviewing the store's opening for the daily *Le Figaro*, extemporized that the place "smelled of the lewd Englishman, the Jewess addicted to morphine, or the cunning Belgian, or an agreeable mix of all three poisons."[8]

In "La Femme devant les peintres modernes," published in 1899, Mauclair took an unusual position for a former Symbolist, praising the new psychological depth granted to female sitters since Manet, as well as the shift in pictorial representation from women as erotic ornaments to moral individuals who share the mores, worries, and responsibilities of modern men.[9] It was Mauclair who, in 1904, wrote one of the first comprehensive studies on Impressionism, praising its anti-academicism (that is, anti-classicism) and its influence abroad, and celebrating it as the greatest renaissance of French painting since the eighteenth century. And finally, Mauclair's continuing opposition to France's insidious forces of reaction led him in 1905 to side with artistic innovation against neoclassicism and the imperialistic overtones assigned to France's so-called *Latinité* by Charles Maurras and his royalist cronies of Action Française, in an article entitled "La Réaction nationaliste en art ou l'ignorance de l'homme de lettres."[10]

Yet if in 1905 Mauclair's own achievements as enlightened *homme de lettres* were acknowledged in a modest monograph—one of a new series published by E. Sansot & Cie dedicated to "Les Célébrités d'Aujourd'hui"—and by the award of the Légion d'Honneur, it can be argued that by then his best years were already behind him.[11] Indeed, Mauclair's whole attitude seems to have changed, in just a few months, by the time he published *Trois crises de l'art actuel* with Editions Fasquelle in 1906.[12] Taking his cue from Nietzsche's ponderous pessimism in *Twilight of the Idols*, Mauclair assumed an entirely negative standpoint. Young artists were unable to create a new form of Symbolism in painting; Impressionism had fallen into some kind of sub-Impressionism with Cézanne and Gauguin; the French decorative arts were being vulgarized by industrialization and mass production; and Bing's Art Nouveau, which he had praised in 1897, he now saw as a manic, hybrid, and ridiculously convoluted style. By far the most premonitory of the tenor of Mauclair's later prose is the last chapter of the book entitled "La crise de la laideur en peinture" ("The crisis of ugliness in painting"). There—without ever mentioning Fauvism by name, although his intimations were clear to all—Mauclair decried the barbaric and willful ugliness that had reached a climax at the 1905 Salon d'Automne and the last (Spring 1906) Salon des Indépendants. These paintings, which draw, he writes, on the "infantile primitivism" of Gauguin and the "pseudo-naivete" of Cézanne—(who "daubs brightly colored folk Images d'Epinal as if he had never seen a painting in his life"), feature "repulsive Africanizing female nudes quartered with a hatchet." They are praised by a slavish, ignorant, howling press, Mauclair goes on, madly fearful of sounding once again *retardataire*. If the art critics are totally confused, the real culprit for this state of affairs, Mauclair claims, is the art dealer who speculates on the art market as if it were the stock exchange. It is the dealers who pull the strings of the salons. Money rules. In the face of all this, Mauclair found solace in the revival of religious painting in the works of Jean-Charles Cazin, Maurice Denis, Georges Desvallières, and Charles Filigier.[13]

There is no doubt in my mind that Mauclair's new obsession with the themes of savagery, decadence, and moral corruption (all of this verging on conspiracy theory) largely stemmed from the shock and frustration he felt, shared by many French Catholics, at the Bloc des Gauches's recent decision to separate Church and State. This decision—taken by the French Parliament without consulting ecclesiastical authorities—led to muscle flexing by the Catholic right and, in the wake of the concommitant rise of anti-German *revanchisme* after the so-called Moroccan Crisis (1905), to a surge of Christian mysticism that constituted an extremely inflammable political mix by the time France marched into the First World War.[14] It also led to a wave of conversions of French intellectuals to Catholicism (among them Mauclair's Jewish friend, the writer Marcel Schwob). This crisis had a strong resonance in Mauclair. For it should be emphasized that, for all of his flirtation with the idea of a Socialist art in the late 1890's, the role of the artist (or writer) for Mauclair had remained fundamentally the same: he had to function as a spiritual and, even more importantly, a moral model, to withdraw from public success, renounce the vanity of Parisian life and the triumph of bohemianism, and avoid excess. He had to epitomize, in short, the Catholic duty of self-renunciation. These values seemed to have been repudiated, even abnegated, by recent art and literature.

Mauclair's sudden outburst of rage in *Trois crises* also reveals, I would argue, a new and profound sense of insecurity on his part in response to the diminished role of the allegedly enlightened *homme de lettres* and, more particularly, the art critic. Indeed, while it can be said that in the last decades of the nineteenth century art production was importantly defined by art criticism, critical discourse in France from the 1900's onward would no longer be blessed by figures of the stature of Zola, Charles Baudelaire, Joris-Karl Huysmans, or even the professional art critic Félix Fénéon. With Guillaume Apollinaire dead from his war wounds in 1919, and the influence of André Breton, Georges Bataille, Louis Aragon, and Michel Leiris confined to a small coterie of readers by what amounts to a conspiracy of silence on the part of the art community, art criticism in France became increasingly mediocre between the wars—average texts churned out by a few too many professional critics in a few too many middle-of-the-road art magazines.[15] While Mauclair himself would have hardly sided, especially by this point, with any of these avant-garde figures, his fears of a power gap in art criticism were well founded. The *fortune critique* of recent art production was no longer primarily informed by critical texts but by dealers and the marketplace.

Mauclair's resentment was given an ideal outlet by the rhetoric of hatred unleashed by the First World War. In 1916 he published *Le Vertige allemand: Histoire du crime délirant d'une race*, a small book which he dedicated to Madame Juliette Adam, a royalist, staunch supporter of Maurras's ultra-nationalist L'Action Française, and close friend of the anti-Semite Léon Daudet. Its main argument, that the Franco-German conflict was only tangentially a territorial, colonial, military, economic, or diplomatic conflict, but in essence a cultural, humanistic, and moral one, was not particularly original. Yet its tone was extraordinarily violent:

> We have to hate Germany and transmit that hatred to our children. We have to make sure that the children of our children hate the crime committed, and that it becomes, in the legend of centuries, as immortally execrated as that of Cain.[16]

In 1919, a year after France's victory over Germany, Mauclair was a co-signatory, with the painter Maurice Denis among others, of the "Manifeste de l'intelligence," published in *L'Action française* by the notable right-wing thinker Henri Massis. The manifesto called for intellectuals to rise in the defense of a Christian, civilized, and humanistic West against the menace of the East—that is, barbarian Germany and, after the 1917 Revolution, Bolshevism. As conservative Catholics went on lamenting the destruction of the medieval churches and cathedrals of the so-called "Villes Martyres" of a victorious yet deeply wounded France, this rhetoric would resonate at least as late as Massis's 1927 *Défense de l'occident*.[17] Massis's title was coined expressly in response to an equally controversial book by the German philosopher Oswald Spengler—*Der Untergang des Abendlandes* (*The Decline of the West*, 1918). According to Massis, Spengler's catastrophic view of history was nothing but a perfidious attempt to exonerate Germany's effort to destroy humanity, as well as to redeem itself for the collapse of its own culture. Calling, as he had in 1919, for a consolidation of Western Europe, whose disunity he traced back to the schism provoked by the Protestant Reformation, Massis warned his compatriots against the infiltration of decadent "Eastern" ideas into Germany, and their leakage from there to France.

By·this point the major ingredients of Mauclair's rhetoric of hatred were well in place: the association of modern painting with pathology, his feelings of impotence as a critic, the fear of the East, the belief in the existence of a "race maudite," and the concept of a conflict to be fought on a moral, rather than territorial and military level. All that remained was to transpose this system of signs which he had associated with Primitivism, Fauvism, Germany, and Bolshevism onto the Jews. The situation in the 1920's gave Mauclair ample opportunity to do precisely that.

As if crouching in preparation for an attack, Mauclair kept a low profile in the early and mid-1920's, writing charming travelogues on Assisi, Venice, and Mont Saint Michel; short monographs on old masters; and another account of recent artistic developments in *Les Etats de la peinture française de 1850 à 1920* (1921), which, while ever fervent in tone, added little to his earlier bitter rhetoric.[18] It was in 1928, aged fifty-six, three years after having received another of France's prestigious awards, the Grand Prix de l'Académie Française, that Mauclair engineered a spectacular comeback to the forefront of the art critical scene, finally earning himself a major public reputation, albeit not so much as a distinguished (if, in the great schemes of things, somewhat unmemorable) *homme de lettres*, but as one of France's leading xenophobes. He did so on three fronts: as a columnist for *Le Figaro*, as a major contributor to the weekly *L'Ami du peuple*, and as a contributor to *La Revue Universelle* (a weekly founded in 1920 by Jacques Bainville and Henri Massis, it basically functioned as a satellite of L'Action Française, featuring the likes of Maurras, Daudet, Robert Brasillach, and excerpts from Barrès). Almost immediately elevated—for reasons that should become clear—from the more mundane and ephemeral status of the daily or weekly column to the "high" and more lasting format of the book, Mauclair's miscellaneous articles were gathered and anthologized by the publishing house La Nouvelle Revue Critique in two volumes: *La Farce de l'art vivant: une campagne picturale 1928–29* and *Les Métèques contre l'art français*, in 1929 and 1930. The first volume reached up to nine reprints in its first year of publication.

Dedicated to "les jeunes peintres français," the first book begins and ends with two disclaimers by Mauclair. First, "this is not a pamphlet, but an impartial, objective exposé written by a man with thirty-eight years as an art historian and critic behind him, and someone who had always defended 'l'art indépendant' from the academicism of the old school;" and second, "precisely because I am a Catholic, I am not an anti-Semite. I have Jewish friends whom I faithfully love." In between these two statements are a series of chapters one more vilifying than the next, ranging from Cézanne's "Negrophilia," Matisse's "odalisques de hammam faubourien," to comparisons between Surrealist art and that of the insane. But Mauclair reserved his most violent attacks for the "unintelligible language" of the painters of the so-called Ecole de Paris, "made up of Bulgarians, Tartars, Valakians, Slovenians, Finns, and Pollacks, for whom the name 'Giotto' is pronounced 'ghetto,' and for 'les mercantis du temple': the Israelite dealers of France and the Jews of Mittel Europa." If the language of the Ecole de Paris was supposedly "unintelligible" to Mauclair, his own, on the other hand, was clear to all. It was the language of cultural pathology: "the whole of European painting is contaminated by a sort of eczema, plague, scabies, or erysipelas, you may pick and choose."

Exhuming the word *métèque*—a vicious term for aliens coined by Maurras at the time of the Dreyfus Affair[19]—Mauclair facetiously dedicated volume two "to Rosenschwein and Lévy-Tripp, to Montparnasse filth of Paris, and to the pseudo-art critics whose businesses I used to run, and whose insults have earned me so much sympathy from my readers." Obsessively reiterating many of the same arguments that consumed him in the first volume, Mauclair lashed out at the "cancer" of Montparnasse, "a nice bourgeois neighborhood until the teens, when, invaded by hordes of savages unfurling from the metro to gather in front of the smallest rat-hole turned into a studio [it became] the gathering place of a crowd eighty percent Semites and every one of them a loser." In a somber harbinger of what had become a fact by the late 1930's, Mauclair went on to urge the police to raid the place and to check the papers of its dwellers.[20]

His course of action was partly prompted, Mauclair tells his reader, by a little book that lifted the mask and almost inadvertently revealed the reality of things to come. The book was *Picasso et la tradition française* (1928) by Wilhelm Uhde who with Daniel-Henry Kahnweiler had been Picasso and Braque's chief Paris dealer before the war. Uhde claimed that the painting of distinct races, *terroirs* (turfs), and motherlands had had its day, and he welcomed the emergence of a truly international European painting. In this respect, he considered the presence of Jews a mixed blessing. Although he opposed Jewish dominance in cultural affairs, Uhde nonetheless considered them an indispensable element in binding the separate nations of

Europe together and in providing some degree of transcultural homogeneity. Coming from a German, these views were doubly suspicious. Seen by Mauclair through the paranoid lens of Massis's *Défense de l'occident*, Uhde's philo-Semitism was perceived as yet another Spenglerian attempt to destroy French culture via Germany's own barbaric orientalism.[21]

On the face of it, Mauclair's views were—once again—hardly original. Rather, they rehearsed a series of allegations that had already been raised on "the Jewish question" in art during the supposedly halcyon decade known as the Golden Twenties. Such allegations were in large part prompted by a significant change in immigration patterns in the 1920's.[22] While the immigration of artists to France in the nineteenth century could still be considered an essentially cultural phenomenon, by the first decade of the twentieth century it had increasingly become a political one. Most of the artists who had come to Paris in the nineteenth century had done so by choice, returning to their country of origin after a few years of study.[23] In contrast, those who arrived during the 1910's were part of a larger flood of refugees from Eastern Europe, who came to France fleeing the pogroms in Russia, Slovakia, and Poland. And as refugees, they came to stay. The flow increased in the 1920's when France began to accept ever more immigrants in order to meet its need for manpower after the population loss of the First World War.[24] For the most part, Eastern European Jews remained in the poorer working-class eastern and central parts of the French capital. As they emigrated en masse to Paris, the 4th, the 11th, and the 13th arrondissements came to be seen as Jewish ghettos, thus reproducing in microcosm Massis's paranoid map of Europe right there in Paris.[25] While settling in Paris was the logical thing for an artist to do, the clustering of Eastern European artists in Montparnasse (in the 14th) turned the neighborhood into an easy target for xenophobic attacks.[26]

For if immigration in general was welcomed by the French, even in the eventuality of a permanent stay, as long as it helped the nation's rapid postwar recovery, its reception in the art world was almost from the start far different. It has long been assumed that the spectacular ascendancy of Jewish artists from Eastern Europe like Marc Chagall, Moïse Kisling, Chana Orloff, Jules Pascin, Chaim Soutine, Ossip Zadkine, and many others attested to the openness of French culture. A closer look at the texts accompanying the reception of these artists in the conservative postwar political and cultural climate known as the *rappel à l'ordre* will reveal, however, a far more disturbing picture.

In 1925, *Le Mercure de France* invited a critic, a scholar, and a dealer—respectively Friz Vanderpyl, Pierre Jaccard, and Adolphe Basler—to answer the question "Is there such a thing as Jewish art?"[27] In the previous three years, a number of precautionary measures intended to distinguish

French art from that merely made in France had already been taken. Starting with the Jew in the text, terminology had been readjusted: the Ecole de Paris, which had been used rather loosely in reference to all modern art produced in Paris in the immediate postwar years, was recast as the polar opposite of the Ecole Française. Accordingly, it was applied solely to foreign—and mostly Jewish artists—working in Paris. Other, more concrete, measures were taken by curators in order to separate things French from things foreign. In 1922 an annex of the Musée du Luxembourg was established in the Musée du Jeu de Paume in the Tuileries Gardens to show foreign art exclusively. The following year the painter Paul Signac, then President of the Salon des Indépendants, decided to exhibit works according to nationalities. This resolve was the result of years of complaints by the most prominent critics in the columns of popular reviews such as *L'Amour de l'art*, *Le Carnet de la semaine*, and *L'Art Vivant*, every time they reviewed the salons. These had become, they argued, swamped and debased by a torrent of foreigners with a noxious and weakening influence on indigenous artists.[28]

Most disturbing within this xenophobic climate was its increasing accommodation by Jewish critics. As Mauclair intimated in his *Trois crises de l'art actuel* of 1906 and was able to confirm in *La Crise de l'art moderne* in 1944, they had indeed come to play a leading role in art criticism by the 1920's. Ranking among the most influential voices in so-called "middle-of-the-road" art in France until they were forced to keep a low profile during the mid- to late 1930's and were "outed" as Jews by the likes of Mauclair during Vichy, were Louis Vauxcelles and Waldemar George—born respectively Louis Meyer and Georges Jarocinsky and thus writing under pen names—and Adolphe Basler.

Much has been said about what Sander Gilman has defined in his book *Jewish Self-Hatred: Anti-Semitism and the Hidden Language of the Jews* as the double-bind of the assimilated or assimilating Jew. On the one hand, the Jew internalizes a self-image generated by the so-called reference group and abides by the rules that define that group and allow the Jew to share its power. But on the other, the Jew is unable to escape the conservative curse that relentlessly whispers in the ear: "the more you are like me, the more I know the true value of my power which you wish to share, and the more I am aware that you are but a shoddy counterfeit, an outsider."[29] True enough, the writings of Vauxcelles, George, and Basler demonstrate the shocking degree to which they were prone to introject ambient anti-Semitism into their own criticism. What they mostly indicate, however, is how great the pressure had become—in supposedly propitious 1920's France—to assimilate into Gentile, normative, French culture. The fact that each successive wave of immigration—first the Sephardic Jews, then the Ashkenazi Jews moving from Alsace to Paris, then the Eastern European Jews, and finally, during the 1930's, the German Jews—tended to submerge the preceding wave, meant that as the interwar years wore on there were more foreign Jews living in France than indigenous Jews. This situation only exacerbated the sense of insecurity, and thus of hostility, between each of the groups. And indeed we find in comparing the writings of Vauxcelles, George, and Basler, that each man was more mindful than ever of the old saying that there is more than one category of Jew in France—from the bottom up—*les youpins, les juifs, les israélites, et les barons.*

Born in Paris in 1870 in what seems to have been an upper-middle-class family—and thus an *israélite*—and having attended a respectable *lycée* before studying literature at the Sorbonne and history of art at the Ecole du Louvre, Louis Meyer (alias Vauxcelles) was of the same generation as Mauclair. Writing at the turn of the century alongside him in the magazine *Gil Blas*, Vauxcelles gained early (and most lasting) critical acclaim from his baptism by fire of both the Fauves and the Cubists in 1905 and 1908. Yet it is as founder and chief editor of *L'Amour de l'art* from 1920 to 1924, while holding onto his art columns for countless smaller art magazines, that Vauxcelles became an authoritative if rarely inspirational voice in the art world. In 1922, he did not hesitate to launch into the "querelle des Indépendants" stirred by the decision to separate native from foreign artists at the annual Spring salon, with an article entitled "Alas! Where are the xenophobes?"[30] In another of his columns we find him writing:

> It seems that the decision has caused the central European high society of Montparnasse to rise in indignation. And I hear that the [Café de la] Rotonde, where all the dialects on earth are spoken, sometimes even French, will be the site of a large demonstration followed by a meeting of protest against the nationalist committee of the Independents.
>
> It isn't a question of chauvinist politics, of expulsion or other pogroms. (A pogrom decreed by me would be quite a piquant idea.)—No! Let's not turn into politico-financial matters what is a simple matter of hygiene, of sanitation, which aims at the proper behavior in Paris of twenty-five or so *moldo-valaques*. And if I am accused of being reactionary, too bad . . .[31]

For all of the critic's cunning reference to his own Jewishness in the most circuitous manner—"a pogrom decreed by me would be quite a piquant idea"—such comments reveal the extent to which the assumed Frenchness of an *israélite* like himself could no longer be taken for granted, even by the early 1920's. With Maurice Barrès singling out the Jew as the ultimate *déraciné* in one of his best-known books, *Scènes et doctrines du nationalisme* (first published in 1905 and reedited in 1925), and in line with the strong anti-metropolitan sentiments of the *rappel à l'ordre*, it was the issue of rootedness in the French soil that became the yardstick of artistic assimilation.[32] It is thus in texts devoted to the *terriens* (native artists) of the Ecole Française— like André Derain, Maurice de Vlaminck, André Dunoyer de Segonzac, and Maurice Utrillo—that one finds the most clamorous precedent for Mauclair's fixation on "Montparno" as the breeding ground for all the ills of France. Vauxcelles, writing under double cover of yet another pseudonym—Pinturicchio—in *Le Carnet de la semaine*, had this to say in reviewing a monograph on Dunoyer de Segonzac written by one of the painter's most devoted champions, another French-born Jewish critic (also blacklisted by Mauclair in 1944) named Claude Roger-Marx:

> A barbarian horde has rushed like a plague, like a cloud of locusts, upon Montparnasse, descending from the cafés of the fourteenth arrondissement onto [the art galleries of] rue de la Boétie, uttering raucous Germano-Slavic screams of war. . . . Their culture is so recent! Are they from our village? no. When they speak about Poussin, do they know the master? Have they ever really looked at a Corot? Have they ever read a poem by La Fontaine? These are people from "somewhere else" who ignore and, in the bottom of their hearts, look down on what Renoir has called the gentleness of the French School, that is, the virtue of tact, the nuanced quality of our race. . . . This painter shows the misled the good old French route to follow. The peril has been exorcised and safe is the honor of the French School.[33]

The need to draw the line between himself and the Jewish "other" was even more pressing for the critic Waldemar George. Born in 1893 in Lodz, Poland, the son of a banker, he had moved to Paris in 1911.[34] After becoming a French citizen and serving in the French army during the war, George studied French literature at the Sorbonne while beginning a career as an art critic. Pro-Cubist, author of essays on Fernand Léger, he yet replaced Vauxcelles as chief editor of *L'Amour de l'art* from 1924 to 1927, and, not too surprisingly in view of his life story, in 1924 made a plea for assimilation vis-a-vis the "querelle": France had always been able to reabsorb outside influences, to impose its discipline, its sense of order, and its laws of harmony on the foreign artists living on its soil.[35]

Known to be a supporter of the Ecole de Paris, George was commissioned in 1928 to write the second booklet for the series "Les Artistes Juifs," published by Le Triangle.[36] However, in his attempt to define the uniqueness of Soutine's art George did not argue for assimilation, but veered rather between praise and ethnic slander, the sublime and the abject. This French-educated urbane Pole, who had emigrated to Paris only one year before Soutine, a poor Lithuanian Jew, began his book by describing Soutine's tiny *shtetl* of Smilovitchi:

the sunken roads, the leprous houses holding onto one another like gangs of cripples, the lame shacks covered with formless [*informe*] graffiti. . . . Here the Slavic East rubs shoulders with the Jewish East which it cannot absorb. Nothing can hold it, the chosen people conserve their Levites, their hooked noses, their beards, their archaic costumes, their language.[37]

In addressing the common anti-Semitic argument that there cannot be a Jewish genius, George remained utterly non-committal:

> Indeed one cannot refute this argument, and it may very well be defendable. Yet the fact remains that Jews play an active role in the art of the twentieth century. Does this role reflect the adaptation of intellectuals from semitic extraction to European culture? Or does one detect, on the contrary, the *enjuivement* (Jewing) of contemporary Europe? Here lies the core of this most anguishing problem. (14–15)

Turning then to the actual paintings he asked:

> What is the meaning of this art, whose origin is undefinable, which knows no law, no *fatherland*, and no directive principles, and is linked to no tradition? An exiled or a *barbarian's* art? I challenge anybody to trace the filiation of Soutine's art. . . . The curse that weighs on his oeuvre extends to his whole race. . . . A muted wind of revolt blows through his dramatic oeuvre. (Isn't the wandering Jew the archetype of the eternal rebel?) . . . What can we say of this *déraciné*? . . . Soutine owes nothing to France, except his thirst for internal balance, which, thank god, he will never reach. (15, 17, 18, 19, my italics)

For George, as for his adopted French countrymen, Soutine's depictions of the sinuous streets of the Provençal villages of Céret and Cagnes, lined with diagonally slanted houses emerging from the ground like withered oak trees, stood as the antithesis to things French. What Soutine's eradication of forms dramatically exposed was the painful psychological dilemma of rootedness versus uprootedness: the very metaphor of the condition of the immigrant Jew in French culture. Reiterating other critics' comments on Soutine's attraction to blood, vermin, and gangrene in his portraits and still lives, George praised them as the sign of spirituality. Adding yet another somatic metaphor, he described this art as one of "expectoration." Soutine is, ultimately, not a wandering Jew, he concludes, but a wandering monk of the Middle Ages whose art announced the apocalypse: "Will people be able to hear one day the funereal calls for help sent by Soutine from his promontory?" (92–3).

Clearly enough, the question raised by this text is how much can one extemporize on thick impasto and oily canvases without having them stand as a synecdoche for the repellent Jewish body? How do you celebrate an artist as the ultimate *artiste maudit* (mad genius)—a well-known trope in art and literary criticism, tributary to romanticism and *fin-de-siècle* anti-materialism—without falling into a rhetoric all too easily appropriated by anti-Semitism? How far can an *exercice de style*—the pleasure of an expressionistic text about a Jew—go, before collapsing into the stereotype?

Less than a year later, while working on a monograph on the sculptor Jacques Lipchitz to be published in Yiddish by Le Triangle, George had established a reputation as one of the staunchest defenders of French art in his new magazine *Formes*. At the same time as accusing Mauclair, in a 1930 article entitled "Le Matamore Mauclair contre l'art français,"[38] of being a bully in calling Picasso, Braque, Léger, Ozenfant, and Lhote "young *métèques*," he held views on French art that, although certainly less conservative, were hardly less exclusionary and xenophobic. In a two-part article entitled "Ecole Française or Ecole de Paris" published in *Formes* in 1931, George went so far as to call for the virtual demise of the Ecole de Paris:

> The School of Paris is a neologism, a new accession. This term, which dominates the world market, is a conscious example of premeditated conspiracy against the notion of a School of France. It not only takes into consideration foreign contributions; it ratifies them and grants them a leading position. It is a rather subtle, hypocritical sign of the spirit of Francophobia. It allows any artist to pretend he is French. . . . It has no legitimacy. It refers to French tradition but it in fact annihilates it. . . . Shouldn't France repudiate the works that weaken her genius? . . . The School of Paris is a house of cards built in Montparnasse. . . . Its ideology is oriented against that of the French School. . . . The moment has come for France to turn in upon herself and to find in her own soil the seeds of her salvation.[39]

As with George, assimilation was initially the solution for the dealer and critic Adophe Basler when asked in 1925 to reply to the series of articles on the "Jewish question" for the *Mercure de France*.[40] The Jews, he explained, having overcome life in the ghettos, were now able to reflect the artistic culture of the country in which they lived, as opposed to continuing to express their ethnic heritage. The more advanced a civilization, the more the Jew is absorbed by it. By means of this argument, Basler managed to rescue the art of the Italian Amedeo Modigliani, the Polish-born Moïse Kisling, and lesser-known Eastern European painters like Simon Mondzain and Adolphe Féder from the onus of their Jewish ethnicity, emphasizing instead their manifest debt to French painting. Finding this more difficult to argue in the case of Chagall, whose work dealt incessantly with Jewish subjects, Basler dismissed him as

> this folkloristic image maker from Vitebsk, who, in his fantastic interpretations of Russian and Judeo-Russian life, unites the wilderness of the *moujik* [Russian

peasant] and the madness of the young Jew who has damaged his brains by reading too much Talmud.[41]

The artists whom Basler chose to attack for obdurate otherness, for their refusal to adhere to the artistic mainstream, were Picasso and his Cubist followers, among them Lipchitz, Zadkine, and Orloff. Indeed, it was Picasso, Basler insisted—propelling the rumor of a Jewish Picasso—who was the authentic incarnation of the "pan-Semitic spirit," the true heir of the Arab ornamentalists and the Spanish Talmudists. In his attack on Picasso, Basler consciously harkened back to a wartime rhetoric that—stressing the heavy involvement of Jews, be they Germans like Kahnweiler and the Berliner Alfred Flechteim or Americans of German descent like Leo and Gertrude Stein—had de facto associated Cubism with "foreign," that is, pro-German and therefore anti-French, sentiment.[42] The very fact that Basler felt the need to revive these demons tells us something about his own low sense of self-esteem in 1920's France as an Austrian Jew.

In 1929, Basler inserted the article verbatim in his book *Le Cafard après la fête, ou, L'esthétisme d'aujourd'hui* (roughly translated, "the hangover after the orgy"), which reads—and here lies the scandal—as a text virtually identical to Mauclair's contemporaneous *La Farce de l'art vivant* and *Les Métèques contre l'art français*. There Basler assailed the "Babel Montparnassienne," invaded yet again by hordes of *"métèques"* affected by "picturomania." In what was becoming a common trope, he collapsed the Jew, the American, and the homosexual, crying out: "what the hell does it matter to the ex-draper of the *sentier* [the French term for the Jewish manufacturing district in the 3rd arrondissement] or the dentist from Odessa? They ape the sodomite gentleman who has found in painting the kick for his perversions." Backtracking for a moment and insinuating himself into the text, he wrote with supreme condescension: "Okay for the little Russian painters. These brothers have, moreover, all my sympathy. I like Soutine, for all of his villainous contortions" (pp. 28–9).

Most interesting to our concern is Basler's inclusion of Waldemar George among those "scribblers who call themselves critics." Writing in *Le Cafard* after the publication of the latter's book on Soutine but before George's nationalist about-face in *Formes*, Basler set out to uncover the "hidden language" of that Jew. It was George who stood as the ultimate

> supporter of a universal ur-style: a boneless and disembodied painting [Cubism] that will free art of all nationalisms, suppress all passports, efface all frontiers. (p. 13)
>
> . . .
>
> Listen to the furor that agitates this great prophet when he writes: My total adhesion to the thesis of salvation from the Orient. Ratifying Spengler's theo-

ries on the decadence of the West, I devote myself to the ruining and corruption of the West! (pp. 39–40)

Taking a route all too reminiscent now of Nazi propaganda for its focus on German and Austrian Jews—his Mittel European countrymen—Basler went on to attack in a single breath a young German critic named Wilhelm Hausenstein, Freudian psychoanalysis, and the French ethnographer Lucien Lévy-Bruhl for their Spenglerian infatuation with the "primitive," the "morbid," the "non-civilized," all of which had reached a climax in Dada and Surrealism.[43] It is ironic that Basler, like his nemesis, Waldemar George, continued all the while to write on Jewish artists: a monograph on Modigliani in 1931, and another for the series "Les Artistes Juifs" in 1932 on the Ukrainian sculptor Léon Indenbaum.[44].

In view of this critical context, what made Mauclair's own rhetoric remarkable was not so much what was said but where it was printed and to whom it was addressed. The prose of Vauxcelles, George, and Basler remained confined within the sphere of culture: books published by small presses, literary journals, and art magazines. Written in the pages of *Le Figaro* and *L'Ami du peuple*, it was Mauclair's text that achieved legitimacy. For it was Mauclair who was able to write among those men (no woman in sight) whom Sander Gilman has called the "reference group," in papers to which a Basler, a George, and even an *israélite* like Vauxcelles—however "hidden" their art critical language—would probably have had no access. And it was he who broke into the "real" world via the popular press.

A few remarks are necessary about the state of this press. *Le Figaro* had always had a distinctively chauvinistic bias, stating the superiority of French culture in almost every field. Yet its backing of Mauclair's diatribes would have been inconceivable in this internationally most respected of French dailies were it not for the fact that its owner during those years was the perfumer François Coty. A billionaire since 1915 when he had conquered America with his Coty perfume, and a man who nurtured political ambitions on the extreme Right, Coty was also a major financial supporter of Maurras's Action Française and of Georges Vallois's Le Faisceau, one of the constellation of tiny fascistic leagues that arose in France during the 1920's.[45] It should be said, however, that Mauclair's years at *Le Figaro* coincided with an all-time trough in the paper's history.[46] Yet lest one may be misled by the reputation of *Le Figaro* to this day, Mauclair's nearly identical column in the now almost forgotten *L'Ami du peuple* (also owned and launched by Coty in 1928) should set the record straight. Under the motto "La France aux français," the weekly functioned as a veritable anthology of xenophobia.[47] More articles were devoted to *les métèques* than in any other right-wing French magazine, including *L'Action française*: the *métèque* as a social and political menace (corruption, scandals, and so on); an economic burden and a source of unemployment, after 1931, and the ravages of the Depression; and finally—thanks to Mauclair's contribution—the *métèque* as cultural (that is, moral) menace. And if *Le Figaro* went through hard times during those years, *L'Ami du peuple* stands as one of the success stories in the French press between the wars. Sold at the modest price of 10 centimes in Paris and 15 centimes in the provinces, the paper was no longer aimed at the urban, sophisticated, and upper-class readership of *Le Figaro*, but at the lower middle class—*le peuple*, as its title indicates—and more pointedly at the inhabitants of *la France profonde* (the countryside), many of whom had never read a newspaper before. Thus if *Le Figaro's* circulation was down to 50,000 in 1928, the success of Coty's other venture was immediate: 800,000 copies in 1928, going up to a million in 1930. What such numbers meant, and as the paper's editorial proudly claimed, was that the friendly prose of *L'Ami du peuple* was read by no less than three million people in a nation which counted about forty million souls in 1930.

Although France remained a land of refuge, the situation of foreigners, and of Jews in particular, deteriorated steadily during the 1930's. As a new wave of immigration of German Jews hit France after Hitler's takeover, followed by Austrian and Italian Jews toward the end of the decade—swelling the alien Jewish population in France from 200,000 to 300,000 between 1930 and 1939—it was agreed by mid-decade, even among political moderates, that there was indeed a "Jewish problem" in France.[48] After having squarely stated his support for Hitler's decision to kick out "false artists" from Germany, and lamenting that "this invasion of Semitic and Marxist runaways" should end up in France, Mauclair gradually withdrew from art criticism.[49] In 1935 he paid a fictional and nostalgic visit to his life-long favorite poet in *Mallarmé chez lui*, finding solace from the crassness of *realpolitik* in Symbolism's most evanescent and luminous poetry. He also went on traveling, projecting his romantic longings for a bygone world into somewhat belated nineteenth-century type orientalist descriptions of France's colonial jewels in North Africa, in *Rabat et Salé* in 1934 and *Tunis et Kerouan* in 1937.[50]

Mauclair could afford to do so, for, by the mid-1930's, the damage was done. After 1933 the number of anti-Semitic publications rose exponentially, including a plethora of weeklies like *Candide*, *Gringoire* (which sold 650,000 copies in 1936), and *Je suis partout*.[51] Exhibitions, books, or articles of any sort on individual Jewish artists were not so much criticized as marginalized, and soon eliminated altogether.[52] Although it had announced future publications on the jacket of its books, the series "Les Artistes Juifs" ceased publication in 1932. When an article did make its way into print after 1935—for instance, on Chagall—it no longer appeared in mainstream publications but almost exclusively in Jewish magazines such as *Shalom* and *Cahiers juifs*, or in genuinely avant-garde periodicals with a liberal, left-wing stance, such as Christian Zervos's *Cahiers d'art*. A reprieve was created during the Popular Front's government under Léon Blum (1936–8), but it proved brief.[53] By 1938, with the implementation of such measures against Jews as quotas, civil restrictions, and the requirement to present papers of identification upon demand, the debate over the status of Jews had shifted to the high echelons of the French administration.

Mauclair's last foray into journalism appeared in the pages of *Cahier jaune*, a racist tract published monthly from 1941 to 1943 by the Institut d'Etudes de la Question Juive, turned into *Le Grand Magazine illustré de la race: Revivre* in 1943–4. Our *homme de lettres* was, it turns out, a lucky man, spared the sudden twists and reversals of history. *La Crise de l'art moderne*, his swan song and vile saga of the "other" that had been so much part of his own career as a critic, came out just a few months before his death, the collapse of the Vichy regime, and the Fourth Republic's *épuration* of many collaborators like himself.

9

Vampires, Viruses, and Lucien Rebatet: Anti-Semitic Art Criticism During Vichy

MICHÈLE C. CONE

There looms, within abjection, one of those violent, dark revolts of being, directed against a threat that seems to emanate from an exorbitant outside or inside, ejected beyond the scope of the possible, the tolerable, the thinkable.

JULIA KRISTEVA, *Powers of Horror*

What might be this thunderbolt, "exorbitant . . . ejected beyond the scope of the possible, the tolerable, the thinkable?" Who is this enormous presence that, Kristeva says, "beseeches, worries, and fascinates desire, which, nevertheless, does not let itself be seduced?" What sprinting demon, "like an inescapable boomerang, a vortex of summons and repulsion places the one haunted by it literally beside himself?"[1] This fantasy creature (it, she, he?), without contours, spreading abjection, terror and envy, lust and disgust, is . . . the Jew in the head of the French anti-Semite (as well as the Jew "inside" the anti-Semite): "Anti-Semitism, for which there thus exists an object as phantasmatic and ambivalent as the Jew is the sociological thrill, flush with history, that believers and nonbelievers alike seek in order to experience abjection."[2]

At no time in recent history did the propensity to paint the Jew in the colors of abjection reach a greater level of sophistication than during the Nazi era. Germans aroused by their Führer, but also Nazi sympathizers in countries occupied by Germany, partook of that activity. In France during the Occupation years, the Institut d'Etudes des Questions Juives (Institute for the Study of Jewish Questions, IEQJ) was the main creator and distributor of thoroughly repugnant and destructive images of Jewish identity. Its art section, according to document CXCIII–162 from the Centre de Documentation Juive Contemporaine (CDJC) in Paris, was handed over to the notorious anti-Semite Lucien Rebatet, who is also listed in the press service (CDJC document XCVI–80).

The influence of the IEQJ's anti-Jewish propaganda exerted itself directly through anti-Semitic pamphlets such as *Journal*, *Bulletin*, and *Cahier jaune*; through the travesty of scientific exhibitions it organized, in particular that called "Le Juif et la France," and through other forms of brainwashing under the guise of learned lectures and technical conferences. And it exerted itself indirectly through its infiltration of the media.[3] Sold on the Nazi point of view, the weekly *Je suis partout* did not need infiltration. Filling the art columns of that nasty sheet, under his own name or the pseudonym of "l'Encadreur," was the man put in charge of artistic matters at the IEQJ, Lucien Rebatet (1903–73).

On the surface, the content of Rebatet's art columns demonstrated a taste for harmony and refinement that was hardly uncommon in Paris then (and probably remains so to this day). "One realizes that almost all these French artists, even the least clever ones, are harmonists by instinct," he wrote after visiting the Salon des Tuileries in 1941. "They are the only race in the world who, after the medieval miniaturists, know how to juxtapose the most vivid blue and green by marrying them, who can vary ad infinitum and continually renew this play on values, from the most discreet and evanescent grays and pinks to the most sumptuous orgies of chrome and vermilion."[4]

To his readers, Rebatet presented himself as a formalist art critic. Reviewing Lionello Venturi's book *Peintres modernes*, he wrote in 1942: "M. Lionello Venturi has made great strides to disengage himself from clichés [*les poncifs*], and from the useless verbiage of contemporary criticism. He has returned to honest formal [*plastique*] analysis as it was practised during the last century, when Eugène Fromentin offered a model of it that is still celebrated . . . In the end it [plastic analysis] is indispensable for providing reference points [*repères*], comparisons, and for discovering the pictorial substance that lies truly within an *oeuvre*. It is far more difficult than a logical improvisation on the picturesque . . . For it demands that one know how to read modeling, values, planes, and volumes, the composition of a painting, of a drawing, or of a print."[5]

How then did Rebatet reconcile artistic refinement with vulgar outbursts against the Jewish "virus?" How did he combine his role of anti-Semitic propagandist with that of a formalist critic of modern art? In order to make sense of the connection, I shall start by unveiling the critical image around which anti-Semitic propaganda at the IEQJ operated. As its major undertaking "Le Juif et la France" reveals, it was the image and myth of the vampire that became a central motif of anti-Semitic messages during the Occupation period.

Why did anti-Semites appropriate the elusive image of the vampire for their propaganda? What were the deep human fears and desires on which the vampire myth played in France for the generation of Lucien Rebatet? These are the issues I shall first address. Only then will I be able to show that Rebatet's voice on modernity was not inconsistent with his role as a mouthpiece for anti-Semitic propaganda. The image of the male Jew as living corpse—vampire—runs subliminally through Rebatet's prose, stirring fear of the virus he carries, and fear of the death of art that his virus causes. Rebatet's notion of the "Jewish virus," of "aryanization" as a form of artistic purification, will be discussed. In lieu of a conclusion, the essay will ask whether the use of the vampire in anti-Semitic propaganda, besides unveiling symptoms of psychopathic traits, was not also a foil for the desire of anti-Semites for a Fascist victory.

Le Juif et la France: The Demonizing of the Jew

The unique function of the IEQJ was the fight against Jews. An anti-Jewish brigade, and a special section in charge of arrests, searches, seizures, and surveillance (in liaison with the Gestapo) made up one branch of its organization. The other branch was divided into "services," among them the Service de la Propagande. That service or section "was in charge of propaganda in all domains, through the press, the radio, the cinema, the theatre, posters, publications, and organization of courses and conferences; it kept an eye on the tendencies of the press, of the cinema, of the radio, and of the theatre (supporting or combating them), on public opinion, and on the effects of anti-German and anti-collaborationist propaganda, and it took charge of counterpropaganda measures, including productions, or suggestions for the German services."[6]

The most visible propagandist undertaking of the IEQJ was the exhibition "Le Juif et la France," inaugurated at the Palais Berlitz in Paris in September 1941. It is that vulgar compendium of misinformation presented as oversized panels with diagrams, photos, texts, caricatures, and as gigantic pieces of sculpture, that demonstrates in sufficient detail the shameless motivations of anti-Semites at that particular moment of French history—to crush the Jews of France.

One way to accomplish this goal was to raise collective consciousness on the "excessive" presence of Jews in the social and cultural national body, by teaching the public how to recognize Jews from non-Jews. C. Laville, who headed the "Service de Recherches Scientifiques" at the IEQJ thus explained the meaning of the diagrams at the exhibition: "As each of us can learn from looking at the illustrated panels exhibited at the Palais Berlitz, Jews result from a triple conjunction between whites, mongols (yellow) and negroes, so that their traits owe something to each of the three great primordial races . . . frequently in opposition to one another." Admittedly, the author went on, Aryans are also of mixed origin. In Jews, however, the originating traits have not become merged: "One Jew is negroid through his eyes and lips, mongol through his hair and nose, while another Jew is mongol through his slanted eyes and heavy lips, negroid through his kinky hair."[7]

One might deduce from this analysis that the Jewish physique is a collage rather than a synthesis of human typologies, and that although existing in various disguises, and hence "ambiguous," the Jewish physique always has some "African" feature—negroid eyes and lips, kinky hair. One might go further and propose that this view of the Jewish physique is not without a connection to early Cubist representations, which were equally abhorred. In the giant three-dimensional head of a generic Jew featured in the exhibition, all the "Jewish" features are seamlessly joined, suggesting an Expressionist caricature rather than the disjointed planes of Cubist figurative sculpture.

On the one hand, the composite typology of the Jew revealed by "Le Juif et la France" connoted a physical monstrosity when compared to Aryan types, but, on the other, the variety of Jewish types was such that imaginary Jews could be seen lurking everywhere, vampire-like, thereby stirring paranoia in the collective psyche. In *Bagatelles pour un massacre* (1937), Louis-Ferdinand Céline, the famous anti-Semite, had put it this way: "The Jews, you know, they're all camouflaged, disguised, chameleon-like, they change names like they cross frontiers, now they pass themselves off for Bretons, Auvergnats, Corsicans, now for Turandots, Durandards, Cassoulets . . . anything at all . . . that throws people off, that sounds deceptive."[8]

The goal of assimilation was widely shared by Jews in France, even after the Dreyfus Affair: "their political theory and their political strategy was that of assimilation. . . . the Dreyfus affair proved to be not a turning-point in the history of the Jews in France, but rather a momentous landmark in their steady march toward the goal of assimilation."[9] Even though during the 1930's, refugee Jews from central Europe and Nazi Germany, more conspicuous than the Jews of France, appeared to arrive in hordes, the total number of Jews living in France in 1939, 300,000, remained less than 1 percent of the French population.

Not only did the exhibition "Le Juif et la France" seek to arouse fear of the "excessive" number of Jews in France but it also raised a fear of their nefarious influence: the guide to the show, a brochure with a long article entitled "Pourquoi une exposition juive?" by J. Marquès Rivière, who liaised between the IEQJ and the Occupation authorities, sought to demonstrate in words what the show did via captioned photographs, drawings, and sculpture, namely that something particularly abject in the Jewish character had undermined society and culture from the beginnings of history to the present. The sayings of famous thinkers from the past were called to testify:

Renan: "The semitic race is recognizable almost solely through its negative traits: it has neither mythology, nor epos [*épopée*], nor science, nor philosophy, nor fiction, nor plastic arts, nor civil life . . ."

Luther: "They are just so many venomous, perverse, cruel, satanic beasts which from 1400 on . . . have been and continue to be the ruin of governments."

Voltaire: "You will merely find in Jews an ignorant, lazy, barbarous people who for a long time have combined the most undignified stinginess with the most profound hatred for all the people who tolerate them and enrich them."

The author added his own list of anti-Jewish traits. He called Jews greedy and conspiratorial: "The Jews control secret societies, which form provisional governments and shift to the benefit of Jews [*la juiverie*] all the political and social upsets [*bouleversements*]"; domineering and destructive: "The Jews were masters of French democracy: She could only die from it;" thriving on the work of others: "From their earliest history, the Jews present themselves as useless businessmen, living off the sweat and the work of others . . ."[10] In all of these characterizations, the Jew threatens now governments, now society, now individuals' wealth, work, life, and soul, by some sort of demonic conspiratorial power.

La France se libérant des juifs (*France Liberating Itself from the Jews*), the thirty-foot-high sculpture of a tall, attractive, and athletic young female (France) subduing a repulsive, greedy old man (the Jew) with her knees, and pushing another one down with her free hand, found in the rotunda of the exhibition, suggested what must be done. France must crush the Jews so that a new genealogical line of pure Aryan types like the baby in France's upheld arm could start.

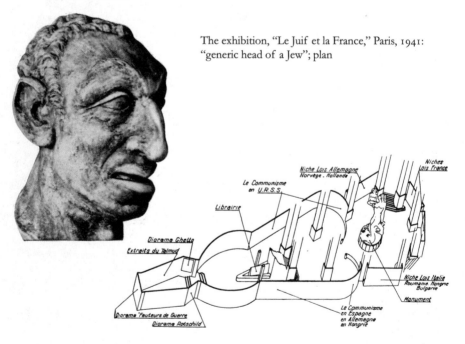

The exhibition, "Le Juif et la France," Paris, 1941: "generic head of a Jew"; plan

The exhibition, "Le Juif et la France,"
Paris, 1941: entrance with poster;
Perron, *France Liberating Itself from the
Jews*

A two-dimensional version of the greedy old man appeared on the cover
of brochures, and on posters advertising the show. It was also the image
that greeted visitors at the entrance of the exhibition. The *Illustration*
reviewer, Robert de Beauplan, described it as "a great allegorical composition representing a kind of vampire with long beard, thick lips, and crooked
nose, whose fingers, like the claws of a bird of prey, clutch the terrestrial
globe."[11]

It does not take a great deal of familiarity with contemporary visual culture to sense that the image being described had as much to do with the
Walt Disney witch (made famous in the 1938 movie *Snow White*, ecstatically

reviewed by Rebatet)[12] as with bloodsucking bats, female ghouls, or the legendary Dracula in Bram Stoker's novel. None of the "vampires" in films that a French critic of those years might have encountered—the actor Conrad Veidt in *The Cabinet of Dr. Caligari*, Max Schreck in *Nosferatu*, the stern old lady in Carl Dreyer's *Vampyr*—wore a wispy beard and a Jewish kaftan.[13] Yet de Beauplan found in "vampire" the image around which the other Jewbaiters had been circling. For as the participation of Jews in the political and cultural life of France increased so did the demonization of the Jew.

The deceptively fascinating male or female vampire of nineteenth-century literature (and twentieth-century film) could feed the myth of a conspiring Jew out to get political power through charm and seduction.[14] Anti-Semites could also use the image of a bloodsucking vampire against Jews whom they accused of living off the wealth and the sweat of others. (In Rebatet's *Les Tribus du cinéma* (1941), Jews are accused of having monopolized that medium to the detriment of French *metteurs en scène*.) In the eyes of anti-Semites, the Jew thus shared with the mythical vampire the status of "an object of hatred and desire, of threat and aggressivity, of envy and abomination."[15] Small wonder that without necessarily being named—the fat capitalist Jew depicted in cartoons by Ralph Soupault wears the elegant top hat and tails of the lethal seducer[16]—the vampire makes an appearance in "Pourquoi une exposition juive?" and other propaganda texts around "Le Juif et la France."

It is curious that "Le Juif et la France" does not seem, from the plan of the show, to have devoted much of its space to a critique of modern art. The section *art juif* is small compared with the bay devoted to the cinema. We do know that the presence of a work by Salvador Dali prompted the General Consul of Spain to send a letter to the IEQJ asking that it be removed since Dali was not a Jew, and that it be replaced by "painters of the same school but of French nationality and Jewish origin."[17] Perhaps the organizers thought that the contrast of style visible in the statue *La France se libérant des juifs* expressed the views of the IEQJ judiciously enough: the Expressionist distortions of the "Jew" denoted *L'art juif* in the process of disappearing; the idealized neoclassical effigy of the goddess France symbolized "art at the end of the vampire age . . ." In any event, the IEQJ had at *Je suis partout* an art connoisseur with a lashing tongue perfect for the task at hand.

Lucien Rebatet on the Jewish Virus

Endowed with a bilious tongue and acerbic verve on the subject of Jews, Rebatet was a minor-league Céline. Like that author of *Voyage au bout de la nuit* (1932), *Bagatelles pour un massacre*, *L'Ecole des cadavres* (1938), and other famous works, Rebatet, using organic metaphors and slang, went out of his way to make Jews responsible for everything that had gone wrong in France.[18] That Céline of the art world detested Salon art as much as what he called the Jewish virus. In 1941 he announced in his first and most polemical piece, "Entre le juif et le pompier" ("Between the Jew and the Pompier"): "If the teaching at the Ecole des Beaux Arts had not been in such decrepitude . . . surely the Jewish virus could not have gnawed into us with such ease."[19] In this way he sketched for us his imaginary Jew, a virus-carrying vampire whose bite poisons and destroys. Modern art, he felt, had been attacked by such a virus, which had drained it of its vitality, and left it "etiolated," like the victims of active vampires, "pale, languishing, without appetite."[20] To recover its energy, art must be "aryanized."

Rebatet explains in "Entre le juif":

It [modern art] is a tree whose trunk is still vigorous, but whose branches are etiolated. Its disease appears that much more evident for its having born magnificent fruit in the course of the XIXth century, and in the first years of this one . . .

It is necessary to cut off the purulent branches. It is necessary to *aryanize* the fine arts. It is an essential task, that which must precede all others. For it is Jews who through their excessive number [*pullulement*] like parasite insects, threaten the beautiful plant . . .

Jews, painters or sculptors propagating the most pernicious example, Jewish dealers with their hideous speculations, critics praising [*glosant*] with unstoppable enthusiasm the mores and works from this vast ghetto, their presence must be forbidden. And they must be told why they are condemned, and how their influence has been devastating [*funeste*] for us, and that even if some of them have talent, that talent is completely foreign to the spirit of our country, and only serves to contaminate our artists.

The notion that the tree that nurtured the beautiful fruits of European culture might have become sickly (or decadent) was a perception shared by a great many intellectuals prior to the world wars. "What generation since Renan and Taine," asks Zeev Sternhell in *Ni Droite ni gauche*, "did not have the feeling of living the end of an epoch? . . . Who did more than the generation of 1890 to shake up the faith in Progress and in Reason? . . . How can one make the war responsible for an ideological phenomenon to which Bergson and Sorel, Barrès and Le Bon, Michels and Pareto contributed several years before 1914?"[21] However, by discounting natural causes for the allegedly "sad" state of the "tree," and naming instead contamination, intentional poisoning by parasites, Rebatet, like other anti-Semitic Fascists, shifted the grounds of discussions to the guilty other, the Jew.

Furthermore, Rebatet's argument that Jewish artists had "infiltrated" the Paris art world and received more attention than their due, thanks to a well-organized network of partisan critics and dealers, was hardly new either. In

1929, the future Director of Fine Arts under Pétain, the art and architecture historian Louis Hautecoeur, had published a book, *Considérations sur l'art d'aujourd'hui*, in which he had spoken of the dangers of the peaceful invasion of foreign artists and complained about their sense of publicity, "so that this foreign colony plays a role in our midst that their production does not always justify."[22] However, only by building on the subconscious fear of a killer-invader (vampirism) of French art could Rebatet utter his solution—doing to Jews what they allegedly did to others, "bleeding them dry" through exclusion from society as individuals, and as alleged practitioners of a certain form of art.

Rebatet on the Aryanization of Art

Although Rebatet entitled his article "Entre le juif et le pompier," his image of a specifically Jewish art was as evanescent as descriptions of vampires by their viewers. Only the sentence "it is necessary to prune the purulent branches" hints at what it might be. For the image of pruning presupposes the idea of excess and of disequilibrium, while the image of organic decay and death is often associated with the Expressionism of Soutine and his followers. The view that Expressionism "mostly practised by Jews and other foreigners" had been a major trend of French art in the interwar years was shared by eminent art historians of modern art. René Huyghe, Bernard Dorival, and again Hautecoeur had made that point.[23] But only Rebatet had a definitive solution for reversing the trend: spread the word that the influence of Expressionism was "funeste," fatal, a harbinger of the death of art. De-vampirize, aryanize art, he said, and the threat of death would go away, leaving art in the state of timeless purity evoked by Baudelaire's famous lines: "*Là, tout n'est qu'ordre et beauté,*/"*Luxe, calme et volupté.*"

Aryanization in Rebatet's rhetoric did not exclusively imply the abject fantasy of "ethnic cleansing." Aryanization had an artistic counterpart—a purifying thrust. Had Rebatet believed that painting ought to be judged through "discovering the pictorial substance that lies truly within an oeuvre"—to quote his own words in his review of Venturi's *Peintres modernes*, he would have welcomed the search for structural essence in painting and sculpture attempted by the international modernisms of the 1920's. For Rebatet, however, artistic purification did not imply a forward glance but a turn of the clock back to an earlier time, a time prior to the invasion of France by the "Jewish virus." That at least is what emerges from his review of the Salon des Tuileries of 1941.

This exhibition, Rebatet told his viewers, was showing signs in the right direction:

Jews, "métèques" from the orient and from central Europe, have fled at last.

They exhibit in Cannes or Toulouse while waiting to depart for ever. Disencumbered of their presence, the new Salon has now an air of probity and of elegance, I would say of good company, if it were not interpretable in a bourgeois sense, which is contrary to my thoughts.

However, Rebatet lamented, the new Salon was far from realizing the fantasy of a totally aryanized vision. The Jewish virus was far from dead: "In front of ... the expressionism of André Marchand (among others) ... we still find many signs of all the disorders, all the facilities, and all the stupid paradoxes that have brought us so low..." The Expressionist influence was still present, and to his great regret, art had not yet "returned" to what it was before the Jewish virus had struck: "What is still lacking is a return to a denser painting, which knows how to define a shape, while keeping this freshness of sensation of which Corot and the Impressionists gave us the secret."[24]

What was so desirable about this "return" to Corot and the Impressionists? In purely artistic terms, both Corot and the Impressionists had, in his view, purified painting from the stranglehold of the academy without contamination by "foreign" influences. In extra-artistic terms, Corot and the Impressionists stood for a vision of the world that rejected the changes in consciousness that occurred at the end of the nineteenth century; they stood for a time when someone named Dreyfus could never have acceded to the rank of captain in the French army.

Coupled with the construction of a myth based on the demonization of the Jew was the construction of a new one, based on the fantasy of a purely "Aryan" society, and Aryan culture. In order to make the new myth attractive, not only did its creator have to promise eternal life and timeless pleasure, but the old one had to be painted in the most abject terms. By transforming the Jew into the equivalent of a virus-spreading vampire, it became possible to proclaim that the Jew must be killed before he destroyed French culture and society.

To read the art criticism of *Je suis partout* is to realize that Rebatet had far more in common with the vampire of the myth, than did the Jews in France whom he was accusing of killing French culture. For, if Jews from central Europe, chased by the threat of Nazism, had descended "vampire-like" on a country already suffering from the effect of the Great Depression, bringing their talents and their traditions to bear on something called French culture, Rebatet welcomed them like the impaler Vlad of the vampire legend.

The Vampire in Anti-Semitic Propaganda

It is tempting to analyze Rebatet's yearning to expel the Jew from the art life of France in psychosexual terms, using Kristeva as a lead. Kristeva is convinced that the anti-Semitic craving of Céline has to do with his fantasy image of the male Jew's sexuality. "The fantasy of a Jewish threat, weighing against the Aryan world . . . in a period when, to the contrary, persecutions against the Jews were beginning, cannot be explained in any other way; but emanates directly out of that vision of the Jew as . . . issuing from the All in which he joys, and especially from the immediate sexualization of that *jouissance*."[25]

Céline, she feels, is envious of the Jew's penis; secretly dreams of being sodomized by him, hates to the point of abjection the thought of submitting to his desire. At the heart of this interpretation is the view that the projection of abjection onto another is inseparable from self-hatred, that is to say, dread of the abject repressed within the self. "To each ego its object, to each superego its abject."[26]

Substitute Rebatet's name for Céline and dread of vampires for fear of sodomists, and the anti-Semite emerges as a psychiatric monster, finding sexual pleasure at the sight of blood and of human body parts, living with the temptation of rape, entertaining the dream of "consuming" human flesh, and, exceptionally, acting on his or her perverse desire, as did Jack the Ripper, Gilles Garnier, Pierre Stumf, Clara Geissler, the originator of the vampire myth, Vlad the Impaler, and . . . Adolf Hitler. "In usual [psychiatric] language, the term vampirism designates . . . the worst of sadism—homicidal monomania, and all forms of necromania," writes Jean Goens, the French authority on real and mythical monsters.[27]

It is also tempting to read the anti-Semites' yearning for the total exclusion of Jews as a cover for the desire of Aryans to regain positions and territory held by Jews. Rebatet himself occupied a position at *Je suis partout* abandoned by François Fosca, a Jew, who returned to his native Switzerland after the Nazi Occupation of Paris. This interpretation harking back to the first vampire legend of Vlad the Impaler, turned into a bloodsucking monster by the usurpers of his throne, has no doubt a great deal of truth, but this form of desire is not specific enough to characterize the anti-Semite of the period 1940–45.

At a time when power was on the side of Fascism, the yearning to expel the Jew, it seems to me, shows evidence of a desire other than sexual perversion (although probably related to it); of more than a desire to recover lost territory (although again not inconsistent with that): it had to do with a passionate desire to help fashion the Fascist victory. For a Fascist like Rebatet, who did not hesitate to say in 1942 in *Les Décombres* (his memoirs) "I have never had an ounce of democratic blood in me," the destruction of Jews was necessary because Jews (and equally, abhorred Americans) were a major force standing in the way of triumphant Fascism, at a moment of crisis for democracy.[28] A cartoon entitled *La Liberté . . . enfin! éclaire le monde!*,

La Liberté... enfin ! éclaire le monde !

Mara, *La Liberté . . . enfin! éclaire le monde!,* published in *La Gerbe,* May 25, 1944

which appeared in the collaborationist newspaper *La Gerbe* on May 25, 1944, shortly before the Normandy landings, makes that point quite clearly: *Liberté*, depicted as a sinister vampire-like giant (America) brandishing a menorah, is shown striding through the air, destroying everything in its path and threatening to "rape" what still stands of a "Fascist" Europe. Once again, threats from an imaginary vampire were being used to help the usurper keep his throne.[29]

The vampire myth always seems to revive in times of paroxystic tension in the social and political realms. Goens proposes in *Loups-garous* that the historical Vlad Tepes of Moldavia (formerly Wallachia), a remote region of central Europe, was "like Richard III, the posthumous victim of political propaganda, that made him a monster in order to justify the presence of illegitimate rivals."[30] Vlad Dracul, in order to protect his region from the Turks, imposed the dreadful punishment of impalement on his enemies, who in turn accused him of reveling in blood, hence his posthumous reputation as Dracul, the vampire, after his death in 1476. (Is there not irony in the fact that Vlad's war took place in central Europe and involved Christians against Moslems?)

The vampire myth was revived, according to Goens, in eighteenth-century France, a period when non-believers and Enlightenment philosophers were seriously questioning Roman Catholic dogma and naive superstition. The priest Dom Augustin Calmet wrote an extremely popular treatise proving the existence of supranatural presences including vampires, *Traité sur les apparitions des anges, des démons et des esprits et sur les revenants et vampires de Hongrie, de Bohême, de Moravie et de Silésie* (1746–51). It was a compendium of testimonies by travelers to central Europe who told of villagers visited by their dead at night, of bloodsucking incidents, and of bizarre deaths.

In 1897, at the height of the Victorian age in England, the most popular of gothic novels, *Dracula* by Bram Stoker, was published. For Goens, "it is significant that Victorian society, haunted by sex and death, should have engendered on the one hand Jack the Ripper . . . and on the other Dracula, the literary sublimation of this obsession, and a transparent metaphor of Jack the Ripper."[31] The Stoker novel was the inspiration of several vampire films, the most recent one being Neil Jordan's *Interview with the Vampire* (1994).

In every moment of its revival, and by whatever means it carries its "abject" work, the "vampire" is double-faced. For, like a magnet, it concentrates onto itself all the givens of abjection, while also acting as a foil for the defense of the status quo and against contamination by ideas contrary to those of the dominant group. The original vampire legend helped the usurper of the throne stay in power and set a precedent for the successful persecution of rivals, religious, political, economic, or cultural. The Calmet "vampire" protected the French church from the sweep of rationalism that was disseminated by the philosophers of the Enlightenment. The Dracula vampire of Bram Stoker put an obstacle in the way of women's sexual revolution. As for the vampiric virus of the age of AIDS, it stands in the way of the gay revolution.

Vampires are thus associated with fear of a "virus" that poses a threat to life—as in the tradition that runs from antiquity to the AIDS virus—but also with fear of the subversion of the status quo, "social fear." It is that enduring feature of the vampire myth that can explain its usefulness to anti-Semitic Fascists, among them critics of modernist culture during the Occupation years in Vichy France.

10

El Lissitzky's "Interchange Stations":
The Letter and the Spirit

JUDITH GLATZER WECHSLER

The idea should be given form through the letters. EL LISSITZKY

The Hebrew word *'oth* means not only letter, but also in the precise meaning of
the term, sign, and more specifically mark (or signature). GERSHOM SCHOLEM

That which seeks to represent, to produce itself in the evolving of languages, is
that very nucleus of pure language. Though concealed and fragmentary, it is an
active force in life as the symbolized thing itself . . . WALTER BENJAMIN[1]

Hebrew letters are primary elements in El Lissitzky's early work, from
1917 to 1923. For Lissitzky (1890–1941), the letter was a building
block, first in his illustrations for Hebrew and Yiddish texts and then for
secular abstract typographical design. Lissitzky parallels certain kabbalistic
ideas in his belief in the letter as an elemental form capable of infinite creative permutations. Underlying his concept of typography is a belief in the
iconic and communicative force of the letter.

Like the projects of other Jewish artists and intellectuals of his generation, Lissitzky's, at least until 1922, was to develop a dynamic relationship
between Jewish culture and the secular world. Most historians who maintain that Lissitzky abandoned Jewish concerns for revolutionary ones after
1923 do not consider how deeply a Jewish upbringing is imbedded.[2]
Although he no longer adhered to religious practice, ways of thinking, both
verbal and visual, continued to inform his life and work. Lissitzky's development, I believe, was not one of radical rejection but of ambiguities, tran-
sitions, and exchanges: he was like a "switching center."[3] His project and
the multivalence of Kabbalah suggest an openness to different paths of
interpretation.

The focus here will be on a few points in Lissitzky's trajectory from
Judaic themes to secular abstraction starting with the one Hebrew text he
illustrated, "Schlomo ha-Melech" ("King Solomon"), by Hayim Nahman
Bialik, published in 1917; followed by his collage for Ilya Ehrenburg's story,
"Shifs Carta," published in 1922; and concluding with Lissitzky's autobio-

graphical self-portrait *The Constructor* (1924), which indicates how he calibrated himself at a critical juncture, setting up the idea that he was an "interchange station" between Judaic tradition and the avant-garde. I see these works as three points on a chart, marking Lissitzky's passage. Each point or position is an "interchange station," as he called his *Proun* paintings, informed by where he has come from and pointing to where he is headed.

First some biographical notes: the story of Lissitzky's life is well known and I will only point to a few factors about the Jewish elements of his early life. Lazar Markovich Lissitzky was born in 1890 in Polshinok, a small market town in the province of Smolensk.[4] Lissitzky's mother was orthodox. His father, a steward of a large estate and manager of an agricultural products factory in the Smolensk region, knew German, English, Russian, and Yiddish and translated Heine and Shakespeare. On a visit to the United States, Lissitzky's father urged his family to emigrate but his mother followed their Rabbi's advice to stay in Russia, and he returned.[5]

Lissitzky grew up in Jewish Vitebsk, a small town in Belorussia in the Pale of Settlement, but returned to Smolensk for high school, living with his grandfather. In the Pale, to be part of the Jewish community was to be orthodox, steeped in Jewish law and lore. Lissitzky knew Yiddish and almost certainly could read Hebrew.[6]

Many Jewish artists born in Russia in the 1880's and 1890's who went through the Russian Revolutions of 1905 and 1917 explored the possibility of a Jewish art, initially based on folkloric tradition. The enthusiastic reception of the play *The Dybbuk* (1922), a tale of spiritual possession, is an indication of the lively interest in Jewish culture at the time. Martin Buber's *Jüdische Künstler*, published in 1902, was found in many middle-class homes. There was a growing literature, both scholarly and popular, on Hebrew language and letters. One assumes that people like Lissitzky's family, educated and middle-class, would have had the Russian *Hebrew Encyclopedia*, published in St. Petersburg before 1912. In it there is a long entry on the Hebrew alphabet, with bibliographical references.[7]

Rejected by the St. Petersburg Academy of Arts because of the Jewish quota, Lissitzky went to Darmstadt in 1909 where he studied architectural engineering at the Technische Hochschule, graduating in 1914. During the period of his studies he traveled to Italy, Belgium, and France as well. At the outbreak of the Great War, he returned to Russia.

From 1916 to 1919 Lissitzky dedicated himself to the Jewish Renaissance. For the Jewish Ethnographic Society, founded by the historian Simon Dubnow and the writer and ethnographer Shlomo An-Sky, Lissitzky made sketches and took notes on the synagogues in Mohilev in the Ukraine. He found sources in Jewish folklore for the development of a revolutionary style, just as other Russian artists—from Malevich to Goncharova—forged similar links with Russian folklore. Lissitzky noted the synagogue in Mohilev: "pictures of holy vessels from Solomon's Temple, ornaments and all manner of living creatures. The artist's treasure-trove of formal invention is inexhaustible."[8] The "Mohilev Synagogue Reminiscences" (1923) was published in *Milgroim* and simultaneously in the Hebrew edition of the same journal, *Rimon*.[9]

Lissitzky is known to have illustrated eighteen Yiddish and Hebrew publications between 1917 and 1923, and current research has identified thirty such publications.[10] Among the most notable were *Sikhes Kholin* ("Small Talk", *Legend of Prague*), a story in prose by Moshe Broderzon published in 1917, and *Khad Gadya* (*One Kid*) in 1919.[11] Mani Leib's *Yingl Tsingl Khvat*, which Lissitzky illustrated during a brief stay in Warsaw in 1921, was published by the Kultur Lige which was committed to a fusion of Jewish folk traditions with contemporary art concerns.[12] Lissitzky was very much part of this group: some historians cite him among its founders. In the catalogue for the Kultur Lige's "Jewish Art Exhibition" in Kiev, in 1920, their manifesto emphasizes the importance of the Hebrew letter for contemporary graphic artistic practice:

> *The first source of our graphics is the Hebrew letter* and the ornaments of old Jewish prayer books and religious articles. . . . [my italics] Modern Jewish artists, who self-consciously seek specifically national graphic art forms, like Altman, Lissitzky, Chagall and others, find in fact a rich selection in our ancient symbols. . . . Modern Jewish art seeks to recreate our artistic inheritance in national forms, in which it expresses the accomplishments of modern art.
>
> The collected primitive folk effort becomes the basis of a higher Jewish art which joins the latest universalist quests with the creative skills of the folk masses.[13]

In 1919 Chagall invited Lissitzky to become professor of architecture and applied arts of the art academy in Vitesbk. There Lissitzky came under the influence of Malevich and it is said that he abandoned representation.[14] While Lissitzky reconstructed his thoughts of 1918 ten years later, saying that "One must be on this side or that, there is no mid-way", his artistic practice and statements indicate otherwise in the years 1918 to 1922.[15] During this period he was producing Hebrew and Yiddish book illustrations, in which he combined folkloric elements with Suprematist traits, as well as paintings he called *Prouns*.

The belief in the power of the letter as icon or hieroglyph rather than phoneme underlies Lissitzky's abstract typographic design.[16] The source of his use of letters has been noted: "The Hebrew script suggested to Lissitzky, under the influence of Suprematism, a new typographic structure in which the geometric characteristics of the letters could be utilized to create a structural order over the entire page."[17]

It is arguable whether it took Suprematism to effect Lissitzky's sense of the structural possibilities of the Hebrew letter. His concept of letters suggests a complex interaction between Jewish tradition and revolutionary ideology. The Hebrew letter is unique in that its structural, lexical, and metaphorical meanings are interlinked.[18]

There is also an underlying architectural idea about the shape of the letter, which one can see in Lissitzky's cover for Ben Zion Raskin's *4 Teyashim* (*Four Billygoats*), published in Warsaw in 1922, an example of avant-garde design principles with Hebrew letters. Lissitzky uses 4 as the structural principle, the word four in Hebrew, the letter *daled* (the fourth letter of the Hebrew alphabet), the number 4 in Arabic and Roman numerals, 4 dots, 4 lines.[19]

Lissitzky's transition to secular revolutionary practice was of its time: to understand the dimensions of his work one must look at the persistence of certain ideas in the Jewish tradition and at the circumstances of the Jewish intelligentsia in the early modern period. For many of Lissitzky's generation—Franz Kafka, Walter Benjamin, Gershom Scholem—there was a deep concern with recovering tradition in a secular world. In Russia, Ilya Ehrenburg and Isaac Babel were caught up in the tension between the call of tradition and secularism. For Benjamin and Scholem, "tradition consists of creative commentary in an effort to reestablish the essential connection between man and the source of language."[20] Kafka, also concerned with the link between Kabbalah and modern creation, wrote in his diaries concerning his own work: "this whole literature is an assault upon the border . . . and it might have developed quite easily into a new esoteric doctrine, a Kabbala."[21]

The interest in our day in the Kabbalah and in its influence on avant-garde Jewish artists probably has to do with the greater openness to interpretation in certain strains of mystical theory and practice than one finds in normative Judaism. The effort to find Kabbalistic links in the work of Kafka, Benjamin, and Lissitzky suggests a critical search for a secret doctrine at the heart of their work.[22]

Lissitzky's understanding of letters as elemental forms parallels kabbalistic hermeneutics with its belief in letters as instruments of creation. I can only begin to suggest the ways in which Lissitzky drew on some of its ideas and principles; the literature on the significance of letters in Jewish tradition is vast and deep: "Discussion of the names and shapes of the letters are already to be found in the Talmud and Midrash. . . . by the time of the Middle Ages the commentaries on the alphabet had become a literature genre widespread in theosophical kabbalah."[23]

The Illustrations to "Shlomo ha-Melech"

Lissitzky illustrated one Hebrew text, a legend about King Solomon recounted by the leading Hebrew poet of the early twentieth century, Hayim Nahman Bialik. Bialik was a key figure in the movement to modernize Hebrew and to create connections with contemporary secular experience. He vivified the midrashic tale in a romantic Hebrew style that is rich in biblical formulations and expressions.

The story appeared in 1917 in a Hebrew journal for young people, *Shtilim* (*Samplings*), published in Moscow bimonthly.[24] Lissitzky drew eleven modest black and white narrative vignettes, ten of which were constructed around a Hebrew letter—in the tradition of historiated letters—with which he divides the story. He makes verbal and visual associations with the alphabet that are part of Jewish lore, and interweaves them with the narrative elements of Bialik's story, drawing on ancient and modern liturgical imagery and iconographic sources.[25]

This one midrashic story Lissitzky illustrated concerns architecture: it is of King Solomon in the process of building the Temple. In the first illustration, the *aleph*, **א**, is embedded in an architectural base with a reverse perspective. The two angels kneeling on the base are shaped like the letter and hold the tablets on which the letter *aleph* is placed.

Aleph, the first letter of the alphabet, is considered the foundation stone of the alphabet and the Torah. According to the Kabbalah, the world was created by the letter *aleph*. Here the story cites the biblical commandment against the use of iron tools in building the Temple. It is this admonition that leads Solomon to capture the demon Asmodeus for his knowledge of where to find the *shamir*, the secret device for splitting stones.

Certain key words in this section begin with the letter *aleph*: *imrei sholomo*, the sayings of Solomon; *Elohim*, God; *avonim*, rocks; *Ashmadai*, the demon Asmodeus; *azikei barzel*, bars of iron.[26]

The second letter, *bet*, **ב**, is framed by a leaf shape, with Asmodeus behind it, like the serpent found at the stem of the vine in the garden of Eden. In the story, Solomon's men have filled Asmodeus's water hole with wine: in great thirst the demon drinks it, gets drunk, and is captured.

Bet is generally associated with the word *bayit*, house or Temple, as in *Bayit Ha-sheni*, the Second Temple. In this segment essential terms begin with the letter *bet*: *banui*, built; *ha-be'er*, the spring; *bor*, hole.

Gimmel, **ג**, shows Asmodeus in captivity, with Solomon holding his chain. In the story the demon tells Solomon that he can find the *shamir* near the nest of the hoopoe bird. In the next illustration, *daled*, **ד**, we see the hoopoe, in Hebrew, *dukhiphat*; the word appears eight times in this section. *Daled* is also the abbreviation of God's four-letter name, the tetragrammaton; the wings in which the letter is embedded imply the divine presence.

The letter *hey*, ה, is another sign of God, deriving from the word *hashem*, the name, used by orthodox Jews to avoid pronouncing the name of God. The letter is located in this illustration in a shield or tear; it is ambiguous. The demon is pictured behind the letter, on fertile ground, within an architectural setting, probably the palace. Solomon asks Asmodeus what has become of his power if it is possible to keep him in captivity. The demon says if Solomon will release his chains and let him hold the magic ring he will explain. Once released, Asmodeus flings Solomon into a distant kingdom, and disguises himself as the king.

The next illustration, around the letter *vav*, ו, seems to be out of narrative sequence. Solomon is back in Jerusalem, indicated by the domes. His body is represented as the continuation of the *vav*: the vertical shape of the letter suggests uprightness, framed by two lions, the traditional attributes of his throne. (Lissitzky had also drawn the lions in the Mohilev synagogue.)

Behind the letter *zayin*, ז, which serves in this picture as a shield, Solomon in exile is shown sleeping on the ground dreaming of a horse-drawn chariot—possibly a reference to the mystical chariot the *merkava*, which also signifies messianic redemption. The numerical equivalent of *zayin* is seven, symbol of a cycle, particularly the creation of the world. Lissitzky may have engaged here in *gemmatria*, the equivalence of letters and numbers, a common practice in Jewish mysticism. In the story, Solomon dreams of the restoration of his kingdom.

There is an old popular tradition associating the letter *khet*, ח, with the word *khet*, sin. Solomon has been cast out of his kingdom for his three sins. The key word here is *khata'av*, his sins.

Solomon is pictured kissing Naamah, the daughter of the Ammonite king in whose house he works as a cook during his exile. Naamah falls in love with Solomon and follows him into the wilderness when he is banished by the king. This illustration may allude to transgression: one of Solomon's sins was having too many wives.

Foraging for food, Solomon brings back a fish, in which he finds the magic ring. Ring in Hebrew is *taba'at*, beginning with the letter *tet*, ט, on which is imprinted the name of god, *Shadai*.

A rabbinic figure is seated behind the letter *yod*, י, blowing a ram's horn, the *shofar*, associated with salvation. Lissitzky features the Magen David, the six-pointed star, which became a common Jewish symbol only in the nineteenth century.[27] The patterns and lines emitted from the *shofar* correspond to the traditional aural pattern of the *shofar* calls: *tekiya*, one blast; *shevarim*, three short calls; *tekiya gedolah*, one long blast. There is here a kind of synaesthesia, a visualization of sounds that interested avant-garde symbolists like the poet and painter Mayakovsky at this time. Certain key words in

El Lissitzky, initial letter *yod*,
illustration for "Shlomo ha-Melech,"
published in *Shtilim*, 1917

this section begin with *yod*: *yoshev*, sat; *va-yisar*, bestow; *yadoah*, to know; *yom*, day; *va-yir'u*, and they saw; *va-yaal*, and he went up; *be-yado*, in his hand.

The ornamental forms in which the *yod* and *aleph* are placed recall the *kaftor va ferakh* (calyx and petal)—the description in Exodus 25:33 and 37:19 of the stylized ornamentation of knops and flowers on the columns in the Temple. In this illustration the ornamentation also resembles a pomegranate, symbol of amplitude and birth. A child, which Naamah bears Solomon, emerges from between the two fruits, like Aphrodite from the shell. (The upraised arms of the child are an ancient symbol of ascension to heaven.)

Whether intentional or coincidental, there are correspondences of letters to key terms using the letters *yod* and *aleph* in sequence. The following words are paired: *yerushalayim* and *or*, "Jerusalem" and "light"; *vayizkor* and *ahavah*, "recall" and "love"; *ka-as* and *ka-asher amar*, "anger" and "when he said"; *va-yeelam* and *ki l'o he-emin*, "disappeared" and "because he didn't believe"; *yisrael* and *elohim*, "Israel" and "God".

The final illustration, which stands alone, draws on both Jewish and Christian iconography and shows the breadth of Lissitzky's frame of reference. Solomon is represented having vanquished the demon, pictured underfoot as in a Byzantine image, and holding a model of the temple in his hand, like a donor or patron saint in Christian iconography. Solomon's scepter and crown is in a stylized fruit form, the *perakh*. On Solomon's turban is the star of David. The wings surrounding the tablets are most unusual. The arc over the tablets has the name of God, which actually was used only in Christian altars, as Jews would not write out the name.[28] The rounded tablets were also a Christian innovation appearing first in 1084, in a Tournai manuscript; they are seen in a number of twelfth-century manuscripts and on a capital at Vézelay.[29]

In Jewish tradition, the idea that letters are building blocks of the universe, is found in the first century C.E. Rabbi Akiba understood the shape of the letters as indicative of certain kinds of powers and was concerned with their transmutational possibilities.[30] There is a remarkable similarity between Akiba's observations and a key statement by Lissitzky concerning the infinity of the text. "The letter is an *element* which is itself composed of elements. . . . The immense text of the world is born from these few non-hierarchical marks, as equal as the text is infinite."[31]

The two main topics in the classic text of the Spanish Kabbalah, *The Zohar*, are "the dynamism of the letters . . . and the secret language as it unfolds in the creative process. . . . the dynamic conception of letters as hypostatic elements . . ."[32] Infinities of meaning are linked to the infinite possibilities of letters.

Gershom Scholem's ideas on language in the Kabbalah may have been influenced by Walter Benjamin who believed that language is not a given but an "'activity' in which man is constantly creating new forms."[33] Against the sign theory of language, Benjamin developed a "'Kabbalistic' conception of language as symbolic."[34] For the kabbalists, symbols are not arbitrary or subjective, but have an essential inner connection with what they symbolize. There may be parallels between Benjamin's theory of language as "*Ursprache*", the fundamental source, and Lissitzky's notion of letters as "elemental form," both inflected by their relation to kabbalistic ideas.[35] There are also analogies between Lissitzky's transference of traits from the Hebrew alphabet to his revolutionary Russian typography and Benjamin's reflections on the role of the translator. Benjamin quotes Rudolf Pannwitz, *Die Krisis der europäischen Kultur*:

> when translating from a language very remote from his own he must go back to the primal elements of language itself and penetrate to the point where work, image and tone converge. He must expand and deepen his language by means of the foreign language. It is not generally realized to what extent this is possible, to what extent any language can be transformed.[36]

Of all the writers on mysticism the one who most stressed the hermeneutic importance of letters was Abraham Abulafia. Various editions of this thirteenth-century mystic's work would have been accessible to Lissitzky. *Sefer ha'Ot* (*The Book of the Letter*) was reprinted in Vienna in 1876, in Breslau in 1887, and in Russia in 1922. Abulafia's hermeneutics involved a method "which deconstructs the text to its letters to reconstruct it in new ways." With Abulafia the "return of focus to the inherent forces of the elements of language in themselves, in comparison to their function in the traditional texts, bears witness to a certain alienation to the ordered linguistic, social and religious universes of medieval Judaism."[37]

The *Sefer ha-Ge'ulah* says that "There is meaning to the visual forms of the letter and every essential aspect of them has implications. This is so regarding the graphic form, the name of the letter, and its numerical value."[38]

For Abulafia, it has been pointed out, language is understood as reality in itself. "The symbolic conception of a text and hierogrammatic perception of letters convey content by their form. The letters are creative elements that enable different kinds of communication." Letters are regarded as microcosms, *Olam ha-otiot*, a world of letters. In Jewish mysticism there is an ontologized or reified conception of language.[39] Lissitzky seeks the visual or visible form of that language.

The Illustration for "Shifs Carta"

In 1921 Lissitzky left for Moscow to direct the faculty of architecture at the recently established Vkhutemas art school. That same year he went to Berlin via Warsaw to make contacts between artists in Germany and the Soviet Union.

While in Berlin, Lissitzky collaborated with Ilya Ehrenburg, producing illustrations to accompany his *Six Stories About Easy Endings*.[40] One of the stories, "Shifs Carta" (ship's ticket), takes place in Berdichev in the Pale of Settlement during the Civil War (which continued until 1922), and tells of a watchmaker, Girtsch, who witnesses the destruction of his Jewish community. Girtsch tries to make sense of the promise of a "shifs carta" which seems to offer salvation. Ehrenburg, with irony, relates the clash of traditional Jewish life with the experience of the Russian Revolution. Using Jewish lore, Girtsch tries to understand the changes but it does not save him.

Lissitzky refers to some underlying elements of the story but none of its narrative details. The illustration is a metaphorical interpretation of Ehrenburg's story. Apparently, Ehrenburg had little to say about the illustration, either in the making of it or in response to it after completion.[41]

The illustration concerns the old world being canceled out and the promise of a new open-ended world, the experience of many Russian-Jewish immigrants. The elements of the collage which served as the basis for the illustration are set in and around an articulated and attenuated Jewish star. In the upper part are symbols of the new world: a United States flag, a flag, with the letters UAL (United American Lines), and a third with an emblem of a ship, which resembles as well as the letter *shin*, **ש**, in Hebrew. There is also an emblem with the acronym H.A.P.A.G. (Hamburg Amerikanische Paketfahrt Aktien Gesellschaft), the main shipping line used by immigrants from Eastern Europe.[42] A black line extends from the ship and forms an upper edge of the star. This part of the collage illustration is lighter and less unconstricted: the flags and ships suggest space and time in motion. The ship starts at the stroke of twelve, the beginning of a new cycle. The point of arrival is left blank but suggests the new world.

The fragment of a clock face links the images of a world of traditional Jewish culture with this new world, bounded by a schedule of the Hamburg–New York line which forms a part of one line of the intersecting triangle of the star of David. In the story, the watch is the clock of history and the universe, with allusions to the hour of the Revolution and the Last Judgment ("[Girtsch] listens with excitement to watches ticking around the world, in the sea, in heaven, in Palestine, Berdichev, Odessa, Warsaw").

The world of traditional Jewish culture, the dark and buried world of the synagogue and the Pale, is symbolically indicated in the lower half of the image. Lissitzky refers here to the synagogue in the story, the Jewish community, and Jewish learning. In Ehrenburg's tale, young Jewish revolutionaries desecrate the synagogue, turning it into a club named after Trotsky. At the sight of all this destruction "The torah flew away". It is ironic that Trotsky's patronymic was Davidovich, son of David, and in the story, Girtsch waits for the Messiah, the son of David, to come.[43]

There are two diagrams of the ancient Temple and a description in the so-called *rashi* script, the Aramaic script used by Sephardic Jews that became the type used for the commentaries on the Bible and Talmud. Here, the *rashi* text concerns the Temple's construction. Individual letters and words indicate places in the Temple. On the plan of the Temple Lissitzky draws lines that create links among elements of the illustration and he introduces black geometric forms that create formal points of emphasis. The inverted pyramid just outside the lines of the star is a diagram of the lintels of the gateway to the Hall of the Temple—the term "*amalterah*," which appears in Hebrew on each line, referring to the lintel beams.

Some historians have mistakenly claimed that the text in the collage comes from the Kabbalah.[44] It has been identified as a portion of the *Mishnah, Order Kodoshim, Tractate Midot*, dealing with the measurements of the temple.[45] But the diagram comes from an illustration for Maimonides' drawings of the temple, in the *Mishneh Torah, Sefer Avodah, Hilkhoth Beit ha-Bekhirah*, based on the tractate just cited.[46]

Over the temple diagram is the imprint of a hand, with the Hebrew letters *pei nun*, ‏נ פ‎, an abbreviation for *po niqbar* (here is buried), an emblem found commonly on burial tombs. It is the hand, the mark, of the artist working on several levels. The hand could be a negation, a blotting out, a stop sign. The *pei nun* could also be burying the artist's hand. There is an-

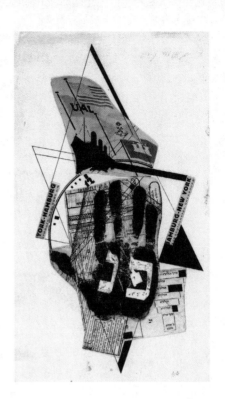

El Lissitzky, illustration for "Shifs
Carta," 1922

other possible reference—to a priestly blessing—suggested by the slight
space between the second and third fingers.[47] There may also be a reference
here to the *hamsa*, the Islamic hand of warning used to ward off the evil eye,
a symbol which entered Jewish art in the fourteenth century.[48]

The collage elements of the texts are made from actual pages of old and
damaged copies of Maimonides found in a genizah, a synagogue depository for damaged holy books.[49] There is an allusion to Lissitzky's hand leafing
through the collage material, using the text to the point of dismembering it,
an avant-garde act that no one else at the time tried—cutting up sacred
Jewish texts for Cubo-constructivist collages. The fragments of religious
texts are like indices; the hand an indexing device, indicating what Lissitzky
is leaving behind—he is laying to rest the old Eastern European Jewish
world. The artist leaves his mark and buries the text under the letters *pei nun*
as a kind of last will.[50] Lissitzky's appropriation is in itself an act of transgression.

The theme of the picture is one of transit and transition, from Eastern
Europe via Germany, to the new world. Lissitzky had gone earlier from
Russia to Darmstadt to study architecture and this illustration was done
during his time in Berlin. Such a trajectory from East to West was true of
other avant-garde artists on whom Lissitzky had a particular influence, like
Moholy-Nagy.[51] Lissitzky is the interchange between Russia and Germany,

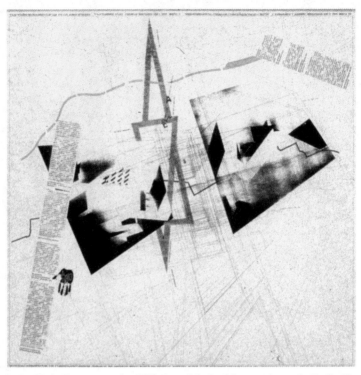

Daniel Libeskind, "Deconstruction III," plan of the Jewish extension to the Berlin Museum,
published in *Architectural Digest,* 1897

which was the purpose of the journal that Ehrenburg and Lissitzky founded in 1922, *Veshch* (*Object*), published in three languages to encourage familiarity with art trends in Western Europe and Russia. Lissitzky attended the
Congrès International des Artistes Progressivistes in Dusseldorf in 1922,
followed later that year in Weimar by the Congrès "Constructiviste," which
included Dada artists. Lissitzky was the only Russian representative.

The dynamics of the "shifs carta" mapping is autobiographical not only
for the relationship to Eastern European Jewry but also for Lissitzky's role
in the middle European avant-garde and its ultimate dissemination via
many artists to the United States during the Nazi period. Many of his typographical ideas were carried on by the new Bauhaus. The image is, in that
sense, prophetic. These associations also appear in a "concept-collage"
published in 1987 for the Jewish Extension to the Berlin Museum by Daniel
Libeskind, with the imprint of the hand marked *pei nun* and the attenuated
Jewish star. There is a lot "buried" in Libeskind's inclusion and displacement of the image; in a sense it marks the passage from Constructivism to
Deconstructivism.[52]

The Constructor

The illustration for "Shifs Carta" was one of Lissitzky's first experiments in montage combining brochures, texts, and drawing. Two years later, in 1924, he made a photographic collage with typography for *The Constructor*, a self-portrait which is another "interchange station." Here the transformation is made to a more technicist conception of art: "if necessary we shall take machines in our hands as well because in expressing our creative ability paintbrush and ruler and compasses and machine are only extensions of the finger which points the way."[53]

Lissitzky's photographic self-portrait is set against a grid. His hand is now not a symbol of death and burial but rather frames an active eye at the center of the active hand.[54] There is a shift from the Hebrew letters, the *pei nun* marked on the hand in the illustration for "Shifs Carta," to the artist's eye, placed iconically in his hand in a substitutive relationship that marks the interchange from tradition to the avant-garde. The hand "holding" the protractor (it is located between his third and fourth finger) is the opposite of the hand marked with the *pei nun*. The ruler and compass replace the mystique of the letter in the hand as self-representation.[55] In this secular self-portrait, the letters *pei nun* are substituted or interchanged for the letters

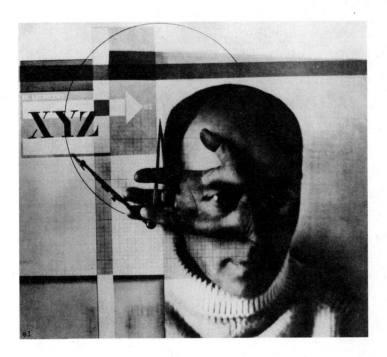

El Lissitzky, *The Constructor*, 1924

XYZ, which may be a secular transformation of the ABC in Hebrew—seeking a new mathematical elemental form with infinite possibilities.[56]

This is not the end of Lissitzky's interchanges. In his subsequent typographical designs the letter continued to have greater importance for him than for most of his contemporaries. Lissitzky's uses of Russian letters preserve some of the lexical traits of Hebrew. The architectural form of the letters, and their consistent size, may be seen, for example, in his cover design for Malevich's *On New Methods in Art* (1919), produced as a fold-out book, like a scroll.[57] For all of Lissitzky's advocacy of new technology, he continued to draw letters by hand, as did Torah scriptwriters.

For Lissitzky, letters are elemental forms, building blocks, which permit endless permutations. From his earliest use of the Hebrew alphabet in illustrating Yiddish and Hebrew texts to the more conflicted and multivalent meanings in the collage for "Shifs Carta," and ending with his personal and universalist references in *The Constructor*, letters are carriers of meaning throughout Lissitzky's oeuvre. Lissitzky partakes of the Jewish consciousness that calligraphic style has communicative force and that letters have iconic effects. That is the legacy of Lissitsky's Judaism in the text.

11

The Jew in Jean-Paul Sartre's Réflexions sur la question juive: *An Exercise in Historical Reading*

SUSAN RUBIN SULEIMAN

... that book is a declaration of war against anti-Semites. JEAN-PAUL SARTRE[1]

Sartre is transformed in the third part of his essay into the antisemite against whom he rails in the first part. ELAINE MARKS[2]

In a sense, this essay will be nothing more than my attempt to fill in the gap between those two statements, both of which I consider true. Can a "declaration of war against anti-Semites" become itself, at least in part, anti-Semitic? The idea, although paradoxical, is not totally surprising: in the heat of battle, much can easily stick to your skin, without your always knowing whether it is your muck or your enemy's.

Sartre was not an anti-Semite, nor did he harbor any love for anti-Semites. His book *Réflexions sur la question juive* (*Anti-Semite and Jew*) was perceived, at the time of its publication in 1946, exactly as he described it more than thirty years later: a declaration of war against anti-Semites. Because of that book, followed by his unwavering support for the state of Israel, Sartre remained a hero to French Jews until his death and beyond.[3] Some of the first Jewish readers of *Réflexions* found their lives transformed by the experience; among them was twenty-year-old Claude Lanzmann, a young assimilated Jew lucky enough to have survived the war in Paris with all his family. "I remember, I walked the streets differently [after reading Sartre's book], I could breathe again, because the simple fact that the war was over had not changed the way one felt inside," Lanzmann told two interviewers in 1987. Even after the Holocaust, he explained, anti-Semitism persisted in France, and so did the shame and fear experienced by many Jews. But Sartre's book "gave us a feeling of recognition." Against a certain hateful French tradition—one for which "the anti-Semitism of the Nazis was not a foreign tongue," Lanzmann grimly notes—Sartre embodied "another way of being French." It was thanks to Sartre's book, Lanzmann concludes, that he was "once again able to walk with head held high." And the ultimate word of praise: "We could compare Sartre's *Reflections on the Jewish Question* to Zola's 'J'Accuse.'"[4]

I too am a Jewish reader with a long-standing admiration for Sartre. Although I was too young to read *Réflexions sur la question juive* when it first appeared, I read it around fifteen years later, when I was in graduate school; the first chapter, "Portrait of the Anti-Semite," became, for a while, my bible. Sartre not only explained the phenomenology of racism but also gave a striking description of how some human beings, possessed by a "nostalgia for impermeability," are "drawn to the permanence of stone" (20–21). Besides its poetic resonance, Sartre's imagery helped me to understand the thornier analyses of his *L'Etre et le néant* (*Being and Nothingness*): the anti-Semite's desire for stone-like permanence was none other than a refusal of the human condition of "l'être pour soi," a state of chronic incompletion and approximation. Furthermore, the "Portrait of the Anti-Semite" complemented and formed a philosophical commentary on one of Sartre's most brilliant works, the novella *L'Enfance d'un chef* (published in 1939), whose antihero-protagonist is a fictional embodiment of the "portrait."[5]

For all these reasons, I considered *Réflexions sur la question juive* a crucially important book. Imagine my surprise when, upon rereading it after many years, I found myself growing more and more angry and offended. My new responses were provoked not by the first chapter, which I still consider magnificent, but by the third, where Sartre discusses "the Jew." The peculiar effects produced by his argumentation and rhetoric in that chapter warrant detailed analysis, for they amount to nothing less than an "anti-Semite effect" (like Roland Barthes's "reality effect," a textual phenomenon). If even a staunchly anti-anti-Semitic work can produce such an effect, that fact is worth pondering.

To return to my two epigraphs, the gap I am seeking to fill is neither psychological nor conceptual; as I have suggested, conceptually the two statements are not contradictory. The gap that interests me is empirical, a gap in reading: by what process can one move from reading this well-known work primarily as an act against anti-Semitism, to reading it *also* as an example of anti-Semitism *malgré soi*? And what are the consequences of such a move, for an understanding both of Sartre and of French anti-Semites and Jews? I call these questions empirical rather than hermeneutic (though, of course, they concern interpretation), because they involve specific instances and experiences of reading in specific historical contexts. They are all the more interesting in that they concern "the Jewish question," a notoriously ambiguous concept with a complicated history.

"La question juive"

From the start, the "Jewish question" was indissociable from reflections on identity and difference. Tracing the history of the term as it emerged in the

1840's, chiefly in Germany, Jacob Toury notes that its meaning was different from earlier "questions" regarding the Jews: "the emerging 'Jewish question' was not the question of individual rights and of equality between private citizens, but rather the question of the corporate status of Jewry as a whole."[6] The "Jewish question" (*die Jüdische Frage*, then *Judenfrage*) in this modern sense could only emerge when a significant number of Jews had entered civil society as fully fledged citizens, after the French Revolution. As long as the Jews of Europe were isolated in ghettos and physically marked off as Other, there was no question about their separate status; that question arose when they were no longer in the ghetto, indeed when they could be perceived as occupying an inordinately large space in mainstream public life. It was the problematic relation between the Jews' "corporate status"—or, as more virulent and "scientific" versions would later formulate it, their "racial identity" as Jews—and their status as citizens of nation-states that "the Jewish question" posed. But in fact, not much real questioning went on in most versions of "the Jewish question," because (as Toury puts it) "the 'Jewish question' as a slogan did not take roots until it had established itself as an anti-Jewish battle-cry" (p. 92). In other words, those who wrote on the question from the start already knew the answer: the Jews were not only unassimilable, a separate "corporation"; they also constituted a threat, as a group, to the well-being of the nation.

Complications occurred when Jewish writers also began writing about the *Judenfrage*, in order to refute the terms in which it was raised by anti-Semites. Most Jews who wrote about the "Jewish question" in Germany in the mid-nineteenth century "utterly denied the existence . . . of a 'Jewish nation' and of a 'Jewish national character'" (Toury, p. 101). For them, Judaism was a religion, not a "corporation": there was no such thing as "the Jewish question," unless it meant simply the right of all citizens to freedom of religion. Still later, however, the question of a Jewish national identity was raised in a positive way by Jewish theorists of Zionism. Theodor Herzl's book on the necessity of a Jewish state, *Judenstaat* (1896), bore the subtitle: *Versuch einer modernen Lösung der Judenfrage* ("Attempt at a Modern Solution of the Jewish Question").

To "reflect on the Jewish question," and even more so to reflect on "Reflections on the Jewish question," is necessarily to grapple with political concepts of identity and difference. Put that way, the question of how one reads Sartre's nearly fifty-year old book takes on a decidedly contemporary ring.

A first ambiguity: why did Sartre choose the title he did, for a book published less than two years after the end of a war whose most notorious slogan was "the final solution"? Solution to what? To the "Jewish question." Clearly, he was being provocative—but provocation is a double-edged sword. For his "war against anti-Semites," Sartre chose a title that evoked tens and hundreds of anti-Semitic pamphlets and articles and special issues of newspapers published in France from the 1880's through the Second World War. From Edouard Drumont to Robert Brasillach, virulent French anti-Semites were concerned about "the Jewish question." In April 1938, Brasillach devoted a whole issue of his weekly newspaper *Je suis partout* (subtitled *Le grand hebdomadaire de la vie mondiale*, "the great weekly of world life") to "La Question Juive." The main message of this special issue, as spelled out by Brasillach and his colleague Lucien Rebatet, was that Jews should be stripped of French nationality: "It is impossible, as many liberals believe, to belong to two nations, the Jewish and the French," wrote Brasillach. "We demand that Jews be returned to their condition as Jews," wrote Rebatet—which meant, for him, "stripping Jews of French citizenship, and of all the rights that go with it."[7]

True, some Jewish publications during those years also used the phrase "question juive"—but after the rise of Nazism, such use was defensive: it was a matter of countering the Nazi or Nazi-inspired use of the term. Thus in 1934, a collective volume titled *La Question Juive* began by citing the persecutions of "Mr. Hitler"; the volume's aim, stated in the introduction, was to "show impartially and clearly the activity undertaken by Israelites [a euphemism preferred by assimilated, upper-middle-class French Jews, instead of "Juifs"] in every domain to make their homeland, France, more prosperous, happier, greater! . . . the Israelites have well served the French family of which they are an integral part, so that they could not be separated from it without doing it grave harm." One "patron" of the volume noted, in a letter reprinted at the end, that in his opinion there should be no "Jewish question" at all. But given what was happening in Germany, he added, it would be both foolish and cowardly to pretend it didn't exist.[8]

By the time of the war, the "Jewish question" had acquired unmistakably anti-Semitic overtones, in France as in Germany. Furthermore, Sartre's title must surely have evoked, for his French readers of 1946, one of the more ignominious institutions of the Vichy regime: the Commissariat Général aux Questions Juives, founded in March 1941, which continued to function until April 1944, shortly before the fall of the regime. The Commissariat was headed during its most active period (May 1942 to February 1944) by Louis Darquier de Pellepoix, who had been a founder of the Comité anti-juif de France (French Anti-Jewish Committee) before the war. During a public speech for the Comité, in May 1937 at the Salle Wagram, Darquier made his memorable statement: "It is extremely urgent to resolve the Jewish question, whether the Jews be expelled or whether they be massacred."[9]

In 1941, before he became Commissaire, Darquier founded a private institute with the support of the Germans, the Institut d'Etude des Questions Juives (Institute for the Study of Jewish Questions, IEQJ), one of whose first activities was the organization of the exhibition "Le Juif et la France." This exhibition, held at the Palais Berlitz on the Boulevard des Italiens from September 1941 to January 1942, brought in, at a conservative estimate, 200,000 paying customers.[10] The catalogue essay (by one J. Marquès Rivière) stated in its opening sentences: "Whether we like it or not, it's a problem. A sore point since forever . . . *the Jewish question dominates the world.*"[11] The proclaimed aim of the exhibition was to instruct and enlighten: the visitor was to learn, by means of "statistics, tables, quotations, documents . . . everything he needs to know in order to defend himself personally and to defend the community of which he is a part against Jewish control."[12] The theme of race dominated both the exhibition and the lectures that accompanied it. More generally, race dominated the preoccupations of the IEQJ, whose secretary-general stated in a public speech in September 1941 that Judaism was not a matter of religion: "for us the Jew is a race and it is on that ground alone that we want to stand."[13] What this meant concretely, in 1941, was that the French Jews who had converted, either in 1940 or before, out of religious conviction or in order to escape persecution, could not count on being "exempted."

Although the IEQJ did not have government status, its position on the "Jewish race" was hardly different from the official Vichy position, as spelled out in the "Jewish laws" of October 1940 and March 1941; the 1941 law defined as Jewish "anyone, regardless of religion, who had at least three grandparents of the Jewish race"—but if the person was married to a Jew, then two grandparents sufficed. As for what constituted "grandparents of the Jewish race," they were grandparents who "belonged to the Jewish religion."[14] Evidently, the "Jewish race" was not easy to define, even for convinced racists. As Michel Leiris pointed out a few years after the war, "the Jews are sufficiently undefinable from an anthropological point of view . . . so that even the Nazis had to fall back on the criterion of religion as a means of discrimination."[15] This difficulty notwithstanding, the IEQJ renamed itself in 1943 as "Institut d'Etude des Questions Juives et Ethno-Raciales" (Institute for the Study of Jewish and Ethno-Racial Questions) under the directorship of an expert in the field of "ethno-racism," Dr. Georges Montandon. Shortly before that, Darquier succeeded in getting the minister of National Education to create a chair at the Sorbonne in the "history of contemporary Judaism," to which a certain Henri Labroue was named in November 1942. He did not have any students, but continued to profess; so much for Jewish Studies under Vichy.[16]

What does all this have to do with Sartre's *Réflexions sur la question juive*, a book whose justly famous opening chapter is the devastating portrait of the anti-Semite? Clearly, Sartre had no connection to Darquier or to his Commissariat or his ethno-racial institutes, other than the connection of an outraged critic. His "Portrait de l'antisémite" (first published separately in *Les Temps Modernes* in November 1945) can be read as a cruelly accurate depiction and analysis of the anti-Semitic personality embodied in Darquier and others of his ilk. But all the more so, the question persists: why did Sartre choose a title as provocatively loaded with anti-Semitic over-tones (in 1946) as "la question juive"? One possible answer is that for him the question did not carry anti-Semitic overtones; just as *die Judenfrage* had been adopted by Jewish writers in Germany in the nineteenth century, so "la question juive" had been discussed by Jews and philo-Semites in France. The only trouble with this answer is that it does not adequately take account of the influence of the war and the years immediately preceding it, when "the Jewish question" was a monopoly of the racist Right. I have a strong suspicion that in the immediate postwar years, the words "question juive" (like *Judenfrage* and "the Jewish question") had become so closely associated with Nazism and with the "final solution" that no Jewish or pro-Jewish writer would use them except in quotation marks. Indeed, even today, many people cringe before a non-quotational use of that phrase. It is not an acci-dent, I think, that the title of Sartre's book in English was not "Reflections on the Jewish Question," but *Anti-Semite and Jew*. The idea is the same, but the words are less tainted.

It is possible, of course, that Sartre wanted to provoke by using a loaded term. Interestingly, his explicit provocation with this phrase is directed not at the anti-Semite but at what he calls "the democrat"—the liberal, human-ist universalist who claims that since all human beings are equal, "There is no Jew, there is no Jewish question" ("Il n'y a pas de Juif, il n'y a pas de 'question juive'," 67). Sartre attacks this figure in the short second chapter of the book, using an argument that will appear familiar to contemporary theorists of identity politics. Despite his goodwill, says Sartre, the democrat ends up paradoxically close to the anti-Semite, for he too wants to destroy the Jew. Whereas the anti-Semite wants to destroy the Jew as a man, leaving only his Jewishness, the democrat wants to destroy the Jew as a Jew, leaving only his humanity (68). By insisting, against the democrat, that there *is* a "Jewish question" (the sentence I quoted above is the only occurrence of that phrase in the book—in quotation marks, attributed to the democrat), Sartre thus prepares the way for his own solution to the question. His solu-tion, laid out in the book's fourth and final chapter, is that Jews must take responsibility for ("assume," in the French sense) their Jewishness instead of trying to deny it or hide it. The "authentic" Jew will claim his rights as a citizen *and* as a Jew. Just as a woman who votes, in societies where she has the vote, is fully equal to a male voter without having to "undergo a sex change when she enters the voting booth," so a Jew has full rights as a citizen without having to strip himself of his Jewishness (177). Only the "inauthentic" Jew tries to hide his Jewishness, or as Sartre puts it, "flees from it." The authentic Jew, by assuming his Jewishness, will achieve what his inauthentic counterpart never succeeded in doing: over the course of time, and with the goodwill of Gentiles who are determined to combat anti-Semitism, he will become assimilated into French society (181–2).

In other words, the authentic Jew will finally cease being a Jew. For as Sartre had stated earlier, "the Jew is a man whom other men call Jew" (83); but once the Jew, having chosen authenticity, becomes fully accepted by others, he will no longer be called Jew. It follows inevitably, although Sartre doesn't actually say it, that the Jew will cease to exist. The insensitivity of this argument—since it ends up denying Jewish existence in a more absolute fashion than any "democrat" ever dreamed of—as well as its ignorance of Jewish history and traditions (since it claims they don't exist) has been pointed out by some Jewish critics from the moment Sartre's *Réflexions sur la question juive* was published.[17] Generally, their criticisms have been circumspect, given Sartre's immense intellectual prestige both at the time of publication and later—and given the undeniable courage and brilliance with which he declared his opposition to anti-Semitism, at a time when already anti-Semitism was making a quiet comeback in France.[18] Also praiseworthy was his sincere assertion, at the end of the book, that anti-Semitism was, finally, not the Jews' problem: it was the French who had to change their attitudes, admit their fault, and mend their ways.

Jewish readers recognized his goodwill and were, on the whole, grateful. Still, in one way or another, many Jewish critics writing in French, then and now, have criticized him for not acknowledging the positive existence of Jews; even Albert Memmi, who considered himself a disciple of Sartre and dedicated his 1962 book *Portrait d'un juif* to him, points a strong criticism when he writes, negating Sartre's own words without naming him: "the Jew is not only one whom others consider a Jew. If he were only that, he would, as a Jew, be nothing but pure negativity. . . . The Jew is also a history and traditions, institutions and customs; he has an abundance of properly positive traits."[19]

Sartre has been rightly criticized for defining the Jew only as an absence, a negative quantity. What very few critics appear to have noticed—and this is especially true of those writing in French—is that Sartre does in fact attribute "positive" traits to the Jew, not in the sense of desirable or positively valued, but in that of a positive quantity opposed to zero. All of Chapter Three, the longest chapter in the book, is devoted to a description of what Sartre calls the "inauthentic" Jew, who is most certainly endowed with presence. It is in this description—which, he emphatically declares, is not a "portrait" (157)—that Sartre himself undergoes the metamorphosis Elaine Marks noticed: he becomes, in the space of his writing, an anti-Semite.

"La race juive"

I repeat, "in the space of his writing." What happens in this third chapter is a textual and discursive event: the production of an "anti-Semite effect." How does this happen? Or put another way, how did I became aware of it? Suddenly, in the middle of a page: "I will not deny that there is a Jewish race" ("Je ne nierai pas qu'il y ait une race juive," 73); and at the same time gradually, through the accumulation of details, as the text repeatedly corrects itself, explains itself, finds exceptions to itself, and squeezes itself into a corner. Only a close reading—and furthermore, only an intertextual close reading that situates this text in relation to the anti-Semitic discourses of the Vichy era and of the 1930's—can fully demonstrate my meaning here. While the whole chapter calls for such a reading, in the interest of concision I will follow a single major track, that of race.

Sartre broaches the matter of race very soon after the beginning of the chapter, in a passage that must be quoted in full:

> Je ne nierai pas qu'il y ait une race juive. Mais il faut d'abord nous comprendre. Si l'on entend par race ce complexe indéfinissable où l'on fait entrer pêle-mêle des caractères somatiques et des traits intellectuels et moraux, je n'y crois pas plus qu'aux tables tournantes. Ce que j'appellerai, faute de mieux, caractères ethniques, ce sont certaines conformations physiques héritées qu'on rencontre plus fréquemment chez les Juifs que chez les non-Juifs. Encore convient-il de se montrer prudent: il faudrait plutôt dire *des* races juives. On sait que tous les Sémites ne sont pas Juifs, ce qui complique le problème; on sait aussi que certains Juifs blonds de Russie sont plus éloignés encore d'un Juif crépu d'Algérie que d'un Aryen de Prusse Orientale. En vérité, chaque pays a ses Juifs et la représentation que nous pouvons nous faire de l'Israélite ne correspond guère à celle que s'en font nos voisins. Quand je vivais à Berlin, dans les commencements du régime nazi, j'avais deux amis français dont l'un était Juif et l'autre non. Le Juif présentait un "type sémite accentué"; il avait un nez courbé, les oreilles décollées, les lèvres épaisses. Un Français l'eût reconnu sans hésiter pour israélite. Mais comme il était blond, sec et flegmatique, les Allemands n'y voyaient que du feu; il se divertissait parfois à sortir avec des S.S. qui ne se doutaient pas de sa race et l'un d'eux lui dit un jour: "Je suis capable de reconnaître un Juif à cent mètres." . . . Quoi qu'il en soit et même en admettant que tous les Juifs ont certains traits physiques en commun, on ne saurait en conclure, sinon par la plus vague des analogies, qu'ils doivent présenter aussi les mêmes traits de caractère (73–5).

(I shall not deny that there is a Jewish race. But we must be clear at the start. If by race is understood that indefinable complex into which are tossed pell-mell both somatic characteristics and intellectual and moral traits, I believe in it no more than I do in ouija boards. What, for lack of a better term, I shall call ethnic characteristics, are certain inherited physical configurations that one encounters more frequently among Jews than among non-Jews. But one is well advised to be prudent: we ought to say Jewish *races*. It is known that not all Semites are Jews, which complicates the problem. We also know that certain blond Jews of Russia are still further removed from a woolly-headed Jew of Algeria than from an Aryan of East Prussia. In truth, each country has its Jews and our picture of an Israelite hardly corresponds at all to our neighbors' picture. When I lived in Berlin at the beginning of the Nazi regime, I had two French friends one of whom was a Jew and one of whom was not. The Jew was of a "marked Semitic type": he had a hooked nose, protruding ears, thick lips. A Frenchman would have recognized him as a Jew without hesitation. But since he was blond, lean, and phlegmatic, the Germans were completely taken in. He occasionally amused himself by going out with S.S. men, who did not suspect his race. One of them said to him one day: "I can tell a Jew a hundred yards off." . . . Whatever the case may be, even admitting that all Jews have certain physical traits in common, one could not conclude from that, except by the vaguest of analogies, that they must also show the same traits of character.)[20]

Following Sartre's tortuous, not to say burlesque, path here, we come up with the following remarkable series of thoughts: he does not deny that there is a Jewish race—a rather uncomfortable affirmation, using a double negative and a verb (*nier*) that requires the subjunctive (*qu'il y* ait), which introduces a shadow of a doubt. But let's be clear, he continues: by race, he does not mean a combination of "somatic" (sounds more scientific than "bodily") traits and character traits. No, by ethnic characteristics (ethnic, racial, the terms are apparently equivalent in his mind) he means "certain inherited physical configurations" that are found more frequently among Jews than non-Jews. Note the careful phrasing, avoiding excessive generalization in this delicate area of ethnic science: those physical configurations are not "always" found in Jews, just "more frequently." Indeed, one must be prudent (*encore convient-il d'être prudent*—a properly ponderous turn of phrase) for "it is known" (*on sait*—an impersonal piece of knowledge, a certainty) that not all Semites are Jews, which complicates the problem (this is becoming very serious science). In truth (*in truth*), every country has its own Jews, and our (*our*—that is, French) representation of "the Israelite" (it is more polite to call them Israelites) is not at all like that of our neighbors. The proof of this important piece of truth is that during the year Sartre spent in Germany, the Germans never realized that one of his friends, *whom a Frenchman would immediately have recognized as jewish* (israelite with a small i) *because of his hooked nose, protruding ears and thick lips,* went totally unrecognized by the Germans! Would you believe it, those stupid S.S. men never suspected his race! One of them even told him, one day, "I could detect a Jew from a hundred meters away." . . . But whatever the case may be, and even admitting that all Jews have certain physical traits in common (here, no subjunctive is used: *même en admettant que tous les Juifs ont quelques traits en commun*), nothing would allow one to conclude, except by the vaguest analogy, that they must also present the same character traits. He has thus circled back to the original position: Jewish race equals physical traits but not character traits. In the process, a subjunctive of possible doubt has been replaced by the indicative, albeit in a concessional phrase ("even admitting that").

But the concessive phrasing appears to be an affectation, for the anecdote that precedes it has already made clear that Sartre and the S.S. man he ridicules are equally certain of their ability to recognize "their own Jews," if not each other's Jews. Was Sartre aware of the perfect symmetry between himself proclaiming that "any Frenchman would have recognized him as Jewish" and the S.S. man who claimed he "could tell one from a hundred meters away"? Another noteworthy thing about the anecdote (is it an *histoire juive,* a Jewish joke?) is that Sartre appears to have a certain trouble deciding whether his friend is a Jew or an Israelite, with or without a capital "i." This trouble occurs often in the book, and in several cases a sudden "Israelite" appears after a series of "Jews," all referring to the same person. Until recently in France, "Israelite" was the polite way of referring to French Jews (especially as opposed to Eastern European Jews), and upper-middle-class Jews preferred that nomination. Since Sartre's point in this book was precisely that Jews should not be ashamed of their Jewishness, it would have been logical for him to use only "Juif" (today, most French Jews prefer that term). Curiously, it is his occasional use of the euphemism that strikes one as jarring, indicating unease. In this instance, after some wavering he finally chooses "israelite" and follows it with a mention of his friend's "race" (without quotation marks).

Now at the Commissariat Général aux Questions Juives, they also had some uncertainty on the point of Israelite versus Jew. So much so that in September 1942, Darquier sent out a circular to his staff: Jews were not to be called Israelites, because that would designate them as a religion, not a race. But since they were a race, they had to be referred to as *Juifs.* The word *israélite* was to be used exclusively as an adjective referring to religion, as in *la confession israélite* or *le culte israélite.*[21] Sartre, less consistent, uses "israelite" but associates it with "race."

Why bring Darquier and his racist nonsense back into this discussion?

Because I cannot help hearing an echo in Sartre's discourse, almost as if he were in dialogue with Darquier—or with the "expert" Dr. Montandon, director of the Institute for the Study of Jewish and Ethno-Racial Questions. Shortly after taking up his post in 1943, Montandon defined the first aim of the Institute as "the study of questions relating to peoples and races and, particularly in the spiritual, social, political and economic realms, the investigation of the field of activity of persons belonging to the people of Jewish race in France and in the world."[22] Sartre, on the contrary, insists that the "physical traits" of the "Jewish race" are not linked to character traits; therefore, we can conclude that he was repudiating Montandon's kind of "ethno-racial" science. Yet, his very use of the term "Jewish race" in a pseudo-scientific sense and his association of it with physical characteristics that "can be recognized by any Frenchman"—characteristics, furthermore, that correspond almost exactly to Montandon's enumeration of the traits of the "Jewish racial type"—hooked nose, protruding ears, thick lips—strike me as troubling.[23] It is as if he were saying to Montandon: "All right, I accept your notions about their physical characteristics; but you're quite wrong if you think I'll go any further. Character traits? Ah ça alors, non!"

The problem is, he has gone too far already. Edith Thomas, a left-wing writer who was roughly the same age as Sartre, noted in her diary in June 1942: "The wearing of the Jewish star has the virtue of proving to us that there is no such thing as the Jewish race; only one Jew in ten has the classical type that people attribute to them and that is also found, even much more so, among Spaniards and Arabs. . . . The Jews are therefore not *a* race."[24] Sartre, by admitting that all Jews "have some physical traits in common," has ventured down a slippery slope. And this is only the beginning: he will slip much further. I am convinced, incidentally, that he was unaware of where his words were leading him. But that is no reason to stop tracking them—on the contrary, it is the most interesting reason for doing so. I offer, briefly, a few more items from his "race track."

After the above passage, the word race is discussed explicitly one more time, in a complicated maneuver that shows Sartre again engaging with the anti-Semite's discourse, again apparently repudiating it but also echoing it in a troubling way:

Cette communauté juive qui n'est basée ni sur la nation, ni sur la terre, ni sur la religion, du moins dans la France contemporaine, ni sur les intérêts matériels, mais sur une identité de situation, pourrait être un lien véritablement *spirituel* d'affection, de culture et d'entraide. Mais ses ennemis aussitôt diront qu'elle est ethnique et lui-même [le Juif], fort embarrassé, pour la désigner, usera peut-être du mot de race. Du coup, il donne raison à l'antisémite: "Vous voyez bien qu'il y a une race juive, ils le reconnaissent eux-mêmes et d'ailleurs s'assemblent partout." Et, en effet, si les Juifs veulent puiser dans cette communauté une fierté légitime, comme ils ne peuvent s'enorgueillir, ni d'une oeuvre collective spécifiquement juive, ni d'une civilisation proprement israélite, ni d'un mysticisme commun, il faudra bien pour finir qu'ils exaltent des qualités raciales. Ainsi l'antisémite gagne à tous les coups (103).

(This Jewish community which is based not on nation, land, religion—at least not in contemporary France—or material interests, but only on an identity of situation, might indeed be a true *spiritual* bond of affection, of culture, and of mutual aid. But its enemies will immediately say that it is ethnic, and he [the Jew] himself, at a loss how to designate it, will perhaps use the word *race*. With that, he justifies the anti-Semite: "You see, there is such a thing as a Jewish race, they themselves recognize it, and besides, they stick together everywhere." And, in fact, if the Jews want to draw a legitimate pride from this community, they must indeed end up by exalting racial qualities, since they cannot take pride in any collective work that is specifically Jewish, or in a civilization properly Israelite, or in a common mysticism. Thus the anti-Semite wins on all counts.)[25]

Besides the appalling ignorance Sartre displays here about Jewish history and about specifically Jewish contributions to culture (it appears that he has never heard of the Hebrew Bible or the Kabbalah, for starters), the most remarkable thing about this passage is its suggestion that the Jews' own racism is what provokes the blame of the anti-Semite, whose words Sartre proceeds to quote: "You see, there is such a thing as the Jewish race, they themselves recognize it, they set themselves apart." Then, to top things off, Sartre *seconds* the anti-Semite: since the Jews have nothing to be proud of, "they must indeed end up by exalting racial qualities. . . . Thus the anti-Semite wins on all counts." But the anti-Semite "wins" here only because Sartre agrees with him—agrees with him about the Jews' lack of history and cultural achievement, and agrees with him that the Jews themselves are racists. It is worth recalling that the theme of "Jewish racism"—with its corollaries, Jewish arrogance and Jewish power—was a commonplace of anti-Semitic propaganda in the 1930's. Thus, the front page of *La France enchaîné*, "Organe du Rassemblement Antijuif de France" (headed by Darquier), carried this banner headline in its issue of April 19, 1938: "L'U-NION SACREE S'IMPOSE contre le Racisme Juif!" ("A Holy Alliance Must Oppose Jewish Racism!").[26] Anti-Semites from Brasillach to Rebatet harped on the "clannishness" of Jews, their refusal to mix with others. Sartre *repeats* the anti-Semitic slogan about "Jewish racism" even as he apparently deplores it.

Note that in this passage, Sartre appears to take his distance from the idea of a "Jewish race," since he has the anti-Semite say: "You see, there is such a thing as a Jewish race," as if addressing someone who contested that notion. Yet—and this is my next item on the list—after this passage I count six explicit uses of the word "race" by Sartre himself, in his own name and without quotation marks, referring to the Jews.[27] This is not counting several other instances where he discusses "Jewish racial traits" without actually using the word "race." For example, in the following extraordinary passage, where he not only offers us his final definition of "ethnic traits," but tells us another anecdote that functions as a fully fledged *histoire juive*:

> Quand les Juifs sont entre eux, en effet, chacun d'eux n'est, pour les autres et, par suite, pour lui-même, rien de plus qu'un homme. Ce qui le prouverait, si c'est nécessaire, c'est que, très souvent, les membres d'une même famille ne perçoivent pas les caractères ethniques de leurs parents (par caractères ethniques nous entendons ici les données biologiques héréditaires que nous avons acceptées comme incontestables). Je connaissais une dame juive, dont le fils, vers 1934, était contraint par sa situation de faire certains voyages d'affaires en Allemagne nazie. Ce fils présentait les caractères typiques de l'Israélite français: nez recourbé, écartement des oreilles, etc., mais comme on s'inquiétait de son sort, pendant une de ses absences, sa mère répondit: "Oh! je suis bien tranquille, il n'a absolument pas l'air juif." (123–4).

> (When Jews are among themselves, in effect, each one is, for the others and consequently for himself, nothing more than a man. What would prove this, if it were necessary, is that very often members of the same family do not perceive the ethnic characteristics of their relatives (by ethnic characteristics, I mean here the hereditary biological givens which we have accepted as incontestable). I knew a Jewish lady whose son had to make some business trips into Nazi Germany around 1934. This son had the typical characteristics of the French Israelite—hooked nose, protruding ears, etc.—but when we expressed anxiety about what might happen to him during one of his absences, his mother replied: "Oh, I am not worried; he absolutely does not look Jewish.")[28]

I want to laugh at the joke, but in another way I want to cry. Note how Sartre has slipped, here, from the earlier concessive construction ("even admitting that all Jews have certain physical traits in common") to pseudo-scientific affirmation, and from statistical probability ("certain physical configurations that one encounters more frequently among Jews") to ethnic essence: "the hereditary biological givens that we have accepted as incontestable." *Who* has accepted these "givens" as incontestable? The fact is, by 1946 very few anthropologists believed in the possibility of defining an ethnic group, or even a race (for the two are not, despite what Sartre seemed to believe, synonymous) in terms of "hereditary biological givens." And absolutely no reputable anthropologist, or any other scientist, believed in the existence of a "Jewish race." That idea had been dismissed, by Ernest Renan and others, as early as the 1890's. By the 1940's, only Nazi theorists of "racial hygiene" and "ethno-racial experts" like Dr. Montandon believed that nonsense.[29] Which leaves one wondering, truly wondering, who Sartre's "we" were. . . .

Perhaps we find an answer twenty pages later: "It is known [*On sait*] in effect that the only ethnic characteristics of the Jew are physical. The anti-Semite has seized upon this fact and transformed it into a myth: he claims to detect his enemy by a mere glance."[30] Sartre, too, can detect a "French Israelite" at a glance. Incidentally, his use of the presuppositional *on sait* and *nous savons* ("we know") in these pages deserves a whole separate analysis, as does his use of pronouns in general. Barbara Johnson has noted that an author "can proclaim 'I am this'; but when the image is repeated as 'you are that,' it changes completely. The content of the image may be the same, but its interpersonal use is different."[31] In the discursive system of *Réflexions sur la question juive*, Sartre never even says "You are that" to the Jew. Instead, he addresses an impersonal *on* or a *nous* and says "*He* is that," pointing to the Jew. Independently of the content of his statements (which, as it happens, is already deplorable), his systematic opposition of *on* and *nous* ("we French") to *il* (the Jew) reproduces on the linguistic level the opposition between Frenchmen and Jews that was (and is) a hallmark of racist anti-Semitic ideology.

The last, and perhaps most disturbing, item on Sartre's "race-track": despite his earlier insistence that Jewish "ethnic traits" were only physical, not moral or psychological or other, Sartre spends a large part of this chapter outlining the psychological, intellectual, moral, and economic character-istics of the "inauthentic" Jew, who turns out to be none other than "the Jew" *tout court*. Once again, Sartre *thinks* he is defending the Jew against the anti-Semite's myth, but actually reinforces the myth. The Jew whose por-trait he draws is hyper-self-conscious and introspective, has perverse sexual tastes, is tactless and anxious, loves money, and has an inordinate taste for abstraction and rationalism. Bergson's concept of intuition, according to Sartre, cannot "rightfully" (*à bon droit*) be called irrationalist, the way Kierkegaard's or Novalis's thought can; it is, rather, simply rationalism by another name—a "*debaptized* rationalism" (*un rationalisme débaptisé*)[32] Is there any clearer way of saying that Bergson's is a "Jewish philosophy"?

Almost invariably, Sartre begins with an *on dit* ("it is said") that sums up a stereotyped trait—and then, instead of contesting "what is said," he pro-ceeds to *explain* it as the result of a choice by the "inauthentic" Jew. Thus, in the matter of money: "The Jew loves money, it is said. . . . In truth, if the Jew loves money, it is not because he has a peculiar taste for copper or gold coins or for bills."[33] No, it's because money is more "abstract" than land or real estate. Conclusion, after three pages of further explanations: "One sees all the background factors involved in the Jew's taste for money" (*On voit tous les arrière-plans que comporte le goût du Juif pour l'argent*), where it is no longer an unidentified, presumably anti-Semitic *on* who says that the Jew loves money, but Sartre himself.[34]

An even quicker switch occurs in the discussion of Jewish anxiety: "We shall content ourselves in conclusion with indicating in broad strokes what is called [*ce qu'on appelle*] Jewish anxiety. For Jews are often anxious. An Israelite is never sure of his position or of his possessions."[35] We are not dealing with a noble, metaphysical angst in the case of the Jew—it is simple material anxiety for possessions and home that Jews are gripped by, as Sartre "explains" them.[36]

Such are "les traits principaux de la sensibilité juive" (157, "the principal traits of Jewish sensibility"). It would seem that Montandon was right after all: "la race juive" is not only a set of physical traits, but a whole complex of character traits as well.

Some years ago, I saw a Charles Addams cartoon in *The New Yorker*: it showed a man in a barber's chair, looking in the mirror held up behind him by the barber. Actually, there was a whole series of mirrors one behind the other, with the man's bland face reflected in them—in all except one, where his face appeared transformed into that of a werewolf. I thought of that cartoon as I reread Sartre's book. In the beginning and the end, the mirror reflects Sartre the sincere enemy of anti-Semitism and generous defender of the Jews. Somewhere around the middle, the werewolf appears.

Conclusion, or, A Question of Reading

Given Sartre's genuine desire to combat anti-Semitism and defend the Jews (recall the ringing sentences of his final paragraph, so often quoted: "Not one Frenchman will be free so long as the Jews do not enjoy the fulness of their rights. Not one Frenchman will be secure so long as a single Jew—in France or *in the world at large*—can fear for his life"[37]), how can we explain the truly unfortunate "anti-Semite effect" produced by his text? And why did none of his French readers, at the time the book came out, notice this effect (or, if they noticed it, why didn't they say so)? Why, for that matter, did so few American readers notice it?

To the first question, there is an almost ridiculously simple, yet compelling answer; and there is a slightly more complicated one as well. The simple answer is that Sartre sounded like an anti-Semite when speaking about the Jews, because all he knew about them he learned from anti-Semites—in other words, he didn't do his homework. Consider the following exchange in his last interview with Benny Lévy, and notice Lévy's growing amazement. He begins by asking Sartre whether he has changed his mind about the Jews not having any history, and Sartre says yes, but he still doesn't know much about Jews and his not knowing Hebrew is a big obstacle; he certainly knew even less when he wrote *Réflexions sur la question juive*, he adds.

> B.L: But when you wrote your book surely you had put together some documentation?
> J.-P.S: No.
> B.L: What do you mean, no?
> J.-P.S: None. I wrote without any documentation, without reading one Jewish book.
> B.L: But how did you do it?
> J.-P.S: I wrote what I thought.
> B.L: But taking off from what?
> J.-P.S:Taking off from nothing, taking off from anti-Semitism, which I wanted to combat.[38]

"Taking off from anti-Semitism," is it surprising that Sartre's portrait of the Jew sounds anti-Semitic? It is the opposite that would be surprising.

The more complicated answer is that, like most Frenchmen during the war, Sartre was bombarded by anti-Semitic discourses in the press, on the radio, in newsreels, posters, not to mention ordinary conversations—before the war as well—with people like his stepfather or Simone de Beauvoir's parents, whose anti-Semitic views were quite strong; and that he "soaked it up" without even being aware of it. This is what Christian Delacampagne has called Sartre's being "a man of his time": "These fragments of antisemitism cannot appear as such to Jean-Paul Sartre himself because, in his youth, they constituted a normal opinion in his milieu, an opinion so normal that it was never questioned, and because it is very difficult to rid oneself of such opinions."[39] When you think about it, both answers make Sartre look bad. I don't know what to do about that.

Perhaps the more interesting question is the second one, about what readers have or have not noticed in Sartre's text. Given the conscious good intentions of Sartre's book, which appeared when he was at the height of his prestige as the leader of the new existentialist philosophy in France, it is understandable why none of his contemporary French readers noticed, or allowed themselves to notice, the text's disturbing underside. All the more so since, by the time the book appeared, the unambiguous first chapter, "Portrait de l'antisémite," had already been published in *Les Temps Modernes* and been greeted as a courageous gesture against a reviving anti-Semitism. (By late 1945 and 1946, anti-Semitism in France was visible again despite the postwar purges.) Still, one wonders: didn't Sartre's contemporary French readers, or at the very least his contemporary Jewish readers, catch any echoes of the Institute for the Study of Jewish and Ethno-Racial Questions? *Le Monde juif,* the monthly journal of the then recently founded Centre de la Documentation Juive Contemporaine, printed documents about Darquier's Commissariat Général aux Questions Juives in practically every issue throughout 1946. Yet, when Sartre's book came out, they published the most hyperbolically positive review of any I have read from that time, praising Sartre's courage, his greatness as a writer, and so on.[40]

It was not that Sartre's Jewish readers had forgotten the wartime propaganda about "la race juive" and "la question juive" when they read his book; on the contrary, they remembered them all to well, but Sartre's whole persona was too prestigious, and too strongly identified in their mind with a pro-Jewish stance, for them to hear the anti-Semitic echoes in his discourse. In other words, they were too close to the historical and intertextual context to "make the mistake" (that is what they would have called it, and undoubtedly that is what it would have been) of putting Sartre anywhere near the anti-Semites. I surmise that they noticed the problem with the "portrait of the Jew," were momentarily troubled, then turned their eyes to the more comfortingly negative portrait of the anti-Semite, and even of the "democrat" who would deny Jewish specificity.

This explanation, although plausible, does not help us much to understand why later admiring readers, even professional reader-scholars and critics, have refused to take a long, hard look at Sartre's representation of the Jew. I recently read a 200-page British thesis devoted to *Réflexions sur la question juive,* which does not once appear troubled: according to the author, Sartre "selects certain common anti-Semitic myths" only in order to demystify them.[41] It is very hard to rid oneself of idolatry, and for many of us Sartre was (continues to be) an idol. When I delivered a first version of this essay at a conference of twentieth-century French specialists at Dartmouth College (March 1994), and a month later in a public lecture at Yale University's French department, I was accused by a few indignant colleagues and graduate students, including some old friends, of having totally misunderstood Sartre's text—and furthermore, of having accused Sartre of "being an anti-Semite." (Others, it is true, congratulated me for having described their own reading experience).

As for the American reception of *Anti-Semite and Jew* at the time of its publication, the prestige and celebrity factor played a big role as well, for Sartre was as famous in the United States by 1948 (when the translation appeared) as he was in France. But that did not prevent some American Jewish critics from picking up the anti-Semitic echoes in his text. Thus Gustav Ichheiser in 1949 noted: "He overtly denounces anti-Semitism but unconsciously is not without sympathy with those values and sentiments which are at the bottom of what he denounces."[42] Harold Rosenberg, in a much longer article that same year, praised Sartre for his courageous action in a historical "moment of intense confusion" after the downfall of Nazism; but he went on to criticize Sartre sharply and extensively: "on the basis of his authentic-inauthentic conception, Sartre has consciously permitted himself to accept the anti-Semite's stereotype of the Jew."[43] Did Rosenberg know about the Commissariat Général aux Questions Juives and the Institut d'Etude des Questions Juives et Ethno-Raciales? Probably not. But he didn't have to, because their stereotypes and theories of the Jew were the same as those of Nazi or Nazi-inspired anti-Semites everywhere. Paradoxically, it was Rosenberg's distance from the specific French context that allowed him to see the similarities between Sartre's "portrait of the Jew" and the standard discourse of virulent anti-Semitism.

The same, I would say, was true of Elaine Marks, writing much later (in 1972). Her remark about Sartre being transformed into the anti-Semite he was attacking was based on her intuitive recognition of the anti-Semitic echoes in his text. What I have tried to do here is to study in detail how the "anti-Semite effect" was produced on the level of Sartre's language and rhetoric, and also to document the intertextual context from which his own discourse unfortunately "took off."

12

"I . . . AM. A": Addressing the Jewish Question in Joyce's Ulysses

STEVEN CONNOR

He thought that he thought that he was a jew whereas he knew that he knew that he knew that he was not.[1]

Opening the Question: How Jewish Is It?

It has not escaped the attention of many readers of *Ulysses* since its appearance in 1922 that its central character is Jewish. (As an agnostic, uncircumcised porcivore, Leopold Bloom is scarcely Jewish in any orthodox sense, but this is not really the point.) Nor has there been any shortage of critical studies of the Jewishness of Leopold Bloom and the treatment of Jewishness more generally in the text.[2] Given the unarguable centrality of Leopold Bloom and the question of his Jewishness in the novel, it would be astonishing if there were. But these studies have concentrated on limited and sometimes banal questions of narrative content, questions like the following. Is Leopold Bloom Jewish? If so, why is he? Is his Jewishness portrayed approvingly or otherwise? Is Stephen Dedalus anti-Semitic? If he is (or is not), is Joyce? Such studies tend, by asking so obsessively what is the Jew in *Ulysses* to focus on the question of how well the Jew comes *out* of *Ulysses*, which is to say, they tend to be drawn into a dichotomous mode of thinking that separates Jewishness and textuality from the outset. The focus on the Jew as a mere constituent of the book inhibits an understanding of Jewishness as constitutive of it.

The purpose of this essay is to lift that inhibition a bit, by looking at the Jew *in* the text of *Ulysses* in parallel with the Jewishness *of* the text of *Ulysses*. This is itself not without precedents, of course. Ira Nadel's erudite and humane book *Joyce and the Jews* (1989) suggests that there may be a close relationship between the proliferating form of *Ulysses* and *Finnegans Wake* and the tradition of open and evolving commentary in Judaism. Even here, though, we see a union predicated on an original cut or dichotomy: the argument about the affinity of Joycean and rabbinical textual modes works by bringing together areas that are held in principle to be distinct or distinguishable. I want to explore what might be called the transferential Jewishness of *Ulysses*, in which Jewishness and textuality do not simply compound or swap places, but themselves undergo processes of mutation that result from partial identifications, projections, and acknowledgments of the other that compromise the self-sufficiency of the self.

I aim, in fact, to detect a preoccupation with Jewishness in the form and force of Joyce's preoccupation with discourse itself in *Ulysses*. In order to do this, I will focus on one particular dimension of discourse (by which I mean simply language in its concrete social use or occasion), namely *address*. I have two reasons for wanting to focus in this way. Firstly, it will become evident that the concern with national or cultural identity in the novel, a concern that manifests itself particularly, of course, with the relations between Irishness and Jewishness, is focused interestingly in a number of occasions or situations in which the addressive function of language—speaking, calling, appealing *to* certain persons—is to the fore. I will suggest that recognizing and acknowledging cultural identity is in *Ulysses* very often a matter of being summoned into it by certain kinds of address, especially public address, which may be inviting or (as is more usually the case in *Ulysses*) hostile.

Secondly, the focus on addressivity may allow me to bring to bear on the question of *Ulysses*'s Jewishness a particular preoccupation of the ethical philosophy elaborated by the principal Jewish philosophers of the twentieth century, Martin Buber and Emmanuel Levinas—the concern with the invocation or implication of the other in every kind of speech or utterance. In alluding to the "philosophy of dialogue" in Buber's work, Michael Theunissen points up the importance of the linguistic relation in the ethical thinking exemplified in and developed beyond the work of Buber.[3] Central to Buber's philosophy of the "I-Thou" is the need to prevent the original openness of a speech directed toward an autonomous other from deteriorating into the closure of a speech-relation in which the other is reduced to an object of representation. Speaking *to* another preserves a primordial relatedness between beings (the "I-Thou") that speaking *of* another shrinks to a relation between subject and object (the "I-It").[4] Emmanuel Levinas borrows extensively from Buber's account of the I-Thou relation, agreeing that "what is important is not thinking *about* the other, even *as* an other, but of directly confronting it and of saying Thou to it,"[5] and develops from it a theory of the ethical force of what he calls "vocativity" in discourse. But for Levinas, Buber actually fails to maintain the radical openness of the "I-Thou" relation he describes, since his emphasis on responsiveness and dialogue establishes the possibility of a completed and symmetrical relationship between two subjectivities conceived as separate and autonomous. This in turn implies the possibility of a side-by-side equivalence or collectivity, which Levinas insists is a reduction of the radical openness and asymmetry of the ethical relation between the self and the other.

One may reasonably ask at this point what this thematic of pure addressivity can have to do with "the Jew" on the one hand and "the text" on the other. For Levinas's demand for such pure addressivity seems to condemn in advance any attempt to name, describe, or instance the addressive relation. The problem, as Jean-François Lyotard has described it in *The Differend* (1984), is how to preserve the authenticity of speaking *to* the other person in a text that tends always to speak *of* that other (or, at best, speak of speaking to that other). Such writing will appear to have betrayed what Levinas and Lyotard agree in seeing as the Judaic instance of ethical address into the persecution of commentary, "the regimen of descriptives . . . the temptation of knowledge."[6] But may it not also be, or under circumstances become, a writing that acknowledges this necessary persecution, testifies in some wise to what commentary and thematization reduce?

I propose to consider in detail a number of passages from *Ulysses* that illustrate the ways in which discursive address bears on questions of national and ethnic belonging, along with the ways in which the figure of the Jew in turn belongs to such questions.

In the Heart of the Hibernian Metropolis (96; 7:1–2)

The first passage occurs toward the end of the "Aeolus" chapter of the novel. Leopold Bloom and Stephen Dedalus are both called upon to visit the offices of the *Freeman's Journal,* Bloom to place an advertisement and Stephen to try to persuade the paper to print a letter from his employer about foot and mouth disease in cattle. In the course of the chapter, both Bloom and Stephen encounter the force of political address. Bloom enters the office in the middle of a discussion between Simon Dedalus, Ned Lambert, and 'professor' MacHugh of a speech given the evening before by Dan Dawson, and reported in the newspaper of June 16. As so often in the novel, Bloom is in transit between states and places, overhearing a nationalist message that is not for him:

– What is it? Mr Bloom asked.
– A recently discovered fragment of Cicero, professor MacHugh answered with pomp of tone. *Our lovely land . . .*
– Whose land? Mr Bloom said simply.
– Most pertinent question, the professor said between his chews. With an accent on the whose. (102–03; 7:271–5)

Here in Bloom's question "Whose land?" is an early instance of a question asked, in different modalities, by and of different characters throughout *Ulysses.* The varieties of this question, and the responses to it, establish the correlation of addressivity and national belonging. The question has been asked about Bloom by Davy Byrne earlier in the day: "What is this he is?" (145; 8:939); the answer, from his interlocutor Nosey Flynn, is that "He's in the craft" (145; 8:960), by which he means that Bloom is a freemason (Flynn is only partly right, for though Bloom has been a freemason he is no longer). However, the tone and nature of Flynn's remarks make it clear that an allusion is also intended to Bloom's Jewishness. The question recurs in pointed form in the Citizen's threatening enquiry of Bloom in "Cyclops," "What is your nation, if I may ask?" (272; 12:1430), and is renewed a little later by Ned Lambert's enquiry after Bloom has momentarily left Barney Kiernan's bar: "Is he a jew or a gentile or a Holy Roman or a swaddler or what the hell is he? . . . Or who is he?" (276; 12:1631–2). There are many forms of the demand on Bloom to say who or what he is in the accusatory cacophony of "Circe": the First Watch asks him "Come. Name and address" (357; 15:718), causing him to pretend to be the "other" Bloom in the book, the dental surgeon; the ghost of his father asks him "Are you not my son Leopold, the grandson of Leopold? Are you not my dear son Leopold who left the house of his father and left the god of his fathers Abraham and Jacob?" (357; 15:260–62); during his hallucination of becoming a civic hero in charge of the New Bloomusalem in Ireland an anonymous voice demands of him, "Bloom, are you the Messiah ben Joseph or ben David?" (403; 15:1834); and the bawd's fan coos the seductive enquiry "Is me her was you dreamed before? Was then she him you us since knew? Am all them and the same now me?" (430; 15:2768–9). The suspicion and uncertainty regarding Bloom's personal and cultural identity seem to be summarized in the following question and answer from the "Ithaca" chapter:

> What, reduced to their simplest reciprocal form, were Bloom's thoughts about Stephen's thoughts about Bloom and about Stephen's thoughts about Bloom's thoughts about Stephen?
> He thought that he thought that he was a jew whereas he knew that he knew that he knew that he was not. (558; 17:527–31).

In his confrontation with the Citizen in the "Cyclops" chapter, Bloom is to lay unequivocal claim to being Irish. In the newspaper office, however, his innocent posing of the question "Whose land?" seems to emphasize the uncertainty of national and racial definitions. It also associates the naming of such identity with the public acts of address that attempt to call a country and its people into community.

Bloom's encounter with nationalist oratory looks forward to the more complex encounter which Stephen undergoes later on in the "Aeolus" chapter, after Bloom has absented himself to check some details of the advertisement he wishes to place. The conversation turns to fine examples of Irish oratory, and professor MacHugh begins to quote from memory a particular example. The speech he quotes—or reconstructs, since no accurate transcription of it survives—was given during the course of a debate about the question of reviving the Irish language that took place at Trinity College Historical Society on October 24, 1901. After a speech made by the conservative Justice Gerald Fitzgibbon, which appealed to the youth of Ireland not to neglect the riches of English culture, a barrister and journalist, John F. Taylor, delivered an impromptu reply, in which he compared the Irish audience to the Jewish people in exile and bondage in Egypt, and Fitzgibbon to an Egyptian high priest demanding arrogantly "*Why will you jews not accept our culture, our religion and our language?*" (117; 7:845). The structure of appropriation in this scene is complex. MacHugh quotes as if from memory the words of John F. Taylor (himself allegedly speaking without notes), which themselves are a parodic citation of the words of Fitzgibbon to which he has just been listening, for which Taylor constructs a parallel between "*the remarks addressed to the youth of Ireland a moment since by my learned friend*" and "*the speech of some highpriest of that land addressed to the youthful Moses*" (116–17; 7:829–30, 832–3). In his own reply, Taylor also perhaps identifies himself with the youthful Moses, who not only hears but also seems to rise to answer the high priest, such that Taylor's parodic seizure of Fitzgibbon's address to the Irish people is itself an imitation of an imaginary address by Moses to his Jewish people: "*And it seemed to me that I heard the voice of that Egyptian highpriest raised in a tone of like haughtiness and like pride. I heard his words and their meaning was revealed to me*" (117; 7:838–40). We move therefore from the simple structure of recapitulated address that is shown in the diagram below (in which the arrow shows the direction of address and the square brackets the recapitulation):

$$\left.\begin{array}{l} \text{Fitzgibbon} \rightarrow \text{Irish youth} \\ \text{highpriest} \rightarrow \text{Jewish people} \end{array}\right]$$

to something like the following stratified citation:

$$\left.\begin{array}{l} \text{Taylor} \rightarrow \text{Irish youth} \\ \text{Moses} \rightarrow \text{Jewish people} \\ \text{highpriest} \rightarrow \text{Jewish people} \\ \text{Fitzgibbon} \rightarrow \text{Irish youth} \end{array}\right]$$

If Taylor's speech already embodies a complex folding over of address and citation in its original performance, its complexities increase when it is taken up by MacHugh. For now its oratorical addressees, the debating society audience in Trinity, are no longer physically present. Their place is taken, or mistaken, by the audience in the newspaper office—consisting at this point, if I have counted right, of J. J. O'Molloy, Matt Lenehan, Myles Crawford, Mr. O'Madden Burke, and Stephen Dedalus. Stephen is a particularly significant member of the party, for he seems to be meant to occupy the place of the youthful Moses invoked by John F. Taylor. The speech calls to him to pledge himself to public, political utterance: seeing MacHugh limbering up, he thinks "Noble words coming. Look out. Could you try your hand at it yourself?" (117; 7:836–7). But MacHugh's rendition of the speech goes on to characterize Moses' resistance to the high priest's impersonal address, in terms which on the one hand draw Stephen into national and political identification and on the other speak of and to his desire to be delivered from the inauthentic servitude of national belonging. MacHugh's evocation of Taylor's evocation of the Jews' release from bondage stands—according to the terms of the analogy between Parnell and Moses which was well established by the end of the nineteenth century in Irish politics—for the Irish release from British domination; but it is available to Stephen as an evocation of his own release from the bondage of politics as such. So Stephen cannot help but be drawn into the address of MacHugh/Taylor's speech, insofar as he is drawn to identify himself as Moses, the lawgiver against the law. To refuse the address as Moses is actually to accept it insofar as it replicates Moses' own refusal of the high priest's assimilating address:

> But, ladies and gentlemen, had the youthful Moses listened to and accepted that view of life, had he bowed his head and bowed his will and bowed his spirit before that arrogant admonition he would never have brought the chosen people out of their house of bondage, nor followed the pillar of the cloud by day. He would never have spoken with the Eternal amid lightnings on Sinai's mountaintop, nor ever have come down with the light of inspiration shining in his countenance and bearing in his arms the tables of the law, graven in the language of the outlaw. (117; 7:862–9)

Voice, oratory, address are here all powerfully identified with the forging of nationhood in discourse. Thinking a few moments later of the nineteenth-century nationalist leader Daniel O'Connell, Stephen says to himself, "A people sheltered within his voice" (118; 7:882). He has himself been invited a few moments earlier to contribute something to the paper by its editor, who urges him to the same act of inclusive address: "Give them something with a bite in it. Put us all into it, damn its soul" (111; 7:621). Addressivity seems to summon and itself be summoned by what one of the mock headlines in the chapter calls the "Omnium Gatherum" of the different professions of Dublin—law, scholarship, literature, journalism, and the turf. Significantly, however, Bloom, standing for "the gentle art of advertisement" (111; 7:608), is absent from the company at this point. This detail is part of a more general association between Bloom's occupation as advertising canvaser and the indirectness of written or technological communication. (Bloom is in fact on the telephone for much of the "Aeolus" chapter.) In *Ulysses*, we might say, speech is to writing as address is to advertisement. But this seems to point to a certain intrinsic incompleteness of the vocative structure, which operates through a relay of voices and lines of address which can be (must be) endlessly renewed, but can never be summed into total simultaneity. Stephen responds to the call of the discursive nation with characteristic scepticism and depression, thinking of O'Connell's words at the great assemblies of the past "howled and scattered to the four winds" and reduced to the condition of "Dead noise" (118; 7:881–2).

So the dynamics of substitution, relay, and transmission involved in the pseudo-Mosaic address of this passage cannot very plausibly stand as an example or allegory of the ethical addressivity on which so much depends for Levinas and which he is inclined to identify as a Judaic counterforce to the analytical and referential language of the Greeks. This is so precisely because the passage constitutes a kind of case study or thematization of addressivity and its conditions. The passage is, so to speak, the demonstration of the ethical call of address decaying into demonstrability. At each point in the addressive relay, in which a previous act of address is quoted and imitated, the immediacy of what Levinas calls the *Saying* is reified into a *Said*, as it becomes in turn the content of a subsequent Saying. The call which Stephen finds oppressive is a call that coerces a community, flattening this dislocated rhythm of transmission into the mythical instantaneity of what has been described as the "enunciative present" of the nation.[7] In a simple sense, the passage shows the stretching and diffusion of the act of national convocation by Stephen's reluctance to respond to the address, which removes him metaphorically from the imaginary "omnium gatherum," just as Bloom is held apart from it by his physical absence. But within that critical demonstration of the limits of addressivity in the passage, there is also a gesture toward a kind of calling that is not wholly assimilable to nationalism. It is, so to speak, the call of discursivity itself, even, perhaps, a certain call of discourse *to* itself, that nevertheless forces the acknowledgment of the "you," bending the accusative case into vocativity. The discomfort experienced by Stephen is in part a discomfort at the capacity of discourse to become a sort of pure "you-saying."

Again: this movement of "you-saying" is neither demonstrable in nor isolatable from the passage, which, as referential language, can present at most a series of muffled aftershocks of vocative immediacy. But the movement is perhaps detectible in this very rhythm of lapse, or abatement of vocativity, in the conjugation of the different addresses and the interpolations of their different hearers, as well as in the intensity with which the passage renews its calls for attention. The structure of address that would compress the present and the past into the homogeneity of "a people" is loosened and diffused by the renewing force of this addressivity, which neither proceeds from nor precipitates definitive agents, objects, contents, or purposes.

This seems to be confirmed by the fact that, when he made a gramophone recording from *Ulysses* in 1924, Joyce chose this very episode in the newspaper office to read.[8] There is something very odd about such a gesture. The artist who had so assiduously proclaimed and practised the art and ethic of authorial self-effacement is here found giving (single) voice to his novel and giving his novel a single voice, within a passage that appears crassly to brandish the oratorical authority of speech. The fact that Joyce's reading isolates the quoted speech from the ironic frameworks that partly give it the lie in MacHugh's recitation seems only to emphasize even more this capacity of speech to give itself the law. But this authoritative gesture is canceled by the very technology of the gramophone, which preserves the immediacy and integrity of the reading that speaks in the name of the text only at the cost of multiplying to infinity the possibilities of its addressive aim and destination.

Perhaps, then, the "Jewishiness" of Joyce's writing in *Ulysses* should be identified, not in any positive qualities of the writing, so much as in its vigilant disinclination to curtail the addressive force of narrative discourse? It will help me in considering this possibility to take a closer look at the effects of addressivity as they combine with some more familiar "Jewish" themes of dispossession, dispersal, and self-division in the presentation of Leopold Bloom.

Strangers in the House

Leopold Bloom has throughout his day to undergo and survive a number of experiences of assimilatory appeal equivalent to that experienced by Stephen in "Aeolus." Perhaps the most significant of these is the effect on him of Ben Dollard's rendition of the Irish republican ballad "The Croppy Boy" in the bar of the Ormond hotel. Like Dedalus, Bloom is both called and excluded by the act of address constituted by the song, and indeed by the siren voices of the music that he hears throughout the chapter. For Bloom, though, the pull is not that of nationalist oratory but of sentimental orality. This is a pull exercised not just by human agents but by impersonal objects, which are here endowed with uncanny powers of utterance. Bloom first encounters this phenomenon at the beginning of the "Aeolus" chapter as he hears the sound of paper delivered from the printing press and thinks to himself "Doing its level best to speak . . . Everything speaks in its own way" (100; 7:275–6). In "Sirens," we begin to approach the condition of

general addressivity that will characterize the "Circe" chapter. The musical-
ization of the style and setting both orchestrates the lines of address in the
chapter, and disorganizes them. The chapter merges and coordinates the
laughter of the barmaids, the conversation of the diners, the words of
Martha Clifford's letter to Bloom, along with Bloom's attempted reply, and
the sounds of Blazes Boylan's progress through the city en route to his
afternoon tryst with Molly Bloom in Eccles Street; even the sound of a tun-
ing-fork is given addressive purpose, for it is heard as "a call . . . long in
dying . . . A call again . . . Longer in dying fall" (217; 11:313–16). The tech-
nique of the chapter charms inanimate noise into vocality and articulate
utterance, as in the shell that Lydia Douce has brought back from holiday,
and the telling reference to a contemporary popular song that it prompts:
"Wonderful really. So distinct. Again, George Lidwell held its murmur,
hearing: then laid it by, gently. – What are the wild waves saying? he asked
her, smiled" (231; 11:947–9). The body too is wakened into address, as
when Bloom thinks of sending a ventriloquial appeal to one of the barmaids:

Say something. Make her hear. With look to look. Songs without words . . .
Ventriloquise. My lips closed. Think in my stom. What?
Will? You? I. Want. You. To. (234; 11:1091, 1095–6)

or when he receives a musical message from his own inner organs: "all of a
soft sudden wee little wee little pipy wind. Pwee! A wee little wind piped
eeee. In Bloom's little wee" (237; 11:11201–3).

The climax of the chapter comes with the singing of "The Croppy
Boy," which converges with the imagined scene of Boylan's arrival at
Bloom's front door. Like the Odysseus who has himself bound to the mast
so that he can listen in enforced safety to the voices of the sirens, Bloom
both succumbs to and refuses its call to affective and political solidarity
attempted by the ballad. Written by William B. McBurney, "The Croppy
Boy" tells the story of a young lad involved in the Wexford uprising in
1798. He goes to the house of a priest to confess, but the priest he tells of
his intention to join the uprising turns out to be a British soldier in disguise, and the croppy boy is arrested and hanged. Bloom appears to be
made uncomfortable by the mingling of sentimental pity and political rage
brought about by the song and rises to leave just as it comes to an end. As
he passes out of the dining room and bar, Bloom, like Stephen listening to
MacHugh's oratory, is both seduced by the song's address and excluded by
the closed emotional solidarity that it creates. The passage describing
Bloom taking his leave runs together allusions to domicile, displacement,
and treachery, Bloom associating the betrayal of the croppy boy with his
own betrayal in his own house:

With a cock with a carra.

Tap. Tap. Tap.

I hold this house. Amen. He gnashed in fury. Traitors swing. (235; 11:1118–20)

The "I" of the phrase "I hold this house" is indeterminate; it embodies the voice of the British yeoman captain in the song, who tells the boy that "We hold his [the priest's] house for our Lord and King," and also speaks for Blazes Boylan, who by now perhaps has taken possession of Bloom's house. But it also gives utterance to the sense of possession and identity established within the circle of the song's address in the Ormond bar. The equivalence of house and country is reinforced throughout *Ulysses*, though perhaps nowhere more emphatically than in the passage in the "Cyclops" chapter, which shows Bloom discussing the details of the advertisement he has been trying to place all day for his client Alexander Keyes while the anti-Semitic violence of the Citizen grows more explicit: "We want no more strangers in our house" (265; 12:1050–51), he growls, in obvious counter-point to the "House of Keyes" advertising motif on which Bloom has been working (and, like Stephen, Bloom has left home without his doorkey). The song of "The Croppy Boy" calls for a lachrymose immersion of the self in a sentimental melancholy: "The voice of the mournful chanter called to dolorous prayer . . . Pray for him, prayed the bass of Dollard. You who hear in peace" (235; 11:1132–41). Bloom, again overhearing rather than hearing this address, is stimulated to a different and more private melancholy about his own houselessness. He is also momentarily transformed into the croppy boy himself, the potential victim of the bullying bonhomie that fills the bar: "Scaring eavesdropping boots croppy bootsboy Bloom in the Ormond hallway heard the growls and roars of bravo, fat backslapping, their boots all treading, boots not the boots the boy" (235; 11:1142–4). In this identification with the croppy boy, who calls himself "a stranger *bouchal* [boy]," Bloom is both inside and outside the house of national belonging, as he stands literally in the hallway of the Ormond bar (just as earlier he shuttles in and out of the newspaper office). The song resembles Taylor's speech in "Aeolus" in that, failing to include Bloom, it defines, or confines, him as what it *excludes*. It is impossible to avoid the address of speech and song, since to decline or fail to be addressed is to be caught in or called to the position of non-addressee that its reflexive address defines.

It is, in fact, in the street that Bloom eventually delivers his response to the sentimental nationalism that has been gathering around him through-out the chapter. Bloom sees the last words of the Irish republican leader Robert Emmet pictured in a shop window; Emmet's exalted address is counterpointed with the inglorious fart that Bloom elaborately contrives in the cadenza-like final words of the chapter:

Seabloom, greaseabloom viewed last words. Softly. *When my country takes her place among.*

Prrprr.

Must be the bur.

Fff! Oo. Rrpr.

Nations of the earth. No-one behind. She's passed. *Then and not till then.* Tram kran kran kran. Good oppor. Coming. Krandlkrankran. I'm sure it's the burgund. Yes. One, two. *Let my epitaph be.* Kraaaaaa. *Written. I have.*

Pprrpffrrppffff.

Done. (238–9; 11:1284–94)

Robert Emmet's final words look toward and in a sense have as their addressee a still undelivered future of full nationhood. Until that time, the words announce, they will remain unheard, even, in the sense that they are themselves the epitaph of which they speak, unuttered. As though in acknowlegment of the analogy between the Irish and Jewish experience of being a people without a nation, Bloom takes possession of these wandering, ghostly words, but refuses their seductive, sepulchral allure. Bloom's musicocorporeal answer and accompaniment to Emmet's words both gives them a final resting place and slackens the fixating force of their address, drawing the anxious intransitivity of the undelivered message of nationhood into a humane circuit of bodily-discursive exchange.

As *Ulysses* proceeds, the focus on addressivity is intensified and the occasions for such interferences in lines of address proliferate, until they reach a climax in the "Circe" episode in the brothel district of Dublin. This chapter is caught between two discursive extremes. One one side, the dramatic mode of the chapter involves a remorseless externalization, in which it seems that nothing can be thought, remembered, dreamt, or alluded to without being embodied in visible and objective form. But this objectification is also a summoning into speech. Objects, animals, and abstract ideas—a clock, a cap, a hobgoblin, a gramophone, a gasjet, a doorhandle, a retriever, a hen, bedsprings, bells, kisses, "beatitudes," "halcyon days," even "the end of the world"—are all given lines to speak in "Circe," thus literalizing Bloom's earlier insight in the printing room into the inanimate world's aspiration to speech. This creates a network of addressivity in the chapter, in which events, ideas, and objects decline to settle for the ignominious condition of a mere referent, energetically refusing to be merely spoken *of.* As a result, there are no objects of discourse in this chapter, but only subjects of discourse, restlessly surging up into speech in a primary language of what we might call "expellation."[9]

It is for this reason, perhaps, that the chapter is so concerned with the vulnerability of both Stephen and Bloom to various kinds of accusatory address, and gives so many opportunities for both characters to develop multiple modes of responsive address on their own account. Much of the early part of the chapter is taken up with Bloom's fantasy of bringing about "the new Bloomusalem in the Nova Hibernia of the future" (395; 15:1544–5), arising no doubt in compensation for his own sense of social exclusion throughout the day, and in response to the Citizen's sneering question in "Cyclops," "Are you talking about the new Jerusalem?" (273; 12:1473). The whole sequence mingles self-aggrandisement and the wish for acceptance with a certain hostility and paranoid fear of being shown to be an impostor. Bloom grandiloquently announces "a new era," consisting of

> New worlds for old. Union of all, jew, moslem and gentile . . . esperanto the universal language with universal brotherhood. No more patriotism of barspongers and dropsical impostors. Free money, free rent, free love and a free lay church in a free lay state. (399; 15:1686–93)

Bloom becomes a patriot hero, inspiring testimonials from bystanders such as "You're a credit to your country, sir, that's what you are" and "He's a man like Ireland wants" (395; 15:1538, 1540); but he also maintains a certain prophetic mystique, imagining himself addressing the Dublin crowds in his sonorous but scavenged Hebrew: "Aleph Beth Ghimel Daleth Hagadah Tephilim Kosher Yom Kippur Hanukah Roschaschana Beni Brith Bar Mitzvah Mazzoth Askenazim Meshuggah Talith" (397; 15:1623–5). But Bloom is also challenged by the enigmatic Man in the Macintosh, whose identity has puzzled him throughout the day, and who springs up through a trapdoor to announce "Don't you believe a word he says. That man is Leopold M'Intosh, the notorious fireraiser. His real name is Higgins," which provokes the uncharacteristic response from Bloom "Shoot him! Dog of a Christian!" (395–6; 15:1561–2, 1564). (Higgins was the name of a Dublin Jewish family to whom Bloom is said in the novel to be related.)

Addressivity is in fact so constitutionally jammed, impeded, and scrambled in "Circe" as to disallow any of its solidary political effects to hold for long. Acclamation, proclamation, exclamation, annunciation, accusation, interrogation, declaration, and denunciation cross and propagate uncontrollably through the chapter. However, if it is true that the chapter resists the various public address systems for forming cultural identity that seduce and rebuff Stephen and Bloom at earlier points in the novel, this is not because the chapter represents a retreat into the privacy of the psyche or the unconscious. Rather, it is the sheer excess of interference between the voices and their lines of utterance, which prevents the crystalization of either addressor or addressee as "I" or "you."

That Other World

In this sense, again, we find no easy congruence between such instances of addressivity in *Ulysses* and the ethical force of vocativity as evoked by Levinas. For Levinas, the vocative dimension of language is disruptive, but in such a way as to conserve the singularity and uniqueness of human encounter, preventing it from being distorted into relations of knowledge and formal equivalence. "Persons who speak to one another confirm one another, unique and irreplaceable," writes Levinas.[10] Vocativity thus sustains "the surplus of sociality" against the reductions of political rhetoric and the whole realm of social and cultural life, insofar as these are constituted upon knowing and universalization. For Levinas, vocativity is an elementary sociality, prior to the formalization of social relationships and systems, "the very essence of language prior to every particular language . . ."[11] In vocativity, "a sign is given from one to the other before the constitution of any system of signs, any common place formed by culture and sites, a sign given from null site to null site . . ."[12] The notorious problem that Levinas's thought poses for ethical thinking is its refusal to derive the ethical encounter from culture and history, or to see its operations within culture as anything other than a purifying disruption. Communication in and between cultures depends upon a "proximity" that works in a mode wholly other than that of a "making common": "The neighbor is ordered to my responsibility; he is already uprooted and without a country as soon as he arises on the earth . . . torn up from culture, law, horizon, context, by reason of an absence which is the very presence of infinity, finding itself in the null site of a trace . . ."[13]

For Joyce, on the other hand, there is no hint of such a precultural encounter between singular beings. For Joyce, the sedimentation of cultures and cultural identities is itself a function and effect of forms of address. However, if this is so, it is also the case that addressivity can exceed its consolidating function; as we have seen, in *Ulysses*, the mobility, indirection, and unfixed nature of addressivity act to disrupt the confirming circles of identity, opening them to time and difference. This is a transcendental addressivity that acts in and through the intervals and spacings of time, history, and culture, not one that lies primordially before them. Jacques Derrida's remarks about the "telegramophonic obsession" that governs the use of the elementary discursive particle "yes" in *Ulysses* may be of assistance here. For Derrida, the actual or implied use of the word "yes" "indicates that there is address to the other."[14] Such a situation of address always opens the ideal time of utterance to the dynamic, unpredictable time of the other's response, which is uncommandable. The link between the lapse of time and the address to the other is what enables

Derrida to connect the addressivity of the "yes" that is diffused throughout *Ulysses* with the alienation and spacing of writing and its mechanical supplements, notably the gramophone and the telephone. All of these establish the disseminating force of an addressivity that, far from standing before the divisive violence of history and culture, operates through and across it. In his account of the "yes" of *Ulysses*, Derrida is no doubt borrowing from Levinas's concern with the vocative dimension of *Saying*, which, in the first of his essays on Levinas, Derrida had described as "not a category, a *case* of speech, but rather the bursting forth, the very raising up of speech . . ."[15] But, here and elsewhere, Derrida also uses Joyce to address Levinas, warning him that the dream of a Judaic discourse capable of a purely vocative opening or approach to the other, as against the Greek *logos* that is always concerned rather to name and make intelligible the truth of the other, may itself commit the violence of asociality. For Derrida, speaking to Levinas as he does with Joyce's voice, the only possible way of ensuring a nonviolent opening to the other is by passing through history and its violences, rather than attempting to abstract oneself from it.[16]

This lesson may conveniently be used to explicate, and itself be explicated by, the moment in *Ulysses* at which Bloom seems most unequivocally to answer all the questions about his racial and national identity. In response to the sneers and tauntings of the Citizen in Barney Kiernan's bar, Bloom declares his Jewishness alongside his Irishness:

> – And I belong to a race too, says Bloom, that is hated and persecuted. Also now. This very moment. This very instant . . .
> – Robbed, says he. Plundered. Insulted. Persecuted. Taking what belongs to us by right. At this very moment, says he, putting up his fist, sold by auction in Morocco like slaves or cattle.
> – Are you talking about the new Jerusalem? says the citizen.
> – I'm talking about injustice, says Bloom. (273; 12:69–74)

In the virulence of his protest (it is, as most readers notice, the only moment at which Bloom shows any anger or propensity to violence in the novel), Bloom attempts to force an acknowledgment of the performative instant of his utterance. "Also now. This very moment. This very instant" refers us both to contemporary persecutions of the Jews in various parts of the world and to the immediately hostile context in Barney Kiernan's.[17] Bloom's assault depends upon forcing an acknowledgment of the power and context of addressivity on the Citizen, whose anti-Semitic discourse wards off the contaminating proximity of the second person by swerving into the abstract violence of general third-person propositions about "the Irish," "the English," "the French," "the Jews," and others. But the ambiguity of Bloom's "very moment," which could include other simultaneous instances in different places, both undermines and in a curious sense reinforces the pure and self-sufficient performativity of his utterance. It undermines it because it introduces the possibility of other contexts of address along with their histories and temporalities; but it reinforces it in redoubling the force of the instant of persecution, refusing to allow the ruses and justifications of history to diffuse that force.

A moment later, however, Bloom seems to retreat from his affirmation, "twisting around all the opposite, as limp as a wet rag" (273; 12:1478–9), as it seems to the cynical, unnamed narrator of the chapter: "But it's no use, says he. Force, hatred, history, all that. That's not life for men and women, insult and hatred. And everybody knows that it's the very opposite of that that is really life" (273; 12:1480–83). Bloom's words seem to suggest, despite what they affirm, that "history" is not the simple opposite of love. The history that Bloom has in mind is a history of heroic gestures and postures, the history that freezes peoples and persons into identification. But the complexity of address that Bloom experiences and is constituted by throughout *Ulysses*, is historical in another, expanded sense, since it is the very time of difference that Levinas himself was arguing as early as 1947 is brought into being in the relationship to the other:

> The situation of the face-to-face would be the very accomplishment of time; the encroachment of the present on the future is not the feat of the subject alone, but the intersubjective relationship. The condition of time lies in the relationship between humans, or in history.[18]

This openness to, and inclusiveness of history is also at work in the other, less determinate answer that Bloom seems to give to "the Jewish question" of the Citizen and others as it is addressed to him in the book, and the more general demands to identify that the Jewish question stands in for. Falling into a doze on Sandymount strand after his voyeuristic masturbation at the sight of Gerty MacDowell in the "Nausicaa" chapter, Bloom starts to write in the sand with a stick:

> Mr Bloom with his stick gently vexed the thick sand at his foot. Write a message for her. Might remain. What?
>
> I . . .
>
> AM. A.
>
> No room. Let it go.
>
> Mr Bloom effaced the letters with his slow boot. (312; 13:1255–65)

The acknowledgment or declaration of self-identity alludes both to Coleridge's triumphant characterization of the imagination as "a repetition in the finite mind of the eternal act of creation in the infinite I AM"[19] and, more locally, to Stephen's meditations on the discontinuity of personality on the same spot earlier in the day. It fails because it is uncompleted, though its uncompletedness, in the sense of its liability to the other, is a necessary part of any completed self-constitution. As Derrida suggests, in commenting on this passage, the ego is constituted in a circuit that cannot but be broken into by the address to the other that it includes: "The self-positing in the *yes* or the *Ay* is . . . neither tautological nor narcissistic; it is not egological even if it initiates the movement of circular reappropriation . . . It holds open the circle that it institutes."[20] The passage asks us, of course, to complete the predication it teasingly withholds. What is Bloom about to acknowledge himself to be? A lecher, a cad, a married man, a fool, a cuckold, a Jew? The last two possibilities seem to be conjoined in the cuckoo clock that strikes nine as Bloom subsides into sleep, the allusion to Bloom as cuckold merging with the scornful reflections of the "Cyclops" narrator on Bloom's alleged Irishness as he "pumps ship" in the back yard of Barney Kiernan's: "Ireland my nation says he (hoik! phthook!) never be up to those bloody (there's the last of it) Jerusalem (ah!) cuckoos" (275; 12:1570–72).

Bloom's uncompleted predication is redoubled and responded to in Gerty MacDowell's words which end the chapter:

> she noticed at once that that foreign gentleman that was sitting on the rocks looking was
>
>
>
> *Cuckoo*
>
> *Cuckoo*
>
> *Cuckoo.*
>
>

(313; 13:1300–05)

Gerty both does and does not answer the question asked by Bloom's unfulfilled declaration. He is identified as "that foreign gentleman," but what he was, or what he was doing is left as unspecified as Bloom leaves it, just as the last words of Gerty's portion of the "Nausicaa" "monologue," which itself has turned into a kind of extended erotic address to Bloom, have had to be supplied by Bloom: "because Gerty MacDowell was . . . Tight boots? No. She's lame. O!" (Joyce's ellipsis, 301; 13:770–71). Neither address can arrive or be completed in response, precisely because of the orientation of address to the other, which is to say, necessarily, to multiple others, and multiple occasions of reception in extended time. For, even in the relatively simple scenario of unrequited erotic address of "Nausicaa," there is complexity and interference. As Bloom prepares to write, he addresses himself with some of the words addressed to him by Martha Clifford in the letter he has received that morning: "What is the meaning of that other world" (312; 13:1261–2). Bloom's recall of Martha's misspelling of "other world" for "other word" brings into proximity the word that passes from one person to another and the other worlds whose separateness is both confirmed and compromised in the very movement of the word. The ghosts of this phrase that haunt Bloom, along with the ghosts who address themselves to and within Stephen and Bloom from their "other worlds" throughout the novel, such as Stephen's dead mother, Bloom's dead father, the recently-deceased Paddy Dignam, and the voice of Shakespeare playing the part of the murdered Claudius, are the evidence of an addressivity which desists and persists across times and persons, which is preserved as well as sent astray in the ghostly conditions of what Stephen Dedalus calls "death . . . absence . . . change of manners" (154; 9:148–9).

je suis . . . juif . . . je ne suis pas juif du tout

It should by now have become clear that I do not think there is any authentically Judaic addressivity to be discovered in *Ulysses*, any "aliorelative" discourse that could be clearly subtracted from the "ipsorelative" address of Anglo-Helleno-Hibernian discourse, to borrow the terms employed in the "Ithaca" chapter (581; 17:1350). It may be nevertheless that the repeated insistence on the vagrant, broken nature of address in the novel is significantly implicated with the complexities of what I want to call "the Jewish question" in it, namely the demand made of "the Jew" that he name and acknowledge himself as such, along with the question that "the Jew" poses in reply to this demand with regard to the processes of national naming and addressing. Addressivity in this novel is concerned both with inclusion and exclusion, as in the Citizen's savage slogans: "*Sinn Fein! . . . Sinn fein amhain!* The friends we love are by our side and the foes we hate before us" (251; 12:523–4). But the violent denial of the "stranger in the house" that secures "ourselves alone" (the meaning of *sinn fein amhain*) is itself a form of address that harbors or insinuates that stranger, a provocation that becomes an invocation. It is after all in this chapter that we hear the (pretty implausible) rumor from John Wyse Nolan and Martin Cunningham that Bloom, the "perverted jew . . . from a place in Hungary" (276; 12:1635), actually advised Arthur Griffith on the establishment of Sinn Fein: "it was he who drew up all the plans according to the Hungarian system," says Martin Cunningham (276; 12:1635–6). The barflies in Barney Kiernan's bar seem to believe this rumor because it accords partially with truth: the original, nonmilitant principles of Sinn Fein did indeed derive from a similar strategy of resistance practised by Hungarians against their Austrian imperial masters in the late nineteenth century.[21] Added to this is the interesting historical morsel that "Griffith was persistently rumored to have a Jewish advisor-ghostwriter . . ."[22] "We" can only be and address "ourselves alone," it seems, through the ghostly intervention, actual or attributed, of the "perverted jew." Martin Cunningham's phrase is less anti-Semitic than it may appear, for he means that Bloom is a lapsed or nonreligious Jew. But his words establish an interesting connection between the perversion and power to pervert associated with the Jew, especially at this historical moment,[23] and the "perverted" Jew who is himself turned away from Jewishness, or no longer quite Jewish. To ask the Jewish question of the closure and fulfilment of national identity in the autoenunciation of "ourselves alone" is to speak as the non-Jewish Jew, that interrupted condition which has seemed to many in the twentieth century to be the most representatively Jewish of all. Thus, there can be no Judaic principle of addressive immediacy to set against what Derrida, following Levinas, sees as the barren lucidity of the Greek *logos*. Rather, *Ulysses* moves toward the historically determinate indeterminacy of the "jewgreek," testifying that, as Derrida has it, "we live in the difference between the Jew and the Greek, which is perhaps the unity of what is called history . . ."[24]

The concern of Joyce's *Ulysses* with the poetics, the erotics, and the politics of address, and its impulse to multiply the indirections of address against the convocational circles of the various public address systems that consolidate national identity, are testimony to the necessarily broken trajectory of every address under historical conditions when there will always be strangers in the house. Nothing illustrates this so well as the story in which Joyce, hearing from Samuel Beckett the names of those who read and admired *Ulysses* in Dublin, replied "But they're all Jews."[25] The transmission of the book here follows the same broken trajectory which characterizes the question of Jewishness as it is posed in the novel. The long and vagrant letter home, in the form of *Ulysses*, which Joyce had sent back to Dublin from Europe in lieu of an actual homecoming, thus appeared to have arrived at an address occupied by the very strangers with whom Joyce had taken up, in the quasi-Judaic community of the book he had gathered around him (consisting in fact of many Jewish writers and intellectuals) during his wanderings between Paris, Trieste, and Zürich. The ironies of identity, address, and belonging persisted in Joyce's life. Three months before he died, Joyce found himself stranded at the Swiss border, struggling to get an entry permit for himself and his family to a country that he described in letters both as "the promised land" (*"la terre promise"*) and, as he grew more desperate, "hermetically helvetic" (*"hermétiquement helvétique"*).[26] Joyce is here a thwarted Moses, being given, in the title of the oblique parable with which Stephen answers the nationalist oratory in "Aeolus," *"A Pisgah Sight of Palestine"* (122; 7:1057); but this is doubly ironic, given the reason initially adduced for refusing him entry, as he explains it in a postcard of October 29, 1940: "Mme. Giedion went to the Aliens' Police at Zurich where they seemed to believe that I am . . . a Jew! I am thunderstruck! There's a remarkable discovery!"[27] A few weeks later, he writes that "I fear . . . that if they did not want me there because they believed me to be a

Jew (Intelligence Service, no doubt?), after reading my declaration they will want me less and less as they perceive that I am not a Jew at all."[28] (Joyce seems to have believed that the authorities would expect a Jew to have much more money than he had.) The Moses denied sight of the promised land because he is Jewish is then denied it because he is not Jewish enough. As so often, Joyce's life, like his writing, submits to the painful hilarity of an error in transmission. In response to the terrible, unanswerable question that has determined so much of the history of persons and peoples in this century, "Are you a . . . ," Joyce's (non)Jewishness, like that of his text, inhabits and exemplifies the hopeful incompletion of the answer "I am a . . ."

13

Assimilation, Entertainment, and the Holywood Solution

CLAIRE PAJACZKOWSKA
AND BARRY CURTIS

In this essay we explore some aspects of the dynamics of assimilation within the wave of immigration to the U.S.A. by Jews from Eastern Europe, at the beginning of the twentieth century. How did the Jewish immigrants' heightened perception of American myths and visual culture enable them to become leaders of the Hollywood film industry?[1] The phenomenon of Hollywood in the twentieth century presents the problems of assimilation in a particularly acute and paradoxical way. In Hollywood, victims of the Czar became "Czars." An industry built on perceptions of generational conflict, of margins and centers, of utopian realization, which seems to have been particularly vivid for Jews and was the persistent victim of anti-Semitic polemics,[2] also provided an opportunity for a relatively small managerial elite to formulate American culture as it should or could be. It has been said that "Hollywood—the American dream—is a Jewish idea in a sense, it's a Jewish revenge on America. It combines the Puritan ethic with baroque magnificence."[3]

In English, "to assimilate" has been a verb since 1578. The Oxford English Dictionary indicates two broad meanings in current usage: the first, "to make or be like," and the second, "to absorb and incorporate." Assimilation is thus described as both active and passive. "To become like" or "to take after," in the sense of adapting and conforming, describes a state of passivity in which a subject is incorporated or absorbed into a system. "To cause to resemble" and "to make alike" are active states in which a subject acts in order "to convert into a substance of its own nature." Both processes can be used figuratively, for instance, to describe the transformation of human identity when subjects are caught in a predicament involving a dialectic of power.

To want to become like the other, or to seek similarities between self and other, is often to be a victim of the passions of envy or jealousy—perhaps, too, a victim of a violation of one's own integrity. This may be unconscious, manifested in one's behavior instead of feeling. To exert power over another, to cause another to be like the self, is to have the power of violence, to violate the integrity of the other. The specific nature of the action at work in assimilation is the violence involved in negating differences. Assimilation (or amalgamation) can be contrasted with integration. The former implies incorporation, with its literal and figurative associations of devouring and the disappearance of difference. The latter is based on a coexistence of respect. Lack of respect leads to a compulsive search for "respectability" and all the forms of repression which that entails.

The paradox of assimilation is that it can never be fully achieved. Its work is unending, always incomplete, its goal always to be reached. It is unsuccessful both for the dominant group, whose values and order are never fully integrated into the immigrant culture—however flattering they may find it to be forever emulated—and for the minority, whose display of their desire to be similar is always a display of their own powerlessness. That is, assimilation can never result in integration. It remains a manifestation of the imbalance of power that gives rise to this process of emulation and the negation of difference. Where there is a plausible emulation of the enviable attributes of the dominant culture this is usually accompanied by amnesia, a disavowal of the "hidden injuries" of race, and a repression of the trauma of difference.

As frequently noted, over the centuries of the Jewish Diaspora within Europe, the significant differences between Jewish and Christian cultures have been subject to certain repeated forms of stereotyping.[4] Differences are often hyperbolized into mutually exclusive opposites or rendered insignificant by being denied. The immigrant's outstanding ability has been called "the genius for survival," which includes an ability to perceive, and act upon, the fantasies and unspoken desires of the cultural majority—surely a defence against the trauma of difference that is in danger of overwhelming the immigrant.

The genius of the Jewish immigrant entrepreneurs who created the economic and ideological system of Hollywood was often recognized by themselves as a patient and acute "ordinariness" of perception. For example, Adolph Zukor (a pioneer of the studio system and head of Paramount Studios) appropriated for the title of his autobiography a "showbiz" truism, attributed elsewhere to other early film entrepreneurs—"The Public is Never Wrong." There he is at pains to describe himself as a particularly observant member of the audience—this is a common autobiographical trope for that generation of Jewish entrepreneurs—sitting in the auditorium, watching the film and the audience at the same time, thus violating the commonplace screen fixation that is normally assumed to guarantee the cinematic experience. The Jewish immigrant entrepreneurs, who often started in the fashion and entertainment industries in the U.S.A., found new ways of analyzing the aspirations of the host culture. This Jewish so-called "duplicity," an obstacle to the membership of any truly national culture, is expressed in a disturbing but relevant way by one of the British novelist John Buchan's heroes: "In Germany only the Jew can get outside himself, and that is why, if you look into the matter, you will find that a Jew is at the back of most German enterprises."[5]

The Jew is often represented as louche and shifty, quick to profit from the knowledge that accrues to obliquity and an ironic consciousness. This is, of course, one of the staple premises of anti-Semitism and provides one of its key icons—the squinting, marginal, and disruptively askance look. The impossibility of the Jews ever becoming fully assimilated is said to lie in their overvaluation of detail and their failure to understand and internalize the inconsequentiality (the sang-froid) and the disinterested mystery of the core (Christian) culture. On the other hand, the danger represented by the successful Jewish cultural entrepreneur—and none were more successful than the "Moguls"[6]—was that this "perversion" of understanding could result in a system of values that somehow enlisted mass support. What is particularly interesting about the success of Hollywood is that the imaginings of the Jewish immigrant "arriviste" could become a format for widely shared representations of American life.

Perhaps it is an anxiety shared by all those who instinctively inhabit the core of a culture that "interlopers" with unnatural energy and drive will misunderstand, asset-strip, travesty, and carnivalize its familiar, but unspoken, "deep" meanings and values, and by so doing will provide a kind of access for the otherwise excluded, peripheral masses. Some processes of assimilation involve an aspiration to inhabit the most central and profound mysteries of the core culture. Outsiders can simplify because they are not intimidated by ritual and protocols, they do not respect boundaries and categories, they misrecognize, but in doing so they mysteriously lay bare something simple and fundamental.

The immigrant is susceptible to being stereotyped by the cultural majority. The stereotyping or hyperbolization that is relevant here is the traditional association of the Jew with an excess of physicality. As noted throughout this book, the traditional characterization of Jewish attributes is in terms of physiognomic difference: Christian traits are designated as unmarked or "normal" while Jewish traits are designated as notable or significant. In its most exaggerated form, such as in caricature, Jewishness is thought of as connoting the body itself, all materiality and carnality, while the Christian has the monopoly of transcendence and the soul. Noses, feet, eyes, hair, darkness, facial expressions, eating rituals, smell, and circumcision are some of the tropes of physical difference that circulate in the signifying economy of anti-Semitism. Related to this ubiquitous fantasy of bodily presence is the traditional characterization of Jewishness as especially "feminine." As stereotypes represent the expression of unconscious, primary-process logic rather than the more rational thinking of conscious, secondary processes,[7] the stereotypes contain paradoxical and contradictory thoughts; hence the Jew who is represented as reprehensibly "physical" is also stigmatized as lacking the genuine unselfconscious physicality of "true masculinity." Traits of compliance, seductiveness, charm, duplicity, and manipulation are often identified as stereotypically Jewish, and these relate to the predicament of passivity in assimilation.[8] The passivity of powerlessness is then transmuted into the exhibitionism of fashion and entertainment, and it is these industries that have become the most significant vehicles of visual culture in the U.S.A. today. However, exhibitionism and passivity have not lost their feminine connotations.

Alongside this confusion of gender identity, implied by the fear and fantasy of its reversibility, there are two other equally "reversible" differences that are present in the representation of the Jew. One is the reversibility of ethnic differences, such as the substitution of Black for Jewish identity, and the second is the reversibility of the generations, for example a confusion of the roles of father and son and, therefore, confusion over historical sequence. The first is the source of much humor in popular cinema. One memorable example is the sequence in *A Day at the Races* where the Marx Brothers, in order to escape pursuit, disguise themselves by "blacking up" and merging with the servants and childen. The hilarity and hysteria of these frequent moments of ethnic reversibility are indices of the immense weight that this carries in the signifying economy of texts.

The amnesia and disavowal which is the high cost of emulating an imaginary success resulted, in the case of the Hollywood Jews, in an absence of films about the origins of Hollywood itself, and a correspondingly excessive presence of films celebrating "show business" as a timeless and absolute fact. Media narcissism replaces a damaged history and damaged self, an example of the distortion of history that results from narcissistic confusion of generations. Of the large number of Jewish performers who appeared in "black face" it has been said: "Black became a mask for Jewish expressiveness, with one woe speaking through the voice of another." Harry Cohn (head of Columbia Studios) is quoted as saying: "Around this studio the only Jews we put in pictures play Indians . . ."[9] H. Stewart Chamberlain, an American racist, who maintained that Jews were a mongrel race because they had intermarried with Blacks, provided an outspoken variant of an argument that is present in more subtle forms in numerous representations of Jews as racially indistinct or transgressive.[10] This generalized sense of hybridity persists in accounts of how the interstitial status of Jewish immigrants rendered them a "mediating category," open to accusations of embodying other racial characteristics and subject to the ambivalence attendant on anxieties aroused by disrupted classification.

The reversibility of Jewish and Black roles in Hollywood representations of jazz has been attributed to a "splitting into two to fulfil transgressive desires"[11]—jazz conceived as linking polyglot America to "the ancient wandering Jews." One writer in 1927 referred to jazz as reaching "from the black South to the black North, but in between it has been touched by the commercial wand of the Jew."[12] In *Duck Soup*, the Marx Brothers in black face not only escape from pursuit but are also revived by the innocence and energy of dancing and singing before they emerge from a "childlike" Black culture into the narrative business of horse trading. Here we have again an instance of how "Blackface exteriorizes Jewishness, embraces the exteriorized identity as regenerative, and leaves it behind."[13]

In many of the narratives of assimilation the reversibility of racial differences becomes confused with the fantasy of the reversibility of generational difference. Not only is Jewishness closely associated with the risible, in many forms of humor, but also with the excessive physicality of the body through singing and performing, as is blackness and its equation with the infantile. The immigrant becomes an apprentice to the codes of a new culture and, without language, is infantilized in his or her relationship to others. Here again the Marx Brothers illustrate this: the three "stages" of assimilation—from silent, childlike, dumbness (Harpo), through the accented, expressive, speaking, and marketeering adaptation (Chico), to the clever, manipulative, and insulting mock professional (Groucho)—are embodied in each of the brothers, and together they rush through meteoric and insecure pathways to assimilation with the "best" of upper-class society. Many of the Hollywood Moguls' biographies testify to the uncomfortable situation of enterprising, precocious sons in families with irresponsible, absent, or damaged fathers.[14] Sons take on the burden of a father's role in supporting their mothers' families. Also present in the fantasy of reversing generations is a compensatory, or consoling, narrative for the tragic loss of history that is the predicament of the immigrant, however exciting the prospect of reinventing a "new self" and life in a "new world."

This reinvention of the self evidently required an extensive understanding of, and investment in, the protocols and signs of success of the host culture. These were pursued with an extraordinary single-mindedness and aggression that became legendary attributes of the studio heads. A persistent mystery which some of the next generation set themselves to investigate was the source of that drive.[15] What Anna Freud (1936) has called "identification with the aggressor"—one of the defence mechanisms central to the paradox of assimilation—may provide an answer: "Faced with an external threat (typically represented as criticism emanating from an authority), the subject identifies himself with his aggressor. He may do so either by appropriating the aggression itself, or again by adopting particular symbols of power by which the aggressor is designated."[16]

One form of aggression that faces the immigrant is the dominant culture's indifference toward his or her predicament. Following the trauma of the loss of an original or native homeland, there is an arduous and often dangerous journey. The loss of the "old country" is then compounded on arrival in the new land by the trauma of difference and the experience of beginning again. Arguably, for Jews the experience was more absolute and produced a more intense dialectic between relief from persecution and habilitation to new and sometimes unwelcome cultural values. For, unlike the southern European immigrants, Jews tended to arrive in the U.S.A. in family groups with no intention of returning. (The Movie Moguls made an exception that proved this rule by combining trips to their European subsidiaries and collaborators with visits to the villages they had left as children and young men. In the case of Adolph Zukor and Carl Laemmle these visits took the form of triumphal and benefactory returns.) For all immigrants, America embodied an important mystique of self-realization, freedom from immediate persecution. The Polish-American writer Eva Hoffman has described America as "a society in which you are what you think you are."[17] The drive to assimilate is often an urgent priority for immigrants and can perhaps be conceived as having a particular intensity for Jewish immigrants to America because, compared with other immigrant groups, there was less nostalgia for a homeland and no strong national identity to be relinquished. The violence of ruptured integrity was often directed inward to self and family and took the form of generational conflict, "passing," and a persistent sense of marginality and insecurity. For the parents the conflict was one of ensuring sufficient grounds for success in the adopted country while maintaining suitable standards of cultural resistance; for the second generation the problems consisted of mediating their adaptive behavior and educating and placating their parents. The problems and rewards of inhabiting the realm of "popular culture" are particularly acute for immigrants since popular culture exacerbates generational conflict but presents an arena in which immigrant groups are often relatively advantaged and can find means of expressing conflicts and aspirations.

The Jewish presence in Hollywood is a model locus for a number of anxieties. The major film studios were predominantly owned and managed by Jews[18] and the humble origins of the first generation of movie entrepreneurs were widely known and publicized: they were described as "the old regime of fur peddlers, second hand jewellers and nickelodeon proprietors who started all the cinema companies . . ."[19]

This generation was part of the one and one half million Jews who left Eastern Europe between the 1880's and 1910, mostly Orthodox, and mostly from beyond the Pale, the boundary established by Russia in 1791 permitting Jews and Slavs to settle in Eastern Poland; most of the Hollywood pioneers came from a relatively circumscribed geographical zone that crossed the borders of Poland, Hungary, and Germany.

Two of the most notable aspects of the rise of the Hollywood Moguls were the ease and rapidity with which they seemed to make the transition from the passivity of spectatorship to the activities of film exhibition, distribution, and production. Some of the conventional wisdom about the early years of cinema has been questioned but it is clear that the early films were popular with Jewish audiences: statistics suggest that there was a particularly high density of nickelodeons in Jewish areas and in the pre-cinema decade of the 1890's Jews already played key roles in the theater as performers and agents. There does seem to be some doubt regarding the role those films played in inculcating immigrant audiences into American life, for many early films were imported from Europe. As an intriguing article from the *Jewish Daily Forward* in 1908 put it, "Our Jews feel very much at home with the detectives, oceans, dogs and cars that run about on screen."[20]

There is general agreement that the cheapness and brevity of the experience of filmgoing, as well as films' expansive subject matter, had particular accessibility and appeal to poor urban immigrants. From early in the history of film exhibition, working-class and ethnic audiences were seen as presenting problems of discipline, hygiene, and limited resources.[21] It seems, too, that the early promoters of film had the positive advantage of familiarity with fashion and public taste and the negative advantage of occlusion from other realms of business where status, credit, and privilege were necessary. The early years of the American film industry were marked by attempts by entrenched business interests to monopolize the technological hardware. The genius of the future Moguls was a complex one, partly sheer business ingenuity, partly ruthless risk taking and a kind of competitive solidarity; but perhaps its most interesting component was coherent with immigrant aspiration and a Jewish prioritizing of "culture." They recognized that the potential of film and the basis for its future appeal lay in the compulsive attractions of narrative, star appeal, and the conspicuous glamor of *mise-en-scène* both on screen and in the theaters in which films were screened. Members of the audience had to be rescued from the crowd which they constituted, offered individualism and intimacy—respected and turned into individual spectators.

The mercurial and piratic Jewish Independents are often pitched against the entrenched unimaginative Wasps in early cinema histories. Recent research, however, has shown that the situation was more indeterminate and fluid. It wasn't the Independents who first set up film making facilities in California, but it is easy to see why the transfer of the industry to the West Coast would appeal to a primarily Jewish industry. California offered cheap land, a literal opportunity to "get the slums out of the movies" (one of Adolph Zukor's aspirations), a "Progressive" Republican culture with few labor laws, a "melting pot" ideal, and an opportunity to reinvent one-self. It provided the Jewish film men with a chance to negotiate an American identity for themselves and share their imaginary America with their clients.

In an important respect, men like Adolph Zukor, Carl Laemmle, Louis Meyer, Harry Cohn, and Jack and Harry Warner became conspicuous examples of the American Dream. "From Poland to Polo in one genera-tion" became a studio joke when the Warner Brothers convened that most Eastern Wasp Ascendancy phenomenon, a polo team.[22] A number of rea-sons have been offered for their success: they range from weak fathers to a genius for risk, but perhaps the most convincing is that a particularly Jewish aspiration to culture made them the perfect agents for mediating between the new underclass and the traditional Protestant dominant culture. The studio heads were modernizers of attitudes and morals, although their sense of a future for the film industry involved drawing on models of tradi-tional high culture: "In their position as immigrants with bourgeois values the Jewish film moguls were ideal middle men for realizing a fusion of styles."[23] However, they were also closely associated with the meretricious ostentation of the industry, with poor morals, bad taste, and the industrial-ization of art. Their apocryphal gauche and ungrammatical expressions have become famous examples of the "baroque" English of the immi-grant. Sam Goldwyn's alleged expostulation "Include me out!" speaks elo-quently the paradox of poor grammar and ambivalence.

Most poignantly for men who embodied a kind of absolute power, which, ironically, led to them being referred to as "Czars," "Emperors," "Princes," "Moguls," was the continually enforced recognition of their dependency on creditors and their subjection to the business interests of Wall Street and the entrenched economic power of the non-Jewish Houses of Rockefeller and Morgan. They were also subject and highly sensitive to successive waves of anti-Semitism, which found different forms of expres-sion—panics about immigration and "hyphenated Americans" in the 1920's; the omnipresence of Fascists in American public life; much publi-cized vilification by prominent figures like Henry Ford and Charles Lindbergh; various Christian fulminations opposed to the immoralities of Hollywood; attacks on the presumed link between Communism and Jews;

and accusations of an inevitable "racial feeling" among Hollywood Jews promoting war with Germany. The American public's attitude to those influential men seems to have shared in the ambivalence expressed by J. B. Priestley who, in his survey of English life and culture of 1933, celebrated "that restless glitter which is the gift of the Jew," and elsewhere in the same book indicated some anxiety at hearing in the slums of Southampton: "Gramaphones (sic) . . . scratching out those tunes concocted by Polish Jews fifteen stories above Broadway . . ."[24]

When the Hollywood film industry is cited as an example of a Jewish success story, the latent paranoia surrounding foreigners tends to be activated in the form of an anti-Semitic conspiracy theory. A recent example is the furore caused by the English journalist William Cash, whose brief article in the right-wing journal *The Spectator* unleashed a correspondence that repeated but hardly illuminated the conspiracy theory of the Jewish "possession" of Hollywood.[25] Latent paranoia becomes overt and manifest whenever a culture's system of classification is thrown into confusion and doubt by an actively unclassifiable element. A central component of the fantasy of the Jewish "conspiracy" is its contradictory belief in the simultaneous marginality and centrality of an infiltrating force, represented in the contradictory belief that the Hollywood Jews were both ostentatiously visible, parading their power, and dangerously invisible, merging too successfully and too rapidly.

The interstitial and undecidable status of the first generation to attain power over the Hollywood film industry can be gauged by the fact that they were regarded by the long established, earlier settled, and mostly German-Jewish community of Los Angeles as culturally suspect interlopers. An interesting class dimension is clearly present here, since the first wave of western, German-Jewish émigrés were not only assimilated into European culture but were also of a higher class than the Eastern European Russian, Lithuanian, and Polish-Jews who followed. All Jews, no matter how wealthy (one estimate places 43 of the 60 highest salaries in America in the mid-1930's as being earned in the film industry) or celebrated, were not allowed to join local country clubs, send their children to local private schools, or attend race meetings at the Santa Anna racetrack. Characteristically, they constructed their own versions of those institutions. There was, however, already a Jewish country club—the Hillcrest Club—which, initially, obstructed membership applications from the newer Eastern European Jews of the film industry, because the newer immigrants, like the "return of the repressed," seemed to threaten the more assimilated, middle- and upper-class, Jews with contamination from the unwanted aspects of their "own kind." It was only after the Depression in the late 1920's, when the number of the more established Jewish members declined, that the newer

Eastern European Jews began to gain entry. Then the Club became a meeting place for the industry. In many respects the Hillcrest Club was a parody of the patrician culture of the Ivy League, its name overtly signifying the upward aspirations of an "elevated" view and the insignia of nobility. It is the club about which Groucho Marx (a more recently arrived Eastern European Jew) quipped that if it would have him as a member he would not want to join, a poignant and complex statement about the impossibility of assimilation. In order to "belong to the club," outsiders have to create their own club which is then marked as inferior to the club that they cannot join. The Hillcrest Club's two "generations" of membership emphasizes the significance of class or status within émigré culture: the first generation identified themselves with the aristocratic or upper class of American society, integrated into its more prestigious financial institutions, and maintained this symbolic distinction by excluding more recent émigrés, who then reversed the humiliation of exclusion by exerting their power as the wealthiest, if not the most prestigious, Jews.

Marks of success for the highly paid studio heads were boats and horses. Scott Fitzgerald's comment in *The Last Tycoon* (1941) on the fascination with horses has been much quoted: "Stahr guessed that the Jews had taken over the worship of horses as a symbol—for years it had been the Cossacks mounted and the Jews on foot. Now the Jews had horses and it gave them a sense of extraordinary well being and power."[26] This unfinished fictional account of Hollywood, full of admiration for the central character Monroe Stahr—who is clearly based on Irving Thalberg, production chief of MGM studios—involves an extraordinary distortion in that it cannot render or admit Thalberg's Jewishness. In that respect it shares in a dilemma of the Moguls themselves.

The Hillcrest Club effect lives on in a wide range of cultural forms. One contemporary example from visual culture is the success and popularity of Ralph Lauren's fashion "looks" or styles, from the popularity of the Great Gatsby revival of the 1970's, through the recent success of the Polo range to the ur-American pioneering, log cabin style. Two "looks" are of interest here: the first is the appropriation of the name and icon of the horseback polo player[27] as the brand name for a range of clothes and the mock "gentleman's club" interior as the setting for point of sale—a style Lauren has successfully marketed to American youth, Japanese industrialists, and the British royal family alike. The second amalgamates associations of late nineteenth- and early twentieth-century European colonial culture to market the "Safari" brand of perfume. Both styles appeal to the yearning for membership of a privileged class and for an imaginary history of ease to substitute for the desperation of diaspora. Born into the Lifschitz family, as a second-generation immigrant (his father emigrated from Lithuania to

New York at the beginning of the century) Lifschitz/Lauren's sensitivity to the yearning for the status of belonging enables him ingeniously to condense a number of symbols of the identity of upper-middle-class American culture, with its idealization of "Britishness."

Lauren's response to the predicament of being without a national history, let alone a colonial history, could be contrasted to the Marx Brothers' use of humor to parody the Jewish relationship to colonialism in the character of Rufus T. Firefly (played by Groucho Marx in *Duck Soup*), where Groucho's pith helmet and jodhpurs become the emblem of the very club that would not have him as a member. Humor is used to liberate us from bondage to the slavish need to emulate and "make love to" cultural indifference. The references to horse riding, polo, and a colonial identity of mastery over baseness were originally conceived by Lauren in terms of his first success, the "Gatsby look." Like the Polo and Safari looks, it signifies a desire for the quiet understatement of a Protestant culture of reserve and control, contrasted with the stereotype of a hysterically helpless, powerless, and traumatized other. Interestingly, the image of the "Roaring Twenties" in the 1974 film version of Scott Fitzgerald's *The Great Gatsby* was created by Ralph Lauren, who designed the film's costumes and then went on to extend the style into a fashion range.

The significance of Gatsby can be derived from the narrative structure of the novel, centered around structural antinomies between two women, Daisy and Jordan, and two men, the protagonist Nick Carraway and the enigmatic and tragic Gatsby. Their differences are clearly marked: Daisy weeps over monogrammed shirts because they are so desirable and Jordan drives a car assertively to her death; their names evoke, respectively, innocence of pastoral idyll, and Negro spiritual or Judaic river; they are whiteness and blackness personified. The narrative seeks a resolution of racial contradictions through the intermediary of Jewishness, the enigma of Gatsby and of his desire. Moreover, Daisy represents the "blondness" of the Ralph Lauren style. Similarly, the male protagonist, the subjective consciousness of the narrator, and the reader's point of view, is contrasted with Gatsby, the remote object of ambivalent desire, of cold curiosity, and fear. The protagonist "I" is characterized as civilized, integrated into a known history, admirable, and actively masculine, while Gatsby is unavailable, unknown, overcivilized, overdressed, overhospitable, and "feminine." The following extract exemplifies the ambivalence and paranoid suspicion that is projected onto the enigma of the unknown man or foreigner:

> Almost at the moment when Mr. Gatsby identified himself a butler hurried toward him with the information that Chicago was calling him on the wire. He excused himself with a small bow that included each of us in turn.

"If you want something just ask for it, old sport," he urged me. "Excuse me. I will rejoin you later."

When he was gone I turned immediately to Jordan—constrained to assure her of my surprise. I had expected that Mr. Gatsby would be a florid and corpulent person in his middle years.

"Who is he?" I demanded. "Do you know?"

"He's just a man named Gatsby."

"Where is he from, I mean? And what does he do?"

"Now *you're* started on the subject," she answered with a wan smile. "Well, he told me once he was an Oxford man."

A dim background started to take shape behind him, but at her next remark it faded away.

"However, I don't believe it."

"Why not?"

"I don't know," she insisted, "I just don't think he went there."

Something in her tone reminded me of the other girl's "I think he once killed a man," and had the effect of stimulating my curiosity. I would have accepted without question the information that Gatsby sprang from the swamps of Louisiana or from the lower East Side of New York.[28]

The novel's narrative is motivated by a set of tensions between categories, tensions between opposing masculinities and femininities, insiders and outsiders, between generations, and between classes. There is a much less explicit tension about ethnicities that motivates the narrative in a more basic and more profound way than the others, and it remains enigmatic even at the resolution of the narrative. As the book begins with a father's liberal advice to his son, on thinking about his own privilege before judging others, and then embarks on a pursuit of the enigma of Gatsby's identity, the narrative is effectively a container for the deep anxieties generated for the narcissism of white, masculine, middle-class Anglo-Saxon American culture by the presence of foreigners, whether from the "swamps of Louisiana or from the lower East Side of New York." An Oedipal anxiety becomes a metaphor for the anxiety of the moral failure of American society. As the racial anxiety is never recognized or spoken, it remains a "structuring absence" in the narrative, a feeling that is so deep and unacknowledged that instead of being experienced as an emotion it is immediately transformed into action.

It is this "structuring absence" at the heart of American culture that has also been broached by the elliptical logic of Jewish humor. When Groucho Marx appears as a colonial explorer, humor arises from the ludicrous juxtaposition of a diasporic culture masquerading as a missionary power. Similarly, Woody Allen has reworked the Gatsby myth with incisive humor in his film *Zelig*, which is, among other things, an allegory of assimilation. In an opening scene Zelig, the lost soul played by Allen, appears in a beautifully crafted bogus documentary, a false history, in conversation with Scott Fitzgerald on the lawn of an opulent Long Island mansion, surrounded by members of the "fast set" of the 1920's. Mysteriously, the same character is then found in the servants' quarters singing with the "Negro" staff whose work underwrites the literary productions of the Scott Fitzgerald set. Who is this character who seems to belong equally amongst the most privileged of the White set and the serving class of Black workers? Zelig, the Jewish immigrant, belongs to both and neither. As an outsider, he cannot fit into the class and ethnic orders of American culture, so he becomes a "mediating category," neither Black nor White, neither serving nor ruling class. He is the unclassifiable element that confounds classification itself. He is therefore elevated into an example of an almost miraculous capacity to mutate, to acquire a range of talents, and to "fit in" with his surroundings, and is simultaneously vilified as reptilian, a chameleon.

Humor can reach a level of understanding that is quite as true and authoritative as theory. Both offer a way out of a constraining paradox generated by the limited forms of belief and classification of mainstream culture. Both offer a way of dealing with aggression generated by being on the receiving end of the constraints of a culture of indifference. Humor liberates us from the conflict of having significant difference recognized; through humor the authority of the symbols of power is undermined, revealed as contradictory and hypocritical. Theory sets out to rethink the categories of classification and to enable significant differences to "make a difference" to thinking. In humor the work of rethinking is transformed into the pleasurable release of energy through laughter. Humor is the creative use of aggression, as Freud observed.

Identity, for all the writing that has recently sought to explore and define it, remains an inexact concept. We take it here to refer to the concept of self that is constructed partly subjectively, through experience, and partly intersubjectively, through representations and the experience of others that a subject uses in order to play an active part in the world. Identities have to be constructed in particular ways in the process of assimilation to a new culture, and the playing of a part is a relevant metaphor here, particularly in the light of the considerable presence of Jews in the entertainment industries in twentieth-century America. It has been suggested that, beyond the practical search for survival, the Jews who pioneered the film industry were motivated by "inchoate yearnings for entertainment and respectability." But "entertainment" seems an incompatible desire. Where "respectability" implies the secure inhabiting of a system of mutual regard, "entertainment means hanging onto a liminal stage where all manner of things are possible because everything is in both transition and suspension, resisting closure in language and in life, bringing disparate elements together, and trying, impossibly, to maintain a state of unsettledness and nomadic consciousness, of un-pin-down-ability."[29]

This meaning of entertainment extends beyond its usual sense of "fun" or escapism, as a counter idea to the difficulty of everyday life, into the more interesting realm of how some aspects of culture can be a form of "holding"—metaphorically keeping people together and stopping them from "falling apart." This is especially the case with the image: it offers imaginary identity in the form of an internalized, unified "picture" of self, mitigating some of the more shattering experiences of émigré life. Film as entertainment provides such a temporarily integrative "holding" experience; the antithetical divisions of the self are reflected in the good and bad objects in a film's narrative, just as the narrative of *The Great Gatsby* illustrates the divisions of "the familiar" and "the stranger." It is significant that the Eastern European Jews, coming from a predominantly verbal and literate culture, were able to seize on the tremendous dependence that Christian culture has on imagery and to create a visual culture that was quite antithetical to the culture of Eastern European Judaism. The influx of this generation coincided with the birth of cinema as a popular form throughout Europe as well as in the U.S.A. The success of Hollywood film culture, however, is largely due to what we have described as the "heightened perception" of the outsider, which arose from the experience of being rendered passive by the trauma of difference. Hollywood film culture thus reveals the antithetical divisions in the fragmented self-identity of the Jewish émigré culture that produced it. One of the most interesting aspects of recent film history is the change in Hollywood's representation of Jewishness. The main theme of most of the films in which Jews appear is the viability of assimilation and the unimportance of cultural difference.[30] Films such as Steven Spielberg's *Schindler's List* (1994) indicate a new attempt to integrate the entertainment of popular cinema with a recognition of historical fact. Would such a film have been made by anyone other than a Spielberg, that is, someone relatively unaffected by virulent anti-Semitism, with the individual power of the producer-director, within a climate of ethnic self-consciousness that was pioneered by the Black struggles of the 1960's? If immigration is a trauma, does it take the passing of several generations before the difficulty of such history can be addressed?

For the immigrant, the entry into another culture, with the losses that this entails, is the founding moment of a number of possible strategies and destinies; in different historical moments and different cultural circumstances, various possibilities emerge. We have concentrated here on the ambivalent structure of assimilation, and on the wave of Eastern

European Jewish émigrés who arrived in the United States at the beginning of the twentieth century. Their predicament motivated some of them to turn failure into success and to transform the trauma of difference into a capacity to generate and elaborate myths for their adopted culture, particularly to create an industry and visual culture of "entertainment" that could hold together the disparate desires and fragmented identity of anyone seeking to belong—the Hollywood Solution.

14

"A Little Child Shall Lead Them":
The Jewish Family Romance

MARSHALL BERMAN

This essay is dedicated to my son Danny, Daniel Shalom Sclan Berman, born 24 June 1994. While I was writing, sitting at my desk through the nights, he was on my chest in a baby carrier called a sling. Was he asleep or awake? I wanted to know, but it was hard to tell. His eyes were open much of the time, but his amazing serenity made me call it sleep. I could feel him as I wrote, and he helped.

One of the ways Jews stay together is by telling stories. The Bible is the world's most spectacular treasury of stories. Our seasonal rituals are pegged to the activities of telling, hearing, and interpreting stories. Our Talmudic tradition is a body of metastories, stories about stories. Our great modern intellectuals—Spinoza, Marx, Durkheim, Simmel, Freud, Einstein, Kafka, Proust, Wittgenstein, and more—have blessed and cursed the world with more grand stories and metastories. Their achievements build on a dense, complex, and psychically rich Jewish culture of narration. We tell each other stories, listen to them, and turn them over and change them around till they fit us. We look for new and better ways to tell them, though sometimes we mask our creativity by saying we're only looking for a new way to tell it the old way. We tell them to the world and hope the world will love us, but we know the world will digest our stories in its own way, and respond with mixtures of love and hate that we can't control, and we hope those mixtures won't blow us up.

One form of story that Jews tell well is the "family romance," a story in which basic family relationships—husband and wife, parent and child, older and younger siblings, older and younger generations, people inside and outside the family—are loaded with metaphysical intensity, and are felt to form the ultimate core of being. In Jewish stories, starting with the Bible, family relationships are intensely dramatized, fraught with tension and crisis, animated by transgression and betrayal, driven by some inner momentum toward a resolution, which is typically a change in the nature of the family. The typical subject of the Christian story, the solitary soul confronting (or seeking) God, is rare in Jewish culture; Jewish happiness is typically family happiness. One important quality of Sigmund Freud's Oedipal triangle is that it is a Jewish family romance.

The family romance, wherever it thrives in the world, serves as a matrix for some of the primary conflicts in human life: between sizes, small versus big people; between ages, young people versus old; between generations, children versus adults; between classes, propertied and rich versus propertyless and poor; between ethnicities, "our people" versus the rest of the world. The family romance enables people to locate themselves in the world, to grow up to be somebody, to achieve identities.

There is a special type of family romance, where a person tells himself (or herself) that the people who have brought him up aren't his "real" parents, that his real parents are "others," greater and more exalted, that his real home is elsewhere, and that a grand mysterious destiny awaits him, if only he has the brains to recognize it and the guts to fight for it. This promissory (and often migratory) romance animates Jewish history, from the sojourn in Egypt and the earliest legends of Abraham and Joseph and Moses, to the mass migrations of the last century, still going on today.

It is hard to tell, or even to think about telling, a story that starts three thousand years ago and stops today. There are vast historical and anthropological differences between the biblical stories in the first part of this paper and the contemporary novels in the second; we need to read in different ways. Still, there are striking continuities in Jewish experience from ancient to modern times, and I want to bring some of them to light. There really is a *Jewish identity* that goes back a long way, but remains alive and well and ready for a future. Much of this identity is rooted in the call and response of storytelling. I want to examine some of the big stories below.

The family romances I explore in detail here focus on the development of male identity, from Second Samuel's story of King David to Henry Roth's novel *Call It Sleep*. But similar themes can be found in Jewish women's stories of growing up, from the Book of Ruth to Anzia Yezeirska's *Hungry Hearts* to Agnieska Holland's *Europa, Europa*.

The Nazi project of genocide engendered thousands of emergency metamorphoses for boys and girls alike: from 1939 to 1945, family romance became a matter of life and death. Many metamorphosed children survived, and became creators of Jewish culture after 1945. (One survived and became the Archbishop of Paris.) This essay is not about their desperate world, the world of *The Painted Bird* and *Tzili*. It is set in relatively normal times and places, where Jews often live precariously but their very survival is not in doubt. Even when Jewish life is "normal," family romance is a crucial theme: it is about the fluid and volatile boundaries between ourselves and the *goyim*, the rest of the world; it helps us to define who we are, and to deal with the existential problems inherent in being us.

The Biblical Dialectic: Israel Grows, Shrinks, Grows

Jewish family romances are, and must be, shaped by the peculiarities of Israel's history. The Covenant between God and Abraham, Isaac, Jacob, Moses, and the others promises that the children of Israel will be as numerous as the sand on the sea and the stars in the sky. And the evil Pharaoh in Exodus 1 was said to believe that "the people of Israel are too many and too mighty for us." But for all the rest of Jewish history, it has been only too clear that Israel is demographically small and not likely to get much bigger. Whether or not Jews have a state of our own, we know that whatever we have will be small. Even when we grow up, we are going to stay small. (Maybe this is why Jews, from Biblical times [2 Samuel 24] to today, have always resisted attempts at an ethnic census.) We have been a small people, either subsumed or surrounded by giant empires which have the power to annihilate us. This predicament has tipped our collective awareness and empathy, and our sentimentality, toward the small, the young, the child. Conflicts of size, age, and generation drive the great dramatic myths in the Book of Genesis—Jacob and Esau, Rachel and Leah, Joseph and his brothers—and drive Israel's history forward. The God of Israel is typically portrayed as one who looks with special favor on the small against the large and the young against the old. God's promise that "the elder shall serve the younger" (Genesis 25:23) is made again and again and again.

The figure of David is one of the most compelling in the Bible, in part because we see him in many phases of the human life cycle, and we see him grow. The Book of Samuel first presents him to us as "Little David." Like the Jack-the-giant-killer youths in world folklore, he defeats Goliath because he is smarter and more resourceful. The author of Samuel suggests that God has a special fondness for those who are young and small but brave and smart, and that somehow these qualities symbolize the Jewish people as a whole, a people that can triumph over its physical limitations. One more Davidic quality takes on heavy counter-physical weight: sensitivity. David's musicality and soulfulness can soothe Saul's soul and drive away his inner demons (1 Samuel 16:14–22). And the Bible seems to consider him worthy of political power precisely because he does not seek it or want it. David, "the younger," is supposed to be not only a rival of Saul, "the elder," but qualitatively better. His ascendancy is supposed to represent a leap forward for the whole people.

At the same time, though, the Books of Samuel portray David in terms that are typical of ancient warrior epics: "Saul has slain his thousands," the people are said to sing, "but David his tens of thousands" (1, 18:7, 21:11, 29:5). In other words, like a typical warrior hero—Gilgamesh, Achilles, Beowulf—he can kill people on a large scale without worrying or holding back. The priests condemn King Saul because he merely commits mass murder against Amalek, but refrains from genocide (1 Samuel 15); but they have no worries about David. By the time he is anointed as king (2 Samuel 5), he has changed from a distinctive "little David" into a typical warrior "big man." Israel, too, has changed, from a small and vulnerable people into a triumphal nation that, in the Middle East, for a little while at least, is Number One.

The biblical account of David and his reign offers one of the rare visions in Jewish history of a sequence of "healthy" development, where small turns "naturally" into large. But this course of growth is ruptured and almost wrecked, first by the scandal that arises from the king's murderous love for Bathsheba (2 Samuel 11–12), and then by the revolt and death of his dearest son Absalom (14–19). It is hard to tell from the narrative just what Absalom's tragic rebellion is about. There is much detail about how this father and son came to the point of killing each other, but no explanation of why. They may be caught up in the chronic conflict between North and South: fifty years after David's death, this broke up the state forever (2 Samuel 20:1–2; 1 Kings 12). Or Absalom may be trapped in a kind of repetition-compulsion of David's own coup d'état against Saul. For a young, handsome, charismatic general in a state whose political institutions are fragile, the pressures could be irresistible to make his move, to blow away the old authority. Absalom's move even has a divine sanction: isn't God supposed to make the elder serve the younger (Genesis 23:25)? David's lament, "O my son, my son Absalom! Would I had died instead of you!" (2 Samuel 18:33–19:8), may be so heartbreaking because in the son he has killed, the father recognizes himself.

In the Bathsheba story David at first exhibits typical "big man" behavior, but then transcends himself. From his palace roof (above) he sees her in the distance (below), a lovely naked woman taking a bath. He wants her and, as the king, he takes for granted his right to have anybody he wants. "So David sent messengers, and took her; and she came to him, and he lay with her" (2 Samuel 11:4). This woman and her soldier husband Uriah are *klayne menshen* next to the king. Before long, Bathsheba gets pregnant, Uriah gets publicly angry, and David gets rid of him, by arranging to deploy him in combat where he will be killed. Bathsheba mourns, but she moves: she comes to the palace and becomes one of the king's wives. At this point, the prophet Nathan denounces David as a murderer, and warns that, because of the crimes he has committed to get that woman, "the sword shall never depart from your house." A Jewish prophet can't arrest a king, but he can create a scandal that will sap the king's legitimacy.

The tragedy heightens and deepens. Bathsheba gives birth, but after a week's illness her baby dies—"the Lord struck the child," the biblical narrator says. While the baby is ill, David mortifies himself, fasts, and sleeps on the ground, in the hope of appeasing God's wrath. But once the baby is dead, he washes and anoints himself, puts on new clothes, and asks for fresh food. The servants are shocked, but David says angrily, "Can I bring him back again?" Biblical kings often fall to pieces when they are faced with disaster, especially when prophets are blaming them. But even though David's child is dead—killed by God, he believes—he is determined to live. "Then David comforted his wife Bathsheba, and went in to her, and lay with her; and she bore a son, and he called his name Solomon. And the Lord loved him" (12:24).

David's first sexual encounter with Bathsheba was portrayed as a form of recreation, but also of domination, a sign that as the king he could have any woman in the kingdom. But now their sexual life is charged with new meanings. In the face of death, it is a way to grasp life. Sex also becomes a form of comfort, balm for a soul in deep distress. Actually, both their souls are in distress, but Bathsheba's has got to be deeper here. She has just lost her child, her lover has killed her husband, she is alone in the king's palace, and her dependence on him is total. Meanwhile, he is being denounced in the streets for his liason with her, and there is no child to legitimize her and hold his love. If King David has spin doctors, they are surely telling him she is a liability and he should get rid of her fast. Instead, to his glory, he does the right thing. The "comfort" that David brings is *nechama*, the Hebrew word that signifies one of the prime rewards that God bestows on Israel: "Comfort, comfort, my people" (Isaiah 40:1); "When the cares of my heart are many/thy comforts delight my soul" (Psalm 94:19). The spiritual exaltation which the Bible sees in the relationship between God and Israel is embodied here in the activity of a man and a woman in bed. After the sadness they have been through, and the external pressure they are under, sex reaffirms them as a couple. Sex is the continuous factor in the David-Bathsheba story, but it gets spiritualized in the course of the story. It becomes a way to choose life against death, and a way to express love beyond expediency. What began as recreational sex has developed into something like sacred marriage.[1] This may explain why the Bible allows a love affair that is both adulterous and murderous to engender not only Israel's wisest king but also what the Bible tells us is Israel's golden age.

If we jump-cut and pick up these themes in the prophetic age, we find ourselves in a world where Israel's bid for imperial glory is gone with the wind. The basic fact of life now, roughly between 750 and 700 BCE, is the gulf between the kingdoms of Judah and Israel—which both separately and together are quite small and about to get smaller—and the neighboring Assyrian empire to the north, which is overwhelmingly big and about to get even bigger, partly at Israel's expense. In this context, the prophet Amos emerges and tries to start a dialogue both with the people and with God. His dramatic encounter with God comes at 7:1–6, about two thirds of the way through his book. It begins with God notifying Amos that he is preparing a series of deadly plagues to use against Israel, first locusts, then fire. God gives the prophet a vivid preview of the mass destruction and death he is about to bring down. Up to now, Amos has been denouncing Israel for a wide variety of sins, from idol worship to violation of the sabbath to oppression of the poor to incest. It seems we are meant to think that God has got the message, and the impending horror is his revenge. The idea of divine plagues also evokes folk memories of Pharaonic Egypt, and sounds a theme that the prophets will often repeat: Israel has become as evil as its worst oppressor. But suddenly Amos seems to recoil in horror from his own dread vision. It is as if a man who has had a splendid career as a prosecutor, and gone so far as to convict his own people, has sudden second thoughts when they are actually on Death Row; he recoils on the eve of the death sentence that he himself has demanded, and strives desperately to get through to the highest authority to make an appeal on their behalf. Twice he intercedes and implores God to have *rachmones*, take pity. The basis for his appeal is a fact that must have been on everybody's mind in eighth-century Israel, but that (so far as I know) commentators have never connected with the prophetic critique. Once the fact is cited, though, its relevance is obvious. What Amos says to God is, "How can Jacob stand? He is so small!"

Amos's question to God embodies a classic strategy in criminal defense: not to deny the defendant's criminal acts, but to claim that he has been driven to them because he is a victim of past abuse. What makes this strategy particularly audacious here is Amos's suggestion that the abuse was committed by God himself: he charged Israel with world-historical responsibilities, but he failed to give it the means, the power and autonomy that it would need to fulfill these ends. As Amos imagines it, this argument brings God up short: at once he relents and cancels his death sentence: "It shall not be." This is one of the great biblical moments where a human being confronts God and forces him to change. The biblical archetype may be Cain's argument about saving his life (in Genesis 4), or Abraham's about saving the city of Sodom (in Genesis 18). Amos believes that once God has heard his voice, he will concede the human point at once, and will accept responsibility for having made Israel chronically, and irreversibly, too small. Amos hears God assure him, in effect, that he won't try this child in adult court, alongside giants like the Assyrians or the Egyptians; he will *hab'rachmones*, take pity, and make sure Israel lives. It isn't only that he will protect the people from the imperial predators that are threatening them; at least as important, he will protect them from himself.

So God promises Israel that it won't be destroyed, it won't die; but its life is going to be permanently precarious and problematical. It may hold onto political power, but there will be far less of it than in its Davidic and Solomonic heyday, and it will be far more subject to the incessant crossfire and convulsion of the great powers that surround it. Or it may lose political identity entirely, and be forced to bear the anguish of exile. In any case, it will have to learn to live small.

In this dark time, our prophets make a great creative leap, and invent a new meaning for Israel, a meaning that is still an important part of our concept of "Jewish identity." At a moment when it is clear that Israel has failed as a great power, Israel instead will become the force that sees through great-power politics. The prophetic political vision is a form of world peace that doesn't dissolve national existence—as the multinational empires of the Middle East were always trying to dissolve it—but that lives in a world of nations who recognize each other's right to live, and recognize that the earth has room for them all.

> For out of Zion shall go forth the law,
>   and the word of the Lord from Jerusalem. . . .
> And they shall beat their swords into plowshares,
>   and their spears into pruning hooks.
> Nation shall not lift up sword against nation,
>   neither shall they learn war any more.
>
> . . .
>
> The wolf shall dwell with the lamb,
>   and the leopard shall lie down with the kid,
> and the calf and the lion and the fatling together,
>   and a little child shall lead them.
> The cow and the bear shall feed;
>   their young shall lie down together;
>   and the lion shall eat straw like the ox.
> The sucking child shall play over the asp's hole,
>   and the weaned child will put his hand on the adder's den.
> They shall not hurt or destroy
>   in all my holy mountain;
> for the earth will be full of the knowledge of the Lord,
>   as the waters cover the sea. (Isaiah 2:3–4; 11:6–9)

Precisely because "Jacob is so small," the prophets believe, "a little child shall lead them." The physical limitations that make Israel a failure as a great power will make it a success as a different kind of power. Ancient Middle Eastern politics seem to have been ruled (as were pre-First World War politics) by the paradigm of a biological food chain; here Israel tells the world that human beings can overcome the zero-sum stark inevitabilities of this model of life.

The prophetic movement marked a break in world culture. Israel was on the verge of fading away—just as dozens, maybe hundreds of other peoples in the ancient Middle East would fade away. But at the moment when it seemed there was no place in the world for Israel, Israel presented the world with a new idea of place, far more expansive and inclusive than the Middle East's deserts and ravines. As the prophetic vision spread, there got to be more room for the Jews. It wasn't simply that they could be legitimately recognized under the new rules: they got special recognition for inventing the new rules. (We have to add that some of the recognition was negative: the vision of Isaiah is radically threatening to those who embrace the warrior morality of the *Iliad* and who want to beat their plowshares into swords.) One minute, the Jews were being ripped to pieces by conflicts with their neighbors, with each other, with God; the next minute—or was it the same minute?—they were offering the whole world a vision that purported to heal conflict between anyone and anyone else. Thus a people forced to live small could extend its life and expand its being by learning to think big.

Modern Times: The Subjective Family Romance

If we make a leap in time, from the biblical to the modern era, we will find Jews still forced to live small, and still searching for new ways to see and think big. But there are important differences. Modern Jews are citizens of national states, and beneficiaries of a social policy that the nineteenth century called "Jewish Emancipation." It is impossible to explain Emancipation on one foot, but it will help if we consider the 1791 debates in the French National Assembly, two years after the Declaration of the Rights of Man and Citizen, on the issue of rights for religious and ethnic minorities. Some members opposed rights for Jews on the grounds that they were an inexorably separate "nation within the nation." The view that prevailed, however, was that of the radical Deputy Stanislas de Clermont-Tonnerre, who said: "One should refuse everything to the Jews as a nation, but one must give them everything as individuals; they should become citizens."[2] The crucial words here are "as individuals" and "become citizens." One of the central forces in modern history has been the mass desire for what Thomas Jefferson called "life, liberty, and the pursuit of happiness." Emancipation created a framework in which Jews, without ceasing to be Jews, could express themselves "as individuals," explore and enjoy individual liberty, pursue their own individual roads to happiness, and, by "becoming citizens," participate actively in modern public life. Hegel, trying to explain this public life philosophically, said: *"The principle of the modern world is freedom of subjectivity."*[3] So many of the men and women who have created modern Jewish culture have been explorers of the most intense subjectivity. But it is usually a blocked, trapped, anguished subjectivity tortured by internal contradictions. A subjectivity that can say to itself, as Kafka said in his diary, "How can I have anything in common with Judaism? I hardly have anything in common with myself."[4] Jewish subjects have had little chance to stretch and evolve into citizens, because not the liberal republics of the modern West or the revolutionary U.S.S.R. or the State of Israel have even begun to fulfill their civic promise.

When Freud wrote his landmark essay "Family Romances" in 1909, he was talking in the language of modern subjectivity.[5] It is a type of fantasy widely held by neurotics, he said, but also by "all comparatively highly gifted people." The fantasy "emerges first in children's play, and then, starting in the period roughly before puberty, takes over the topic of family relations." It surges up in dreams and in daydreams: "the child's imagination becomes engaged in getting free from the parents . . . and of replacing them by others, occupying, as a rule, a higher social station." The subject imagines that he (or she) is really "a stepchild or an adopted child," that the people who have brought him up are not his real parents. Sometimes it's the father who's a fraud, sometimes the mother, sometimes both. The "real" parents may be landed proprietors, aristocrats, the Lord of the Manor, even the Emperor; the basic principle is that the child's "parents are replaced by others of better birth." As the child grows older, "learns about sexual processes," and "tends to picture to himself erotic situations and relations," the romance takes on a sharply sexual focus. Although Freud says (rightly, I think) that both sexes go through the family romance, his detailed account is almost entirely male. The growing boy now "desires to bring [his] mother, who is the subject of the most intense sexual curiosity, into situations of secret infidelity and into secret love affairs." The more ardently he idealized her before, the more luridly he portrays her now; he "has no hesitation in attributing to his mother as many secret love affairs as he himself has competitors." These mental and emotional processes—the demonization of the mother, the reincarnation of the self as an "other"—are likely to be intensely painful, for both the child himself and the family of his romance. Nevertheless, the family romance enables the growing child to separate inwardly from his parents:

> The freeing of an individual, as he grows up, from the authority of his parents is one of the most necessary though one of the most painful results brought about by the course of human development. It is quite essential that this liberation should occur. . . . Indeed, the whole progress of society rests on the opposition between successive generations.

In other words, every one of us has got to go through the pain of a family romance in order to free ourselves from our family. If we do go through it, we can come out the other end and grow into modern "free subjectivity," and furthermore we can help bring about the "progress of society." But if Jacob doesn't wrestle, he can't become Israel.

Call It Sleep: Romance on the Lower East Side

The family romance I want to discuss is Henry Roth's 1934 novel *Call It Sleep*. Since the 1960's, students of American literature have recognized this radiant lyrical novel as one of the great works of fiction of the twentieth century. Its historical context is the great migration of Eastern European Jews to the U.S.A., which began in 1881, when the Czarist government sponsored a wave of pogroms, and lasted till 1924, when the U.S. Congress closed the gates. Its world is the immigrant ghetto that developed in every late nineteenth-century American city. New York's Lower East Side, where Roth grew up and where his book is set, was by far the biggest and most tumultuous of these ghettos, with more than 540,000 people (the 1910 census figure, which counted only legal immigrants) in one square mile, the world's highest urban density.[6] Roth attended the City College of New York in the 1920's, and got a degree just before the Great Depression made college men chronically unemployed. Early in the 1930's, he joined the American Communist Party. Roth was a Communist when he wrote *Call It Sleep*, and when it came out, and for at least another twenty years.[7] You will see why this matters later on.

The novel begins in 1907, just after Roth's birth. Roth offers us a grand, Whitmanesque panorama of New York harbor, Ellis Island, the Statue of Liberty, and the immense crowds of immigrants, thousands coming every day, from dozens of nations—Slovaks, Armenians, Greeks, Danes, Irish, Poles, Italians, Jews—and each people, Roth says, has its own distinctive style of joy as they set foot in the New World and meet their loved ones. But the hero, David Schearl ("Little David") and his mother Genya are cut off from this public happiness, and thrown into a nightmare of private dread. Albert, his father, greets them with scorn and violent rage: "What do you do? You refuse to recognize me. You don't know me. That's all the greeting I get." David and his mother were detained and re-examined at Ellis Island; the father translates this as "You . . . made a laughingstock of me!" He focuses on David's straw hat, a gift from an old nurse:

> " . . . You don't think it's pretty?"
>
> "Pretty? Do you still ask?" His lean jaws hardly moved as he spoke. "Can't you see those idiots lying back there [on the ferry] are watching us already?

They're mocking us! What will the others do on the train? He looks like a clown in it. He's the cause of all this trouble anyway!"

The harsh voice, the wrathful glare, the hand flung out toward the child frightened him. Without knowing the cause he knew the stranger's anger was directed toward himself. He burst into tears and pressed closer to his mother.

"Quiet!" the voice above him snapped.

Cowering, the child wept all the louder.

"Hush, darling!" His mother's protecting hands settled on his shoulders.

"Just when we're about to land! . . . he begins this! This howling! And now we'll have it all the way home, I suppose. Quiet! You hear?"

"It's you who are frightening him, Albert!"

"Am I? Well, let him be quiet. And take that straw gear off his head."

. . . A snarl choked whatever else he would have uttered. While his wife looked on aghast, his long fingers scooped the hat from the child's head. The next instant it was sailing over the ship's side to the green waters below. The overalled men in the stern grinned at each other. The old orange-peddler shook her head and chuckled.

"Albert!" his wife caught her breath. "How could you?"

"I could!" he rapped out. "You should have left it behind."

His teeth clicked, and he glared about the deck. She lifted the sobbing child to her breast, pressed him against her. (13–15)[8]

This short scene contains most of the novel's main themes. David's father, a lineal descendant of Strindberg's *The Father*, is one of the most terrifying characters in modern literature. He is gripped by violent impulses that don't get repressed but erupt in public. His rage at his wife and son is crudely paranoid: they got themselves examined and detained at Ellis Island to spite *him*; his two-year-old son is crying to insult *him*; this boy just off the boat is dressed like a boy just off the boat so that strangers on the train will mock *him*. (In the 1990's, after twenty years of public discussion of domestic violence, David's father's problems have a far clearer context than they did in the 1960's, when I first read *Call It Sleep*, or in the 1930's, when the book first appeared.) He is a skilled worker, but his great rage drives him from job after job; eventually he will find stability as a milkman, where, he says, he doesn't have to be with other people. David's mother loves her son in a way that is protective—and he needs protection—but also sexual and hot. David, a smart and sweet but weirdly introspective kid, is terrified by his father, but also, in a strange way, thrilled by him: here, and later, he seems to aestheticize that harsh voice, that wrathful glare, that snarl, that proud outstretched hand, so that even as his father looks monstrous he feels sublime.

David's story begins with a grand panorama of New York, and of America; by the first chapter's end, his horizon shrinks into a claustrophobic tenement cell that could be marked NO EXIT, where his parents will torture and destroy each other for six years and four hundred pages, while he struggles desperately to breathe and grow. But his tenement life is not all bleak. Its beauty, Roth shows us, flows from Genya's overpowering sexuality, and from the sexual chemistry that flows between mother and son. *Call It Sleep* is an intensely beautiful representation of the Oedipal romance, suggestive of D. H. Lawrence's *Sons and Lovers* (whose influence Roth acknowledged), and just as powerful. It is especially striking in its poetic language, which creates an aura around the mother and around the mother and son.

After its start at the Harbor, Roth's story resumes four years later, now from inside David's head. "Standing in the doorway, she looked as tall as a tower." David and his mother are home alone together on a hot summer day. They are sort of flirting, in a way that parents and children flirt. He asks for a drink, and she gives him a glass of water from the tap. His question takes up our central theme of Israel's size. In Roth's family romance the issue carries special urgency, because this boy's father takes advantage of his size to beat and threaten people.

> "When am I going to be big enough?" he asked, resentfully.
> "There will come a time," she answered, smiling. "Have little fear."

Genya speaks in an idiosyncratic but luminous voice that Roth creates for her. (It is likely that he wants us to imagine her speaking a "pure" Yiddish, as distinct from the supposedly "corrupt" English and "Yinglish" that most other people speak.) She tells her son to go play in the street so she can clean the house, but she really doesn't want him to leave, and he says he's leaving but he doesn't really want to go. As he is set to go, she asks him,

> "Whom will you refresh with the icy lips the water lent you?"
> "Oh!" he lifted his smiling face.
> "You remember nothing," she reproached him, and with a throaty chuckle lifted him in her arms.
> "There!" she laughed, nuzzling his cheek, "but you've waited too long; the sweet chill has dulled. Lips for me", she reminded him, "must always be cool as the water that wet them." She put him down. (17–20)

They flirt some more. David wants to see his birthday on the calendar, and to know when he is going to grow. But instead he notices the days in red, Sunday, the one day his father will be home. Downcast by this fact of life, he finally leaves his mother's kitchen for the street.

As David grows, he becomes sexually aware, but in twisted ways. First, he is invited by Annie, a crippled girl in his building, to "play bad" (51–5), and their encounter gives him garbled ideas: that sex is something that people do "down there", in the lower parts of their bodies, and in the dark cellars of tenements; that it is a process initiated by women; that it makes them crippled (like Annie), but also makes children; that it gives him a tremendous physical force that makes him ("Who puts id in is de poppa. . . . Yaw de poppa"), potentially at least, like his father.[9] It takes David another couple of years before he can imagine sex between his parents (296–9): he can't accept that this radiant being who loves him so much can also do that unspeakable thing with that dreadful man. Meanwhile, however, he comes to see that his mother's sexuality does not exist for him alone. Luter, the family boarder, his father's coworker, and a sleazy, hateful man, comes alive in Genya's presence. He picks up this signal (as his father does not), but misreads its meaning: not only have they "played bad" together, he thinks, but his mother has initiated and invited it (89). She is degraded, guilty of some sort of sexual pollution, but he shares her guilt by knowing all. Angry and distraught, he flees from her, from the house, the block, the neighborhood. He promptly gets lost. Ironically, given his sense of guilt, he is picked up by the police. They locate his mother and summon her: she, too, has never been so far from home. As they head home together, threading their way through strange streets, mother and son feel a sense of adventure and comradeship. They have become close in a whole new way. The father, of course, is angry at them both: "How did you ever let him get so far?" (114). David is getting things all wrong (he thinks of his mother and himself as partners in crime, when there has been no crime), yet his family romance has an inner dynamism of its own that is helping him grow up.

David's first misreading of his mother sets him up for a far more serious misreading of himself. He overhears her confess to her sister Bertha a disastrous love affair, back in Europe, with a *goy* (195–207). She has been treated horribly by her lover, the organist in their village church, and by her parents; she is lucky to be alive. In her heartrending tale of love and betrayal, we pick up echoes of the "Chava" story in the *Tevye* cycle and of the Gretchen Tragedy in Goethe's *Faust* (and of hundreds of tragic folk tales from Eastern Europe and all over the world). But David, who understands only fragments of the story, since the sisters are talking in Polish, picks up something that isn't there: he feels instinctively that he must be the love-child of this affair, and the son of this *goy*. It is like a revelation, and suddenly his life seems to make sense to him. Now, he thinks, he understands why he feels so alienated from the life around him, and why his father seems to hate him so much: he is truly an "other," a Polish bastard, and not a Jew at all.

From this point on, David's inner life splits in two; it is only at the book's dramatic climax that these contradictory tracks comes together. On one track, his father creates a deeper bond with him through Judaism: he asks his wife to put David in a *cheder*, so he can get a basic Jewish eduction, learn something of the Hebrew language and the Bible, have a *bar mitzvah* at age thirteen, and say *kaddish* (blessing) for his father when he is dead. Here David's father briefly stops being the raving *meshugginer* we know so well, and acts as millions of normal Jewish fathers have acted through the ages. David is instantly comfortable in *cheder*, he learns Hebrew fluently, and he has a gift of empathy that enables him to project himself into the biblical world: here, at last, he feels he "fits." But, ironically, his perfect fit propels him into a situation where he appears radically unfit. His favorite text is Isaiah 6, a vision of God in the Temple, surrounded by his angels, exploding with his light and power. David feels he has seen the light, the luminous explosion, over by the electric trolley on Avenue D. (We can recognize the explosion of light as an electrical breakdown, a short circuit, but David can't.) Isaiah is terrified, he is too impure to bear what he has seen. But an angel touches his mouth with a burning coal: "Behold, this has touched your lips; your guilt is taken away, and your sin forgiven" (6:6). Now he can speak to Israel, and he says it will be utterly wasted before it can be saved. David identifies himself totally with this prophetic vision, and dreads his own impurity. His spiritual anguish leads him to tell his *rebbe* his mother's confession. The *rebbe* is stunned: can it be that his once-in-a-generation star pupil, "a true Yiddish child" (365), "a seraph among Esau's goyim" (387), is not a Jew at all?[10]

Meanwhile, David presses toward transgression and betrayal on another front. As he grows and feels more confident, he dares to go up on the roof, where he can see the harbor and the whole city, and feel free. There he meets Leo, a Catholic boy who flies kites, skates through the streets, gets into fights, and lives a loose and unsupervised life ("no parents to interfere, no orders to obey—nothing" [319]). Leo is not only a Catholic, but a Catholic from Poland, his parents' Old Country, hence magically connected to the *goy* whom David dreams is his real father. Leo explains Catholic theology, and claims he is free to do anything because he is protected by the Holy Family; he gives David a set of his magical rosary beads. David is in awe and utterly abject before Leo, and offers him anything he wants. What he wants, it turns out, is to be a sexual predator, and he wants David to smuggle him into David's aunt's candy store and into her house, to give him a crack at her two preadolescent girls. Leo's caper falls flat, but meanwhile it leads David to humiliate both his family and, everybody feels, the Jewish people. "And exactly the same way—a goy!" David's uncle screams at his wife, "It's a family trait by now!" (382). David's family romance has driven him to reenact his mother's primal crime. He tried to overcome ethnic prejudices, but in a way that seemed designed to prove these prejudices are right. He reached out, but in a poisoned embrace.

Roth constructs an unbearably intense, Dostoevskian "scandal scene," where the *rebbe* and David's aunt and uncle simultaneously arrive at David's tenement, and their two stories together break over his head (384–403). David's father explodes in a series of paranoid diatribes, increasingly hysterical and unbalanced. He springs on the company a confession that he murdered his father back in Poland; though it is likely, from the way he tells the story, that what he was really guilty of was Ivan Karamazov's crime, *desire* to murder his father.[11] But his sense of guilt includes no contrition; it only magnifies his self-righteous fury in assigning guilt to others.

> "Hear me!" He was slavering at the mouth. . . . "All these years my blood told me! Whispered at me whenever I looked at him, nudged me and told me he wasn't mine! From the very moment I saw him in your arms, out of the ship, I guessed, I guessed! . . . It's been in my way, tangled me. . . . Haven't you ever seen it? That weeks and weeks go by and I'm no man at all? No man as other men are? You know of what I speak, having known others!" (391–3, 401–02)

By paranoid logic, Albert's own sexual difficulties become proof of his wife's and child's conspiracy against him.

At the end of his last tirade (401), Albert announces that he is going to kill his son. The rest of the family seems numb, in a state of shock. Maybe they are so inured to his emotional violence, they don't recognize (as Roth's readers do) that this time he is over the edge. David, whimpering, in shock along with everyone else, drenched in guilt, offers his father a broken horsewhip (a fine Dostoevskian black-comic detail), one of Albert's own discards, to beat him with. He commences, slowly, with a sadistic glee. And now, in a stunning climax, as Albert hits David and he falls, Leo's rosary beads fall out of his coat. Albert lets loose a final barrage:

> "God's own hand! A sign! A witness!" his father was raving, whirling the whip in his flying arms. "A proof of my word! The truth! Another's! A goy's! A cross! A sign of filth! Let me strangle him! Let me rid the world of a sin!" (402)

The rosary, sensational detail, jars the family out of their trance and mobilizes them to resist the child sacrifice that is about to happen. Albert lunges forward for the kill. But David's aunt Bertha is "hanging like a dead weight from his father's whip-hand. 'He'll slay him,' she shrieked, 'He'll trample on him as he let his father be trampled on. Hurry, Genya!'" At the last minute, Genya flings herself against the door, and pushes David out of the house and down the stairs to the street.

David escapes a sacrifice, yet now he seems ready to sacrifice himself. He runs for the trolley tracks: he will touch the third rail, set off a luminous explosion, and give himself a massive electric shock. He seems to know that he can get himself killed by doing this. Why is he doing it? As David runs for the tracks, he is hysterical, but purposeful; but it is hard for us to grasp just what his purpose is. In a world where Israel is chronically small, he is working in a great prophetic Jewish tradition by trying to think big. But what is he thinking of? First, he wants to create a dialogue with God: he wants to evoke God's presence and power; he wants God to forgive his real and imagined sins, and to take away his guilt, just as God did for the prophet Isaiah (6:7). A little while ago he was taken in by a *goy*, not only by Leo's sleazy *macho*, but by his magic and fetishism. Now he doesn't need Leo—or his mythical father the organist—anymore: he is making an existential leap on his own. He is confronting God directly in a Jewish idiom, affirming his Jewishness, even flaunting it before the world.

In addition, David feels he is showing his good faith and ultimate seriousness by putting his life on the line. In fact, this particular act of faith has been central to the mass politics of the past two hundred years. It was only in the Age of Revolution, when the *proste menshen* of the modern world, the common people, were ready to stake their lives, that they won respect and power and made human rights real.[12] David has been cut off from collective politics both by his size and age and by his family's isolation. But he makes a revolution of his own in a subjective and existential way.

After he risks and nearly destroys himself, David at last wins recognition from his angry God. It happens indirectly—maybe only Shakespeare or Dostoevsky could have written a scene where these two look into each other's eyes—but it is for real. David nearly electrocutes himself, but he is saved, and carried home under the protection of a crowd, a doctor, and a cop. A neighbor, "a fattish, bare-armed woman" who lives on the same floor as the Schearls, but whose name we never learn, tells the policeman what transpired after David ran away. She narrates in excruciatingly broken English, which even suggests a vaudeville parody of "Yinglish."

> En dey vas fighdingk, Oy-yoy-yoy! Vid scrimms! . . . En vee vus listeningk, en' dis man vos crying. *Ah'm khrezzy! I dun know vod I do! I dun' know vod I said. . . . Yes, Yes, he was saying, My sawn, Mine, Yes.* (436–7, italics mine)

Albert finally says the magic words that he has resisted, and then actively denied: *My son.* And he finally accepts Genya's story of David's birth: "Awld eight. Eight en'—en vun mawnt'. He vas bawn in—". The cop cuts Albert off impatiently, because David's age (eight years, one month) and date of birth mean nothing to him. But they mean everything to David, and to Genya, and to us. After abusing his wife and nearly destroying his child, Strindberg style, Albert has turned and repented. He has come to trust Genya and accept her calendar, in which David's father is nobody but himself.

Just before David falls asleep, "His father stood in the doorway, features dissolved in the dark. Only the glitter in his eyes was sharply visible, fixed on the puffy grey ankle." The doctor has written a prescription, Albert uncharacteristically volunteers to go get it, then quotes the doctor, that David should be better in a day or two. Then there is a long silence. Then they converse (in articulate Yiddish instead of broken English):

> "It—it's my fault, isn't it?"
> She shook her head wearily. "What use is there to talk about faults, Albert? None foresaw this. No one alone brought it on. And if it's faults we must talk about it's mine as well. I never told you. I let him listen to me months and months ago. I even drove him downstairs to—to—"
> "To protect him—from me?"
> "Yes."
> "I'll go get it." He turned heavily out of the doorway. (440)

Albert accepts a reality that has been visible to everyone but himself, till now: he was an overwhelming menace from whom his son needed protection. Now that he has affirmed himself as a father, he is implicitly pledging to provide his son with protection from now on. And now that Genya does not have to act as a single parent anymore, she can afford to surrender at least some of her saintliness. And now that David had been out on the farthest edge, and come through the valley of the shadow of death, he can relax and let himself be taken care of. Because he has risked everything, and won recognition, he can even afford magnanimity: as he hears his father's steps out the door, "A vague, remote pity stirred within his breast." And he can embrace all the realities that have assaulted him, and that he has confronted, "and feel them all and feel, not pain, not terror, but strangest triumph, strangest acquiescence. One might as well call it sleep. He shut his eyes" (440–1).

David's family romance drove him to grow up fast, too fast; but through Roth's dialectical imagination, his growth transforms his real family, so that it at last can take care of him. David is a modern Jacob, underage and underweight, who still has the courage to wrestle with his angel, and who is finally blessed and becomes Israel. Israel's reward for growing up prematurely is to be reborn into a new life where he can live like a child, where he can regress and rest.

Where does the Schearl family romance fit in the long waves of Jewish history? Readers of the Bible will surely notice that Roth's portrait of the father, seen through his child's eyes, sounds a lot like a portrait of Yahweh in his cruelest, most murderous incarnations.

"Answer me."

Answer me, his words rang out. Answer me, but they meant Despair. Who could answer his father? In that dread summons the judgment was already sealed.

. . .

"Your only son!" she wailed, pressing David convulsively to her. "Your only son!"

"Don't tell me that! He's no son of mine! Would that he were dead at my feet!" (83, 84)

And his child's vision of his mother recalls some of the Canaanite goddesses in whose being sexuality, nuturance, and fertility converged. At some points in the Bible, Yahweh appears as a kind of sexual terrorist who is consumed by jealousy and determined to destroy utterly the mother goddesses and all the guilty pleasures they embody. The opposition between the male and female gods appears total, Yahweh would rather see Israel dead than shared—"Not pitied", he tells Hosea, "Not my people" (1:6–8)—and Israel seems like a child in a custody struggle, in the process of being ripped to pieces. But our Bible offers green oases. Our prophets imagined a God who has the power to evolve, to develop and grow. Up to now, they said, not just Israel but even God has lived in the dark. We have transgressed, we have sinned, they say, but there are also vital things that God has missed; but through dialogue and struggle, our God can learn even as we learn ourselves. Then God and Israel can come together in a *new covenant* (Hosea 2:18–20; Jeremiah 31:31). Yahweh's sexual jealousy and uncontrolled rage have become a mortal danger to his child Israel. The prophets imagine a God who can overcome, who can recognize, who can accept and include, who can incorporate male and female and bring them together in peace.

Every new generation of Jews has to wrestle with the problems of Jewish identity on its own. In modern times, when, as Hegel says, "The principle of the modern world is freedom of subjectivity," identity questions force themselves on every single subject. Thus every Jew is both forced and free to work out what kind of Jew he or she is going to be. And it is a question of sexuality as well as a question of observance and belief. It is nice that both the Bible and modern Jewish literature offer us visions in which, like Albert and Genya on Roth's last page, male and female forces, father and mother, can recognize each other and unite, and children can be reborn in peace.[13]

I have been arguing that the Jews, forced by nature and history to live small, have survived and thrived by learning to think big. This argument is rooted in Nietzsche, and I don't want to quit without giving him due credit. Take, for instance, this fabulous passage from *The Genealogy of Morals*:

Whatever else has been done to damage the powerful and great of the earth seems trivial compared with what the Jews have done, that priestly people who avenged themselves on their enemies and oppressors by radically inverting their values, that is, by an act of the most spiritual vengeance.

For two thousand years and more, Jewish life has been animated by "the furious hatred of the underprivileged and impotent." Driven by this hatred, by "rancor turning creative," we

> dared to invert the aristocratic value equations—good/noble/powerful/beautiful/happy/favored by the gods—and to maintain that only the poor, the powerless, are good; only the suffering, the sick, are truly blessed. But you, noble and mighty ones of the earth, will be, to all eternity . . . the godless, the cursed, and the damned![14]

Surely Nietzsche was right to say that visions and ideals are rooted in a will to power. And he was right to think that Jewish expressions of the will to power have been radically innovative. But then what's his complaint? Why shouldn't we fight for our lives in any way we can? Nietzsche is always saying the will to power makes the world go round; fine, so why shouldn't it drive and inspire the small and weak as well as the big and strong? What Jews did to the will to power long ago, and are still doing to it today, has been to sublimate it, to create structures where people could struggle without anybody getting killed. We should be able to enjoy some post-Nietzschean *nachis* for that.

The Crowd in the Family Romance

I have presented the family romance in *Call It Sleep* as an essentially subjective phenomenon, typical of modernity, located within an individual and within his family, disconnected from any collective life. But in fact collective life plays a crucial role in the story:

> Humanity. On feet, on crutches, in carts and cars . . . Human voices, motion, seething, throbbing, bawling, honking horns, and whistling. Troubling the far clusters of street lamps, setting lights guttering with their passing bodies like a wind. (407)

In a remarkable stretch of bravura writing (403–31), Roth makes the whole neighborhood pass through David's head—warehousemen, push-cart peddlers, working girls, gamblers by the river, customers in a saloon, sailors on a ship, a revolutionary orator and his (mostly skeptical) crowd—as he passes them by. These people are living lives that sound insular and hermetically sealed, with no apparent relationship to each other. Their fragments of conversation are surprisingly personal. It is as if

David becomes magically gifted, so that he not merely overhears people's voices, but actually, in a second or two, penetrates into their whole lives.[15] This power to enter into people's lives may be Roth's idea of the closest thing to prophetic power in modern times, the age of free subjectivity. It is the power of the novelist.

David touches the third rail. He gets a tremendous electric shock, which nearly kills him. For an instant he feels in touch with overwhelming primal force. Then he blacks out, and blows out all the power in the neighborhood. Suddenly, all the different worlds of the Lower East Side come to a stop. They stop short in a dozen different languages and dialects:

"W'at?"
"W'ut?"
"Va-at?"
"Gaw blimey!"
"W'atsa da ma?"

Jesus!"
"Give a look! Id's rain—
"Shawt soicit, Mack—"
"Mary, w'at's goin—"
"Schloimee, a blitz like!"
"Hey mate!"

On Avenue D, a long burst of flame spurted from underground, growled as if the veil of earth were splitting. . . . On Avenue C, the lights of the trolley-car waned and wavered. The motorman cursed, feeling the power drain. In the Royal Warehouse, the blinking watchman tugged at the jammed and stubborn window. The shriveled coal-heaver leaned unsteadily. . . .

The street was filled with running men, faces carved and ghostly in the fierce light. . . .

"Christ, it's a kid!"
"Oy! Oy vai! Oy vai! Oy vai!"
"Git a cop!"
"Don't touch 'im!"
"Bambino! Madre mia!"
"Mary. It's jus' a kid!"
"Helftz! Helftz! Helftz Yeedin! Rotivit!" (419–21)

Up to now, the people of the Lower East Side have lived in contiguous but segregated worlds, hermetically sealed by barriers of language, ethnicity, class, sex, barely aware of each other's existence, or else aware of each other as taboo. What little David achieves—perhaps inadvertently, but authentically—is to get these strangers to recognize each other and work together for the first time in their lives.

Although the people in this crowd can barely communicate (in the everyday street, they probably could not communicate), the state of emergency of a child in lethal danger inspires them to overleap ethnic and cultural barriers and focus on what matters most. Thus they pull David off the third rail and perform some rough sort of artificial respiration that brings him back to life; although their relations with officials appear to be at best shaky, they manage to summon an Irish cop who certifies that the boy has broken the law and a WASP doctor who certifies that he will live. They then bear David home in a triumphal procession; they congratulate him for surviving, but also congratulate each other for helping him survive. In these anonymous people, Henry Roth has created what may be American literature's first multicultural crowd. They are a modern, and American, incarnation of the multicultural world where Isaiah imagined a little Israel could belong almost three thousand years ago: the wolf will live with the lamb, the leopard will lie down with the goat, the lion will eat straw like the ox, and a little child, the one with the vision, will lead them.

This vision of a multicultural crowd, talking different languages yet able to understand each other and work together in an emergency, is important not only in the history of Judaism, but also in the history of Communism. I mentioned before that Roth was a Communist when he wrote *Call It Sleep* and for many years after. His book got a frigid response from the Party journal *New Masses*, which said, "It is a pity that so many young writers drawn from the proletariat can make no better use of their experience than as material for introspective and febrile novels." Roth was understandably upset by this: as he told Leonard Michaels in the 1980's, "I thought I was writing a proletarian novel."[16] The Party's stupidity and rigidity, which help define the word "Stalinism," do not define all periods of Party history. *Call It Sleep* was a victim of the very end of the Comintern's "Third Period," from 1928 to 1935. In those disastrous years, the Party, through its utter refusal to share space and make alliances with any other leftists or liberals, helped Hitler come to power. After 1933, the Party saw what it had done, and recoiled in horror. But the recoil mechanism, made in Moscow, took some time to work. Finally, in the summer of 1935, the Comintern proclaimed a new strategy, which it called the "Popular Front," a "union of all democratic forces against fascism."[17] Now Communists could work, politically and culturally, with all sorts of people who weren't communistic or revolutionary at all. The Popular Front, roughly from 1935 to 1946 (minus the two years of the Hitler-Stalin pact), is the one really creative period of American Communism. Their greatest achievement was to organize the major American industries under the banner of the C.I.O. The culture of the Front included (and this is only a little) the Works Progress Administration Guides, the great folklore collections, James Agee and

Walker Evans's *Let Us Now Praise Famous Men*, John Steinbeck's and John Ford's *Grapes of Wrath*, Martha Graham and Aaron Copland's "Appalachian Spring," Robert Rossen-Abraham Polonsky-John Garfield's *Body and Soul* and *Force of Evil*, and a series of giant murals that framed public buildings and public spaces all over 1930's America. (Many have been bricked or painted over, or disintegrated beyond repair, but a surprising number can still be recognized and admired.) The main theme of these murals, and of Popular Front culture in general, is that America is so great because it is "trans-national," so open to so many different kinds of people.[18]

Roth's vision of a multicultural crowd places him in the vanguard of creators of the Popular Front, the high point of Communism in the U.S.A. But even now, fifty years later, after the eclipse of Communism, his portrait of the urban crowd still has visionary power, whenever we try to dream of what we want America to be.

David in Israel

At the very end of 1994, a reading of King David's story almost brought Prime Minister Yitzhak Rabin's government down. The trouble started when Shimon Peres, Rabin's Foreign Minister, addressing the Knesset (the parliament), said that his idea of Judaism did not include "occupation and ruling over other people."[19] A member of one of the far-right parties shouted that King David had done plenty of both. Peres replied: "Not everything King David did is acceptable to a Jew, on the ground [or] on the roofs." Those roofs clearly allude to David's desire for Bathsheba (discussed earlier in this essay), which not only leads him to homicide, but also ensures an age of permanent warfare. Peres's characterization of King David set off a riot among the Orthodox and right-wingers, who ran through the streets screaming and vilified Peres (and Rabin) for heresy. They cited Talmudic authority to show that no man has the right to say King David sinned.[20] They stirred up a vote of No Confidence, and although the vote failed (as expected), the political atmosphere grew even more hysterical than usual. It took some weeks before the hermeneutic wars abated and the Knesset focused on the present again.

It is fascinating to see the vitality of the Bible in Israel's political culture, and the way ancient Scripture is assimilated by modern and secular politicians like Peres and Rabin, Begin and Shamir. In the twentieth century, as Israel has become a state again, the Bible has emerged as one of the primary sources of legitimacy for all the state's contending forces. It has become the basis of cultural traditions that are vivid and desperately relevant, but that have radically opposite and contradictory meanings. The Israeli Right acted as if they were using the Bible simply, naively, as a source of role models: David had taken what he wanted, and so would they; as David's acquisitiveness was blessed by God, so was their own; as David had grabbed land and people, so Israel should do today; as God blessed it then—by success—so he would bless it now. Peres, a longtime supporter of peace (and sharer of the Nobel Peace Prize with Rabin and Yasir Arafat), was suggesting that Israel's past and present wars and militarism "on the ground" were poisoned by the same greed and overreaching that had turned King David's lustfulness into murderousness "on the roof." For Peres, the Biblical story's point is not only that power corrupts, but also that Israel's ancient and modern abuses of power have endangered its own survival. Peres and Rabin were making the same claim I have been making here: that for the Jews, survival means recognizing our limits, and thinking big means understanding how to live small. The argument between them and those Jews who recognize no limits on Israel at all will probably never end. It is likely to reappear in an endless variety of forms so long as the Jews remain alive on earth.

15

Parvenu or Palimpsest: Some Tracings of the Jew in Modern France

ADRIAN RIFKIN

The Jew, it has to be admitted, is only one among many visions of alterity that frame the special illusion of a self we give the name of "nation." Whether a nation is the victim or a conqueror, whether it emerged over a long historical period or as an effect of a short war of liberation, its history will be, in part, an assemblage of texts that articulate never having been with being, origin with temporariness, annihilation with persistence. Conquering or being conquered alike deposit the violent archeology of a fragile and unstable identity, which is made out of nothing if not effacements, now of self and now of other, in a complex, unfinished reinvention. "France" is one such palimpsest, "Israel" another. Matching the Emperor Napoleon to Charlemagne in 1806, for example, placed the very name of France at risk in its elision of the recent, revolutionary past. Just as, in another timescale, the modern state of Israel might be thought to undermine the all-important myth of origin for diasporic Judaism that was the destruction of the Second Temple, which is also the founding myth of the Jew's place in the Western world. If Jew and France alike are palimpsests, then their writing over of each other might be thought of as a paradigm of the ways in which this "one among many" others of the Western "I" is, after all, a crucial figure.

The idea of a writing and a showing through, a doing and an undoing that amount to an involuntary assimilation in the very process of demarcating self from other, suggests how "other" is not necessarily illuminating as a concept.[1] For "other," in even the subtlest of its gradations, normally asks for a line that will be neat—even though the reason why the line is drawn may not be clear and though what lies on either side of it be not clearly different. On the contrary, it is bound to be overdetermined. The same line may be drawn around more than just one "other"—something all too often forgotten in the articulation of the "being-other" that is being a Jew. The other and not-other are "always and already" in each other's presence with all the difficulty of knowing what it is, this self made out of presence and of lack. This lack is a blank space or an unreadable text, waiting to be written

Lithuanian prayerbook, 1613

Italian manuscript, 1323, with
erased passage from
Maimonides

on or over, to be filled out or corrected with a history that will name it, matching the desire to know for sure.

This puts me in mind of an exhibition of Hebrew manuscripts at the Bibliothèque Nationale in Paris in 1991. In one showcase there was a Lithuanian manuscript of the seventeenth century, whose caption explained that such items were extremely rare because, generally speaking, they were destroyed along with their Jews in major pogroms. The lettering was a dirty grey, steep and exaggerated, spiky, grim, and without grace. It was more like a defensive picket than an invitation to study or prayer, a limit round communication rather than an opening out. A way of being Jewish in its gestures as in its meanings. Its contrast with some Italian medieval manuscripts was as stark as its calligraphy: from thorny rigor to sweetness and light, from cruel scratchings to delicate cursions. But these Italian manuscripts had also been cruelly scratched and whitened in entire blocks. Passages from Maimonides or commentaries on the psalms, for example, that could not in *that*, irremediably Jewish, version be read as confirming Christian theology, had been removed under the Counter-Reformation. The text is preserved as a precious and religious object while erasing its embarrassing specificity. As the social philosopher Zygmunt Bauman has pointed out, the Jewish refusal of Christianity forces the latter to these elaborate stratagems both to assert and renounce its origins, here with a double gesture of elimination and retouching.[2] To establish something of the normality and the particularity of this cultural process, I shall range across a few of the richly overwritten figurations of the Jew in modern France, thinking through some of the ways in which the two words "Jew" and "France" cannot be written without each other, yet ever at the threat of each other's effacement. If I use the word "figure" rather than "image," then this is, as we will see, because we are coping with the very structures of utterance, and not with some more or less pretty pictures.

Henri Murger, the Parisian writer who more than any other codified the romance of artistic bohemia, badly needed such a figure. In his *Scènes de la vie de bohème* (1851), the painter Marcel sells a canvas, *Crossing of the Red Sea*, to the rascally dealer "Médicis"—the bohemians' name for the Jew Salomon, who works "in all forms of bric-à-brac."[3] Médicis/Salomon is a complex character, far more so than the bohemians themselves, who conform to one of those simple typologies that were a currency of journalistic entertainment throughout the July Monarchy. Unlike the bohemians, he is as much a social mechanism as an individual type. His trade can be confined neither to a specialized and restricted range of things nor well delimited commercial spaces. He will as readily buy or sell an idea as an old shoe, exchanging "cigars for the plan of a serial novel, slippers for a sonnet, fresh fish for a paradox" (247). He "works in the ideal," Murger remarks, and in his head he holds the whole structure of social relations in the city, the addresses of anyone who matters or who can fix. He can get a play put on or a favor extended. Murger gives us two pages of extracts from his account books, of which a selection reads like this:

> Bought from M. V. . ., journalist, the complete works, uncut, of M.***, member of the Académie, 10fr.
> Sold to same a critical article on the works of M.***, member of the Académie, 30fr.
>
> . . .
>
> Bought from the little D. . . her hair, 15fr.
> Bought from M. B. . . a lot of scandalous articles and the last three spelling mistakes made by the Prefect of the Seine, 6fr., plus a pair of Neapolitan shoes.
> Sold to mademoiselle O. . . a blond hair-do, 20 fr.
>
> . . .

Indicated to M. Ferdinand the time at which the Baronne R. . . de P. . . goes to mass. Rented to the same for one day the little entresol of the faubourg Montmartre, the lot for 30fr. (248–9)

Utterly protean, then, is this figure of Salomon the Jew, exceeding the stereotype of the grasping, rasping moneybags that is his superficial form. For what we see in him is the pure and abstract production and movement of profit, reified profit, freed from any sullying relation to the exaction of the surplus value of labor, distanced from the common world of labor as from the ownership of the means of production. As in Marx, capital's substance and superego alike are Jew. And the profit exacted in each of this Jew's transactions at one and the same time facilitates the ensemble of social relations and condenses a fantastic image of a society's unconscious weavings of unities and fragments. The doings of Salomon the Jew flow out into every narrative of city life, an image of complex, urban porosity satisfying in its poetic grotesqueness. As much an armature of the city's mythic shape was the *Spleen* (1869) of Baudelaire, which itself could not exist without the trade in poems. Salomon's maneuvring, like the instalments of the serial novel, activate relations of individual desire with the unpredictable narratives of city life. When Marcel goes out hoping to see his painting at a distinguished exhibition, as he has been promised, he chances on it only in another, unexpected episode of its being. It is hanging outside a food shop. A steamboat has now been added to it and it is retitled *At the Port of Marseille*. Clearly, Murger's Jew is hardly sentimental about the biblical theme of his own deliverance from Egypt. The scene becomes folklorically French. The present of cash is more immediate than the theologies of Jewish memory. When Médicis sits to deal with Marcel, his pockets rattle with gold; when Marcel agrees to the deal in cash, Médicis rattles the "orchestra of his purses" (252). This Jew is a creator, a creator of conjunctions and chance encounters. And yet this Jew, even as he creates, edges out the true artist, who now lives through him, by procurement. He feeds the bohemians' bellies, starves their ambition. His contemporary homologue is the fully anti-Semitized social type of Richard Wagner's *Judaism in Music*, the Halévy and the Meyerbeer who snip out their scores like financial coupons and force the authentic musician off the stage.[4]

The Jew Salomon is one of those isolated individuals who belongs, as a matter of common definition, to what was called the "bohemia of work;" but not to the bohemia of the soul. Maybe the two are incompatible because of the intervention of the word Jew. Jews are not inevitably represented as second-hand or wheeler dealers, yet to class a dealer as a Jew is to class *that* dealing as abject and irredeemable. Turned into a "sociological" description in Maxime Ducamp's *Paris, ses organes, ses fonctions* . . . (1875), the Jewish rag merchant becomes the squalid, lowest form of trash dealer, whose qualities just happen to become those of every Jew.[5] A figure like Ducamp's ragman is to emerge again, some seventy years later, in Marcel Carné's film *Les Enfants du Paradis* (1944). Here, in the glorious, displeasing ambivalence of the character Jéricho, the Jew's dealing and the city's form turn out still to be inseparable—but now at the very moment of the liberation of Paris from the Nazi rule that had eliminated its population of living Jews.

Between Salomon and Jéricho there sits a tomb at the cemetery of Père Lachaise. The sepulcher of Michel and Calmann Lévy, who were, after all, the creators of the modern industry of French publishing, is modest enough and free from any maudlin rhetoric of grief or show of wealth. Editors of Gustave Flaubert, of Maxime Ducamp, of Murger, and of Ernest Renan, more than a few of their authors grappled with the image of the Jew as vile or sacred. Renan's Catholic enemies, in condemning his *Vie de Jésus* (1863), insisted that he was really running with the Jews. As has been pointed out, not only was Renan supposed to have accepted a million from Rothschild to accomplish his historical relativizing of Jesus as a Jew, but this "author and sometime abbot and the Jewish [*israélite*] editor [Michel Lévy] have made a packet" in their common anit-Christianism.[6] And here is a crucial figure of abjection; the capitalist Jew dealing Catholicism back to itself, corrupted. Indeed, the capitalist is the only truly convincing figure of arrival for a Jew, who, having come from nowhere, can hardly inherit any social *merit*. Inevitably, and in this sole capacity for arriving, she or he figures the decline of feudal and aristocratic France, as the diminishing of landed wealth brings with it dependence on the Jew's successful dealings.

This theme of dependence is at the heart of the most famous of all French anti-Semitic texts, Edouard Drumont's *La France juive* (1887), where the vampiric nightmare of a naive, pleasure-loving aristocracy, overgenerous and free from any trace of hatred, offering itself to the bloodsucking, plutocratic, rasping, wheezing, Germanic Jews, is fully dreamed:

> The heraldic *goym* who rush to visit the Rothschild are not attracted just by the perfume of some Romanée [the famous vineyard then owned by them]. Many amongst those who seek this humiliating hospitality have got at home their own little wine that is not bad, an old hotel and family portraits . . . For them to visit the Rothschild is to go to the court. The king of Jews, the Jew of kings is not quite Louis XIV, but they have the illusion of being in a palace.[7]

The Jew illuminates the aporia of French identity that has failed itself, that, through revolution and economic change, is insufficient to its own glorious

Père Lachaise cemetery, Paris: Michel and Calmann Lévy's tomb seen from Rachel's;
Rachel's tomb seen from Michel and Calmann Lévy's

history. And this impasse structures the ambivalence of the enemy, the mapping of the foreign Jews, pronouncing "p" for "b" and "b" for "p," onto the Germanness of their origins, and of Germanness as enemy onto the sickly, "prematurely decrepit" Jew's easily available foreignness. The Rothschilds wanted to conquer France—was not the armistice of the Franco-Prussian war of 1871 signed at their château of Ferrières?—"they conquered her, and they felt that she was dying in their noxious breath, that it was only a corpse they had got themselves" (107). Yet the German, enemy of this weak Judaic France, is also ally of a strong Frenchness that counts on it to counter the Jew within. Wagner and Wagnerism in music, which Drumont had already invoked against feeble Frenchness in his *Richard Wagner, l'homme et le musicien* (1869), fulfilled at one and the same time both of these roles. For over half a century it was to excite hatred of its author, the great German musician who had laughed at the French defeat in 1871. And it was to be recruited as a weapon to undo the hated if irresistible effects of "Jewish music," Meyerbeer or Bizet, through the alternative modernity of Débussy, of Chausson, of d'Indy.

Near where the Lévy brothers lie in the cemetery lies the actress Rachel, an altogether more stylish sepulcher. According to Ducamp, it was the center of an impassioned cult in the years after her death. Alongside the Lévys' lie the Rothschilds, substantial if more discreet in death than in life. And there is one vault for a "M. X from Pesth, born in Vienna, died in Paris," a fair enough trajectory for the homeless Jew, a "from," a "born," an arrival, pure and simple. No one today comes to this part of the cemetery, or certainly not by intention to see these tombs.

Père Lachaise cemetery, Paris: detail from the Rothschilds' tomb

You can note a few gay men, who have been advised by various guides that this southern sector is a *lieu de drague*, and who are surprised and disappointed by its emptiness. But this is not the Quai des Tuileries. It was my own surprise at the guide's directions that took me there, to see if Père Lachaise could really be a temple of libidinous vivacity. Out of one text, then, I found another, out of the *Spartacus* or *Gai Pied* guides came Hebrew inscriptions to efface their simple if mistaken indications. And I found this article, too, which began with Michel Lévy's tomb.

In this unexpected disjuncture it seemed worth thinking about the desire, so commonly expressed in our own day, of gay Jews to identify with their religion as practising Jews, some even forming their own synagogues (and of gay Christians to be communicants and priests), in the teeth of a scripture (and a Christian priesthood) that is structured by homophobia. Is it not the perfect instance of the aporetic argument that the "norm" should both be and not be, embrace and differentiate, exclude and celebrate? Does the text which rules out "that" rule out this Jew? Is this Jew the subject of that text? Or is this Jew not just the subject of that text, because she or he is anyway the faithful subject of the whole text as a historical identity, as an ethic, in all its argued forms? And why do this and that have to be identified with each other, above the right to civil status?

The strategy of essentialism may exceed itself in a self-realized as well as self-realizing defeat, no less shattering than that either of being assimilated or of maintaining one's culture, and yet ending up in the same *vélodrome* or concentration camp. Indifferently the Nazi régime in France did away with Max Jacob, good-Catholic-ex-Jew; Maurice Sachs, likewise, gay and Nazi-admirer, too; or Marc Bloch, who was a historian and nothing more complicated than just a Jew. Civil status may in the end come only as an effect of learning not to need the "other" to represent and so efface one's own diffraction, which would be an ultimate test of the capacity for self-reflection. Otherwise, "others" will appear to end up in the same grave whether they deserve this similarity or not.

In the cemetery the Jews are hemmed in by the phoney, pre-Disney monument to Héloise and Abelard, and the great hostess and poetess Anna de Noailles, whose tomb stands at the limits of the supposed trysting place. The visitors who do go to Père Lachaise for Jewish tombs are more inclined to the ones higher up on the hill, clustered around the monuments to the deportation. These are often quite pathetic, doubly so as the photographic ceramics of long-dead deportees are even now abused, and because the terrible, profoundly kitsch representations of suffering, in the form of the concentration camp memorials, cast a black shadow over the records of their life. As has been pointed out, even these monuments are dedicated to the Resistance rather than the Jewish victims of the Holocaust.[8]

They are somewhat showily grouped around the more discreetly showy tombs of the first-generation leaders of the French Communist Party, facing the Federals' Wall, the memorial to the massacred Communards of 1871. People, slaughtered revolutionaries, so much despised by the brothers Lévy and their famous authors. The matter is not an easy one. For was not one of the most virulent anti-Semitic documents of the *fin-de-siècle*, *Du Molochisme juif* (1884), penned by the ex-communard Gustave Tridon? And if Tridon's objective in his obscene fantasy of Judaism was the perfectly worthy, republican discrediting of Christianity through its assumed origins, then his language far exceeded the virtue of this aim.

The ensemble—the Wall, the Party tombs, the concentration camp memorials—adds up to one of those preemptive strikes on history that used to preoccupy the Communist Party in its desire to be at the very end of grand narratives, here of both resistance and class struggle. Be this as it may, it is this, no doubt, that the visitors prefer. Better by far the dramatic *dénouement* of a set of social relations, a rhetorical closure that satisfies the maudlin desire for the grim spectacle of moral finality, than traces of the complex, slow unfolding of a civilization in all its rich uncertainty. Holocaust here effaces history, doubly, of the Jews and so of holocaust itself.

But let us note another effacement of this place, one which the Right could recognize. These Jews buried in the middle of the last century have acquired a homeland. In the strictest of right-wing, monarchist definitions, to have a home is to have a burial ground, and if the buried Jews have won this place, or bought it rather, then have they effaced a bit of France, or have they been made French in death? Consider these lines of Maurice Barrès, as well as the problem that the buried Jews might pose for his ecstatic morbidity:

> In certain islands without a recorded history, where prehistoric homesteads remain on the surface of the earth, everything is raw, the water, the milk, the eggs, and flavorless. Man can find nothing but insipidity on this too new earth that has not been made by corpses. The cup of pleasure needs the taste of ashes. I need tombs that speak for me to halt before the most beautiful landscape. Every living being is born from an earth, a race, an atmosphere, and the genie does not show itself as such unless it is tightly bound to the land and to its dead. The cemetery is the fatherland. The nation, this is the ownership in common of an ancient cemetery and of the will to set a worth to this joint heritage. With a seat of education and a cemetery one has the basics of a fatherland.[9]

The flavor of the nation, it cannot but follow, its acquired and death-won savors, must in part become Jewish, tasting of a man from Pesth, born in Vienna but dying in Paris, slipping into the tomb despite his being born elsewhere, his foreign atmosphere around him. Irremediably his bond with the funeral land of France makes her atmosphere what it is, changing a taste. In a sense, the Deportation solved the problem by sending them to Germany or Poland to die, to the sites demarcated solely for this purpose, sites that now make the atmosphere of Europe what it is. And, after all, the negative connotation of Jew with German was strong enough, even for the Vichy client, for a reactionary France to pile one abjection upon another—the abject, Jewish part of France to be cast out into the land of the German ally of and in abjection, the ally-conqueror of 1870, 1914, and 1940.

There is a famous scene in Jean Renoir's once scandalous, filmic comedy of social manners *La Règle du jeu* (1939), the scene after the guests have installed themselves in the great Solognais Chateau belonging to the duc de la Chesniet. At the heart of the film's critique lies the class struggle of master and servant, respectable servant and gamekeeper, bohemian and bourgeois, a social typology where the overflow of narratives, desires, needs, from one stratum to another, delineates the brink of disaster for all. In this scene the camera leaves the upper class to settle in to their accommodation, and we are cut to the dinnertime conversation in the servants' quarters. It turns to the mores, fads, and origins of their masters and mistresses. "At

Jean Renoir, *La Règle du jeu*,
1939: Dalio (*far right*) as la
Chesniet; (*below*) the hunt

least," one servant ripostes to another, defending some fun at his boss's expense, "he's not a Yid like la Chesniet." The reply is surprised, "La Chesniet a Yid?" . . . "Yes, he had a grandmother who was a Rosenthal from Frankfurt." The cinema-going audience of 1939 already knew that something was afoot with this aristocratic la Chesniet, elegant, supple, and subtle in his speech and manners, for he was played by Dalio, the specialized actor of stereotypically poor or outcast Jews. He had been a Semitic Judas to Robert le Vigan's rather more northern-looking Jesus in Julien Duvivier's conservative, Catholic film, *Vie de Christ* (1934). The original public for *La Règle du jeu*, largely scandalized by its almost callous parody of refined

manners, was equally invited to view it as both pro- and anti-Semitic, with so eminent an anti-Semite as Lucien Rebatet arguing that it should satisfy both tendencies.[10] And so too the notorious hunt scene—a crucial moment in the film, if it is seen against Barrès and Drumont—begins to deny its usual and rather easy reading as the image of a destructive and self-seeking bourgeoisie on the eve of national catastrophe. Rather, the hunt resonates in its very failure to escape from these questions of the Jew-arrived to a more general politics: how does the land taste if la Chesniet is a Yid, and what is a hunt if it is a Jewish hunt? For Drumont, a compelling image of the Jewish enslavement of France could be made in the Jewish social hunt of the aristocracy on the one hand, and their buying up of ancient hunting domains on the other: "Fontainebleau is Ephrussi's, Versailles belongs to Hirsch, Ferrières to Rothschild" (82). Just as in the film the useless "hunters" stand stock still in their hides while the gamekeepers drive the helpless animals, rabbits and birds, to their line of fire, in Drumont it is the Jews who elaborate the "economic" hunt—the hunt with a deer driven to its pursuants, only to be rescued, given alcohol, and recycled. Through this farce it is the Jews who admit the ancient families of Rohan and Chabot back to their ancestral land.

In the end Renoir writes over Drumont not in his cinema of social critique, which is hard put to escape him, but through the slippage of the signs of Jew, of those very "p's" and "b's" that mark out Jewish speech. The foreign voice in *La Règle* is not that of the exquisitely spoken Dalio–la Chesniet, but that of his blamelessly Aryan, Austrian wife, whose clumsy, generous elocution haunts the soundtrack. It is her social and amorous ineptitude that sets her apart from French manners, be they pure or purely Jewish, and sets them in crisis. The destructive force that leads the film to tragi-farce with the shooting of the honest, simple French aviator, is the heavily accented gamekeeper Schumacher, the Frenchman who, as an Alsatian, represents the historical ambiguity of the very distinction between French and German on which the defining of Jew as Germanic must be founded or, in foundering, must make this much too clear: that the self is not easily named and circumscribed.

One of the insights that might be attributed to Joseph Losey's film *M. Klein* (1977)—in which the eponymous hero, Alsatian too, suspected of Jewish origins, but proven to be "purely" French, nonetheless willfully joins the train from the Vél d'Hiver—is that the Jews bore as much the weight of desire as of hatred, sacrificial victims with whom to reenact the history of French abjection to German might. When the fastidious Klein, an art dealer, at this moment specializing in mopping up Jewish property in wartime Paris, first fears that he is suspected of being Jewish it is because he finds a copy of the "official" wartime paper *Informations juives*, apparently

Joseph Losey, *M. Klein*, 1977: Klein faces the Gestapo

addressed to him, on his doormat. And this just as he sees out one of his commercial victims, a Jew. He tries to find the (other) M. Klein to whom the paper must have been addressed. He seeks and interrogates the editors of *Informations*, he traces an address, he waits for contacts, meets lovers of a man who may not even exist, who might be he. Among guests in a fashionable apartment he glances cautiously, fearfully into a mirror. He sees nothing but himself. Certainly not the race-science measurements of Jewish noses, breasts, and hips with which the film has opened in its fearful sequence of a middle-age couple being measured, hoping against hope that their measurements are "wrong." Must he become a Jew to himself, to efface his own reflection as French? Yet he cannot be sure, he is trapped by a system of imagery already bearing the signs of Jew. When he buys a painting from a Jew just before the fatal discovery on his doormat, Klein throws the gold on the table in an excessive gesture that is as vulgar as it's mean. Like Médicis. Commerce itself, fair or unfair, honest or dishonest, is impossible without the risk of a contamination that is already of the social body, with or without the Jew. The Jew is nothing but a name for another inevitability as well as for the denial of that inevitability. When the Gestapo come for Klein's property, he refuses to give up only the Jew's painting: "It's not for commerce," he insists, "it's family property." Good Frenchman that he is, he chooses deportation—at the very moment when certificates arrive to prove his racial purity. The Jew is desire, pure and the compelling mystery of lack.

But not all Jews bought a site in Père Lachaise. In 1841 the *Archives israélites de France* exposed some of the complicated dimensions of Jewish dying in Paris. In an article of the May issue, there is a debate concerning the emergence of a serious difference between the Consistoire (the Jewish board of community self-governance set up under Napoleon I) and the community on the organization of burial. The journal remarks that:

> As far as their death is concerned, even those who are the most detached from religious practice are loath not to conform to established custom. There is nothing extraordinary about the luxury of the tombs in which, these days, the opulent Jewish (*israélites*) families wish to imitate the Christians; already the Bible offers these sepulchral vaults (Gen. 23), types of monument and family tombs . . .

The problem is that, with the reorganization of the cemeteries by the city authorities, the land of the paupers' burials will be leveled off and topped up for reuse, breaking both Jewish law and erasing the memory of poorer Jews. The Eastern cemetery (Père Lachaise):

> opens its graves only to the coffins of the rich, and if the family of a deceased person lacks 543fr to spend on a tomb, then the hearse that bears his remains must roll toward the northern cemetery . . .[11]

The slightly anxious tone forestalls and oddly chimes with Maxime Ducamp's remarks on the cemetery written in the 1870's, another strange alliance in the making, with Ducamp writing over the Jew's self-evident truth with a pure ideology of race. In *Paris, ses organes* Ducamp comments:

> The new section of Père Lachaise, where the showy tombs affect all sorts of pretentious and sterile forms, looks like an improvised city whose inhabitants have not turned up. It's displeasing to see. There's nothing there but white stones which the workers sculpt while they whistle: all is new, the monuments, the epitaphs, the grills, the wreaths, even the names that no one has heard pronounced: you could call these the little palaces of a people of "parvenus." Eternity for a self-love that wants to survive beyond unbeing. Which makes the most efforts to escape being forgotten? Is it glory? Is it nobility? Is it money? It is money. (190)

Ducamp is not writing directly of the Jewish part of the cemetery. He does a few pages later, discussing the cult of Rachel, whose tomb might be flashy enough to lend some credence to his irritable description (192ff.).

But who can say what enough might be? And he is interested to note its physical separation from the Christian area for the observation of religious rites. But while he writes of industrialists' tombs, the tombs of a new class who are always fair game for satire, the point is not just that money counts beyond the grave. On the contrary, the argument is ridiculous, and therein lies its meaning. For Ducamp is not about to denounce the grandiose and dramatic tombs of the nobles or of the French kings and queens at Saint-Denis. It is this slightly unhinged illogic and the use of the words "parvenus," "not heard pronounced," "self-love," that alert us to the subject of Jew. And if the workmen whistle irreligiously, there is something utterly Parisian about the image. Their work is not dishonest, even though the tombs are a sham. Set to work, they disturb a peace that should, in the best of all possible, timeless worlds, have been primordial, a pure relation of soil and flesh such as was to nourish Barrès's unpleasant invocation.

In the cemetery the right to emancipation is inscribed on the tombs of the substantial and well-heeled dead who could pay the cost of a sepulcher. But the Jewish dead of the common grave were ploughed over every few years, sharing the land in common with their compatriots in death rather than their coreligionists of life. In this sense Jews were no different from anyone else, even if their demands on the rite and hence the site of burial were quite particular. They belonged to social classes. One result of this is that in memory one class of Jew stands in for the other, through the inscriptions they could afford to leave. As the *Archives israélites* insisted, the poor in their common grave could not even ensure their memory. Yet memory is the very medium through which Israel lives:

> Israel lives first and foremost in its memories, fighting still with David in mind, thinking with Solomon, weeping with Jeremiah, and it is above all in the cemetery that this genius for the past has established its solitary empire. There, should we pull together our history with contemporary life, we let our memories wander in a long gone world, we breathe the air of times that are no more
> ... (332)

The very alignment of the graves, the winding paths, their citylike topography, is a metaphor for a way of living in the past. The cemetery is required for this, no more. Here the Jews neither need nor desire to give their flavor to the nation. Alone they record the timescale of their persistence. And this a century before Walter Benjamin invented Messianic Time as a category of historical experience! Yet the inadequacy of the common grave in Paris to the enduring memory of difference and the right to emancipation is as striking as its adequacy at Auschwitz. The inscription "M. X from Vienna, born in Pesth, died in Paris" is a dead letter since the Holocaust, and for this reason utopian. Once upon a time it was simultaneously an effacement of

Marcel Carné, *Les Enfants du Paradis*, 1944: Jéricho rattles the stolen spoons

being Jewish and of being French, both perhaps felt as some mere contingency.

Anyway, Salomon reappears in *Les Enfants du Paradis* as the clothes seller Jéricho, who was not intended by Carné as an anti-Semitic figure. Indeed, Carné was surprised at the very suggestion—"it never ocurred to me," he said in an interview. It is not hard to see why. Even in a newsreel film of 1932, in a reportage on *Rosh Hashanah*, there was no other way of showing Jews than with big noses, even if this meant, for newsreel's sake, taking some footage of Jews who did have big noses.[12] When Jéricho inspects some stolen spoons for the murderer-thief Lacenaire, he rattles them, running them between his hands. He knows they are only plate by the sound they make. He was to have been played by a real-life anti-Semite, the specialist in true French roles, Robert le Vigan, to whose Jesus of 1934, Dalio, the perfectly stereotyped actor of Jews, had played Judas. But while the film was being shot le Vigan, along with his admirer the novelist and anti-Semitic propagandist Céline, had made the enforced pilgrimage to Sigmaringen—the resort offered by the defeated Nazis to their closest collaborators—and the more neutral Pierre Renoir was substituted. But had

Carné wanted his figure to be Jewish, he could have cast a Dalio. After all, caricatures have to be of something, to have some historical substance and finally be thought of as embodied in a figure of cultural experience. So Jéricho, who is a form of knowledge, of the kind that derives its power from the empathy with the commodity, from always knowing its price and value and mode of circulation, which is also the circulation of feelings between people, Jéricho makes connections and rattles silver. More Jewish than Salomon, his voice rasps like Wagner's Jew: "who has not been shocked and held to the spot, partly in horror and partly by a sense of their absurdity, at hearing those gurgling, jodeling and babbling sounds confusive of all trace of sense and spirit . . ." (27).

By all these established relations of image to image, more or less partial and complete slippages and substitutions of the one for the other—Jéricho's disreputability and greed, his clinking of cash, his secretive, self-serving linking of the narratives of other people's lives—Jéricho could not but be a figure bearing the name of Jew. But if he were not a Jew, there would be no text. The social life of the capitalist city would be without an image. There would be no non-Jews. There would be no connections or procurements between them, fabricated out of commodities and circulating like commodities. No, ironically, there would be no text at all. Just babble. Pace Wagner, Jew and culture form the perfect palimpsest of the self and other that culture is.

Nonetheless, it is important not to become sentimental. What I have come to argue is simply that, for a certain moment in the history of capitalist democracies, and at certain sites, the Jew becomes more than a sign pointing to alterity or abjection; an embodied grammar, a means for making sense, an indispensable structure of the self.

16

The U.S. Holocaust Memorial Museum: Memory and the Politics of Identity

JAMES E. YOUNG

In 1964, when a group of Jewish American survivors of the Warsaw Ghetto Uprising submitted a design for a Holocaust memorial to New York City's Arts Commission, they were turned down for three reasons. First, according to the Arts Commissioner, Eleanor Platt, the proposed design by Nathan Rapoport was simply too big and not aesthetically tasteful. It would, in her words, set a regrettable precedent. Second, such a monument might inspire other "special groups" to be similarly represented on public land—another regrettable precedent. And finally, according to the Parks Commissioner Newbold Morris, the city had to ensure that "monuments in the parks . . . be limited to events of American history."[1] That is, he suggested, the Holocaust was not an American experience.

For the Jewish survivors of the Holocaust who had emigrated to America after the Second World War, and who regarded themselves as typical "new Americans," such an answer challenged their very conception of what it meant to be an American in the first place. For the first time in their minds, a distinction had been drawn between "events of American history" and those of "Americans' history." Did American history begin and end within the nation's geographical borders? Or did it, as most of these immigrants believed, begin in the experiences abroad that drove them to America's shores? With the dedication of the U.S. Holocaust Memorial Museum in Washington, D.C. in 1993, it could be said that America has finally recognized the survivors' experiences as part of a national experience—and has in this way made the Holocaust part of American history.

At the same time, such a museum necessarily raises other difficult questions, among them: what role does the Holocaust play in American thought and culture, in American religious and political life, in relations between Jewish Americans and other ethnic groups? To what extent will it necessarily be universalized in a society defined by pluralist and egalitarian ideals? To what extent has it become a defining preoccupation for Jewish Americans, a locus of memory and identity? The answers to these questions are complicated and ever-changing.

For as the shape that Holocaust memory takes in Europe and Israel is constrained by political, aesthetic, and religious coordinates, that in America is no less guided by both American ideals and experiences of that time. Unlike European memorials, however, often anchored in the very sites of destruction, American memorials are necessarily removed from the "topography of terror." Where European memorials located *in situ* often suggest themselves rhetorically as the extension of events they would commemorate, those in America must gesture abstractly to a past removed in both time and space. If memorials in Germany and Poland composed of camp ruins invite visitors to mistake them for the events they represent, those in America inevitably call attention to the great distance between themselves and the destruction. The meaning in American memorials is not always as self-evident as that suggested at the camps, places of deportation, or destroyed synagogues. In this sense, American memorials seem not to be anchored in history so much as in the ideals that generated them in the first place.

In America, the motives for memory of the Holocaust are as mixed as the population at large, the reasons variously lofty and cynical, practical and aesthetic. Some communities build memorials to remember lost brethren, others to remember themselves. Some built memorials as community centers, others as tourist attractions. Some survivors remember strictly according to religious tradition, while others recall the political roots of their resistance. Veterans' organizations sponsor memorials to recall their role as camp-liberators. Congress members support local monuments to secure votes among their Jewish constituency. Even the national memorial to the Holocaust in Washington, D.C. had been proposed by then-President Jimmy Carter to placate Jewish supporters angered by his sale of F-15 fighter planes to Saudi Arabia. All such memorial decisions are made in political time, contingent on political realities.[2]

Indeed, of all Holocaust memorials in America, none can begin to match in scope or ambition the national memorial and museum complex that opened in April 1993 in the heart of the nation's capital. Situated adjacent to the National Mall and within view of the Washington Monument to the right and the Jefferson Memorial across the Tidal Basin to the left, the U.S. Holocaust Memorial Museum is a neighbor to the National Museum of American History and the Smithsonian Institution. It has enshrined, by dint of its placement, not just the history of the Holocaust, but American democratic and egalitarian ideals as they counterpoint the Holocaust. That is, by remembering the crimes of another people in another land, it encourages Americans to recall their nation's own, idealized reason for being.

By the time it opened, over 150,000 people had donated some 200 million dollars to its construction. These funds were used not just to build its enormous edifice but also to collect some 10,000 artifacts from around the world, including what is believed to be a Treblinka boxcar, a Danish fishing boat used in the rescue of that country's Jews, an actual barrack from Birkenau, and 2,000 pairs of shoes from Auschwitz, among thousands of other remnants. The projected holdings of the archives and library of 100,000 volumes make them the largest Holocaust repository and study center in America. To the amazement of its curators and consternation of its maintenance staff, more than 2 million people visited the museum in its first year, more than three times what the Museum had anticipated.

"What is the role of [this] museum in a country, such as the United States, far from the site of the Holocaust?" the historian Charles Maier has asked: "Is it to rally the people who suffered or to instruct non-Jews? Is it supposed to serve as a reminder that 'it can happen here?' Or is it a statement that some special consideration is deserved? Under what circumstances can a private sorrow serve simultaneously as a public grief?"[3] Before such a museum could be built on the Mall in Washington, D.C., explicitly American reasons would have to be found for it.

The official American justification for a national memorial in the nation's capital was provided by President Carter in his address to the first Days of Remembrance commemoration in the Capitol Rotunda, April 24, 1979:

> Although the Holocaust took place in Europe, the event is of fundamental significance to Americans for three reasons. First, it was American troops who liberated many of the death camps, and who helped to expose the horrible truth of what had been done there. Also, the United States became a homeland for many of those who were able to survive. Secondly, however, we must share the responsibility for not being willing to acknowledge forty years ago that this horrible event was occurring. Finally, because we are humane people, concerned with the human rights of all peoples, we feel compelled to study the systematic destruction of the Jews so that we may seek to learn how to prevent such enormities from occurring in the future."[4]

Not only would this museum depict the lives of "new Americans," but it would reinforce America's self-idealization as haven for the world's oppressed. It would serve as a universal warning against the bigotry and anti-democratic forces underpinning such a catastrophe and call attention to the potential in all other totalitarian systems for such slaughter.

For as a national landmark, the national Holocaust museum would necessarily plot the Holocaust according to the nation's own ideals, its pluralist tenets. In the words of the Memorial Council, therefore, the Holocaust began "before a shot was fired, with persecution of Jews, dissenters, blacks, Gypsies, and the handicapped. The Holocaust gathered force as the Nazis excluded groups of people from the human family, denying them freedom to work, to study, to travel, to practise a religion, claim a theory, or teach a value. This Museum will illustrate that the loss of life itself was but the last stage in the loss of all rights."[5] In being defined as the ultimate violation of human rights and as the persecution of plural groups, the Holocaust encompasses all the reasons that immigrants—past, present, and future—ever had for seeking refuge in America.

When cultural critics protested that such a museum, though necessary, would be a blight on the Mall, the U.S. Holocaust Memorial Council countered, "This Museum belongs at the center of American life because as a democratic civilization America is the enemy of racism and its ultimate expression, genocide. An event of universal significance, the Holocaust has special importance for Americans: in act and word the Nazis denied the deepest tenets of the American people."[6] That is, the U.S. Holocaust Memorial defines what it means to be American by graphically illustrating what it means not to be American. As a reminder of "the furies beyond our shores," in one columnist's words, the museum would define American existence in the great distance between "here" and "there."[7]

This would be the beginning of what the Museum's project director, Michael Berenbaum, has termed the "Americanization of the Holocaust." In Berenbaum's words, the museum's story of the Holocaust would have to be

> told in such a way that it would resonate not only with the survivor in New York and his children in Houston or San Francisco, but with a black leader from Atlanta, a midwestern farmer, or a northeastern industrialist. Millions of Americans make pilgrimages to Washington; the Holocaust Museum must take them back in time, transport them to another continent, and inform their current reality. The Americanization of the Holocaust is an honorable task provided that the story told is faithful to the historical event.[8]

Of course, as Berenbaum also makes clear, the story itself depends entirely on who is telling it—and to whom.

The story also depends on several other layers of meaning created in the memorial's location in Washington, in the heart of America's monumental civic culture; the form of the edifice itself, its place in relation to nearby buildings, to architectural trends and fashion; and the exhibition narrative housed by the museum. Each makes different meaning, each in some relation to the other dimensions of the memorial's total "text."

From the beginning, there were many who, like the New York City Parks Commission, were unsettled by "the symbolic implications of the memorial's placement [adjacent to the National Mall]—that the Nazi extermination of 6 million Jews [could be] an integral part of the American story."[9] Even local survivors came forth with their reservations, testifying against the Memorial for its not being relevant to the American national experience and for enlarging the idea of the Holocaust to include other, non-Jewish victims of the Nazis. Still others feared that such a memorial contradicted the very essence of the National Mall, that by recalling such horrible events, the Memorial would cast a dark shadow across a monumental landscape dedicated to all that was high and virtuous in America's origins.

To all of which the Memorial Council's chairperson, Harvey Meyerhoff, responded that precisely because the Mall celebrates human history and creativity, the Holocaust Museum belongs on it, a reminder of the dark side of humankind's civilized works. "If the Smithsonian represents the accomplishments of civilization, the Holocaust raises fundamental questions about the capacity of individuals and of society, of technology and human genius for evil," Myerhoff wrote.[10] This too, he seemed to say, is part of Western civilization; this too can become part of a past on which we now build a "more perfect union."

Meyerhoff went on to acknowledge that "Because the Holocaust Memorial is located in the heart of our nation's capital and because it is a national memorial, the uniquely American dimension of the Holocaust will be consistently represented in the museum." To this end, the American dimension has included not only the soldiers' part in defeating Nazi Germany and in liberating the camps, but also the less "memorable" parts—that is, restricting immigration, turning away refugees during the war, and refusing to bomb the death camps. In this sense, the "Americanization" of the Holocaust has meant presenting both the laudable and lamentable aspects of "the American Holocaust experience," exhibiting both the power and limitations of American ideals. After the Vietnam Veterans' Memorial nearby, the Holocaust Memorial has become the second anti-memorial on the Mall: a national memorial institution that celebrates American ideals by challenging them.

As it turns out, putting the Memorial on the Mall has not only Americanized the Holocaust, but has also set a new national standard for suffering. By formally monumentalizing the Holocaust, the Museum also proposes it as an ideal of catastrophe against which all other past and future desstructions can be measured. Moreover, the Museum has issued an implicit invitation—some might say challenge—to two other long-suffering American ethnic groups, African and Native Americans, who have responded by proposing their own national institutions for the Mall. Indeed, when informed that the National African American Museum would be located in an existing building of the Smithsonian Institution, the Illinois Representative Gus Savage responded angrily that since "Jews and Indians had their own place on the Mall," so should African Americans.[11]

Given the Mall's own dark past as the site of holding pens for newly arrived African slaves, the National African American Museum will be placed in an especially difficult position: not only will it be asked to share an authentic site of African American suffering with other groups, but it will also be faced with the unenviable task of teaching Americans that the topographical center of their national shrine is also the site of America's greatest, ineradicable shame.

The next layer of meaning was negotiated in the building design itself. Chosen from a large field of competitors, James Ingo Freed, a principal in Pei Cobb Freed & Partners, began by articulating the fundamental problems facing him on all fronts. He would have to begin, he said, by bridging the two landmark buildings on either side of the memorial's 1.7 acre lot: the grey limestone and neoclassical lines of the hulking Bureau of Engraving to the south, and the ornate red-brick Victorian Auditors Building to the north. From here, his aim would be to "take the conditional [that is, situational] circumstances of [the museum's] location and weave them together with its content."[12] This is, in some ways, the dilemma facing any architect and monument builder: how will design and materials used for the way they speak to the environment now speak to the Museum's content? Specifically, in the case of a Holocaust memorial, how will the brick and limestone chosen for its neighboring architectural resonance generate meaning in Holocaust memory?

At the same time, Freed wanted to use this space to challenge—or at least to offer a critique of—Washington's monumental facade. How to challenge the Mall's monumentality from a monumental structure on the Mall? How to do this while remaining answerable to the capital's Fine Arts Commission, whose first principle is to regulate and keep a relatively uniform appearance on the Mall? How to make a building that would disturb consciousness on the one hand, while having to conform to a highly regulated and uniform architectural set of guidelines on the other?

For the self-conscious architect, every structure is also a metaphor, created for one physical purpose but also to stand figuratively for an idea, a time, an event, a people. In Freed's eyes, for example, "The metaphor of the guard tower was the watching, the overview, the distancing of the persecutors from the prisoners" (p. 63). How then would his building figure the memory it was designed to house? The essential problem of design for a plural nation was resolved by Freed in a relatively simple, yet profound formulation. It is important, in Freed's words, that "memory be sufficiently ambiguous and open ended *so that others can inhabit the space, can imbue the forms with their own memory*" (p. 64, my emphasis). Like other memorial designers before and after him, Freed has insisted on keeping forms open-ended, abstract enough to accommodate all rememberers, especially those who

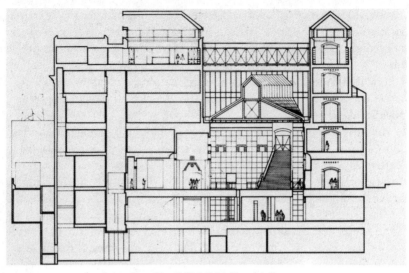

James Ingo Freed/Pei Cobb Freed & Partners,
elevation of the United States Holocaust Memorial Museum, Washington, D.C., 1993

come after his generation. "We wanted an evocation of the incomplete," he wrote. "Irresolution, imbalances are built in. For instance, the screen in the front portal is not there to force a reading, but to make evident the need for interpretation" (p. 64).

"It is my view," Freed wrote, "that the Holocaust defines a radical, but hopefully not a final, break with the optimistic conception of continuous social and political improvement underlying the material culture of the West."[13] This view led to a fundamental architectural dilemma: how to represent the Holocaust as a radical breach in the Western mind without violating the enforced architectural harmony of the nation's capital? Freed's answer was an exterior that conformed to the Fine Arts Commission's strict guidelines and an interior that metaphorically removes visitors from the capital. "When you walked out of Washington," Freed wrote, "I wanted to separate you from the city formally and spatially; but before you stepped into the Hall of Witness, I also felt that you had to go through an acoustical change, a disturbance like a drumbeat. Something to tell you that you are coming to this place, to make you pay attention" (p. 65).

When visitors now enter, they find themselves in a great "raw steel structure, without cover or enclosing planes, except that the walls have panels of glass. These panels are the Walls of Nations, where every nation that suffered deaths is identified by a panel of glass" (p. 70). Visitors proceed diagonally through the Hall of Witness, the path lighted by a diagonally cut

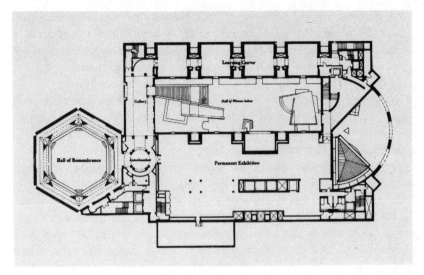

James Ingo Freed/Pei Cobb Freed & Partners,
plan of the United States Holocaust Memorial Museum, Washington, D.C., 1993

skylight high above. Elevators take visitors to the fourth floor, where the historical exhibition begins. But to enter the exhibition, visitors must cross a bridge made of glass blocks, what Freed describes as "a dangerous path" (p. 70).

Where structure and form figuratively reflect senses of brokenness and irreparability, the steel trusses and brick more literally recall the materials out of which the Nazis built their own houses of destruction. The roof and its skylight are thus both skewed and fragmented, even as they are bound with steel trusses, representing lines inside that are deliberately twisted, without reassuring angle or form. After finishing the exhibition walk-through, the visitors' last stop at the detached Hall of Remembrance, like their first, also resonates brokenness, an irresolution of form and meaning. In this great, open skylit gallery, absence reigns, and an architectural empti-ness recalls the void left behind by a people's mass murder.

The discontinuity and fragmentation preserved in the museum's interior architectural space cannot, however, be similarly conveyed in the exhibition narrative itself. For like all narrative, that created in the exhibition necessar-ily depends on the continuous sequence of its telling, the integrative coher-ence of a history being told. Though housed in a structure reverberating brokenness and the impossibility of repair, the exhibition itself exists sole-ly on the strength of its internal logic, the linear sequence by which events of the Holocaust are ordered in their telling.

In this museum, the telling begins with the visitors' own immediate, personal leap of identity.[14] On entering the museum, visitors can choose an identity card of a man or woman, someone like themselves who was caught up in the Holocaust. At each floor, visitors are asked to turn the pages of their cards to reveal what happened to their identity-card companion at each stage of the Holocaust—1933–39, 1940–44, 1945 and the aftermath. At the end of the permanent exhibition, visitors touch the ID-card number on a computer monitor, where the *Encyclopedia of the Holocaust* is stored, to learn the fate of their phantom-guides.

On the one hand, such a device allows individuals a chance to personalize such history, to know it "as if it happened to us," in the Passover refrain. For a moment, at least, the victims are rehumanized, invigorated with the life force of the visitors themselves. But while the "experiential mode" has come into increasing favor with museums, it is also a mode that encourages a certain critical blindness on the part of visitors. Imagining oneself as a past victim may not be the same as imagining oneself—or another person—as a potential victim, one of the kinds of leap necessary to prevent other "holocausts." All of which obscures our contemporary actual reality of the Holocaust, which is not the event itself, but *memory* of the event, the great distance between then and now, between there and here. For this, not the Holocaust itself, is our preeminent reality now, no less than the Holocaust was the victims' preeminent reality then.

A further twist has been detected by Jonathan Rosen: "The irony is that many Jews during the Holocaust scrambled to acquire false papers in order to survive the war—the papers of non-Jews. There is a reverse principle at work here, as if everyone were expected to enter the museum an American and leave, in some fashion, a Jew."[15] If this is true, then precisely the opposite effect of a unifying experience has been achieved: Americans enter whole, only to exit in their constituent parts.

In addition, by insisting on our identification with the victim, this device may also generate a certain complacency in visitors, the self-righteousness of the persecuted. For even though the Holocaust was, after all, a Holocaust only for the victims, without looking into the minds and hearts of the killers, we may ignore our own capacity as potential persecutors. In fairness, several excellent film compilations near the beginning of the exhibition present the rise of the Nazis in their political and historical contexts. But by asking us to identify only with the victims, the museum closes off the critical self-examination that might have accompanied an even fleeting identification with the murderers: the professor who collaborated, the school child who taunted her Jewish classmates, the Hitler Youth who ended up in the S.S., a concentration camp guard. How people became killers might be almost as important here as how people became victims, though not nearly as inviting a motif as the latter, or much of a basis for a national museum meant to affirm national ideals and values.

Despite their identity cards, the visitors' experience begins appropriately with America's first direct Holocaust experience—that is, through the eyes of the American GI's who liberated Buchenwald and Dachau. In this opening section, we view footage of the camps at their liberation filmed by the Army, images that convey both the shock of the Americans and the gratitude and relief of survivors on being liberated, many of them about to become new Americans. With a little chronological slippage, in fact, it could be said that as potential Americans, many of the victims in these films were already American somehow. For them, the Holocaust was the beginning of their becoming American, making the Holocaust an essential part of their American identities.

And then, unlike European Holocaust museums that begin and end with the destruction of Europe's Jews, and unlike some museums in Israel that show the prewar European diaspora as already half-dead, the U.S. Holocaust Memorial Museum reflects an essentially exilic bias, showing the great vibrancy and richness of Jewish life lost in the Holocaust. The tragedy in this context is not just how European Jewry was destroyed, or the gruesome remains at the end, but the richly complex life lost—the 1000 years of civilization extirpated, unregenerated, unrepaired. The Holocaust is defined here not as mere killing, but as an immeasurable loss. (Even Israeli museums that include life before and after the Holocaust are not so generous in their appraisal of pre-Holocaust Jewish life in Europe—so decayed and decrepit in the Zionist view, so defenseless and weak, that it almost deserved to perish. For to do otherwise, to represent diaspora Jewry in overly generous terms would be to undercut one of Israel's very reasons for existence.)

Because the American experience of Nazi Germany in the 1930's was necessarily mediated by newsreels, newspapers, and radio broadcasts, the media experience itself is recreated in the next section. Visitors enter an installation recalling a typical American living room in 1939, complete with a radio broadcasting news reports, newspapers and magazines discussing what was reported at the time. This was the American experience, in all of its limited and necessarily mediated ways.

To reach a section about the ghetto, visitors traverse a narrow bridge like the ones that once linked one side of the ghetto with another. Then they walk on authentic cobblestones from the Warsaw ghetto and view other artifacts, such as a sewing machine, a milk can, a cart, and other items showing the range of life in the ghetto—each artifact a metonymic reminder of the actual life once animating it. The former director Jeshajahu Weinberg believes such artifacts make the factuality of the Holocaust self-evident—

an immunization against the negationist lies denying the Holocaust. In addition, the museum shows entire cases of victims' shoes, photographs of mounds of hair, and other remnants brought from the Auschwitz museum and Majdanek.

Although this museum also shows images of Jewish life before and after the Holocaust (for example, a moving temporary exhibition that depicts the rich life of a young Jewish boy before the war), when an entire people is represented by their scattered belongings, memory of life itself is lost. Nowhere among this debris do we find traces of what bound these people together into a civilization, a nation, a culture. Heaps of scattered artifacts belie the interconnectedness of lives that made these victims a people. These lives and the relationships between them are lost to the memory of ruins alone—and will be lost to subsequent generations who seek memory only in the rubble of the past. Indeed, by adopting such artifacts for their memorial presentations, other Holocaust museums in America, Europe, or Israel risk perpetuating the very figures by which the killers themselves would have memorialized their Jewish victims.

After the ghetto experience in this museum narrative comes mass murder, beginning with the Einsatzgruppen, the mobile killing units of the S.S. responsible for murdering some 1.5 million Jews in the Soviet Union. Film images of these killings are simultaneously presented and hidden: a four-foot high concrete wall will keep young children from looking into the abyss, visible only to their elder siblings and parents. Or, for those survivors who, in Berenbaum's words, "don't need to see or feel what they can never forget" (p. 7), or who grow claustrophobic, or who just cannot bear the horrible images, or who want to avoid the rail car, there will be a detour.

A section on concentration camps follows, replete with half an actual barrack imported from Birkenau. Again, according to Berenbaum, this and other artifacts are used to refute the lies of Holocaust negationists. Once inside the barracks, visitors view a scale model of the gas chambers designed after a similar model on view at Auschwitz. Cannisters of Zyklon-B, long de-activated, attend this section alongside mention of contracts of the construction companies who built the gas chamber and crematorium complexes, guaranteeing a longevity of 25 years. "Issues of corporate behavior—with all their ethical ramifications—must be confronted squarely in this tower," Berenbaum writes.

After the death exhibits, visitors find both respite and some sense of vindication in sections on resistance and "the courage to care." Here the stories of ghetto fighters and partisans are told alongside those of other heroes, such as Raoul Wallenberg (who saved 100,000 Jews in Budapest) and the French villagers of Chambon, where Jewish children were hidden and protected.

Finally, like the museum narratives in Israel, where lives were rebuilt after the Holocaust, this exhibition also ends with the "return to life." For this is the story of an ideal shared by America and Israel: both see themselves as lands of refuge and freedom. What follows is then a story of immigration, the long journey from "old world" Displaced Persons Camps, ravaged towns, and anti-Semitism to the "new worlds" of Jewish statehood and American egalitarianism. It is the story of America's absorption of both immigrants and their memories, the gradual integration of Holocaust memory into American civic culture. For at the end, the museum suggests itself as the ultimate triumph of America's absorption of immigrants, the integration of immigrant memory into the topographical heart of American memory.

In his introduction to the museum walkthrough, Berenbaum addresses the reciprocal exchange between a monument and its surroundings that takes place on leaving the Museum. It is not only a matter of the memorial's meaning being shaped by its context—the Holocaust Americanized in this case—but also of the surroundings being re-viewed in the light of the Holocaust memorial. "When people leave the U.S. Holocaust Memorial Museum," Berenbaum writes, "the monuments to democracy that surround it—to Lincoln and Jefferson and Washington—will take on a new meaning." Such American icons of democracy will either be affirmed for the ways their ideals prevented similar events in America or, in the eyes of Native Americans, African Americans, and Japanese Americans, reviewed skeptically for the ways such ideals might have prevented, but did not, the persecution of these groups on American soil. Every visitor will bring a different experience to the museum, as well as a different kind of memory out of it.

In America, the traditional impulse to anchor memory in historical crisis is further complicated—and exacerbated—by a number of additional factors unique to the contemporary Jewish American experience. For in America's culture of assimilation, where explicitly religious differences are tolerated and deemphasized, it is almost always the memory of extreme experience that serves to distinguish the identity of minority groups from the majority population. Indeed, one of the central topoi of American "new world" identity that began with the progenitors of America's "majority population"—the pilgrims—is the memory of "old world" oppression.

With the rise of ethnic pride among African Americans, Jewish Americans, and Native Americans during the 1960's, the power of a vicariously remembered past to bind otherwise alienated groups grew increasingly attractive. As African Americans recalled their enslavement and Native Americans their genocide, Jewish Americans began to recall the Holocaust as the crux of their common heritage. At the same time as the memory of mass suffering was binding together the members of these communities, it also set the stage for an implicit competition between the various cults of victimization. Two-dimensional identities constructed solely around the memory of past suffering began to clash as groups asserted the primacy of their tragic pasts over that of others.

One of the results has been a narrowing of each group's experience, a dividing of these groups' histories from one another. Instead of learning about the Holocaust through the larger study of Jewish history, many Jews and non-Jews in America now learn the whole of Jewish history through the lens of the Holocaust. Likewise, all that many Americans know about African Americans is their degraded condition as slaves, or about Native American history is its grisly end. In each case, entire centuries of rich life and culture are reduced to the detritus of destroyed civilizations.

Today, the Holocaust continues to occupy a central place in both Jewish and non-Jewish consciousness. In a plural and diverse society, it has also entered a universal realm, becoming a standard and currency by which many disparate groups measure their pasts, even as they come to know a part of Jewish history. Over time, however, Holocaust memorials and museums in America will also be asked to invite many different, occasionally competing groups of Americans into their spaces. At the same time, such museums have already inspired other persecuted minorities to demand national museums as well, to commemorate their catastrophes. In the most ideal of American visions, the memory of competing "holocausts" would not continue to divide Americans from one another but may lead each community to recall its past in the light of another group's historical memory. In this way, each group might also come to know more about their compatriots' experiences in the light of their own remembered past.

NOTES
NOTES ON THE CONTRIBUTORS
INDEX

Notes

Introduction: Starting with the Self

1. Sander L. Gilman, *The Jew's Body.* New York and London: Routledge, 1991.

2. Cited in Doris Grumbach, *Coming into the End Zone: A Memoir.* New York: W. W. Norton, 1991, p. 41.

3. The Pinkas Synagogue stands over the 11th-century foundations of what was possibly the first synagogue in Prague. The present building was begun in 1479. It was enlarged in 1535 and received its present facade in 1625. 77,297 Czech Jews were killed by the Nazis, and their names were inscribed beneath the vaults of the synagogue after the war. The synagogue was reopened in 1991, after being closed for over 20 years of so-called restoration, during which the Communist authorities permitted the written memorial to sink into invisibility. This information comes from the invaluable and accurate guide to Prague by Sadakat Kadri: *Prague.* London: Cadogan Books, 1993, p. 166.

4. Trans. K. O'Neill and D. Suchoff. Lincoln: University of Nebraska Press, 1994 (originally published as *Le Juif Imaginaire*, 1980), p. 83.

5. Alain Finkielkraut, *The Imaginary Jew*, p. 83.

6. Kathleen Adler, *see below*, p. 90.

7. *The Hebrew Lesson* was one of Lévy's most frequently shown works. Not only was it published in the prestigious *La Plume*, it was represented in the artist's one-person show of 1897 on the premises of the journal. See *Atelier d'Alphonse Lévy à Alger* (sale cat.), Paris: Hôtel Drouot, 1993, no. 112.

8. See *Ludwig Knaus, 1829–1910* (exh. cat.), Museum Wiesbaden, 1979, no. 96, p. 96, for extensive information about this painting and Knaus's attitudes toward his Jewish subjects.

9. It is perhaps not without rele-vance to the attitudes embodied in this painting to discover that 1878, the year it was created, was also when the Christian Socialist Party was founded in Berlin, the first political party grounded on anti-Semitic doctrine. See *Knaus*, p. 97.

10. Cited in *Knaus*, p. 169. The same boy appears again, as a single full-length figure, in *The First Profit*, another work from 1878 with a Jewish subject, an oil painting now in the Hermitage in St. Petersburg (*Knaus*, no. 97, pp. 169–70.) A pendant to *Solomonic Wisdom*, the young Jewish boy represented here has a certain youthful charm but also a feral look that bodes ill for the future. His racial "otherness" and associated moral insufficiency are conveyed by subtle hints rather than outright caricature: the slanted green "cats" eyes, the prominent spaces between the teeth, the big ears; above all, the complacent leer with which the youth shares his triumph with the spectator as he puts his first-earned coin into his purse.

11. See Elie Szapiro, "Réflexion sur les représentations et l'image du Juif en France au temps de "l'Affair Dreyfus," *Actes de la Journée d'Etudes autour de l'Affaire Dreyfus*, December 12, 1991, Paris: Ecole des Hautes Etudes du Judaisme, 1992, p. 45, and *Atelier d'Alphonse Lévy*, no. 112. However, as Szapiro himself points out, despite the fact that the issue is not in itself anti-Semitic, "son titre extérieur est la première impression qu'il donne le soit franchement." Nevertheless, as this author contin-ues, "il offre pourtant huit autres reproductions d'oeuvr d'Alphonse Lévy, reproductions qui montrent, au contraire, avec quelle tendresse évidente, même si elle reste souvent teintée d'ironie, ce peintre savait représenter les aspects très dif-férents du judaisme français de son temps." *Actes*, pp. 45–6.

12. For the best account of Lévy's career, see Elie Szapiro, "Alphonse Lévy et l'image du Juif en France au temps de l'affaire Dreyfus (1895–1902)," *Archives Juives: Revue d'histoire des Juifs de France* (Dossier: Les Juifs et l'Affaire Dreyfus), no. 27/1, vol. a, 1994, pp. 72–8.

13. Original, large-scale litho-graphs of these works, including a color version of the poster, and many more are available in two albums in the Salle d'Estampes, Bibliothèque Nationale, Paris: *Oeuvre d'Alphonse Lévy, Peintre, graveur et lithographe français, 1843–1918* (AA.4. Supplt. relié) and *Oeuvre d'Alphonse Lévy* (Dc. 356/in-fol. Form 3)/Mobile. Another volume of the artist's work, Alphonse Lévy, *Scènes familiales juives*, preface by Bernard Lazare, Paris: F. Juven, 1902 (In-dol., 10 p.m.h.) is missing from the collection. Several of the prints were exhibited at the Galerie Saphir Rive Droite, Paris, Summer, 1994. The *Scènes familiales juives*, in various avatars, keep popping up as illustrations, most recently for an English translation of Daniel Stauben's *Scenes of Jewish Life in Alsace*, a work originally published in serial form in the *Revue des deux mondes*, 1857 and 1859, and, translat-ed by Rose Choren, by Methuen in London in 1979. The American edition contains numerous pale and worn-out versions of Lévy's richly modulated lithographs: see Daniel Stauben, *Scenes of Jewish Life in Alsace*, illustrations by Alphonse Lévy, ed. and trans. Rose Choren, Malibu, Joseph Simon: Pangloss Press, 1991.

14. Cited in Elie Szapiro, *Actes*, pp. 72–3.

15. See Gale Murray, *below*, p. 58. Of course John Singer Sargent, as Kathleen Adler points out, could create a positive, if ambiguous, image of wealthy, sophisticated urban Jews in his portraits of the Wertheimer family, *below*, pp. 83–96.

16. Marshall Berman, *All that Is Solid Melts into Air: The Experience of Modernity.* New York: Simon and Schuster, 1982.

17. For the extensive literature devoted to the Jewish nose, see "The Jewish Nose: Are Jews White? Or, The History of the Nose Job," in Sander Gilman's pioneering work *The Jew's Body*, pp. 169–93, as well as three significant articles on the subject: Marie-Josée Baudinet Mondszain, "Juif—Face et Profil", *Judaisme, Judaïcités: récits, narrations, actes de langages* (textes du colloque C.N.R.S. 84) (*Traces*, 9/10, n.d.), pp. 170–83; Alfred David, "An Iconography of Noses: Directions In the History of a Physical Stereotype," in *Mapping the Cosmos*, ed. Jane Chance and R. D. Wells, Jr. Houston: Rice University Press, 1985, pp. 76–97; and Jay Geller, "(G)nos(e)ology: The Cultural Construction of the Other," in *People of the Body: Jews and Judaism from an Embodied Perspective*, ed. Howard Eilberg-Schwartz. Albany: State University of New York Press, 1992, pp. 243–82. Has the nose of any other ethnic group received so much attention; or had so much plastic surgery performed upon it?

18. Of course, not all deviations from the ideal are necessarily read as negative. The single tooth and the sunken features marking the face of Donatello's *Magdalene* are not read as anti-Magdalene or anti-Christian, but rather as the insignia of her exemplary self-sacrifice. Nor, in the well-known double portrait of an old man and his grandson in the Louvre (Ghirlandaio, *Old Man and his Grandson*) does the swollen, wart-covered nose of the old man transform the image into a sinister or abject one: on the contrary, it would seem to underline the tenderness of the relationship between old and young. See Alfred David, in *Mapping the Cosmos*, for a historical consideration of the relativization of physiognomic elements in Western representation.

19. For Lévy's intentions, see pp. 13–14 and note 7 *above*.

20. Alphonse Lévy, *Scènes familiales juives*. Elie Szapiro characterized the lithographs as both tender and caricatural in "Réflexions sur les représentations el l'image du Juif ...," p. 45.

21. James E. Young, *The Texture of Memory: Holocaust Memorials and Meaning*. New Haven and London: Yale University Press, 1993, p. 254.

Introduction: Modernity, Identity, Textuality

1. For the position of the Jew in Christian consciousness, see Frank E. Manuel, *The Broken Staff: Judaism Through Christian Eyes*. Cambridge, M.A: Harvard University Press, 1992; Amos Funkenstein, *Perceptions of Jewish History*. Berkeley and Oxford: University of California Press, 1993; Sander L. Gilman, *Jewish Self-Hatred: Anti-Semitism and the Hidden Language of the Jews*. Baltimore: Johns Hopkins University Press, 1986, 1990. For one contemporary philosophical use of "the jews" as distinct from the Jews, an indentifiable group, see Jean François Lyotard, *Heidegger and "the jews."* Minneapolis: University of Minnesota Press, 1988. For a discussion of the notion of the stranger within Western consciousness, see Julia Kristeva, *Strangers to Ourselves*. Hertfordshire: Harvester, 1991, and for a discussion of the Jew as the stranger within European consciousness, see Zygmunt Bauman, *Modernity and Ambivalence*. London: Polity Press, 1991.

2. For the suggestive juxtaposition of the notions of "a part of" and "apart from," I am grateful to Andrew Benjamin who used this formulation at a graduate seminar delivered at University College London, Spring 1994.

3. For a psychoanalytic discussion of anti-Semitism as projection, see Theodor Adorno and Max Horkheimer, "Elements of Anti-Semitism: Limits of Enlightenment," *Dialectic of Enlightenment*, first published 1944, Eng. trans. New York: Herder & Herder, 1972. All quotations in this essay from the 1979 edition, London: Verso, pp. 168–208.

4. For a brilliant collection of essays on racism and universalism, see E. Balibar and I. Wallerstein, *Race, Nation, Class: Ambiguous Identities*. Paris, 1988, Eng. trans. London: Verso, 1991. For a discussion of the role of "race" in the formation of liberal ideology and Enlightenment thought, see David Theo Goldberg, *Racist Culture: Philosophy and the Politics of Meaning*. Cambridge, M.A: Blackwell, 1993. See esp. p. 29. For a discussion of the relatioship between racial and

class hierarchies, see George Lukacs, "Social Darwinism, Racial Theory and Fascism," *The Destruction of Reason*. London: Merlin Press, 1962.

5. For a discussion of the move from Judaism as a religious belief to Jewishness as a racial category, see Hannah Arendt, *The Origins of Totalitarianism*. London: George Allen and Unwin, 1958.

6. See Adorno and Horkheimer, *Dialectic of Enlightenment*, pp. 185–6.

7. See Sander L. Gilman, *The Jew's Body*. London and New York: Routledge, 1991, and *People of the Body: Jews and Judaism from an Embodied Perspective*, ed. Howard Eilberg-Schwartz. Albany: State University of New York Press, 1992.

8. For a critical discussion of Christian universalism and Jewish separatism, see Daniel Boyarin and Jonathan Boyarin, "Diaspora: Generation and the Ground of Jewish Identity," *Critical Inquiry* 19 (Summer 1993), pp. 693–725.

9. Manuel, *The Broken Staff*, p. 286.

10. Cited in ibid.

11. Cited in ibid., p. 294.

12. Adorno and Horkheimer, *Dialectic of Enlightenment*, p. 175.

13. See Gilman, *Jewish Self-Hatred*, pp. 205–07.

14. Brian Cheyette, *Constructions of "The Jew" in English Literature and Society*. Cambridge and New York: Cambridge University Press, 1993.

15. On the feminization of the male Jew, see Gilman, *Jewish Self-Hatred*, pp. 74–6.

16. For Carol Ockman's important essay on the sexualization of the Jewess, see "'Two large eyebrows à l'orientale': Ethnic stereotyping in Ingres's *Baronne de Rothschild*," *Art History* 14, no. 4 (December 1991), pp. 521–39. For Adler, see her essay here, ch. 4.

1. Neither Black Nor White

1. Apart from the current Virago edition of Dorothy Richardson's *Deadlock* (1921) and the Penguin editions of John Buchan's *Prester John* (1910) and *The Three Hostages* (1924), I will be referring to contemporary editions of the literature in parentheses in the text.

2. Martin Bernal, *Black Athena: The Afroasiatic Roots of Classical Civili-*

zation, vol. 1. London: Free Association Books, 1987.

3. Henry Louis Gates, Jr., *Loose Canons: Notes on the Culture Wars*. Oxford and New York: Oxford University Press, 1992, p. 47 and ch. 3.

4. Cited in Bernal, *Black Athena*, p. 340.

5. See Wendy Katz, *Rider Haggard and the Fiction of Empire: A Critical Study of British Imperial Fiction*. Cambridge and New York: Cambridge University Press, 1987, pp. 47–50.

6. See Katz, ibid., pp. 148–52.

7. See Sander L. Gilman, *Difference and Pathology: Stereotypes of Sexuality, Race, and Madness*. Ithaca: Cornell University Press, 1985.

8. Bryan Cheyette, *Constructions of "the Jew" in English Literature and Society: Racial Representations, 1875–1945*. Cambridge and New York: Cambridge University Press, 1993, p. 186 and ch. 5.

9. See Jacqueline Rose, "Dorothy Richardson and the Jew," in Bryan Cheyette, *Between "Race" and Culture: Representations of "the Jew" in English and American Literature*. Stanford University Press, 1996.

10. See also Marshall Grossman, "The Violence of the Hyphen in Judeo-Christian," *Social Text* 22 (Spring 1989), pp. 115–22, and Bryan Cheyette, "White Skin, Black Masks: Jews and Jewishness in the writings of George Eliot and Frantz Fanon" in *Cultural Identity and the Gravity of History: On the Work of Edward Said*, ed. Keith Ansell-Pearson, Benita Parry, and Judith Squires. London: Lawrence & Wishart, 1996.

2. Charles Dickens' Oliver Twist

1. Mrs. Eliza Davies, letter to Charles Dickens, June 22, 1863, cited in *Anglo-Jewish Letters (1158–1917)*, ed. Cecil Roth. London: Soncino, 1938, p. 305.

A distinction is marked throughout this essay by the convention that whenever *Jew* is italicized it refers to the regulating idea of Jew, while Jew signifies *real* Jew. Usually, I write Jew in the singular to connote something of the violence that is for me inextricably associated with the histories and discourses of Jew and *Jew*.

My thanks to Tamar Garb,

Richard Appignanesi, and Joan Key for their insightful comments and suggestions which informed and reformed this essay.

2. L. Poliakov, *The History of Anti-Semitism*, vol. 3. London: Routledge and Kegan Paul, 1975, p. 324, argues that while there may have been feelings of "unease," nonetheless anti-Semitism, in Britain in the 19th century, was at "low ebb." Many historians, including Poliakov, have celebrated Jewish integration into British society, which has been seen as more tolerant than those of other European states. However, David Cesarini has identified and criticized this interpretation, which has adopted what he calls an "apologetic stance." This attitude has been shaped by Anglo-Jewry's particular route to modernity. See *The Making of Modern Anglo-Jewry*, ed. David Cesarini, Oxford: Basil Blackwell, 1990.

Oliver Twist was first published in 20 parts in *Bentley's Miscellany*, 1837–9. It was the first novel to appear under Dickens' own name. See Edgar Johnson, *Charles Dickens: His Tragedy and Triumph*, 2 vols. Canada: Little, Brown, vol. 1. 1952, p. 223. Dickens paid Bentley £1,500 for the rights of *Oliver Twist* and in June 1842 Chapman and Hall agreed to finance him; thereafter, they published all his books: see Johnson, *Charles Dickens*, p. 252.

3. Charles Dickens, letter to Mrs. Davies, July 10, 1863, cited in Roth, *Anglo-Jewish Letters*, p. 306.

4. Charles Dickens, Preface, *Oliver Twist*. London: Chapman and Hall, n.d. [1842?], p. 3. Subsequent quotations in the text are from this edition, with page numbers in parentheses.

5. Dickens, letter to Mrs. Davies, cited in Roth, *Anglo-Jewish Letters*, p. 306.

6. Ibid., p. 306.

7. Edward Said, *Orientalism*. Harmondsworth: Penguin, 1985, p. 145.

8. "Statement of the Civil Disabilities and Privations affecting Jews in England," London, 1829, reported in *Edinburgh Review*, (January 1831), p. 369.

9. T. B. Macaulay, "The Jews," *Hansard*, House of Commons, April 5, 1830, p. 1309. There were 14 attempts to remove parliamentary

disabilities. One bill was presented in each of the years 1830, 1833, 1834, 1836, 1847–8, 1849, 1851, and 1856 and 4 more measures were considered in 1857 and 1858. Lionel de Rothschild was able finally to take his seat in Parliament in 1858, when the obligation to take a Christian oath was waived.

10. Ernest Renan, cited in Said, *Orientalism*, p. 149.

11. "Identity thinking" in Theodor Adorno refers to the idea that the particular is subsumed under the general concept as the individual is subsumed under the "plan." See David Held, *Introduction to Critical Theory: Horkheimer to Habermas*. London: Hutchinson Library Press, 1980, p. 202.

12. Dickens was instructing Cruikshank as he wrote the installments, 1837–9.

13. Dickens, letter to Cruikshank, *Letter 1*, 152 [1838], cited in Johnson, *Charles Dickens*, p. 216.

14. See Michael Hollington, "Dickens and Cruikshank as Physiognomers in Oliver Twist," *Dickens Quarterly* 7, no. 2 (1990), p. 251.

15. See Sander L. Gilman, *The Jew's Body*, London and New York: Routledge, 1991, p. 189.

16. Eden Warwick (George Jabet), *Notes on Noses*, 1848, cited in Gilman, *The Jew's Body*, p. 179.

17. Ibid., p. 179.

18. Sigmund Freud, *Civilization and its Discontents*. Harmondsworth: Penguin, 1987, p. 289.

19. Sander L. Gilman, *Jewish Self-Hatred: Anti-Semitism and the Hidden Language of the Jews*. Baltimore: Johns Hopkins University Press, 1990, pp. 174–5, 300.

20. See Mary Douglas, *Purity and Danger: An Analysis of the Concepts of Pollution and Taboo*. London and New York: Ark Paperbacks, 1989, p. 38.

21. See Theodor Adorno and Max Horkheimer, *Dialectic of Enlightenment*, first published 1944, Eng. trans. New York: Herder & Herder, 1972; London: Verso, 1989, p. 175.

22. Gilman, *Jewish Self-Hatred*, p. 77.

23. Julia Kristeva, *Powers of Horror: An Essay on Abjection*. New York: Columbia University Press, 1982, p. 5.

24. Zygmunt Bauman, *Modernity and Ambivalence*. Cambridge: Polity Press, 1991, pp. 60–61.

25. Adorno and Horkheimer, *Dialectic of Enlightenment,* passim.
26. Matthew 16, King James Bible.
27. Jessica says: "Alack, what heinous sin is it in me/To be asham'd to be my father's child!/But though I am a daughter to his blood,/I am not to his manners . . ./I shall end this strife/Become a Christian, . . ." William Shakespeare, *The Merchant of Venice,* Act 2, Scene 3.
28. Hannah Arendt, *The Origins of Totalitarianism.* London: George Allen and Unwin, 1958, p. 87.

3. Toulouse-Lautrec

1. When asked to make a political cartoon, presumably on the Affair, for *L'Aurore* in November, 1897, Lautrec refused, stating that he had "never done any *current events.* It's not my style." See Herbert D. Schimmel, ed., *The Letters of Henri de Toulouse-Lautrec.* Oxford University Press, 1991. Cf. letter 489, p. 309.
2. See Riva Castleman and Wolfgang Wittrock, eds., *Henri de Toulouse-Lautrec: Images of the 1890s* (exh. cat.), Museum of Modern Art, New York, 1985, p. 16. However, Lautrec was incapacitated for much of 1899, following his internment in a sanitarium for an alcoholic and nervous breakdown. The petition appealed against the imprisonment of Colonel Picquart for maintaining that Dreyfus had been mistakenly condemned in place of Esterhazy.
3. Thadée Natanson, *Un Henri de Toulouse-Lautrec.* Geneva: Pierre Cailler, 1951, p. 275.
4. Wolfgang Wittrock, *Toulouse-Lautrec: The Complete Prints* (London: Sotheby's 1985), p. 3. A reduced version served as the frontispiece of the book and was used for advertisements in the press: Victor Joze [Victor Dobrski], *Reine de Joie.* Paris: Henry Julien, 1892.
5. Henry H. Weinberg, "The Image of the Jew in Late Nineteenth-Century French Literature," *Jewish Social Studies* 45, no. 3–4 (1983): pp. 242, 246. See also Moses Debré, *The Image of the Jew in French Literature from 1800 to 1908,* trans. Gertrude Hirschler. New York: Ktav, 1970, pp. 25–34; Robert F. Byrnes, *Antisemitism in Modern*

France: The Prologue to the Dreyfus Affair. New Brunswick: Rutgers University Press, 1950, pp. 103–10; Charles C. Lehrmann, *The Jewish Element in French Literature,* trans. George Klin. Rutherford, N.J: Fairleigh Dickinson University Press, 1971, pp. 157–63; Earle Stanley Randall, *The Jewish Character in the French Novel: 1870–1914.* Evanston, Ill: George Banta, 1941, pp. 23–59.
6. Victor Joze, *Mon Album: Les Petites Démascarades.* Paris: Ernest Kolb, 1889, pp. 39–41, 72, 87–8, 106–7.
7. Robert Wistrich, *Between Redemption and Perdition: Modern Anti-semitism and Jewish Identity.* London and New York: Routledge, 1990, pp. 39–41. See also Edmund Silberner, "French Socialism and the Jewish Question, 1865–1914," *Historia Judaica* 16 (April, 1954): pp. 3–38; Albert S. Lindemann, *The Jew Accused: Three Anti-Semitic Affairs (Dreyfus, Beilis, Frank), 1894–1915.* Cambridge University Press, 1993, p. 70; Byrnes, *Anti-Semitism in Modern France,* pp. 156–8; Nancy L. Green, "Socialist Anti-Semitism, Defense of a Bourgeois Jew and Discovery of the Jewish Proletariat: Changing Attitudes of French Socialists Before 1914," *International Review of Social History* 30, no. 3 (1985): p. 374.
8. Stephen A. Schuker, "Origins of the 'Jewish Problem' in the Later Third Republic" in *The Jews in Modern France,* ed. Frances Malino and Bernard Wasserstein. Hannover, N.H: University Press of New England, 1985, p. 148; Zeev Sternhell, "The Roots of Popular Anti-Semitism in the Third Republic" in Malino and Wasserstein, p. 103; see also pp. 109, 113–14. See also Pierre Birnbaum, "Anti-Semitism and Anticapitalism in Modern France" in Malino and Wasserstein, p. 215.
9. Joze probably commissioned Lautrec to make the poster during the spring of 1892; it was exhibited at the Association pour l'Art in Antwerp, May–June, 1892; cf. Schimmel, *The Letters of Henri de Toulouse-Lautrec,* letter 221, p. 171. On June 4, 1892 *Fin de Siècle* announced the poster's appearance on the streets of Paris, to coincide with the publication of Joze's novel. Joze, in "Toulouse-Lautrec,"

La Plume, April 15, 1900, later recalled the circumstances of the commission.
10. Joze, *Reine de Joie,* p. 159 (my translation).
11. Ibid., pp. 143–4.
12. Ibid., p. 164.
13. Richard Thomson, *Toulouse-Lautrec.* London: Oresko, 1977, p. 79.
14. Stephen Wilson, *Ideology and Experience: Antisemitism in France at the Time of the Dreyfus Affair.* Rutherford, N.J: Fairleigh Dickinson University Press, 1982, pp. 585, 597; 584–5 and passim. See also Lindemann, *The Jew Accused,* pp. 222, 239.
15. Lautrec's preparatory sketches lack this ambiguity; see M. G. Dortu, *Toulouse-Lautrec et son Oeuvre.* New York: Collectors Editions, 1971, D3224, D3225. In them the baron's arm either hangs limply by his side or rests on the table.
16. This interpretation is suggested by Nora Desloge, *Toulouse-Lautrec: The Baldwin M. Baldwin Collection* (exh. cat.), San Diego Museum of Art, 1988, p. 204.
17. Wittrock, *Toulouse-Lautrec,* no. 30, published in *L'Escarmouche,* November 12, 1893. The same male figure watches La Goulue and Valentin le Désossé, the racy stars of the Moulin Rouge, slither through a waltz in a lithographed sheet-music cover, designed by Lautrec in 1894. See Wittrock, *Toulouse-Lautrec,* no. 65, *La Goulue.*
18. Arthur Symons, *Parisian Nights.* London: Beaumont, 1926, p. 8. See Dortu, *Toulouse-Lautrec et son Oeuvre,* P399.
19. Félix Fénéon, "Chez les Barbouilleurs: Les Affiches en Couleurs," *Le Père Peinard,* May 7, 1893, p. 5 (my translation).
20. Ernest Maindron, *Les Affiches illustrés, 1886–1895.* Paris: G. Boudet, 1896, pp. 111–12; Octave Uzanne, *Les Maîtres de l'estampe et l'affiche.* Paris, 1896, p. 821. See also Frantz Jourdain, "L'Affiche Moderne et Henri de Toulouse-Lautrec," *La Plume* 4, no. 110 (November 15, 1893): 490, who called *Reine de Joie* "a superbly harsh and psychological poster of the upper class at play" and the male figure "a shady-looking banker, obviously a millionaire . . . the lustful old dodderer, paying a whore to slobber kisses all over his sagging shriveled flesh." Thadée Natanson praised the

poster for its "lucid, pretty, exquisitely perverse" forms in "Oeuvres de M. de Toulouse-Lautrec," *Revue Blanche* 4, no. 16 (February 1893): 146. He referred to it as one of a group that have "surprised, disturbed, or delighted us," but did not discuss its subject.

21. *Fin de Siècle*, June 18, 1892, p. 1, "Echoes" by "Diable Rose." *Fin de Siècle*, June 29, 1892, p. 1, "Echoes", noted: "Following a complaint addressed by M. Victor Joze to the public prosecutor, the chief of criminal investigations went to the rue Guénégard to search for some posters of *Reine de Joie* that had been fraudulently taken from the Bonnard-Bidault establishment by some disloyal employees. Two poster-hangers were to be arrested."

22. See Phillip Dennis Cate, "The Paris Cry: Graphic Artists and the Dreyfus Affair," in *The Dreyfus Affair: Art, Truth, and Justice*, ed. Norman L. Kleeblatt (exh. cat.), The Jewish Museum, New York, and Berkeley, Los Angeles, and London: University of California Press, 1987, pp. 62–95. In several of Steinlen's song illustrations the Jew is the archetypal "john"; see, e.g. Aristide Bruant, *Dans la Rue*. Paris: Aristide Bruant, 1895, vol. 2, pp. 155; also Eduard Fuchs, *Die Juden in der Karikatur: Ein Beitrag zur Kulturgeschichte*. Munich: Klaus Guhl 1921, pp. 214–16.

23. Linda Nochlin, "Degas and the Dreyfus Affair: A Portrait of the Artist as an Anti-Semite," in Kleeblatt, *The Dreyfus Affair*, pp. 109–10; on Pissarro, see Nochlin, pp. 98–9.

24. Victor Joze, *La Tribu d'Isidore*. Paris: Antony, 1897. *La Conquête de Paris*, 1904, and *Jérusalem sur Seine*, 1914.

25. Joze, *La Tribu d'Isidore*, p. vii.

26. Ibid., p. ix. P. vii draws a parallel between the fictional Rozenfeld family and actual contemporary French Jewish families: "les Mayer, les Meyer, les Wolff, les Dreyfus" explaining that "even though they were of foreign extraction, they succeeded in worming their way into all of the ranks of French society. At present, they are very strong and do nearly everything they wish to in Paris."

27. Ibid., p. x.

28. Wittrock, *Toulouse-Lautrec*, no. 234.

29. Joze, *La Tribu d'Isidore*, p. 7.

30. Desloge, *Toulouse-Lautrec*, p. 170, has suggested that it was an image near at hand, since he had made at least two other driving scenes in 1897 (Wittrock, *Toulouse-Lautrec*, nos. 227, 228). See also Wittrock, no. 303, which is nearly identical in composition and placed in 1897 by Götz Adriani, *Toulouse-Lautrec: The Complete Graphic Works, a Catalogue Raisonné*. London: Thames and Hudson, 1988, no. 230, p. 292.

31. Joze, *La Tribu d'Isidore*, p. vii.

32. Stephen Wilson, "Antisemitism in France during 'La Belle Epoque,'" *Wiener Library Bulletin* 29 (1976): p. 6.

33. Georges Clemenceau, *Au Pied du Sinaï* (Paris: Henri Floury, 1898). Unless otherwise noted all translations are from the Eng. ed: Georges Clemenceau, *At the Foot of Sinai*, trans. A. V. Ende. New York: Bernard G. Richards, 1922. For Lautrec's illustrations, see Wittrock, *Toulouse-Lautrec*, nos. 187–201. Lautrec also designed six *cul-de-lampes*, which were photomechanically reproduced; see Loys Delteil, *Henri de Toulouse-Lautrec*, vol. 6 of *Le Peintre-Graveur illustré, XIXᵉ et XXᵉ siècles*. Paris, 1920, reprinted New York: Da Capo, 1969, no. 320 (mistakenly identified as belonging to *Histoires Naturelles*). N.B: the deluxe edition consisted of the first 25 impressions of the publication.

34. See Schimmel, *The Letters of Henri de Toulouse-Lautrec*, letter 475A, p. 301, dated April 15, 1897, from Lautrec to the publisher, regarding the payment; letter 477, p. 302, a telegram from Lautrec to Clemenceau on May 1, requesting a meeting so that Clemenceau could give him "the subject of the two stories to be illustrated"; letter 478, p. 303, May 1897, in which he reported to his mother that he was "working on a book with Clemenceau"; letter 480, p. 304, also May 1897, in which he told her "I'm finishing a book with Clemenceau on the Jews."

35. Samuel Isaac Applebaum, "Clemenceau: Thinker and Writer," Ph.D. diss., Columbia University, 1948, f.85. The addition of illustrations by Lautrec must have been arranged by their mutual friend, the journalist and art critic Gustave Geffroy. In 1894 Clemenceau had

written a lengthy rave review of Lautrec and Geffroy's collaborative album on Yvette Guilbert. See "Au Café-Concert," *La Justice*, September 15, 1894.

36. Wilson, *Ideology and Experience*, pp. 235–6; Barnett Singer, "Clemenceau and the Jews," *Jewish Social Studies* 43–44 (Winter 1981): p. 49 and *passim*; Julien Benda, *La Jeunesse d'un clerc*. Paris: Gallimard, 1937, p. 161.

37. Wilson, *Ideology and Experience*, p. 66; article of December 25, 1894, reprinted in Georges Clemenceau, *L'Iniquité*. Paris: P.-V. Stock, 1899, pp. 1–4; Jean Ratinard, *Clemenceau ou le colère et la gloire*. Paris: Fayard, 1958, p. 119. David Robin Watson, *Georges Clemenceau: A Political Biography*. New York: David McKay, 1974, p. 146, relates that Clemenceau was still convinced of Dreyfus's guilt when he agreed in October 1897 to join *L'Aurore*. His condition was that Bernard Lazare "should not continue his campaign for Dreyfus in its columns." See also Janine Ponty, "La Presse quotidienne et l'Affaire Dreyfus en 1898–1899: Essai de typologie," *Revue d'Histoire Moderne et Contemporaine* 21 (April–June 1974): p. 207, who notes that Clemenceau finally affirmed the innocence of Dreyfus in *L'Aurore*, October 28, 1898.

38. Watson, *Georges Clemenceau*, pp. 146–7. Jean-Baptiste Duroselle, *Clemenceau*. Paris: Fayard, 1988, p. 450. Robert L. Hoffman, *More than a Trial: The Struggle Over Captain Dreyfus*. New York: Free Press, 1980, p. 207. See also Schuker in Malino and Wasserstein, p. 150, who states, "The principal issue was the fate of the Republic, not the status of Jews." On the changing position of the Left see Wistrich, *Between Redemption*, pp. 133–49; Sternhell, "The Roots of Popular Anti-Semitism," pp. 119–21; Green, "Socialist Anti-Semitism."

39. Clemenceau, *L'Iniquité*, pp. 146–7. See also his articles of January 7, pp. 111–12; January 25, pp. 163–6; January 27, pp. 172–5; January 29, pp. 180–82. For articles of 1899 see his *La Honte*. Paris: P.-V. Stock, 1903, esp. pp. 6–11.

40. Clemenceau, *At the Foot of Sinai*, p. 67; see pp. 171–2 of the French edn. ("il a voulu se reprendre et s'achever par la domination de la terre"), trans. in the Eng. edn., p. 133, as "he has wanted to redeem himself and to perfect himself by overcoming untoward circumstances." The Eng. edn. frequently downplays the anti-Semitism of Clemenceau's remarks. The translation I have used is that of Léon Poliakov, *Suicidal Europe: 1870–1933*, trans. George Klin, *The History of Anti-Semitism*, vol. 4. New York: Vanguard, 1985, p. 64; see also pp. 64–5. Clemenceau's anti-Semitic remarks in these pieces were pointed out with great satisfaction by the anti-Semitic journalist and author François Bournand, *Les Juifs et nos contemporains*. Paris: Librairie A. Pierret, 1899, pp. 65–78.

41. Nochlin, "Degas and the Dreyfus Affair," p. 110.

42. Joseph Pennell, *The Jew at Home: Impressions of a Summer and Autumn Spent with Him in Russia and Austria.* London: Heinemann, 1892, pp. 44, 110, 103; Pennell's articles were originally published in *The Illustrated London News*, 1891. See also the discussion of Warsaw in Karl Baedeker, *La Russie: Manuel du voyageur.* Leipzig, 1893, pp. 12–13. Baedeker distinguished the "imposing bearing, fine, lithe build, and graceful gait" of the native Poles from "the extremely filthy external appearance of the Jews" which made "a disagreeable contrast with the elegant aspect of the streets," and went on to point out the Jews' "domination" of Poland through their skill at "commerce," and their crippling of the Polish nobility through moneylending. Gustave Larroumet, *Vers Athènes et Jérusalem.* Paris: Hachette, 1898, pp. 305–12, similarly spoke of "the great defects and profound lacunae of the Jewish heart and spirit" and the Jews' "wealth and power over the entire world."

43. Quoted in Poliakov, *Suicidal Europe*, p. 64.

44. Clemenceau, *At the Foot of Sinai*, pp. 64, 110–11, 137, 135.

45. Ibid., xiv; Poliakov, *Suicidal Europe*, p. 63.

46. Schimmel, *The Letters of Henri de Toulouse-Lautrec*, letter 478.

47. Nochlin, "Degas and the Dreyfus Affair," p. 111.

48. This analysis was proposed by Linda Nochlin, "Toulouse-Lautrec, the Performer and the Prostitute:

Advertising and the Representation of Marginality," lecture, Museum of Modern Art, New York, 1985.

49. Yvanhoé Rambosson, "Publications d'Art," *Mercure de France* 27, no. 103 (July 1898): p. 283. This was one of very few press notices of Clemenceau's book. See also Emile Berr, "Petite Chronique des lettres," *Revue Bleue* 9, no. 19 (May 7, 1898): pp. 605–6. Maurice Joyant, *Henri de Toulouse-Lautrec.* Paris: Henri Floury, 1926, vol. 1, p. 204, noted that Lautrec's illustrations indicate the direction his career would have taken had it not been cut off by alcoholism and illness.

50. Because of the imprecision of Lautrec's rendering, its identification as the Polish eagle cannot be certain. Numerous other Eastern European regimes, including the Russian and the Austrian, used an eagle standard, as did the German. Cate in Kleeblatt, *The Dreyfus Affair*, p. 74, sees this as the German imperial eagle. The implication of Jewish connections with the Germans would make the lithograph's message even more anti-Semitic, and more immediately relevant to the Dreyfus Affair. However, there is no reference in Clemenceau's book to support this interpretation. Moreover, the German imperial eagle is black and sports a rounded, not pointed, crown.

51. Jan Goldstein, "The Wandering Jew and the Problem of Psychiatric Anti-semitism in Fin-de-Siècle France," *Journal of Contemporary History* 20 (1985): p. 535. See also Hyam Maccoby, "The Wandering Jew as Sacred Executioner" in *The Wandering Jew: Essays in the Interpretation of a Christian Legend*, ed. Galit Hasan-Rokem and Alan Dundes. Bloomington: Indiana University Press, 1986, pp. 255ff.

52. Wilson, *Ideology and Experience*, p. 394, quoting Auguste Chirac in April 1898.

53. Adolf L. Leschnitzer, "The Wandering Jew: The Alienation of the Jewish Image in Christian Consciousness" in Hasan-Rokem and Dundes, pp. 234; Maccoby, in Hasan-Rokem and Dundes, pp. 257–8; Joshua Trachtenberg, *The Devil and the Jews: The Medieval Conception of the Jew and Its Relation to Modern Antisemitism.* New Haven: Yale University Press, 1943; Wilson,

Ideology and Experience, pp. 543–53.

54. Clemenceau, *At The Foot of Sinai*, p. 137. The Eng. edn. uses "fear" for "exterminer" and "reaching out for" for "en voie de leur voler"). See Castleman and Wittrock, *Henri de Toulouse-Lautrec*, p. 15. See also Wilson, *Ideology and Experience* p. 263, who notes that Balzac asserted that money was "the God of the Jews."

55. Georges Clemenceau, "Le Baron Moise," *L'Illustration*, July 11, 1896, no. 2785, pp. 22–3, 26.

56. Clemenceau, *At the Foot of Sinai*, pp. 1, 23, 15, 35.

57. Ibid., p. 13.

58. See, e.g., Wittrock, *Toulouse-Lautrec*, no. 179.

59. Clemenceau, *At the Foot of Sinai*, p. 32. In one other selection of *Au Pied du Sinai*, "How I Became Farsighted", originally published in *La Dépêche de Toulouse*, November 1894, Clemenceau also focused on the capitalistic instinct of the Jew. This humorous anecdote about how he was "conned" and vastly overcharged by the Parisian Jewish optometrist Mayer seems somewhat incongruous in this anthology of Eastern European sketches; presumably it was included for its Jewish theme and its attempt to say something about the Jewish character.

60. Georges Clemenceau, "Chronique: Histoire Juive," *La Dépêche de Toulouse*, August 29, 1895, no. 9879, p. 1.

61. Clemenceau, *At the Foot of Sinai*, pp. 46–7, 48, 49, 50.

62. Nochlin, "Degas and the Dreyfus Affair," p. 111.

63. Clemenceau, *At the Foot of Sinai*, pp. 53–5.

64. Nochlin, "Degas and the Dreyfus Affair," p. 111.

65. Green, "Socialist Anti-Semitism," pp. 375–6 and *passim*; see also Silberner, "French Socialism and the Jewish Question, 1865–1914," p. 37; Wistrich, *Between Redemption and Perdition*, pp. 146–9; and Green, *The Pletzl of Paris: Jewish Immigrant Workers in the Belle Epoque.* New York: Holmes & Meier, 1985.

66. Clemenceau, *At the Foot of Sinai*, p. 61.

67. Nochlin, "Degas and the Dreyfus Affair," p. 111.

68. Georges Clemenceau, "En Israël: Carlsbad", *Le Journal*, August 24, 1895, no. 1061, p. 1.

69. Georges Clemenceau, "Impressions de Galicie," *La Dépêche de Toulouse*, May 15, 1897, no. 10, p. 501; "Impressions de Galicie: Busk," May 20, 1897, no. 10, p. 506; and May 27, 1897, no. 10, p. 513. The series was also published in *La Justice*, May 18, 1897, no. 6339; June 2, 1897, no. 6851; and June 3, 1897, no. 6852.

70. Joyant, *Henri de Toulouse-Lautrec*, vol. 1, p. 204.

71. "Crasseux", p. 149 in the French edn., is translated in the Eng. edn. as "unkempt"; see Clemenceau, *At the Foot of Sinai*, pp. 113, 65.

72. Clemenceau, *At the Foot of Sinai*, pp. 62–7.

73. Pennell, *The Jew at Home*, pp. 33 and 104.

74. Clemenceau, *At the Foot of Sinai*, pp. 69–71.

75. Ibid., p. 73.

76. Ibid., pp. 96–7.

77. Ibid., pp. 104–5.

78. Wilson, *Ideology and Experience*, pp. xv–xvi.

4. Sargent's Portraits of the Wertheimers

1. Sargent wrote this to Lady Lewis in 1898; cited in Evan Charteris, *John Sargent*. London: William Heinemann, 1927, p. 164. The nine paintings in the Tate Gallery are: *Asher Wertheimer* (1898); *Mrs. Wertheimer* (1904); *Hylda Wertheimer* (1901); *Ena and Betty Wertheimer* (1901); *Alfred Wertheimer* (1901?); *Edward Wertheimer* (1902); *Essie, Ruby, and Ferdinand Wertheimer* (1902); *Hylda, Almina, and Conway Wertheimer* (1905); and *Almina Wertheimer* (1908). The first portrait of Mrs. Wertheimer (1898) is in the New Orleans Museum of Art, an oval portrait of Betty is in the National Museum of American Art, Washington, D.C. and the portrait of Ena, *A Vele gonfie* (1905), is still in the possession of the family.

I should like to thank Andrew Wilton, David Fraser Jenkins, Robert Upstone, and especially Anna Southall at the Tate Gallery for giving me access to the Tate's Wertheimer portraits and for their enthusiasm for the paintings; Mrs. Victoria Jarvis, for the opportunity to see *A Vele gonfie*; Carol Ockman, for inviting me to participate in the

session she organized at the 1994 College Art Association conference in New York on negotiating stereotypes, for her friendship, and for the work she has done on representations of "la Juive;" Laura Marcus and Bryan Cheyette, for the chance to develop this project in a paper given at the conference on "Modernity, Culture and 'the Jew'" at Birkbeck College, London, in 1994; Malcolm Baker for his support and encouragement; Linda Nochlin, for her helpful comments; and, most of all, Tamar Garb for many hours of discussion, support, and incisive criticism.

2. Todd M. Endelman, "German-Jewish Settlement in Victorian England," in *Second Chance: Two Centuries of German-Speaking Jews in the United Kingdom.* ed. Werner E. Mosse. Tübingen: Mohr, 1992, p. 42.

3. On the Rothschilds as collectors, and Wertheimer's connections with them, see Virginia Cowles, *The Rothschilds: A Family of Fortune.* London: Weidenfeld and Nicolson, 1973, esp. p. 191; and Mrs. James de Rothschild, *The Rothschilds at Waddesdon Manor.* London: Collins, 1979, esp. p. 32.

4. Details of Wertheimer's travels to Russia from his (unsigned) obituary in *The Times*, August 12, 1914, "Death of Mr. Asher Wertheimer, A Fine Judge of Art."

5. Bernard Berenson intervened in the distribution of this collection, arguing with Gutkunst that Isabella Stewart Gardner in Boston should be allowed some plums from the collection. He selected two undisputed Rembrandts and a Ter Borch, for which Mrs. Gardner paid $150,000. See Colin Simpson, *The Partnership: The Secret Association of Bernard Berenson and Joseph Duveen.* London: Bodley Head, 1987, p. 83.

6. Roger Fry, *New Statesman*, January 13, 1923, reprinted in *Transformations: Critical and Speculative Essays on Art.* London: Chatto & Windus, 1926, p. 132.

7. John Russell, "Art" in *Edwardian England*, ed. S. Nowell-Smith. London, 1964, p. 333.

8. Cited in Colin Holmes, *Anti-Semitism in British Society 1876–1939.* London: Edward Arnold, 1979, p. 59.

9. Ibid., p. 112.

10. W. D. Rubinstein, "Jews among the Top British Wealth Holders, 1857–1969: Decline of the Golden Age," *Jewish Social Studies* 34 (January 1972), p. 73.

11. See A. Allfrey, *Edward VII and his Jewish Court.* London: Weidenfeld and Nicolson, 1991, and Holmes, *Anti-Semitism in British Society*, p. 87.

12. A. White, *The Modern Jew.* London: William Heinemann, 1899, p. xv.

13. J. A. Hobson, *Imperialism: A Study.* London: Unwin Hyman, (1902) 1988, p. 57.

14. Ibid., p. 283. On "Jewish involvement" in the Boer War, see Holmes, pp. 66–80, and D. Feldman, *Englishmen and Jews: Social Relations and Political Culture 1840–1915.* New Haven and London: Yale University Press, 1994, pp. 264–7.

15. See Holmes, ibid., p. 42

16. On the issue of Jewish identity, see Feldman, *Englishmen and Jews*, pp. 2–17.

17. Mrs. Meyer was the wife of Carl Meyer, who came to England from Hamburg, and was a Lieutenant of the City of London, Director of the National Bank of Egypt, and Chairman of the London Committee of De Beers. He became a baronet in 1910.

18. Cited in William Howe Downes, *John Singer Sargent: His Life and Work.* London: Thornton Butterworth, 1926, p. 49.

19. Henry James, *The Painter's Eye: Notes and Essays on the Pictorial Arts.* Madison, Wi: University of Wisconsin Press, 1989, p. 257.

20. Cited in Trevor Fairbrother, *John Singer Sargent.* New York: Abrams, 1994, p. 6.

21. Wilfred Scawen Blunt, for example, wrote in *My Diaries.* London, 1922, vol. 2, p. 171: "He [Sargent] paints nothing but Jews and Jewesses now, and says he prefers them, as they have more life and movement than our English women."

22. Cited in Fairbrother, *John Singer Sargent*, p. 22.

23. M. Birnbaum, *John Singer Sargent: A Conversation Piece.* New York, 1941, cited in Fairbrother, ibid., p. 22.

24. See n. 21.

25. Fairbrother, *John Singer Sargent*, p. 8, and "Sargent's Genre Paintings and the Issues of Suppression and

Privacy," *Studies in the History of Art* 37 (1990), pp. 29–49.

26. Henry James, *The Painter's Eye*, p. 254.

27. Unsigned review, *The Times*, April 30, 1898, p. 14. The reference to Cromwell alludes to Cromwell's wish to be painted "warts and all."

28. On the physical "characteristics" of the Jew, see Sander L. Gilman, *The Jew's Body*. New York and London: Routledge, 1991.

29. Cited in Fairbrother, *John Singer Sargent*, p. 94. This quotation was attributed to Henry James by Charles Merrill Mount, *John Singer Sargent: A Biography*. London, 1957, p. 186.

30. Cited in Stanley Olson, *John Singer Sargent: His Portrait*. London: Macmillan, 1986, p. 209. Sargent also stayed at the Wertheimers' country house, the Temple, a rare indication of friendship on his part: see Olson, ibid., p. 209.

31. Robert Ross, "The Wertheimer Sargents," *The Art Journal* (January 1911).

32. J.-E. Blanche, *Portraits of a Lifetime*. London: Dent, 1937, p. 158.

33. Unsigned review, *The Times*, May 4, 1901, p. 13.

34. Family legend has it that Ena's dresses often fell down, and indeed the engineering of her dress appears to defy the probability of it remaining up.

35. My thanks to Anna Southall for showing me this portrait in the conservation studio at the Tate and for pointing out this detail.

36. Unsigned review, *The Times*, April 29, 1905, p. 14.

37. Marjorie Garber, *Vested Interests: Cross-dressing and Cultural Identity*. London: Routledge, 1992, p. 17.

38. Carol Ockman, "'Two large eyebrows à l'orientale': Ethnic Stereotyping in Ingres's *Baronne de Rothschild*," *Art History* 14, no. 4 (December 1991), pp. 521–39.

39. A typical comment was that made by Alice Meynell: "The Hebrew portraits present more obviously, but also not less subtly, the characteristics of race." *The Works of John S. Sargent RA*, with an introductory note by Mrs. Meynell. London: William Heinemann, 1903, p. 5.

40. Unsigned obituary in *The Times*, August 12, 1918.

41. As Sander L. Gilman has discussed in *Difference and Pathology: Stereotypes of Sexuality, Race, and Madness*. Ithaca and London: Cornell University Press, 1985, esp. pp. 15–29.

42. This was not the real issue, since the National Gallery had accepted works by living artists, such as Daubigny, before the Sargent paintings entered the gallery in 1923, two years before Sargent's death.

43. Letter in the archives of the Tate Gallery, dated April 11, 1924.

44. Frank Rutter, "Wertheimer and Sargent," *Arts Gazette*, January 13, 1923, describes the hang. W. J. Turner, *The London Mercury*, April 1923, p. 652, notes: "The crowds which flocked to the National Gallery to see the Wertheimer bequest of Sargent's portraits of the Wertheimer family rivalled in numbers those which went to see Gainsborough's *Blue Boy* before its journey to America."

45. Quoted in Olson, *John Singer Sargent*, p. 245.

46. Forbes Watson, "Sargent—Boston—and Art," *Arts and Decoration* 7 (February 1917), pp. 194–7.

47. Cited in Fairbrother, *John Singer Sargent*, p. 132.

48. The *Protocols of the Elders of Zion* was published in English by Eyre and Spottiswoode, His Majesty's Printing Office, early in 1920, and was rapidly followed by further editions. Although it was exposed as a fraud in *The Times* in 1921, the resonance of its "arguments" lingered on. The widespread belief that "Jews were always after personal gain" is to be found in all forms of writing, from pamphlets to T. S. Eliot's "Burbank with a Baedeker, Bleistein with a Cigar" of 1920, *Collected Poems 1909–1935*, London: Faber and Faber, 1936, p. 40: "The rats are underneath the piles/The Jew is underneath the lot." On this see, e.g., Holmes, *Anti-Semitism in British Society*; Shmuel Almog, "Antisemitism as a Dynamic Phenomenon: The 'Jewish Question' in England at the End of the First World War," *Patterns of Prejudice* 21, no. 4 (1987), pp. 3–18; Gisela C. Lebzelter, *Political Anti-Semitism in England 1918–1939*. London and Basingstoke: Macmillan, 1978, esp. pp. 13–28;

Robert S. Wistrich, *Antisemitism: The Longest Hatred*. London: Thames Methuen, 1991, pp. 101–13.

5. Salome, Syphilis, Sarah Bernhardt

1. See Sander L. Gilman, *The Jew's Body*. New York and London: Routledge, 1991.

2. See Felix Gilbert, *Bismarckian Society's Image of the Jew*. New York: Leo Baeck Institute, 1978.

3. Cited by Maurice Paléologue, *An Intimate Journal of the Dreyfus Case*, trans. Eric Mosbacher. New York: Criterion, 1957, p. 247.

4. Ibid., p. 104.

5. On the masculinization of the prostitute, see Sander L. Gilman, *Difference and Pathology: Stereotypes of Sexuality, Race, and Madness*. Ithaca and London: Cornell University Press, 1985, pp. 95–6; on the "bluestocking" see Gilman, *Inscribing the Other*. Lincoln: University of Nebraska Press, 1991, p. 21; on the feminization of the male Jew, see Gilman, *The Jew's Body*, pp. 60–104.

6. "Im Zorn hat Gott den Juden geschaffen, in der Wut aber die Jüdin (d.h. Die Jüdin ist noch schlechter als der Jude)," from the Nazi compilation of anti-Semitic proverbs by Ernst Hiemer, *Der Jude im Sprichwort der Völker*. Nuremberg: Der Stürmer, 1942. See Wolfgang Mieder, "Proverbs in Nazi Germany: The Promulgation of Anti-Semitism and Stereotypes through Folklore." *Journal of American Folklore* 95 (1982): pp. 435–64.

7. H. Naudh [H. G. Nordmann], *Die Juden und der deutsche Staat*. Chemnitz: Schmeitzner, 1883, p. 76.

8. Hans F. K. Günther, *Rassenkunde des jüdischen Volkes*. Munich: Lehmann, 1930. Page numbers in the text refer to this edition.

9. Paul's *Deutsches Wörterbuch* (1921), cited by Günther, *Rassenkunde*, p. 254.

10. Johann Jakob Schudt, *Jüdische Merkwürdigkeiten*, 3 vols. Frankfurt: S. T. Hocker, 1714–18, vol. 1, p. 369, cited by Günther, p. 254.

11. Richard Wagner, "Das Judentum in der Musik" (1850); cited by Günther, *Rassenkunde*, p. 254.

12. Bernhard Blechmann, *Ein Beitrag zur Anthropologie der Juden*. Dorpat: Wilhelm Just, 1882, p. 11.

13. Sander L. Gilman, "Opera, Homosexuality, and Models of Disease: Richard Strauss's *Salome* in the Context of Images of Disease in the Fin de Siècle," *Disease and Representation: Images of Illness from Madness to AIDS*. Ithaca: Cornell University Press, 1988, pp. 155–82.

14. Thus Fritz Kahn, *Die Juden als Rasse und Kulturvolk*. Berlin: Welt, 1922, p. 154, notes that Salome is a Jewish princess but racially an Edomite!

15. *The New York Times*, January 23, 1907, p. 9.

16. See Hyam Maccoby, "The Delectable Daughter," *Midstream* 16 (November, 1970): pp. 50–60; Livia Bitton Jackson, *Madonna or Courtesan? The Jewish Woman in Christian Literature*. New York: Seabury, 1982; Stephen Wilson, *Ideology and Experience: Antisemitism in France at the Time of Dreyfus*. Oxford University Press, 1983, ch. 15.

17. See his statement before the Munich court on December 1, 1895, reprinted in Kurt Boeser (ed.), *Der Fall Oskar Panizza: Ein deutscher Dichter im Gefängnis*. Berlin: Hentrich, 1989, p. 46.

18. See Michael Bauer, *Oskar Panizza: Ein literarisches Porträt*. Munich: Hanser, 1984.

19. Oskar Panizza, *The Council of Love*, trans. O. F. Pucciani, New York: Viking, 1979, p. 79. Page numbers in the text refer to this edition. See the discussion of Panizza in Claude Quétel, *History of Syphilis*, trans. Judith Braddock and Brian Pike. London: Polity, 1990, pp. 45–9.

20. Schudt, *Jüdische Merkwürdigkeiten* 2: 369. On the later ideological life of this debate, see Wolfgang Fritz Haug, *Die Faschisierung des bürgerlichen Subjekts: Die Ideologie der gesunden Normalität und die Ausrottungspolitiken im deutschen Faschismus*. Berlin: Argument, 1986.

21. Franz Kafka, *The Sons*, trans. Willa and Edwin Muir. New York: Schocken, 1989, p. 3.

22. See the discussion in Gilman, *The Jew's Body*, pp. 38–59.

23. See the first-rate study by Anna Foa, "Il Nuovo e il Vecchio: L'Insorgere della Sifilide (1494–1530)," *Quaderni Storici* 55 (1984): pp. 11–34, trans. Carole C. Gallucci, in *Sex and Gender in Historical Perspective*, ed. Edward Muir and Guido Ruggiero. Baltimore: Johns Hopkins University Press, 1990, pp. 24–45. On Jews and syphilis, see also Klaus Theweleit, *Male Fantasies*, trans. Erica Carter and Chris Turner, 2 vols. Minneapolis: University of Minnesota Press, 1987–9, vol. 2, p. 16.

24. Ignatz Kohn, "Salome," *Ost und West* 2 (1902): p. 167. As this text is hardly known, I am also reproducing it in its original language.

25. On the background of this production and its reception, see Norbert Kohl, *Oscar Wilde: Das literarische Werk zwischen Provokation und Anpassung*. Heidelberg: Winter, 1980, pp. 288–95. See also Martine C. Thomas, "La Salomé d'Oscar Wilde: Épanouissement au tournant du 19ème siécle d'une figure des début de l'ère chrétienne," Ph.D. diss., Strasbourg, 1985, and Ewa Kuryluk, *Salome and Judas in the Cave of Sex*. Evanston: Northwestern University Press, 1987.

26. On the image of Sarah Bernhardt, see Simon Koster, *De Legenden van Sarah Bernhardt*. Zutphen: De Walberg Pers, 1974. See also Mme. Pierre Berton, *The Real Sarah Bernhardt, whom her Audience Knew, told to her Friend*, trans. Basil Woon. New York: Boni and Liveright, 1924; Maurice Baring, *Sarah Bernhardt*. New York and London: Appleton-Century, 1934; William Emboden, *Sarah Bernhardt*. New York: Macmillan, 1975; Sarah Bernhardt, *Memories of My Life: Being My Personal, Professional, and Social Recollections as Woman and Artist*. London: Peter Owen, 1977; Eric Salmon (ed.), *Bernhardt and the Theatre of Her Time*. Westport, CT: Greenwood, 1984; Elaine Aston, *Sarah Bernhardt: A French Actress on the English Stage*. Oxford and New York: Berg, 1989; Arthur Gold, *The Divine Sarah: A Life of Sarah Bernhardt*. New York: Knopf, 1991.

27. Anatole Leroy-Beaulieu, *Israel Among the Nations: A Study of the Jews and Antisemitism*, trans. Frances Hellman. New York: Putnam's, 1895, p. 150.

28. Kikeriki [i.e., Ottokar Franz Ebersberg], *Sarah's Reisebriefe aus drei Welttheilen (Amerika, Europa, Skobolessia)*. Würzburg: L. Kreßner, n.d. Page numbers in the text refer to this edition.

29. I am grateful to the master's thesis by Jeanette Jakobowski, "Antisemitismus und Antifeminismus von Johann Andreas Eisenmenger bis Houston Stewart Chamberlain," Free University, Berlin, 1991, pp. 309–60, for drawing my attention to this text. See also *Jüdische Kultur und Weiblichkeit in der Moderne*, ed. Sabine Schilling, Inge Stephan, and Sigrid Weigel. Cologne: Böhlau, 1993.

30. Nadine Sine, "Cases of Mistaken Identity: Salome and Judith at the Turn of the Century," *German Studies Review* 11 (1988): pp. 9–29.

31. See Joanna Richardson, *Sarah Bernhardt and her World*. London: Weidenfeld and Nicolson, 1977, pp. 104–6, about the rumor that Sarah Bernhardt was a man.

32. Cited in Ute Frevert, *Frauen-Geschichte zwischen bürgerlicher Verbesserung und neuer Weiblichkeit*. Frankfurt: Suhrkamp, 1986, p. 77.

33. Else Croner [-Kretschmer] (1878–?), *Die moderne Jüdin*. Berlin: Junker, 1913. Page numbers in the text refer to this edition. She wrote *Fontanes Frauengestalten*. Langensalza: Beyer, 1931, and edited *Das Tagebuch eines Fräulein Doktor*, hg. Else Croner. Stuttgart: Deutsche Verlagsgesellschaft, [1908–?]. On the general background see Atina Grossmann, "'Girlkultur' or Thoroughly Rationalized Female: A New Woman in Weimar Germany?" in *Women in Culture and Politics: A Century of Change*, ed. Judith Friedlander et al. Bloomington: Indiana University Press, 1986, pp. 62–80, as well as her "The New Woman and the Rationalization of Sexuality in Weimar Germany," in *Powers of Desire: The Politics of Sexuality*, ed. Ann Snitow, Christine Stansell, and Sharon Thompson. New York: Monthly Review Press, 1983, pp. 153–71.

34. See Riv-Ellen Prell, "Why Jewish Princesses Don't Sweat: Desire and Consumption in Postwar American Culture," in *People of the Body: Jews and Judaism from an Embodied Perspective*, ed. Howard Eilberg-Schwarz. Albany: State University of New York Press, 1992, pp. 329–60.

35. Wilhelm Stapel, *Volk: Untersuchungen über Volkheit und Volkstum*. Hamburg: Hanseatische Verlagsanstalt, 1942, p. 268.

36. Helene Deutsch, *The Therapeutic Process, The Self, and Female*

Psychology, ed. Paul Roazen. New Brunswick: Transaction, 1993, pp. 49–61; all quotations are from pp. 59–60. See also Gertrud Lenzer, "On Masochism: A Contribution to the History of a Phantasy and Its Theory," *Signs* 1 (1975): pp. 277–324. On Deutsch see Janet Sayers, *Mothering Psychoanalysis: Helene Deutsch, Karen Horney, Anna Freud and Melanie Klein*. London: Hamish Hamilton, 1991, and Paul Roazen, *Helene Deutsch: a Psychoanalyst's Life*. New Brunswick: Transaction, 1992.

6. When Is a Jewish Star Just a Star?

1. I would like to thank Mlle Cécile Giteau, *Directeur*, and Noëlle Giret, *conservateur en chef*, of the Département des Arts du Spectacle at the Bibliothèque Nationale de France; Mlle Noëlle Guibert, *conservateur en chef* of the Bibliothèque de la Comédie Française; Baronne Elie de Rothschild; M. Hubert Heilbronn; and Helena Warburg, librarian at Williams College, for facilitating the research for this essay.
Sarah Bernhardt's activity and success as a sculptor was greater than as a painter. She regularly exhibited sculpture at the Salon from 1874 to 1891 and received an honorable mention in 1876 for *Après la tempete*. Enthusiasm for her painting and sculpture in England surpassed that in France; see Nicole Savy, "Talents d'artistes," in *Stars et Monstres sacrés*, ed. Jean-Michel Nectoux. Paris: Réunion des Musées Nationaux, Les Dossiers du Musée D'Orsay, 1986, p. 17. Unless otherwise specified, factual information about Bernhardt comes from Arthur Gold and Robert Fizdale, *The Divine Sarah: A Life of Sarah Bernhardt*. New York: Vintage, 1992.
2. For Bernhardt and her Jewishness, see especially Sarah Bernhardt, *Ma Double Vie: Mémoires de Sarah Bernhardt*, ed. Claudine Hermann. Paris: Des Femmes, 1980, vol. 2, p. 209; see also vol. 1, p. 220. For Bernhardt and the Dreyfus Affair, see Cornelia Otis Skinner, *Madame Sarah*. New York: Paragon House, 1966, p. 259; Catherine Simon Bacchi, *Sarah Bernhardt: Mythe et réalité*. Paris: Catherine Simon

Bacchi, 1984, p. 63; Gold and Fizdale, *The Divine Sarah*, pp. 274–8.
A letter of support from Bernhardt to Dreyfus dated July 1906 was exhibited as cat. no, 479 in *The Dreyfus Affair: Art, Truth, and Justice*, ed. Norman L. Kleeblatt (exh. cat.), The Jewish Museum, New York, and Berkeley, Los Angeles, and London: University of California Press, 1987; an autograph by Zola reading "La vérité est en marche," also signed by Bernhardt and Réjane in 1906, is in a private collection in Paris.
3. Forrest and Lewes cited in Rachel M. Brownstein, *Tragic Muse: Rachel of the Comédie Française*. New York: Knopf, 1993, pp. 95, 236.
4. Quotation from a letter to her mother cited in Brownstein, *Tragic Muse*, p. 36. On Rachel's origins, see ibid., pp. 72–107 and Sylvie Chevalley, *Rachel: "J'ai porté mon nom aussi loin que j'ai pu."* Paris: Calmann-Lévy, 1989, pp. 8ff.
5. Unidentified clipping in Bernhardt dossier, Bibliothèque de la Comédie Française, Paris.
6. Even a cursory examination of the period calls into question the supposed rarity of successful Jewish performers. The list of famous women performers who were Jews includes Giuditta Pasta, Carlotta Grisi, Mademoiselle Judith, Delphine Fix, Dinah Félix, and Marthe Brandès.
Mirbeau's rabidly anti-Semitic formulation that the theater was composed solely of Jews is in his "Le Théâtre juif," *Les Grimaces* (November 3, 1883): pp. 728–9. For his renunciation of anti-Jewish sentiments the following year, see Pierre Michel and Jean-François Nivet, *Octave Mirbeau: L'Imprécateur au coeur fidèle*. Paris: Séguier, 1990, pp. 161ff.
7. The definition of *puff* is from Pierre Larousse, ed., *Grand Dictionnaire universal du XIXe siècle*. Geneva and Paris: Slatkin, 1982, vol. 13, pp. 399–400. The entry on Barnum begins "famous American charlatan," in ibid., vol. 2, p. 244. See also Barbey d'Aurevilly's assessment of Barnum as an "American humbug," cited and trans. in A. H. Saxon, *P. T. Barnum: The Legend and the Man*. New York: Columbia University Press, 1989, p. 1. Unless otherwise specified, English translations are mine.

8. All quotes are from Mousk, "Théodora Puff," *La Vie Parisienne* (November 22, 1884), p. 694–5. Unless otherwise specified, English translations are mine.
9. On this equation, see Béatrice Philippe, *Etre juif dans la société: du moyen âge à nos jours*. Paris: Montalba, 1979, pp. 56ff. and Léon Poliakov, *The History of Anti-Semitism*, trans. Miriam Kochan. New York: Vanguard Press; London: Routledge and Kegan Paul, 1975, vol. 3, pp. 356ff.
10. Marie Colombier, *Les Mémoires de Sarah Barnum*. Paris: Tous les Librairies, 1883. Page numbers in parentheses in the text refer to this edition.
11. For descriptions of *la belle juive*, see Carol Ockman "'Two Eyebrows à l'orientale': Ethnic Stereotyping in Ingres's *Baronne de Rothschild*," *Art History* 14, no. 4 (December 1991): pp. 521–39, reprinted, slightly revised, in Ockman, *Ingres's Eroticized Bodies: Retracing the Serpentine Line*. New Haven and London: Yale University Press, 1995, pp. 66–83.
12. Mirbeau, "Un Crime de Librairie," *Les Grimaces* (December 15, 1883), p. 1002. Mirbeau reports that the book had 92 editions (letter cited in Michel and Nivet, *Octave Mirbeau*, p. 239).
13. Mirbeau describes a "work of girlish spite" in Mirbeau, "Un Crime de Librairie," p. 1001; Auriant speaks of "a woman's revenge" in *Mercure de France* (March 3, 1934); p. 444; Zi-Zim calls it "this feminine pamphlet" in *Les Femmes du Jour* (April 1886), n.p.
14. For Mirbeau's exhortation, see "Un Crime de Librairie," pp. 1004–05. On the duel, see the *procès-verbal* in *L'Intransigeant* (December 20, 1883) and Michel and Nivet, *Octave Mirbeau*, p. 170.
15. On her unruly hair, see Bernhardt, *Ma Double Vie*, vol. 1, pp. 28, 125–7. The portrait is reproduced in Marie-Madeleine Aubrun's catalogue raisonné, *Jules Bastien-Lepage 1848–1884*. Paris: Marie-Madeleine Aubrun, 1985, pp. 55, 167.
16. "Plus triste que la passion," *Le Grélot* (December 10, 1882). For the nose as a sign of Jewishness, see also Sander L. Gilman, *The Jew's Body*. New York and London: Routledge, 1991, pp. 169–93.

17. Robert F. Byrnes's examination of publications attacking Jews records a marked increase only in 1886: see his *Antisemitism in Modern France: The Prologue to the Dreyfus Affair*. New Brunswick, N.J: Rutgers University Press, 1950, p. 155. On graphic artists and the Dreyfus Affair, see Phillip Dennis Cate, "The Paris Cry: Graphic Artists and the Dreyfus Affair," in Kleeblatt, *The Dreyfus Affair*, pp. 62–95.

18. The term *hydropathe*, coined by Emile Goudeau, refers to a group of writers committed to Truth, Art, and Beauty who began to meet around 1878. The group eventually included Abram, Emile Goudeau, Georges Lorin, Rives and Maurice Rollinat, André Gill, Jean Moréas, and Jean Richepin; see Jules Lévy, *Les Hydropathes*. Paris: André Delpeuch, 1928, pp. 5–7. Photographs of Bernhardt in studio dress are reproduced in Gold and Fizdale, *The Divine Sarah*, figs. 19, 20.

19. Gershom Scholem and Gunther W. Platt argue that for most of human history the hexagram had no specific Jewish connotation whatsoever. Although the Zionist movement adopted the star as its emblem in 1897, Platt suggests that it was not officially adopted until the 18th Zionist Congress in 1933, and Scholem concludes that, more than the Zionists, the Holocaust made the star a genuine symbol of Judaism. See Scholem, "The Star of David: History of a Symbol" in *The Messianic Idea in Judaism and Other Essays on Jewish Spirituality*. New York: Schocken, 1971, pp. 257–81; Platt, *The Magen David: How the Six-Pointed Star Became an Emblem for the Jewish People*. Washington, D.C: B'nai Brith, 1991, pp. 23–4. See also Scholem, "*Magen David*" in *Encyclopaedia Judaica*. New York: Macmillan, 1971, vol. 11, p. 696.

20. Leigh Woods, "Sarah Bernhardt and the Refining of American Vaudeville," *Theatre Research International* 18, no. 1 (Spring 1993), p. 22.

21. Images emphasizing Rachel's brow are reproduced in Brownstein, *The Tragic Muse*, pp. 203, 204. For the comparison of Bernhardt's hair to "negro's wool," see Bernhardt, *Ma Double Vie*, vol. 1, p. 126. On the likeness of Rachel to a marble statue, see Brownstein, ibid., pp. 172–83.

22. The portraits are reproduced in Brownstein, *Tragic Muse*, facing pp. 112, 113. Stanley Kauffmann suggests that the paintings belie the fact that Rachel was fully corsetted on stage: see Kauffmann, "Performing a Life," *Salmagundi* (Fall 1993), p. 201.

23. Melandri's photograph of Bernhardt in a coffin is reproduced in Gold and Fizdale, *The Divine Sarah*, fig. 27, facing p. 53. On dress reform, see John Stokes et al., *Bernhardt, Terry, Duse: The Actress in her Time*. Cambridge & New York: Cambridge University Press, 1988, p. 9.

24. For Bernhardt on her thinness, see Bernhardt, *Ma Double Vie*, vol. 1, p. 89; vol. 2, pp. 45, 50, 104, 150, 151. On her ill health, see passim. For instances where she berates her public, see esp. p. 150.

7. Marcel Proust: In Search of Identity

1. Marcel Proust, *A la Recherche du temps perdu*, 4 vols. Paris: Gallimard, Pleiade, 1954, vol. 4, p. 344; Eng. edition, *Remembrance of Things Past*, trans. C. K. Scott-Moncrieff, rev. Terence Kilmartin, 3 vols. Harmondsworth: Penguin, 1983, vol. 3, pp. 788–9. Hereafter, vol. and page numbers in parentheses in the text refer to this Eng. edition.

2. Jacques Rivière in *Cahiers Marcel Proust*, no. 13, 1985. Paris: Gallimard, p. 83.

3. *Ethos* meant the usual place of residence, originally of animals, which then came to refer to a usual way of being, customs, character.

4. Jules-César Scaliger, *Poetices libri septem*. Lyon, 1581.

5. *Cahiers Marcel Proust*, no. 8, 11976, p. 83.

6. See Hannah Arendt, "Anti-Semitism," *The Origins of Totalitarianism*. London: George Allen and Unwin, 1958; New York: Harcourt Brace Jovanovich, 1973, pp. 3–120.

7. J. C. Combes (1837–1921), the French statesman who formed an anticlerical ministry declaring the separation of church and state.

8. Proust, "Un esprit et un génie innombrables: Léon Daudet," "Nouvelles Mélanges," March 1920, in *Contre Sainte-Beuve*. Paris, 1954, p. 603.

9. Among the studies of Proust and Judaism see esp. Albert Mingelgrun, *Thèmes et structures bibliques dans l'oeuvre de Marcel Proust*. Paris: L'Age d'homme, 1978; Jean Recanti, *Profils juifs de Marcel Proust*. Paris: Buchet-Castel, 1979; Marcel Muller, "Préfiguration et structure romanesque dans *A la Recherche du temps perdu*," *French Forum*, 1979; Erwin Spatz, "Les Juifs dans l'oeuvre de James Joyce, Marcel Proust, et Robert Musil," Ph.D., EHESS, Paris, 1979; Jeanne Bem, "Le Juif et l'homosexuel dans 'A la Recherche'," *Littérature* 37 (February 1980).

10. As demonstrated by Mingelgrun, *Thèmes et structures*, p. 40.

11. In the synagogue a Jewish groom must trample on and break a glass while reciting Psalm 137:5–6: "If I forget you, O Jerusalem, let my right hand wither! May my tongue cleave to the roof of my mouth ..."

12. B. Brun, "Brouillons et brouillages: Proust et l'antisémitisme," *Littérature* 70 (May 1988), p. 111.

13. Letter to Charles Bugnet, January 4, 1921, cited by A. Compagnon, "Racine is more Immoral!" in *Proust Between Two Centuries*. New York: Columbia University Press, 1992.

14. Arendt, *Origins of Totalitarianism*, p. 83.

15. See ibid., p. 84.

16. Ibid., p. 194.

17. Translator's note: *puant* has the double meaning of stench and, when describing a person, of pretension. The themes of contagion, aspiration, and purging add specific meaning to the term.

18. Translator's note: *secret de polichinelle* is an "open secret" but "polichinelle" also refers to the character Punch, and hence to a stereotype of a buffoon, and someone with an overly large nose.

8. From Fin de Siècle to Vichy

1. Camille Mauclair, *La Crise de l'art moderne*. Paris: C.E.A., 1944, p. 10. Further page numbers in parentheses in the text refer to this edition. All the quotations in this essay are my translation.

2. On the fate of Jewish dealers, collectors, and artists during the years of Vichy see Michèle Cone.

Artists Under Vichy: A Case of Prejudice and Persecution. Princeton University Press, 1922; Laurence Bertrand Dorléac, *L'Art de la défaite.* Paris: Seuil, 1993.

3. On this issue, and the problematic and still controversial notion of a French grass-root leftist current as the source of Fascism, see Zeev Sternhell, *Ni Droite ni gauche: L'Idéologie fasciste en France.* Paris: Seuil, 1983; see also Michael Curtis, *Three Against the Republic: Sorel, Barrès, and Maurras.* Princeton University Press, 1959.

4. Little is known about Mauclair's personal life and family origins, only that he was born in an old Parisian family—presumably from the upper bourgeoisie—with some distant antecedent in Denmark. My account of Mauclair's early career is largely indebted to Charles Clark Williams, *Camille Mauclair and the Religion of Art.* Ann Arbor, M.I: University of Michigan Research Press, 1976; and Georges Jean Aubry, *Camille Mauclair.* Paris: E. Sansot, 1905.

5. See Mauclair, "Stéphane Mallarmé," *La Nouvelle Revue* 114 (October 1, 1898): pp. 531–3; and "Souvenirs sur Stéphane Mallarmé et son oeuvre," *La Nouvelle Revue* 115 (December 1, 1898): pp. 433–58.

6. Mauclair's "Souvenirs sur le mouvement symboliste en France, 1884–1897" (*La Nouvelle Revue* 108 (October 15, 1897): pp. 670–93) rang the death knell of Symbolism. The movement had gone too far in its obscurantism, mannerism, and idealism, degenerating into confusion and an obsessive search for the rare. Its writers and painters had sold out to the public.

7. On the ever transforming and accommodating tactics of the Third Republic, see Robert J. Anderson, *France 1870–1914: Politics and Society.* London and Boston: Routledge & Kegan Paul, 1977, and Jean Marie Mayeur and Madeleine Rébérioux, *The Third Republic from its Origins to the Great War 1871–1914,* trans. J. R. Foster. Cambridge and New York: Cambridge University Press, 1984.

8. On the anti-Semitic overtones of the reception of Samuel Bing see Kenneth Silver's review of Gabriel Weisberg's exhibition "Art Nouveau Bing: Paris Style 1900"

(New York: The Cooper Hewitt Museum, 1986), in "The Outer Fin de Siècle," *Art in America* 75 (December 1987): pp. 105–11, 173. On the politics of Art Nouveau, see Deborah L. Silverman, *Art Nouveau in Fin-de-Siècle France: Politics, Psychology, and Style.* Berkeley: California University Press, 1989.

9. Mauclair, "La Femme devant les peintres modernes," *La Nouvelle Revue* no. 1 (1899): pp. 190–213.

10. Mauclair, "La Réaction nationaliste en art ou l'ignorance de l'homme de lettres," *La Revue* 54 (January 15, 1905): pp. 151–74. On the ideological dimension and intricacies of the North vs. South debate in France ca. 1905, see James D. Herbert, *Fauve Painting: The Making of Cultural Politics.* New Haven and London: Yale University Press, 1992.

11. See Aubry, *Camille Mauclair.* Focusing on *fin-de-siècle* literary figures, the series included monographs on Octave Mirbeau, Anatole France, Péladan, Jean Moréas, and many other by now almost forgotten writers.

12. I would like to thank Sarah Wilson for reading the present essay, for drawing my attention to this particular book, and for giving me the unpublished text of her lecture on Mauclair delivered at a symposium on Fauvism, Royal Academy of Arts, London, June 17, 1991.

13. See also Mauclair, "Puvis de Chavannes et Gustave Moreau," *The International Quarterly* 12 (1905–06): pp. 240–54.

14. See John McManners, *Church and State in France 1870–1914.* London: SPCK, 1972. On the fundamental ideological link between Catholicism and right-wing nationalism in France, see also Pierre Birnbaum, *"La France au Français": Histoire des haines nationalistes.* Paris: Seuil, 1993.

15. See Malcolm Gee, *Dealers, Critics, Collectors of Modern Paintings: Aspects of the Parisian Art Market between 1910 and 1930.* New York: Garland, 1981, and Yves Chevrefils Desbiolles, *Les Revues d'art à Paris, 1905–1940.* Paris: Ent'Revues, 1993.

16. Mauclair, *Le Vertige allemand: Histoire du crime délirant d'une race.* Paris: Hélios, 1916, p. 129.

17. For a further analysis of 1927 as a pivotal year for France's self-

image, see my *Modernity and Nostalgia: French Art and Politics between the Wars.* New Haven and London: Yale University Press, 1995.

18. During these years Mauclair extended his discontent to other fields; see, e.g., his "Enquête sur les maladies de la littérature actuelle," *Les Marges* 37 (September 15, 1926): p. 88; and "Allons-nous vers le crétinisme?" *Les Marges* 40 (September–October 1927): pp. 43–4.

19. Derived from *metoikos* (*oikos*, house), the word was used by the ancient Greeks to refer to a foreign resident with no rights as a citizen.

20. Calling for a defense of French art in an exhibition, "Contre le Sabbat de la peinture" ("Against the Sabbath of Painting"), Galerie de la Palette Française in 1930, Mauclair denounced once more the deceitfulness of the term Ecole de Paris to describe a school that was in fact composed of foreigners who had the nerve to pretend to teach the French how to paint. Around 1930, Mauclair was also president of the Association des Critiques d'Art Français, founded to defend and promote a nationalist agenda in the realm of art criticism. The group even demanded that foreigners be prevented from writing on contemporary French art in the French press. I am grateful to Matthew Afron for this information.

21. In the chapter "La hantise extrême orientale" in vol. 1, Mauclair had already exposed in great detail Massis's argument on the Germans' fascination for the East.

22. On this topic see also my "The Ecole Française versus the Ecole de Paris: The Debate about the Status of Jewish Artists in Paris between the Wars," in Kenneth Silver and Romy Golan, *The Circle of Montparnasse: Jewish Artists in Paris 1905–1945* (exh. cat.), New York, The Jewish Museum, 1985: pp. 80–87; and ch. 6 in my *Modernity and Nostalgia.*

23. See *Le Paris des Etrangers depuis un siècle,* ed. André Kaspi and Antoine Mares. Paris: Imprimerie Nationale, 1989.

24. See Arthur Cohen, "From Eastern Europe to Paris and Beyond," in Silver and Golan, *The Circle of Montparnasse,* pp. 60–67. There were 150,000 Jewish immi-

grants from 1918 to 1939 (in contrast to the only 30,000 Jews who emigrated to France between 1881 and 1914), multiplying thus by seven their number in France since 1906. Of these, 90,000 were from Eastern Europe, including 50,000 Polish, 15,000 Russian, 11,000 Hungarian, 10,000 Romanian, 1,500 Lithuanian and Latvian. By 1930, France counted three million aliens. See David Weinberg, *A Community on Trial: The Jews of Paris in the 1930s*. University of Chicago Press, 1977, and Ralph Schor, *L'Opinion Française et les étrangers en France 1919–1939*. Paris: Presses Universitaires de la Sorbonne, 1985.
25. By 1939 the 200,000 Jews living in Paris represented 7% of the metropolitan inhabitants, but less than 1% of the total French population. The other main cities of Jewish immigration were Metz, Nancy, and Strasbourg. See Philippe Bourdrel, *Histoire des juifs de France*. Paris: Albin Michel, 1974.
26. For a detailed mapping of the Montparnasse art community, see billy Kluver and Julie Martin, "Carrefour Vavin," in Silver and Golan, *The Circle of Montparnasse*, pp. 68–79.
27. See Fritz Vanderpyl, "Existe-il une peinture juive?" *Mercure de France* (July 15, 1925): pp. 386–96; Pierre Jaccard, "L'Art Grec et le spiritualisme hébreux," *Mercure de France* (August 15, 1925): pp. 80–93; and Adolphe Basler, "Y-a-t-il une peinture Juive?" *Mercure de France* (November 15, 1925): pp. 111–18.
28. A map of the 1924 Salon des Indépendants at the Grand Palais was reproduced the following spring in *Le Bulletin de la vie artistique* so that its readers would not "get lost in the meanders of the quarrels." According to this plan, not only would foreigners be boxed into separate national categories but they would also be relegated to the four aisles of the building, with the Ecole Française in the middle.
29. Sander L. Gilman, *Jewish Self-Hatred: Anti-Semitism and the Hidden Language of the Jews*. Baltimore: Johns Hopkins University Press, 1986, pp. 2–6. See also Linda Nochlin, "Degas and the Dreyfus Affair: A Portrait of the Artist as Anti-Semite," in *The Dreyfus Affair: Art, Truth, and Justice*, ed. Norman Kleeblatt (exh. cat.), The Jewish

Museum, New York, and Berkeley, Los Angeles, and London: University of California Press, 1987.
30. "Hélas! ou sont les xénophobes?" under Vauxcelles, "Le Carnet des ateliers," (Le Carnet de la semaine (1923), file 91, Fond Vauxcelles, Bibliothèque Doucet, Paris.
31. Vauxcelles, "La Semaine artistique," *Excelsior* (1923), file 91, Fond Vauxcelles.
32. Maurice Barres, *Scènes et doctrines du nationalisme* (Paris, 1905 and 1925): 67–8. For an ideological analysis of the "return to the soil" in interwar France see my *Modernity and Nostalgia*.
33. Vauxcelles (under the pseudonym Pinturicchio), "Le Carnet des ateliers," *Le Carnet de la semaine* (1925), file 5, Fonds Vauxcelles.
34. He apparently fled Poland to avoid arrest by the Russian police for having published a collection of patriotic poems.
35. Waldemar George, "Le Salon des Indépendants," *L'Amour de l'art* (February 1924): p. 42.
36. The first was Florent Fels, *Kisling* (1928), the rest: Waldemar George, *Soutine* (1929); Waldemar George, *Lipchitz* (1929); Georges Charensol, *Jules Pascin* (1928); André Salmon, *Léopold Lévy* (1931); Maximilien Gauthier, *Eugène Zak* (1932); Adolphe Basler, *Indenbaum* (1932); Florent Fels, *E. Terechkovich* (n.d., ca. 1932); Emile Tériade, *Menkes* (n.d., ca. 1932).
37. George, *Soutine*, p. 7. Subsequent page numbers in parentheses in the text refer to this edition.
38. Waldemar George, "Le Matamore Mauclair contre l'art français," *Formes* no. 7 (July 1930): pp. 11–12.
39. Waldemar George, "Ecole Française ou Ecole de Paris," part I, *Formes* (June 1931): pp. 92–3; part II, *Formes* (July 1931): pp. 110–11.
40. See note 22 above.
41. Basler, "Y-a-til une peinture Juive?", reprinted in *Le Cafard après la fête, ou, L'esthétisme d'aujourdhui*. Paris: J. Baudry, 1929, p. 137. Subsequent page numbers in parentheses refer to this edition.
42. On these *revanchiste* anti-Cubist campaigns see Christopher Green, *Cubism and Its Enemies: Movements and Reaction in French Art 1916–1925*. New Haven and London: Yale

University Press, 1987; Kenneth Silver, *Esprit de Corps: The Art of the Parisian Avant-Garde and the First World War, 1914–1925*. Princeton University Press, 1989; and on the dispersal of Kahnweiler's collection at auction in 1920, see Gee, *Dealers, Critics, Collectors of Modern Paintings*, passim.
43. On the French anti-Semitic resistance to psychoanalysis see Elisabeth Roudinesco, *La Bataille de cent ans: Histoire de la psychanalyse en France*. Paris: Ramsay, 1982.
44. Equally paradoxical is the fact that Basler wrote two books on "primitive art" during those years: *L'Art précolombien* in 1928 and *L'Art chez les peuples primitifs* in 1929.
45. On Vallois see Sternhell, *Ni droite ni gauche*.
46. In spite of a boost of popularity thanks to a big infusion of funds by Coty, allowing sales to rise from 20,000 copies in 1921 to 50,000 in 1928, the paper's distribution was down again to 10,000 in 1932, a small number indeed for a Parisian daily. After Coty's dramatic bankruptcy and death in 1934, overtly polemical articles "à la Mauclair" were banned from the paper and it recovered its conventional, moderate, right-wing stance. By 1939, it was back with its old-time status of grand newspaper of quality, and the Coty episode forgotten. See Jacques Godelet et al., *Histoire générale de la presse française (1871–1940)*, vol. 3. Paris: Presses Universitaires de France, 1972.
47. For a detailed rundown of the contents of this paper, see Ralph Schor's excellent article, "Xénophobie et extrême droite: l'example de *L'Ami du peuple* (1928–1937)," *Revue d'histoire moderne contemporaine* (January–March 1976): pp. 116–44; and Godelet, *Histoire générale de la presse française*.
48. See Jean Michel Palmier, *Weimar en exil: le destin de l'émigration intellectuelle allemande antinazie en Europe et aux Etats Unis*, vol. 1, Paris: Payot, 1988; Ralph Schor, *L'Antisémitisme en France pendant les années trente: prélude à Vichy*. Brussels: Editions Complexe, 1992.
49. See *L'Ami du peuple* (September 10, 1933).
50. Mauclair wrote 3 books for a series published in Paris by Henri Laurens: *Fes, Ville Sainte*, 1930;

Rabat et Sale, 1934; and *Tunis et Kerouan*, 1937.

51. See Schor, *L'Antisémitisme en France*.

52. Among the last monographic books written on Jewish artists during the 1930's were René Schwob's *Chagall et l'âme juive* in 1931 and Vauxcelles's *Lipsi* in 1935.

53. On the cultural policies of the Popular Front, see Pascal Ory, *La Belle Illusion: Culture et politique sous le signe du Front Populaire, 1935–1938*. Paris: Plon, 1994.

9. Vampires, Viruses, and Lucien Rebatet

1. Julia Kristeva, *Powers of Horror: An Essay on Abjection*, trans. Léon Roudiez. New York: Columbia University Press, 1982, p. 1.

2. Ibid., p. 180.

3. Centre de Documentation Juive Contemporaine, Paris, XCVI–80, pp. 58–68.

4. Lucien Rebatet, "Le Salon des Tuileries," *Je suis partout*, June 23, 1941. All translations are mine, unless otherwise noted.

5. Rebatet, "La Critique des Livres: Peintres modernes," *Je suis partout*, April 11, 1942.

6. See CDJC, XCVI–80, pp. 59–63.

7. C. Laville, "A quoi reconnait-on les juifs?" *Cahier jaune* 1 (November 1941).

8. Cited in Kristeva, *Powers of Horror*, p. 181.

9. Michael Marrus, *The Politics of Assimilation: A Study of the French Jewish Community at the Time of the Dreyfus Affair*. Oxford: Clarendon Press, 1971, pp. 85, 196.

10. See J. Marquès Rivière, "Pourquoi une exposition juive?" CDJC, XIg–118, pp. 11–30.

11. Robert de Beauplan, "L'Exposition Antijuive," *L'Illustration*, September 1941, from typewritten document, CDJC, DLVI–18.

12. F. Vinneuil [alias Lucien Rebatet], "Un grand et ravissant chef d'oeuvre," *Je suis partout*, May 6, 1938.

13. Curiously, there was a lot of interest in film in the anti-Semitic camp; Rebatet wrote film reviews in the 1930's; Robert Brasillac and Maurice Bardèche coauthored *Histoire du cinéma*. Paris: Denoel, 1942.

14. See Jean Perrin, "La femme vampire dans la poésie romantique anglaise," in *Les Vampires*, ed. Antoine Faivre and Jean Marigny. Colloque de Cerisy. Paris: Albin Michel, 1993.

15. Kristeva, *Powers of Horror*, p. 178.

16. See Christian Delporte, *Les Crayons de la propagande*. Paris: CNRS, 1993, p. 129.

17. CDJC, XIb–546.

18. For more on the organic metaphors of Rebatet's art criticism, see my *Artists under Vichy: A Case of Prejudice and Persecution*. Princeton University Press, 1992, ch. 2.

19. Rebatet, "Entre le juif et le pompier," *Je suis partout*, February 14, 1941; "n'aurait certainement pas pu morde sur nous avec cette facilité."

20. Jean Goens, *Loups-garous, vampires et autres monstres: Enquêtes médicales et littéraires*. Paris: CNRS, 1993, p. 71.

21. Zeev Sternhell, *Ni Droite ni gauche: L'Idéologie fasciste en France*. Paris: Seuil, 1983, p. 289.

22. Louis Hautecoeur, *Considérations sur l'art d'aujourd'hui*. Paris: Librairie de France, 1929, p. 72.

23. René Huyghe, *Les Contemporains*. Paris: Tisné, 1949, p. 108; Bernard Dorival, *Les Etapes de la peinture française contemporaine*. Paris: Gallimard, 1946; Louis Hautecoeur, *Littérature et peinture du XVIIème au XXème siècle*. Paris: Armand Colin, 1942, p. 306.

24. Rebatet, "Le Salon des Tuileries," *Je suis partout*, June 23, 1941.

25. Kristeva, *Power of Horrors*, p. 183.

26. Ibid., p. 2.

27. Goens, *Loups-garous*, p. 75.

28. Rebatet, *Les Décombres*. Paris: Denoel, 1942, p. 20.

29. For Kristeva, *Powers of Horror*, p. 178, the anti-Semite is in a "*rage against the symbolic*" (namely, Jewish monotheism) that leads him to "the attempt to substitute *another Law* for the constraining and frustrating symbolic one," something she names "*material positivity . . .*" It is "a full tangible reassuring and happy substance [which] will be embodied in the Family, the Nation, the Race, and the Body." (Kristeva's italics)

30. Goens, *Loups-garous*, p. 67.

31. Ibid., pp. 83–4. The most thorough bibliography on vampires and vampirism is found in Goens, *Loups-garous*. Faivre and Marigny, *Les Vampires*, also contains many references. A history of the original "vampire" from central Europe and its successive metamorphoses is found in Denis Buican, *Les Métamorphoses de Dracula: L'Histoire et la légende*. Paris: Edition du Felin, 1993. Film versions are discussed in Lotte H. Eisner, *L'écran démoniaque*. Paris: Eric Losfeld, 1990; and in Francis Courtade, *Cinéma Expressioniste*. Paris: Henri Veyrier, 1984. Although these are French-language books, their bibliographies include titles in other languages.

10. El Lissitzky's "Interchange Stations"

1. El Lissitzky "*The Book*," "Topography of typography," 1923, reprinted in Sophie Lissitzky-Küppers, *El Lissitzky: Life, Letters, Texts*, trans. Helene Aldwinckle and Mary Whittall. Greenwich, C.T: New York Graphic Society, and London: Thames and Hudson, 1980, p. 355. Gershom Scholem, "The Name of God and the Linguistic Theory of the Kabbalah," part 2, *Diogenes* 80 (1972), p. 166. Walter Benjamin, *Illuminations*. New York: Schocken 1969, p. 79.

Professor Moshe Barasch led me through the intricacies of Jewish iconography. Dr. Louis Kaplan suggested modes of analysis and offered many thoughts and suggestions. I am very grateful to both of them. Discussions with the following scholars were informative and helpful in diverse ways: Professors Zvi Werblowsky, Bezalel Narkiss, Moshe Idel, Michael Fishbane, Ziva Amishai Maisels, and Christopher Ricks; also Peter Nisbet, Ruth Apter-Gabriel, Joshua Rubenstein, and Mark Kuchment.

2. Chimen Abramsky, "El Lissitzky as Jewish Illustrator and Typographer," *Studio International* 172, no. 82 (1966), pp. 182–5. See also P. Nisbet, *El Lissitzky 1890–1941* (exh. cat.), Harvard University Art Museums, 1987; Yve-Alain Bois, "El Lissitzky. Radical Reversibility," *Art in America* (April 1988), pp. 160–81. Alan C. Birnholz, in "El Lissitzky and the Jewish Tradition," *Studio International* 186, no. 959

(1973), p. 131, is the first to argue that Jewish elements continue in Lissitzky's work but I think he overstates and underdevelops the case for the artist's kabbalistic beliefs. I have found no evidence for Birnholz's assertion of "the Jewish mysticism Lissitsky experienced so intimately as a youth in the Pale." I shall argue that the parallels with mysticism function on a different level.

3. Jean Baudrillard, in "The Ecstasy of Communication," in *The Anti-Aesthetic: Essays on Post-Modern Culture*, ed. Hal Foster. Port Townsend: Washington Bay Press, 1983, p. 133, uses the metaphor of a switching center in negative terms. He observes of the modern circumstance, a new form of schizophrenia. "It is the end of interiority and intimacy, the overexposure and transparence of the world which traverses him without obstacle. . . . He is now only a pure screen, a switching center for all the networks of influence."

4. Lissitzky-Küppers, *El Lissitzky*, p. 15. The town is variously spelled. Nisbet, *El Lissitzky*, refers to it as Pochinok. The Jewish community of Smolensk, which was outside the Pale of Settlement, had before 1917 a population around 11,100 and may well not have had the institutions of a larger Jewish community.

5. In "Lissitzky Speaks," 1932, reprinted in Lissitzky-Küppers, *El Lissitzky*, p. 326, he writes somewhat contradictorily, "Reaction against the Czarist regime drove my father, an official in the Smolensk government, to America and from there back to the approved settlement area."

6. Nisbet, *El Lissitzky*, pp. 59–61, reprints an essay written originally in Yiddish by Lissitzky, "The Conquest of Art," in the Warsaw literary-cultural journal *Ringen* [*Links*] 10 (1922), pp. 32–4.

7. *Hebrew Encyclopedia* [in Russian]. Warsaw: Akhiasaf, 1906, vol. 2, cols. 36–73; in the bibliography, p. 71, it cites *Sefer Tagin*. Paris, 1866, which discusses letters as ornaments; W. Gesenius, *Geschichte der Hebraischen Sprache und Schrift*. Leipzig: P. C. W. Vogel, 1815; Hermann Leberecht Strack, "Schreibkunst und Schrift bei den Hebraen," in *Real encyklopädie für protestantische theologie*.

Hamburg, 1881; M. Lidzbarski, *Handbuch der nordsemitischen Epigraphik, nebst ausgewahlten Inschrift*. Weimar: E. Felber, 1898. Other key works on Hebrew letters were Leopold Low, *Graphische Requisiten und Erzeugnisse bei den Juden*, reprinted in *Gesammelte Schriften*. New York: Hildesheim, 1979, and M. Steinschneider, *Vorlesungen uber die Kunde hebraischer Handschriften deren Sammlungen und Verzeichnisse*. Leipzig: Otto Harrassowitz, 1897, pp. 27ff.

8. Cited in Nisbet, *El Lissitzky*, p. 57.

9. Nisbet, ibid., p. 53, notes, "He stresses the international parallels to the Jewish search for folk-art, the transmission of images and ideas across borders via printed texts."

10. See Chimen Abramsky, "El Lissitzky as Jewish Illustrator and Typographer." These include non-Jewish works translated into Yiddish. Some of these publications, including cover sheets for music, have recently come to light, in part with the Russian immigration to Israel. Conversation with Mordechai Omer, Tel Aviv, June 12, 1994.

11. See Haia Friedberg, "Lissitzky's 'Had Gadia'," *Jewish Art*, vol. 12–13. Jerusalem: Hebrew University, 1986–7, pp. 292–303.

12. Nisbet, *El Lissitzky*, p. 183, points out that for this edition he did a "Proun" version, the original drawings having been done in 1918.

13. Cited in *Tradition and Revolution: The Jewish Renaissance in Russian Avant-Garde Art 1912–1928*, (exh. cat.), ed. Ruth Apter-Gabriel, trans. from Yiddish by Seth L. Wolitz, The Israel Museum, Jerusalem, 1987, p. 230. See also Seth L. Wolitz, "The Jewish National Art Renaissance in Russia," ibid., pp. 21–42.

14. Lissitzky-Küppers, *El Lissitzky*, p. 20. Nisbet, *El Lissitzky*, p. 17, and others maintain that in 1919 Lissitzky underwent a conversion to geometric abstraction that is "abrupt and total. For all the cubistic devices and quasi-modernist air of the later Jewish illustration . . . the artist himself saw this step as a radical break with his past practice. . . . The catalyst for this change was Kazimir Malevich." Dr. Alexandra Shatskikh, a leading Russian Lissitzky expert, informed me that Lissitzky knew Malevich in 1917

when they worked together in the Moscow Soviet Deputies and that their meeting did not catalyze a sharp break for Lissitzky with Judaic tradition. Conversation in Jerusalem, June 5, 1994.

15. "The Film of El Lissitzky's Life," cited in Lissitzky-Küppers, *El Lissitzky*, p. 325.

16. Yve-Alain Bois, "El Lissitzky: Reading Lessons," *October* 11 (Winter 1979), pp. 113–28.

17. Kenneth Frampton, "The Work and Influence of El Lissitzky" in *Urban Structures*, ed. David Lewis. *Architect's Year Book*, vol. 12. London, 1968, p. 254.

18. In other cultures the associative values of the letter differ from its place in Jewish tradition. I discussed this issue with Zvi Werblowsky, professor of comparative religion at the Hebrew University, Jerusalem. The Chinese ideogram functions more aesthetically and does not carry theological implications. See Lothar Ledderose, "Chinese Calligraphy: Its Aesthetic Dimension and Social Function," *Orientations* (October 1986), pp. 35–50. In Islam, where the calligraphy is more fluid and letters connect, there is greater importance accorded to words rather than to individual letters.

19. In regard to design after the October Revolution, Lissitzky writes about "the architecture of the book," which he contrasts with other directions in typographic design, like "figurative montage." In "El Lissitzky: Reading Lesson," p. 114, Bois quotes Lissitzky's article, "The Artist in Production," *Catalogue of the Graphic Arts Section*, Polygraphic Exposition of the Union of Republics, Moscow, 1927.

20. Benjamin, *Briefe*, 2 vols. Frankfurt: Suhrkamp, 1966, vol. 1, p. 130. Letter to Scholem, June 1917, cited in David Biale, *Gershom Scholem: Kabbalah and Counter History*. Cambridge, M.A: Harvard University Press, 1979, p. 108.

21. "Diese ganze Literatur ist Ansturm gegen die Grenze, und sie hätte sich, wenn nicht der Zionismus dagwischengekommen wäre, leicht zu einer neuen Geheimlehre, einer Kabbala, entwickeln können," *Tagebucher*, January 16, 1922. Frankfurt: Fischer, 1990, p. 878.

22. On Benjamin's interest in Kabbalah and his possible influence on Scholem see Biale, *Gershom Scholem*. See also Karl E. Groezinger, *Kafka und die Kabbalah*. Frankfurt: Eichborn, 1992, and Frank Schirrmacher, *Verteidigung der Schrift Kafkas Prozess*. Frankfurt: Suhrkamp, 1987. Moshe Idel concludes *Kabbalah: New Perspectives*. New Haven, C.T: Yale University Press, 1988, with Kafka's parable before the Law. Susan Handelman, *The Slayers of Moses: The Emergence of Rabbinic Interpretation in Modern Literary Theory*. Albany, N.Y: State University of New York Press, 1982, links contemporary Jewish deconstruction with kabbalistic thinking. Scholem, in "The Name of God and the Linguistic Theory of the Kabbalah," part 1, *Diogenes* 79 (1972), p. 61, writes about linguistic theory in the kabbalah: "What exactly is this 'secret' or 'hidden' dimension of language, about whose existence all mystics for all time feel unanimous agreement—it is the symbolic nature of language which defines this dimension."

23. Moshe Idel, *Language, Torah, and Hermeneutics in Abraham Abulafia*. Albany, N.Y.: State University of New York Press, 1989, p. 4, n. 20.

24. *Shtilim* 6–7 (October 23, 1917).

25. Moshe Barasch suggested to me ways of "decoding" the iconography of these images. For a compendium of information (in Hebrew) on the Hebrew alphabet, see Elias Lipiner, *Hazon ha-otiyot torat ha-ideot shel ha-alfabet ha-Ivre* (*The Metaphysics of the Hebrew Alphabet*). Jerusalem: Hotsaat Sefarim, al shem Y. L. Magnes, Hebrew University, 1989.

26. In Hebrew, words such as "and" (*ve*) and "the" (*ha*), and certain tenses, appear as prefixes to the word, so that looking at the English transliteration, the root of the word and its initial letter may not be apparent without knowledge of Hebrew.

27. Gershom Scholem, "Magen David," in *Kabbalah*. New York: Dorset Press, 1974, p. 367. Franz Rosenzweig, *Der Stern der Erloesung*. Frankfurt: J. Kauffmann, 1921, interprets the star and gives his ideas about the relationship of God, man, and the world.

28. Conversation with Werblowsky, Jerusalem, June 8, 1994.

29. See Ruth Mellinkoff, "The Round-Topped Tablets of the Law: Sacred Symbol and Emblem of Evil," *Journal of Jewish Art* 1 (1974), pp. 28–43.

30. A modern edition of Akiba's ideas exists in Adolph Jellinek, *Bet haMidrash*, II. Leipzig, 1853. This idea is also conveyed in the kabbalistic text *Sepher Yitzirah*.

31. Cited in Lissitzky-Küppers, *El Lissitzky*, p. 356.

32. Eliot R. Wolfson, "Letter Symbolism and Merkavah Imagery in the Zohar," in *'Alei Shefer: Studies in the Literature of Jewish Thought*, ed. Moshe Hallamish. Ramat Gan: Bar Ilan University Press, 1990.

33. Benjamin, *Illuminations*, p. 80, and David Biale, *Gershom Scholem*.

34. Biale, *Gershom Scholem*, p. 105: "Since belief in symbols had waned in the modern world, the task of philosophy, which Benjamin opposed to science, is to 'reestablish the symbolic character of the world, in which the idea comes to self-understanding in its primacy,'" citing Benjamin's *Ursprung des deutschen Trauerspiels*.

35. Patricia Railing, *More About Two Squares*. Cambridge, M.A: MIT Press, 1991, pp. 32 and 34, writes about Lissitzky and his book *The Two Squares* that the "literal, object-based meaning was sacrificed—or played with—in favour of pure meaning without object. To discover meaning in sound itself, in the letter, in the root of a word as the basis for the creation of new words . . . This meaning found within the very medium of language itself, complemented the search for the painters to find meaning within the language of art (in colour, line, form, space, movement). The collaboration between poet and painter was also a collaboration in the arts in which the language of the word and the language of the image came together." "Letter and word are the essential and fundamental creative units with which man constructs his relation to the world and the universe, and thus should be understood in the same way as are number and geometry."

36. Benjamin, *Illuminations*, p. 81.

37. Idel, *Language, Torah, and Hermeneutics*, pp. vii and xvi; see also p. xv: "This dissolution of the canonical text is evidently connected to the assumption that the ele-ments that construct the text have a meaning by themselves, namely even in their isolated existence."

38. *Sefer ha-Ge'ulah*, MS. Leipzig 39, fol. 7b, cited in Idel, *Language, Torah, and Hermeneutics*, pp. 4–5.

39. Moshe Idel, "Reification of Language in Jewish Mysticism," in *Mysticism and Language*, ed. S. Katz. Oxford and New York: Oxford University Press, 1988, pp. 42–79.

40. Ilya Ehrenburg, *Shest povestie o legkikh kontsakh* (*Six Stories About Easy Endings*). Moscow and Berlin: Knig-oizdatelstno Gelikon, 1922. Tonya Lifschutz recounted the story to me in English and Mark Kuchment amplified the translation and helped elucidate a number of references.

41. Related to me by Boris Frezinski, the foremost expert on the life and work of Ehrenburg. Joshua Rubenstein put me in touch with Frezinski in St. Petersburg on May 31, 1994, translating my questions about the collaborative relationship on the illustrations for *Six Stories About Easy Endings*. Among other things, Frezinski said that Ehrenburg was not an admirer of Lissitzky's graphic work!

42. After consulting with many people, Christoph von der Decken, Manager, Corporation Quality Assurance for HAPAG-Lloyds (America) Inc., was able to provide the information. Fax of June 8, 1994.

43. Conversation with Mark Kuchment, Cambridge, M.A., June 1, 1994.

44. Birnholz, "El Lissitzky and the Jewish Tradition," p. 134. I showed this image to Professor Moshe Idel who said, emphatically, that it was not from the Kabbalah.

45. Chimen Abramsky, "Yiddish Book Illustrations in Russia: 1916–1923," in *Tradition and Revolution*, pp. 61–70, esp. p. 66. He is not far off: Maimonides' *Mishneh Torah* is his presentation of the midrash in clearer terms.

46. Communication with Bezalel Narkiss, Jerusalem, May 13, 1994. The diagram has been reproduced in the Index of Jewish Art (Maimonides, *Sefer Avodah, Hilkhoth Beit ha-Behirah*, viii.1.15), and more accessibly in Rachel Wischnitzer, "Maimonides' Drawings of the Temple," *Jewish Art*, vol. 1, 1974, pp. 16–27, from which comes the following information. The illustrations are first found in an edition of the *Mishneh Torah*, in France in 1296 (1386 for the *amalterah*), but do not appear in all editions of Maimonides.

Lissitzky probably studied Maimonides as a youth; editions of the *Mishneh Torah* were published in St. Petersburg in 1852 and in Lublin in 1884. Most educated Jewish households had a copy, often given at a *bar mitzvah* or at marriage and there would have been a copy in every house of worship, Professor Barasch informs me.

47. This was suggested to me by Moshe Barasch. It would be interesting to know whether Lissitzky might have been a Cohen, the priestly caste that gave such blessings.

48. Both Moshe Idel and Bezalel Narkiss suggested this intepretation.

49. Lissitzky writes about the depository of books and their images in his essay on the Mohilev synagogue, cited in Nisbet, *El Lissitzky*, p. 58: "Let the scholars flounder as they navigate the sea of art history, I can only cite the following from my own field of observation. Every synagogue always had a small library. The cases hold some of the oldest editions of the Talmud and other religious texts, each with frontispieces, decorative devices and tailpieces. These few pages fulfilled the same function in their time as illustrated journals do in our own day; they familiarized everyone with the art trends of the period. . . . a heap of loose pages from Amsterdam editions of the 16th and 17th centuries [are] preserved (in a *genizah*) in the Druja synagogue."

50. Birnholz and Frampton have suggested that *pei nun* may also refer to the *Prouns*—a nice idea, but I'm not convinced.

51. Louis Kaplan, a Moholy-Nagy scholar, brought this and related matters to my attention.

52. Louis Kaplan pointed out this relationship to me. For more on the design of the Museum see "Daniel Libeskind: An architectural Design Interview," *Architectural Design: Profile No. 87, Deconstruction III* (1990), pp. 14–19. No reference is made to Lissitzky in this interview; see also *Daniel Libeskind:*

Architecturen und Schriften. Munich and New York: Prestel, 1994.

53. Lissitzky, "suprematism in world reconstruction" 1920, in Lissitzky-Küppers, *El Lissitzky*, p. 327.

54. Birnholz's reading of *The Constructor*, in "El Lissitzky and the Jewish Tradition," p. 134, as the image of a martyr I think is misguided.

55. Louis Kaplan suggested to me this way of looking at the image. Werner Hofmann, "Sur un Auto-Portrait de El Lissitzky", *Gazette des Beaux-Arts* 107 (January–June 1986), p. 44, interprets this self-portrait as sanctifying the image of the artist by attributing to him "all the traditional tools of God the creator: the hand, the eye, a pair of compasses and a circle." Another article places the work in the tradition of self-portraits: Joachim Heusinger von Waldegg, "El Lissitzky 'Der Konstrukteur' (Selbstbildnis) von 1924," *Pantheon* (Munchen) 50 (1992), pp. 125–34.

56. Peter Nisbet in conversation, March 24, 1994, commented that the stenciled letters XYZ in *The Constructor* represent unknown quantities; this is one of the few places where the letter has autonomy. Lissitzky wrote: "In the new mathematics of x,y,z, there is no definition of the quantity. They are signs of the connection between an infinite number of possible positions within one and the same character: taken as a whole, they equal a number. . . . x,y,z, are numbers only inasmuch as the signs + or – are." Cited in Esther Levinger, "Art and Mathematics in the Thought of El Lissitzky: His Relationship to Suprematism and Constructivism," *Leonardo* 22, no. 2 (1989), p. 228.

57. Alexandra Shatskikh confirmed that Lissitzky's use of letters differed from that of Rodchenko and other contemporaries in the primacy of its importance and in the even sizes of the Russian letters, in which Lissitzky may have been unique. She also pointed out the resemblance of the Malevich book to a traditional Hebrew scroll. Conversation, Jerusalem, June 5, 1994.

II. The Jew in Sartre's *Réflexions*

1. Interview with Benny Lévy, "The Last Words of Jean-Paul

Sartre," trans. Rachel Phillips Belash, *Dissent* (Fall 1980), p. 418. Sartre died in April 1980; the interview appeared in French in *Le Nouvel Observateur*, March 10, 17, and 24; reprinted in J.-P. Sartre and Benny Lévy, *L'Espoir maintenant*. Lagrasse: Verdier, 1990.

I wish to thank the following for their help: Sharon Bhagwan for her superb research assistance; Michel Contat, Dorothy Kaufmann, and Stanley Sultan for their careful reading of the manuscript and their critical suggestions; Denis Hollier and Sandy Petrey for disagreeing with me, forcing me to make my own position clearer.

2. Elaine Marks, "The Limits of Ideology and Sensibility: J.-P. Sartre's *Réflexions sur la question juive* and E. M. Cioran's *Un Peuple de solitaires*," *The French Review* 45, no. 4 (March 1972), p. 784.

3. See, e.g., Salomon Malka, "Une couronne pour Sartre," *L'Arche: Le mensuel du judaisme français* (May 1981), who eulogizes Sartre one year after his death, mentioning *Réflexions sur la question juive* as one indication of Sartre's lifelong "fidelity to Judaism and Israel" (p. 61). I discuss the critical reception of *Réflexions* at the end of this essay. Jean-Paul Sartre, *Réflexions sur la question juive*. Paris: Gallimard, "Folio essais," 1954, p. 54; originally published (by P. Morihien), 1946. Page references, to the 1954 French edition, will be given in parentheses in the text. Unless otherwise stated, all translations from French and German are my own.

4. Interview with Gertrud Koch and Martin Löw-Beer, "Sartre's 'J'accuse.' Ein Gespräch mit Claude Lanzmann," *Babylon: Beiträge zur jüdischen Gegenwart*, 2/1987, pp. 75, 76, 77.

5. I have analyzed *L'Enfance d'un chef* in detail in my *Authoritarian Fictions: The Ideological Novel as a Literary Genre*. Princeton University Press, new edition with new preface, 1993, pp. 244–56.

6. Jacob Toury, "'The Jewish Question': A Semantic Approach," in *Yearbook of the Leo Baeck Institute*, vol. 11. London: Horovitz Publishing, 1966, p. 95. Subsequent page references are given in parentheses in the text.

7. Brasillach's article, "La Question Juive," appeared on the front page of *Je suis partout*, 15 April 1938; Rebatet's "Esquisse de quelques conclusions," p. 9. A note on p. 1 states that the articles in this special issue—which also contains a large number of anti-Semitic cartoons—were written and asembled by Rebatet.

8. *La Question Juive vue par vingt-six éminentes personnalités*, ed. W. Simon. Paris: E. I. F., 1934, introduction by W. Simon pp. 11–12; the "patron" is Louis Schmoll, a lawyer, letter p. 108.

9. "Il faut de toute urgence résoudre la question juive, que les Juifs soient expulsés ou qu'ils soient massacrés." Cited in Jean Laloum, *La France antisémite de Darquier de Pellepoix*. Paris: Editions Syros, 1979, p. 17. Laloum gives a detailed history of the Commissariat Général aux Questions Juives, on which my own account is largely based. See also Michael Marrus and Robert Paxton, *Vichy France and the Jews*. New York: Basic Books, 1982.

10. For a detailed study which cites that figure as the low figure, see André Kaspi, "'Le Juif et la France,' une exposition à Paris en 1941," *Le Monde Juif* 79 (1975), pp. 8–20. The exhibit ran from September 5, 1941 to January 15, 1942.

11. "Qu'on le veuille ou non, c'est un problème. Agitée depuis toujours . . . *la question juive domine le monde*," *Le Juif et la France*, exh. cat., Palais Berlitz, Paris, 1941, p. 7; emphasis in text. Besides the essay, the catalogue contains photographs of installations and a map of the two floors of the exhibition, as well as a preface by the secretary-general of the IEQJ, P. Sézille. As befits the exhibition's didactic mission, the catalogue essay is divided into sections on "Jews in the Middle Ages," "Jews and Revolutions," "Jewish Customs and Mores," "The Secret Power of the Jews," "The Jews Masters of Peoples," and so on.

12. "Les chiffres, les statistiques, les tableaux, les citations, les documents de toute nature que nous avons réunis pour l'édification du public . . . lui apprendront sans effort tout l'essentiel de ce qu'il doit savoir, et pour se défendre personnellement, et pour défendre la collectivité dont il est solidaire, contre l'emprise judaïque," ibid., preface (2 pp., unnumbered) by P. Sézille.

13. "Pour nous le Juif est une race et c'est sur ce terrain seul que nous voulons rester." Cited in Kaspi, "'Le Juif et la France,'" p. 13.

14. The texts of the various laws of 1940 and 1941 which defined persons of the "Jewish race" are quoted in Laloum, *La France antisémite*, pp. 90–92.

15. Michel Leiris, "Race et Civilisation" (1951) in *Cinq études d'ethnologie*. Paris: Gonthier, 1969, p. 22.

16. See Laloum, *La France antisémite*, p. 73 and pp. 67–8; Marrus and Paxton, *Vichy France and the Jews*, p. 298. Dr. Montandon was the author of several works of "ethnoracial science," including the notorious little pamphlet *Comment reconnaître et expliquer le Juif?*. Paris: Nouvelles éditions françaises, 1940, in which he enumerates the physical and moral characteristics of the "Jewish race." Montandon's clinical work as an "ethno-racial expert" (consisting in measurements to determine whether a given person was "of the Jewish race" or not) is described by Marrus and Paxton, in tragicomico-grotesque terms, pp. 300–01.

17. See, e.g., the long article signed Rabi, "Sartre, portrait d'un philosémite," *Esprit* (October 1947), pp. 532–46. Rabi notes that Sartre reduces Jews to objects, whereas they want to be subjects: "We know that we have a common history . . .," p. 539; Arnold Mandel, "Retour aux 'Réflexions,'" *L'Arche* 61 (February 1962), p. 48: "In Sartre's postulate there is a categorical negation of Jewish being as belonging to a culture and inheriting a history; Albert Memmi, *Portrait d'un Juif*. Paris: Gallimard, 1962, offers an indirect criticism of Sartre, as I discuss below.

18. Tony Judt, *Past Imperfect: French Intellectuals, 1944–1956*. Berkeley: University of California Press, 1992, pp. 184–6, has faulted Sartre for not condemning Communist anti-Semitism in the Soviet Union and Czechoslovakia in the early 1950's, at the time of the Slansky trial. Sartre's silence, as Judt rightly points out, was due to his anti-anti-Communism at the height of the Cold War. This moral lapse inspired by "global politics" does not diminish the importance of Sartre's denunciation of anti-Semitism at home right after the war.

19. Memmi, *Portrait d'un Juif*, p. 81: "le Juif n'est pas uniquement celui que l'on considère comme Juif. S'il n'était que cela, il ne serait, en tant que Juif, que pure négativité. . . . Le Juif est aussi histoire et traditions, institutions et coutumes, il déborde de traits proprement positifs."

20. Sartre, *Anti-Semite and Jew*, trans. George J. Becker. New York: Grove Press, 1960, pp. 61–2. I have modified the translation somewhat for the sake of precision. Most notably, I have removed the quotation marks around "Aryan." Evidently, the translator felt bothered by Sartre's uncritical use of that disreputable word—he puts it into quotation marks almost each time it occurs. Werner Cohn, "The 'Aryans' of Jean-Paul Sartre: Totalitarian Categories in Western Writing," *Encounter* (December 1981), pp. 87–8, has shown that Sartre referred to "Aryans" quite frequently in this book (17 times), mostly without quotation marks; but Cohn cites evidence to show that even some Jewish writers in the 1940's, in Germany and the United States, used the term uncritically—a fascinating case of being contaminated by the words of the enemy.

21. Cited in Laloum, *La France antisémite*, pp. 76–7.

22. Cited in Laloum, ibid., p. 74, "l'étude des questions se rapportant aux peuples et aux races et, en particulier, dans les domaines spirituel, social, politique et économique, l'investigation du champ d'activitée des personnes appartenant au peuple de race juive en France et dans le monde."

23. Montandon's *Comment reconnaître et expliquer le Juif?* is divided into 2 parts: "Caractères physiques du Juif" and "Portrait moral du Juif." Under physical characteristics (p. 23), Montandon mentions "a strongly convex nose," "fleshy lips," and "eyes not deeply set into their orbits" as primary traits; secondary traits are "curly hair" (indicating "negroid ancestry") and "large, protruding ears."

24. Edith Thomas, *Pages de journal, 1939–1944*, ed. Dorothy Kaufmann. Paris: Viviane Hamy, 1995, pp. 181–2: "Le port de l'étoile juive a ceci d'excellent c'est qu'il nous prouve que la race juive n'existe pas; un sur dix juifs seulement a le type classique qu'on a l'habitude de leur attribuer et qui se retrouve aussi bien et même beaucoup mieux chez les espagnols, les arabes. . . . Les juifs ne sont donc pas *une* race." Entry dated June 24, 1942. Thomas would fit Sartre's definition of the "democrat," since she also states, 18 days before (June 6, 1942), p. 180, that "there is no such thing as the Jewish question" (*il n'y a pas de question juive*). According to her, "the Jewish problem is an imposture." "Democrat" or not, Thomas's views here strike me as less problematic than Sartre's. Thomas, incidentally, was actively involved in the Resistance; Sartre was not.

25. *Anti-Semite and Jew*, p. 84; translation slightly modified.

26. Reproduced in Laloum, *La France antisémite*, following p. 88.

27. In some recent discussions with French friends, I have been repeatedly reminded that the word "race" in French is often used in a general way, with no racist overtones, to mean nation or community linked by a common heritage. Nevertheless, Sartre's use of "Jewish race" is astonishing given the shameful history of that term in the 1940's; besides, as was clear in the first passage quoted, he uses the word "race" in connection with Jews not in its loose sense but in a pseudo-scientific sense.

28. *Anti-Semite and Jew*, pp. 101–02, translation modified. Inexplicably, the English version *omits* the first sentence of this passage (which occurs in the middle of a page). Did the translator consider it too compromising?

29. For a detailed study, see Robert N. Proctor, *Racial Hygiene: Medicine under the Nazis*. Cambridge, MA: Harvard University Press, 1988. Although the concept of "race" is still a subject of debate, it is clear that by the 1940's—partly in response to Nazi theories—the supposedly biological "givens" of race were largely discredited. Ashley Montagu's study, *Man's Most Dangerous Myth: The Fallacy of Race*, first came out in 1942. New York: Columbia University Press; later editions 1945, 1952, 1961. For a contemporary synthesis, see (among many) Anthony Appiah, "The Uncompleted Argument: Du Bois and the Illusion of Race," in *"Race," Writing, and Difference*, ed.

Henry Louis Gates, Jr. University of Chicago Press, 1986, pp. 21–37. As for the "Jewish race," a good brief account of early uses of this term in France is in Michael Marrus, *The Politics of Assimilation: The French Jewish Community at the Time of the Dreyfus Affair*. Oxford: Clarendon Press, 1971, ch. 2. Marrus notes that although at that time French Jews themselves often used the term, they "did not mean by 'race' the same thing as Drumont . . . they meant a sense of community with other Jews" (p. 27). Marrus points out that the enormously influential Ernest Renan *revised* his idea about a "Jewish race" in response to Drumont's anti-Semitic racism: by the early 1890's, he strongly opposed the idea that there was a "distinctly Jewish racial type" (pp. 21–2).

30. *Anti-Semite and Jew*, p. 118, translation modified. "On sait en effet que les seuls caractères ethniques du Juif sont physiques. L'antisémite s'est emparé de ce fait et l'a transformé en mythe: il prétend déceler son ennemi sur un simple coup d'oeil," *Réflexions*, p. 144.

31. Barbara Johnson, "Thresholds of Difference: Structures of Address in Zora Neale Hurston," in Gates, *"Race," Writing, and Difference*, pp. 322–3.

32. *Réflexions*, p. 141. Becker's translation does away with Sartre's Christian image: "a rationalism that has undergone a change of name," p. 16.

33. *Anti-Semite and Jew*, p. 126, translation modified. "Le Juif aime l'argent, dit-on. . . . A vrai dire, si le Juif aime l'argent, ce n'est pas par un goût singulier pour la monnaie de cuivre ou d'or ou pour les billets," *Réflexions*, p. 153.

34. *Anti-Semite and Jew*, p. 128, translation modified; *Réflexions*, p. 156. Again, Becker softens the Eng. version by inserting a crucial adjective, not in Sartre's text: "Thus we see all the background for the Jew's *alleged* taste for money."

35. *Anti-Semite and Jew*, p. 132, translation modified. "Nous nous contenterons, pour finir, d'indiquer à grands traits ce qu'on appelle l'inquiétude juive. Car les Juifs sont souvent inquiets. Un Israélite n'est jamais sûr de sa place ou de ses pos-

sessions," *Réflexions*, p. 161.

36. Again, the demon of intertextuality confronts me: Montandon entitled his book "How to recognize and explain the Jew?" (*Comment reconnaître et expliquer le Juif?*). Sartre, *Anti-Semite and Jew*, p. 124, translation modified, writes, in the midst of a whole series of "explanations": "It seems to me that one might explain in the same way the famous Israelite 'lack of tact.' Of course, there is a considerable amount of malice in this accusation." "Il me paraît que l'on pourrait expliquer de la même façon le fameux 'manque de tact' israélite. Bien entendu, il y a dans cette accusation une part considérable de malveillance," *Réflexions*, p. 151. If the accusation is malicious, why "explain" the trait it points to? Sartre's own uneasiness, or perhaps his own split personality with regard to the Jew in this text, is particularly apparent here. Could it also be that—being himself an ultra-rationalist, introspective, anxious man with "perverse" sexual tastes, uncomfortable with his body—he identifies with the "inauthentic" Jew?

37. *Anti-Semite and Jew*, p. 153. "Pas un Français ne sera libre tant que les Juifs ne jouiront pas de la plénitude de leurs droits. Pas un Français ne sera en sécurité tant qu'un Juif, en France et *dans le monde entier*, pourra craindre pour sa vie," *Réflexions*, p. 185, emphasis in text. Suddenly, I notice even here: is Sartre *opposing* Frenchmen to Jews? Or are French Jews included among the "Frenchmen who will not be free," etc? Oh dear. Maybe it is impossible to speak about Jews, or any other ethnic group, from outside the group without running into such problems.

38. "The Last Words of Jean-Paul Sartre," pp. 418–19. Fourteen years earlier, Sartre had already stated in an interview that he had some regrets over his approach in the *Réflexions*: "I should have treated the problem from a double point of view, historical and economic. I limited myself to a phenomenological description"; quoted in Michel Contat and Michel Rybalka, *Les Ecrits de Sartre*. Paris: Gallimard, 1970, p. 140.

39. Christian Delacampagne, *L'invention du racisme: Antiquité et*

Moyen-Age. Paris: Fayard, 1983, p. 27. I discovered Delacampagne's discussion of *Réflexions* only after writing the first draft of this essay (thanks to the author himself). In the few pages he devotes to Sartre's book, Delacampagne cites many of the same phrases and passages I found most disturbing; he concludes that the anti-Semitic echoes are typical of "the most traditional anti-Semitism, that of the French Right before the war" (p. 27). Delacampagne informs me, however, that he no longer believes in his demonstration. I do!

40. Review by Jean-Albert Hesse, *Le Monde juif* (May–June 1947), p. 33.

41. Anthony Blend, "Sartre and the Jewish Question," M. Phil. thesis, University of Southampton, 1988, p. 138 (at the library of the Centre de la Documentation Juive Contemporaine, Paris).

42. Gustav Ichheiser, book review, "*Anti-Semite and Jew*" by Jean-Paul Sartre, trans. by George J. Becker," *American Journal of Sociology* 55, no. 1 (July 1949), p. 111.

43. Harold Rosenberg, "Does the Jew Exist? Sartre's Morality Play About Anti-Semitism," *Commentary*, 7, no. 1 (January 1949), p. 15.

12. "I . . . AM. A."

1. *Ulysses: The Corrected Edition*, ed. Hans Walter Gabler. Harmondsworth: Penguin, and New York: Garland, 1986, p. 558. References to the novel will be given hereafter in my text in the following form: page number; chapter number: line number. Hence, for this quotation, 558; 17:530–31.

2. In addition to the texts referred to more specifically below, the critical discussion of Jews and Jewishness in *Ulysses* is represented by Louis Hymen, *The Jews in Ireland*. Dublin: Irish University Press, 1972; Erwin Steinberg, "James Joyce and the Critics Nothwithstanding, Leopold Bloom is Not Jewish," *Journal of Modern Literature* 9 (1981–2): pp. 27–49; G. Y. Goldberg, "Ireland is the Only Country: Joyce and the Jewish Dimension," *The Crane Bag* 6 (1982): pp. 5–12; Edmund L. Epstein, "Joyce and Judaism," in *The Seventh of Joyce*, ed. Bernard Benstock.

Brighton: Harvester Press, 1982, pp. 221–4; Morton P. Levitt, "The Humanity of Bloom, the Jewishness of Joyce," ibid., pp. 225–8; Marilyn Reizbaum, "The Jewish Connection, Continued," ibid., pp. 229–37; Ira B. Nadel, *Joyce and the Jews: Culture and Texts*. London: Macmillan, 1989; Timothy P. Martin, "Joyce, Wagner and the Wandering Jew," *Comparative Literature* 42 (1990): pp. 49–72; Bryan Cheyette, "'Jewgreek is greekjew': The Disturbing Ambivalence of Joyce's Semitic Discourse in *Ulysses*," *Joyce Studies Annual* 3 (1992): pp. 32–56.

3. Michael Theunissen, *The Other: Studies in the Social Ontology of Husserl, Heidegger, Sartre, and Buber*, trans. Christopher Macann. Cambridge, M.A: M.I.T. Press, 1984, p. xi.

4. Martin Buber, *I and Thou* (1923), trans. Ronald Gregor Smith. Edinburgh: T. and T. Clarke, 1947, pp. 3–4.

5. Emmanuel Levinas, "Martin Buber and the Theory of Knowledge," trans. Seán Hand, in *The Levinas Reader*, ed. Seán Hand. Oxford: Blackwell, 1989, p. 64.

6. Ibid., p. 114.

7. Homi K. Bhabha, "Dissemi-Nation: Time, Narrative, and the Margins of the Modern Nation, in *Nation and Narration*, ed. Homi K. Bhabha. London: Routledge, 1990, p. 310.

8. The recording runs from the beginning of MacHugh's rendering of Taylor's reply to Fitzgibbon, "*My chairman, ladies and gentleman: Great was my admiration . . .*" (116: 7:828) to "*Vagrants and daylabourers are you called: the world trembles at our name*" (117:7:858–9). The 78 r.p.m. record was released in a limited edition of 30 copies on the Shakespeare and Co. label. I am grateful to the National Sound Archive of London for their assistance.

9. I offer a different and more extended reading of the ventriloquial mobility of speech between the human and the nonhuman world in "Circe" in my "Jigajiga . . . Yummyyum . . . Pfuiiiiiii! . . . Bbbbblllllblblblblobscb!': 'Circe"s Ventriloquy," in *Reading Joyce's 'Circe' (European Joyce Studies*, 3), ed. Andrew Gibson. Amsterdam: Rodopi, 1994, pp. 93–142.

10. Emmanuel Levinas, "Martin Buber's Thought and Contem-

porary Judaism," *Outisde the Subject*, trans. Michael B. Smith. London: Athlone Press, 1993, p. 10.

11. Emmanuel Levinas, "Language and Proximity," *Collected Philosophical Papers*, trans. Alphonso Lingis. Dordrecht: Martinus Nijhoff, 1987, p. 122.

12. Ibid.

13. Ibid., p. 121.

14. Jacques Derrida, "Ulysses Gramophone: Hear Say Yes in Joyce," trans. Tina Kendall and Shari Benstock, in *Acts of Literature*, ed. Derek Attridge. London: Routledge, 1992, pp. 269, 299.

15. Jacques Derrida, "Violence and Metaphysics: An Essay on the Thought of Emmanuel Levinas," *Writing and Difference*, trans. Alan Bass. London: Routledge and Kegan Paul, 1978, p. 103.

16. The last couple of sentences attempt to summarize swiftly the triangular relationship of Joyce, Derrida, and Levinas which I describe in more detail in my *Theory and Cultural Value*. Oxford: Blackwell, 1992, pp. 203–30.

17. Edwin R. Epstein, "'Persecuted . . . Sold . . . in Morocco Like Slaves,'" *James Joyce Quarterly* 29 (1992): pp. 615–22, provides some details of the massacres and maltreatments undergone by Jews at the hands of the Moroccan authorities in 1903, the year before *Ulysses* is set, as this was widely reported in the Irish and American press. The other contemporary instance of anti-Semitism that Bloom may be meant to have in mind was the riots in Limerick in the early months of 1904. These are described in Marvin Magalaner's "The Anti-Semitic Limerick Incidents and Joyce's 'Bloomsday,'" *PMLA* (1953): pp. 1219–23.

18. Emmanuel Levinas, *Time and the Other, and Additional Essays*, trans. Richard A. Cohen. Pittsburgh: Duquesne University Press, 1987, p. 79.

19. S. T. Coleridge, *Biographia Literaria*, ed. George Watson. London: Dent, 1965, p. 167.

20. Derrida, "Ulysses Gramophone," p. 302.

21. See Don Gifford and Robert J. Seidman, *Ulysses Annotated: Notes for James Joyce's "Ulysses,"* 2nd edn. Berkeley: University of California Press, 1988, p. 366.

22. Hugh Kenner, *Ulysses*. London: Allen and Unwin, 1980, p. 133.

23. Robert Byrnes describes the ways in which Bloom's physical and psychological characteristics are made to accord ironically with contemporary stereotypes of the degenerate Jew, in "Bloom's Sexual Tropes: Stigmata of the Degenerate Jew," *James Joyce Quarterly* 27 (1990): pp. 303–23.

24. Derrida, "Violence and Metaphysics," p. 153. Gillian Rose, *Judaism and Modernity: Philosophical Essays*. Oxford: Blackwell, 1993, p. 18, has argued in similar terms against the tendency, both among Jewish and non-Jewish commentators, to represent "Judaism or the Jewish community eschatologically as irenic and sequestered—beyond rationalism, violence, the history of the world," and has urged, here and elsewhere in her work, that the relation between philosophy and Judaism, or "Athens" and "Jerusalem," "be explored neither in terms which presuppose self-identity, nor in terms of mutual opposition but in terms of their evident loss of self-identity."

25. Richard Ellmann, *James Joyce*, 2nd edn. New York, Oxford, and Toronto: Oxford University Press, 1982, p. 702.

26. *Letters of James Joyce*, vol. 3, ed. Richard Ellmann. London: Faber and Faber, 1966, pp. 499, 501.

27. "Mme Giedion est allé [sic] au bureau de la police des étrangers à Zurich où l'on semble croire que je suis . . . juif! Tonerre [sic] m'enlève! Voilà une fameuse découverte!," ibid., p. 491.

28. "Je crains pourtant que si l'on ne me voulait là-bas parce que l'on me croyait juif (Intelligence Service, sans doute?) après lecture de ma declaration l'on me voudra de moins en moins en s'apercevant que je ne suis pas juif du tout;" ibid., p. 499.

13. Assimilation, Entertainment, and the Hollywood Solution

1. It must be stressed that there are many ways of assimilating and that Jews in Hollywood, particularly in screenwriting, were very actively engaged in working to raise painful social issues in ways which were not amenable to simple "law and order" or utopian solutions. The case for

Yiddish as a *lingua franca* of popular culture, and a Jewish creativity that could be put to subversive as well as affirmative uses, was made very convincingly by Paul Buhle "The Hollywood Reds and Their Influence" at a conference on Cold War culture at University College London, October 22–23, 1994, organized by the Bartlett School of Architecture and the Department of History of Art, UCL.

Thanks to Lynda Nead and Juliet Steyn for useful suggestions and to Jacob Curtis who admired and enjoyed Hollywood culture and enabled us to think about it in these terms.

2. As we discuss on p. 246, a recent manifestation of this is an article published in *The Spectator*, October 29, 1994 by the son of Bill Cash, a British Conservative M.P., purporting to investigate a "new Jewish establishment." The journalist argues, in ways that echo previous attacks on Jews in Hollywood, that the predominantly Jewish establishment—a "Cabal"—excludes outsiders, that Jews are "compulsive story-tellers and talented negotiators" (i.e., fabulists and manipulators). His defenders—the editor of *The Spectator*, Dominic Lawson, and the editor of *The Modern Review* Toby Young—have sought to redeem him from accusations of anti-Semitism by suggesting that he used racial stereotypes "unthinkingly" and that he is merely "snobbish." The extent to which anti-Semitism is both unthinking and an aspect of other kinds of discrimination is explored in this essay.

3. Jill Robinson in Studs Terkel, "American Dreams Lost and Found", cited in Lester D. Friedman, *The Jewish Image in American Film*. New Jersey: Citadel Press, 1987.

4. See Sander L. Gilman, *Difference and Pathology: Stereotypes of Sexuality, Race, and Madness*. Ithaca, N.Y.: Cornell University Press, 1985; Gilman, *Freud, Race, and Gender*, Princeton University Press, 1993.

5. John Buchan, *Greenmantle* (1916). London: Wordsworth Editions, 1994, p. 55.

6. The term "Mogul" was first used in this way during the First World War and implies an absolute power of indeterminate oriental

origins, combined with a sense of barbarian threat to the cultural interests of the West. The Mogul was part autocrat, part invader, the term suggesting levels of despotism, nepotism, extravagance, and ruthlessness supposedly alien to American culture.

7. For an explanation of the difference between primary and secondary processes of thinking, see Martin Wangh "National Socialism and the Genocide of the Jews: A Psychoanalytic Study of an Historical Event," *International Journal of Psychoanalysis* 45 (1964): pp. 386–95.

8. See Sander L. Gilman, ch.5 above, and n.4. Julia Kristeva explores the feminization of the Jewish man, and the sexualization of the woman as representations of the projected perversity of an anti-Semitic culture; see "Proust, Issues of Identity" in this volume.

9. Cited in L. Friedman, *The Jewish Image*. R. Stam and L. Spence discuss the substitution of ethnicities in "Colonialism, Racism and Representation: An Introduction," *Screen* 24, no. 2 (March/April 1983): pp. 2–21. See also Brian Henderson, "The Searchers: An American Dilemma" in *Movies and Methods II*, ed. B. Nicholls. Bloomington: University of Indiana Press, 1985, pp. 429–49, which presents a convincing analysis of the textual substitution of Red (Indian) for Black (Negro) in John Ford's *The Searchers*.

10. Cited in Sander L. Gilman, *Reading Freud in English*, p. 205, collected in his *Inscribing the Other*. Lincoln and London: University of Nebraska Press, 1991, p. 21.

11. Michael Rogin, "Blackface White Noise: The Jewish Jazz Singer Finds his Voice," *Critical Inquiry* 18 (Spring 1992).

12. Isaac Goldberg, "Aaron Copeland and his Jazz," *American Mercury* 12 (September 1927), cited in Rogin, ibid.

13. Rogin, ibid.

14. See Neal Gabler, *An Empire of Their Own: How the Jews Invented Hollywood*. London: W. H. Allen, 1989, for biographies of Jewish personnel in the film industry.

15. Most notably in Budd Schulberg (himself the son of the studio executive B. P. Schulberg), *What Makes Sammy Run* (1939), a notorious book much resented by his father's generation.

16. Anna Freud, cited in *The Language of Psychoanalysis*, ed. J. Laplanche and J. B. Pontalis. London: Hogarth Press, 1973, p. 208.

17. Eva Hoffman, *Lost in Translation: Life In a New Language*. London: Minerva, 1991, p. 97, cited in Madan Sarap, "Home and Identity" in *Travellers' Tales*, ed. Robertson, Mash, Tickner, Bird, Curtis, and Putnam. London: Routledge, 1994.

18. Adolph Zukor, Jesse Lasky, Marcus Loew, Carl Laemmle, William Fox, Louis Meyer, the Schenk and Warner Brothers, and Harry Cohn dominated the Hollywood studio system in the interwar years. All Jewish, they controlled all the main studios except RKO and Disney.

19. Article on Metro-Goldwyn-Meyer in *Fortune Magazine*, December 1932, pp. 51–8, cited in *The American Film Industry*, ed. Tino Ballio. Madison, W.I: University of Wisconsin Press, 1976, p. 265.

20. Cited in Gabler, p. 57.

21. See Miriam Hansen, "Early Cinema: Whose Public Sphere" in *Early Cinema: Space, Frame, Narrative*, ed. Thomas Elsaesser. London: British Film Institute, 1990, p. 230.

22. See Gabler, p. 255.

23. Lary May, *Screening Out the Past: The Birth of Mass Culture and the Motion Picture Industry*. New York: Oxford University Press, p. 175.

24. J. B. Priestley, *English Journey* (1933). Leipzig: Tauchnitz Edition, 1935, pp. 193 and 21.

25. See n. 2.

26. F. Scott Fitzgerald, *The Last Tycoon* (1941). Harmondsworth: Penguin, 1960, p. 90.

27. Irene Mayer Selznick, *A Private View*. London: Weidenfeld and Nicolson, 1983, p. 39, says "There was much ado about horses in Southern California in those years (the early 1920's), and I don't mean cowboys or Western pictures. Proper saddle horses and English riding habits were quite the thing. High-class stars were photographed in wonderfully tailored habits, always carrying a riding crop. It was also rather dashing to wear riding clothes for casual attire and just skip the horses." Appropriately, Freud in "The Ego and the Id" (1923), *The Complete*

Psychological Work of Sigmund Freud, vol. 19. London: Hogarth Press, 1962, p. 25, discusses the symbol of horse and rider as a metaphor for id and ego, with the ego mastering the animal power of the id.

28. F. Scott Fitzgerald, *The Great Gatsby* (1926). Harmondsworth: Penguin Modern Classics (numerous printings), p. 55.

29. Maria Damon, "Talking Yiddish at the Boundaries," *Cultural Studies* 5, no. 1 (January 1991): p. 21.

30. See Friedman, *The Jewish Image in American Film*.

14. "A Little Child"

1. In the Book of Hosea, one of the earliest prophetic books, the image of sacred marriage becomes the primary symbol of the bond between God and Israel. In the earlier parts of the book, this image is introduced as an attribute of Canaanite religion, and blended with an image of sacred prostitution, supposedly connected to local fertility cults and rites. Hosea's life, as he describes it, is a textbook case of "The personal is political." He marries a woman who betrays him, taking many lovers and also worshipping many gods. He denounces her infidelity, but also proclaims his steadfast love (*chesed*), and lyrically implores her to return. Hosea grows hysterical in denouncing the Canaanites' sacred orgies (whose existence scholars now doubt). One especially intriguing aspect of *Hosea* is a subtext of divine self-criticism. Why, the prophet asks, did this beautiful marriage (Hosea/Gomer, Yahweh/Israel) fail? The prophet, who personifies God, recognizes that he was carried away by his own desires and fantasies, and inadequately sensitive to his wife's real needs. He hopes to renegotiate their marriage on a new and more authentically mutual basis, something like the "new covenant" promised in Jeremiah 31:31. Hosea is at once a tragedy of adultery and a comedy of remarriage, *Anna Karenina* merged with *Adam's Rib*.

2. Cited in Arthur Hertzberg, *The French Enlightenment and the Jews: The Origins of Modern Anti-Semitism*. New York: Schocken, 1970, p. 360. See also Werner Keller, *Diaspora: The Post-Biblical History of the Jews*, trans.

Richard and Clara Winston. New York: Harcourt, Brace & World, 1969, "The Beacon of the French Revolution," pp. 376–9.

3. Hegel, *Philosophy of Right*. Addition to Paragraph 273, ed. and trans. T. M. Knox. Oxford University Press, 1945, p. 286. Italics mine.

4. *The Diaries of Franz Kafka, 1910–23*, trans. Joseph Kresh, Martin Greenberg, and Hannah Arendt. Harmondsworth, Middlesex: Penguin, 1964.

5. Freud, "Family Romances" (1909), reprinted in *Collected Papers*, trans. and ed. James Strachey. Basic Books, 1959, vol. V, pp. 74–8. Freud's essay originally appeared as a chapter in Otto Rank's 1909 book, *The Myth of the Birth of the Hero*. Freud's original title was "The Family Romances of Neurotics," but in fact he saw family romance as part of a process of normal growth and development.

6. The best overall account of this migration, and of the culture that grew from it, is Irving Howe, assisted by Kenneth Libo, *World of Our Fathers*. New York: Harcourt Brace Jovanovich, 1976.

7. Roth has given many different accounts of his past politics. I interviewed him in Albuquerque, New Mexico, Summer, 1980. At that time, he placed his rupture with Communism in 1956 (the year of Khrushchev's revelations about Stalinism, followed by a revolution in Hungary, and its suppression by the U.S.S.R.) and, an hour later, in 1967 (Israel's victory in the Six-Day War, followed by waves of official anti-Semitism in all Communist countries). In the later 1980's, however, he began to tell interviewers that he was never a Communist at all, but only a victim of Communist bullying and intimidation. My reasons for doubting this will become clear.

8. Page numbers cited are from the beloved (and endlessly reprinted) 1964 Avon paperback edition. That edition features a critical afterword by the British critic Walter Allen, and a beautiful tenement photograph on the cover by Jay Maisel. The photo is evocative of Jacob Riis and Lewis Hine, but contains many emphases that are especially appropriate to Roth's book: in the foreground, clotheslines display men's and women's underwear, and fire escapes lead up to roofs; in the background, visible only in faint shadows, there is a panorama of New York City skyscrapers. The Avon edition went out of print in the late 1980's, and there is now a new edition on the market, published in 1990 by Noonday/Farrar, Straus & Giroux. It is sewn-bound, as if built to last (let us hope so), and it has a fine introduction by Alfred Kazin, and an Aferword by Hana Wirth Nesher, "Between Mother Tongue and Native Language in *Call It Sleep*." Page numbers in the body of the novel are identical in the Noonday edition, making life easier for critics and their readers, and helping the Jewish culture of narration live on.

9. In a novel by a writer who lived in Greenwich Village in the 1930's, "id" has to be a crude psychoanalytic allusion.

10. David's Jewishness cannot be problematic according to rabbinic law, where descent comes through the mother, regardless of the father's identity. After the rabbis have heard David's story of his mother's story, they began to worry about whether David was circumcised: "Let us hope they saw to it he was made a Jew" (375). But even if "they" hadn't seen to it, circumcision can legitimately take place anytime in a man's life. We need to understand that David fears an excommunication, an existential otherness, far deeper and more total than anything that would be possible in normal Jewish life.

11. "Why, is there anyone here who doesn't wish his father's death? . . . They all long for their father's death, because one beast devours another!" *The Brothers Karamazov*, Book XII, Ch. 4, trans. Andrew MacAndrew. New York: Bantam, 1970, p. 825. This is a basic element of Freud's Oedipus Complex, and a central theme in his *Interpretation of Dreams* (1900): that we are all guilty of this and other evil desires.

12. In his *Phenomenology of the Spirit* (1807), Hegel argued very forcefully that the enslaved masses had to risk their lives before they could become free. See Herbert Marcuse, *Reason and Revolution: Hegel and the Rise of Social Theory*. Boston: Beacon, 1960, for an incisive dis-

cussion of this theme, including its influence on the young Marx.

In Jewish mass politics of the 1900's, both in the Russian Empire and on the Lower East Side of New York, thousands of Jews staked their lives, and many were killed, in differently configured but equally urgent fights for collective freedom. On Eastern Europe, see esp. Jonathan Frankel, *Prophecy and Politics: Socialism, Nationalism and the Russian Jews, 1862–1917*. Cambridge, 1981; on the sweatshops of New York, see Howe, *World of Our Fathers*, esp. Chs. 9–10.

13. These readings and formulations owe something to David Biale's fascinating book, *Eros and the Jews*. Basic Books, 1992, though I have no idea whether Biale would be comfortable with them.

14. Nietzsche, *The Birth of Tragedy/The Genealogy of Morals*, trans. Francis Golffing. Anchor, 1956, pp. 167–8.

15. Montage was one of the most important innovations of modernism. It became a force in all arts—painting, music, photography, drama, cinema. The most brilliant creators of montage in modernist fiction were James Joyce, especially in *Ulysses* (1922), and William Faulkner. It is easy to see their influence here, but Roth is distinctive in the intimately personal character of his montages: this is David's way of breaking up the world, shaped by what he needs and what he knows; the street would sound a lot different through the prism of his mother's or father's or *rebbe*'s mind.

16. Leonard Michaels, "Life and Art in Henry Roth," *New York Times Book Review*, August 15, 1993, reprinted as the Introduction to the paperback edition of *Shifting Landscape*, Roth's collection of short pieces, letters, and interviews, ed. Mario Materassi. New York: St. Martin's, 1994.

17. Robert Daniels, *A Documentary History of Communism*, 2 vols. New York: Vintage, 1962, vol. 2, pp. 107–17, reprints basic Third Period and Popular Front manifestos. Coser and Howe, in their history of the CPUSA, and Daniel Aaron, in *Writers on the Left* (New York: Avon, 1962), say some interesting things about the Popular Front, but the great work on the worldwide cul-

ture of the Popular Front remains to be written.

18. This concept was coined in a brilliant 1916 essay by Randolph Bourne, "Trans-National America," in *War and the Intellectuals: Collected Essays, 1915–1919*, ed. Carl Resek. New York: Harper, 1964, pp. 107–23; note also "The Jew and Trans-National America," pp. 124–33. Bourne is one of the heroes of Christopher Lasch's *The New Radicalism in America, 1889–1963: The intellectual as a Social Type*. New York: Vintage, 1967. See also, on the pre-1960's, John Higham, "Ethnic Pluralism in Modern American Thought," in *Send These To Me: Jews and Other Immigrants in Urban America*. New York: Atheneum, 1975, pp. 196–230.

Ironically, although Bourne was a notorious opponent of the First World War, his "trans-national" idea was eagerly appropriated by the war propaganda machine, which claimed that our transnational character made us better than the old, homogenous nations of Europe, and that this was why it was urgent for us to win. The idea was appropriated again in the Second World War, and incarnated in dozens of Hollywood movies (e.g., Frank Sinatra/Albert Maltz's stirring short film *The House I Live In*), but this time the Communists of the Popular Front, who were often writing and directing those movies, didn't mind.

19. *New York Times*, stories by Clyde Haberman, December 16 and 26, 1994, and anti-Rabin letter from Richard Horowitz, dated December 26, published January 2, 1995. My citation from Peres preserves his words but changes their order.

20. The *New York Times* story of December 16, 1994, which first reported this controversy, concluded with a rare exegetical intervention. After citing Orthodox insistence that King David could not have sinned, Clyde Haberman ended with the (accurate) observation that "The final verse of [2 Samuel] Chapter 11 states unequivocally, 'The thing that David had done displeased the Lord.'"

15. Parvenu or Palimpsest

1. From an immense range of materials, see Edward Said,

Orientalism, 1978; Jean-Pierre Vernant, *La mort dans les yeux: Figures de l'autre en Grèce ancienne—Artémis, Gorgô*. Paris: Hachette, 1990; Homi K. Bhabha, *Nation and Narration*. London: Routledge, 1990.

2. Zygmunt Bauman, cited from his plenary paper, *Allosemitism: Premodern, Modern, Postmodern*, given at the conference "Modernity, Culture and the 'Jew'," Birkbeck College, London, May 12–14, 1994. See Michel Garel, *D'une main forte, manuscrites hébreux des collections françaises*, Paris: Seuil/Bibliothèque Nationale, 1991, items 100 and 115.

3. Henri Murger, *Scènes de la vie de bohème*, 1845–1851, collected and published by both Hetzel and Michel Lévy, Paris, 1851. These quotations and all page references from Folio edition, Paris, 1988. All translations from the French are mine.

4. Richard Wagner, *Judaism in Music, being the original essay together with the later supplement*, translated from the German and furnished with explanatory notes and introduction by Edwin Evans, senior, F. R. C. O. London: William Reeves, 1910.

5. Maxime Ducamp, *Paris, ses organes, ses fonctions et sa vie dans la seconde moitié du XIXe siècle*. 6 vols. Paris: Hachette, 1869–75, sections on the rag trade and on cemeteries in vol. 6.

6. Pierre Birnbaum, *"La France aux France aux Français"—Histoire des haines nationalistes*. Paris: Seuil, 1993, pp. 118 and 346.

7. Edouard Drumont, *La France juive*. Paris: Marpon et Flammarion, 1886, vol. 2, p. 105. This and all further quotations from vol. 2 of the 1887 edition.

8. Annette Wieviorka, from her paper given at "Modernity, Culture and the 'Jew'," see n. 2.

9. Cited in Georges Eckhoud, *Voyou de velours, ou l'autre vie* (1904). Brussels: Editions Labor, 1991, pp. 157–8.

10. For a good coverage of Jews and the cinema in France, see *CinémaAction No. 37—Cinéma et judéité*. Paris: Cerf, 1986. See the

chapter by Jacques Gerstenkorn, *A la recherche d'une judéité perdue: M. Klein de Joseph Losey*, pp. 188–191, for a summary of the fierce debates aroused by the film. For the reception of Renoir, see Francis Vanoye, *La Règle du jeu*. Paris: Nathan, 1989. Vanoye and other film historians give disparate versions of which critics wrote what, though there is agreement on Rebatet's intervention.

11. *Archives israélites de France: Recueil mensuel, historique, biographique, bibliographique et littéraire, par une société d'hommes de lettres sous la direction de S. Cahen, traducteur de la Bible*, Supplément no. 5. Mai (1841), 11e année, pp. 318, 326.

12. This newsreel in in a selection of anecdotal news items, *Actualités Gaumont—la Fête de Roch Hachana*, 1932, in the Vidéothèque de Paris, found under subject-search "juifs." For Carné's view on Jéricho, see Edward Baron Turk, *Child of Paradise: Marcel Carné and the Golden Age of French Cinema*. Cambridge, M.A: Harvard University Press, 1989, p. 266.

16. The U.S. Holocaust Memorial Museum

1. Both Platt and Morris are cited in "City Rejects Park Memorials to Slain Jews," *New York Times*, February 11, 1965, p. 1, and in "2 Jewish Monuments Barred from Park," *New York World Telegram and Sun*, February 10, 1965, p. 1.

2. For more on the political dimension of memorials, see Michael Berenbaum, "On the Politics of Public Commemoration of the Holocaust," *Shoah* (Fall/Winter 1981–82), p. 9. See also Berenbaum's collection of essays, *After Tragedy and Triumph: Modern Jewish Thought and the American Experience*. Cambridge and New York: Cambridge University Press, 1991, pp. 3–16. For further details on the controversy surrounding the establishment of the U.S. Holocaust Memorial Commission, see Judith Miller, *One*

by One by One: Facing the Holocaust. New York and London: Simon and Schuster, 1990, pp. 255–66.

3. Charles Maier, *The Unmasterable Past: History, Holocaust, and German National Identity.* Cambridge, MA, and London: Harvard University Press, 1988, p. 165.

4. From an undated press release of the U.S. Holocaust Memorial Council.

5. *The Campaign for the United States Holocaust Memorial Museum.* Washington, D.C: U.S. Holocaust Memorial Council, [n.d.], p. 4.

6. Ibid.

7. George Will, "Holocaust Museum: Antidote for Innocence," *The Washington Post*, March 10, 1983.

8. Berenbaum, *After Tragedy and Triumph*, p. 20.

9. See Benjamin Forgey, "In Search of a Delicate Balance," *The Washington Post*, May 23, 1987, pp. B1–B2.

10. Harvey M. Meyerhoff, "Yes, the Holocaust Museum Belongs on the Mall," *The Washington Post*, July 18, 1987.

11. Cited in Cassandra Burrell, "Supporters of African-American Museum Object to Smithsonian Control," Associated Press, September 15, 1992.

12. James Ingo Freed, "The United States Holocaust Memorial Museum," *Assemblage* 9 (1989), p. 61. Subsequent page references appear in parentheses in the text.

13. Freed, "The United States Holocaust Museum: What Can It Be?", printed by the United States Holocaust Memorial, Washington, D.C. [n.d., n.p.].

14. For details from the exhibition walkthrough, I rely here on both my own visits and on the Museum Project Director Michael Berenbaum's provisional walkthrough, "A Visit to The Permanent Exhibition: The United States Holocaust Memorial Museum," which he generously provided me before the Museum's opening.

15. See Jonathan Rosen, "America's Holocaust," *Forward*, April 12, 1991, p. 7.

Notes on the Contributors

KATHLEEN ADLER is Senior Lecturer in History of Art at the Centre for Extra-Mural Studies, Birkbeck College, University of London. She is the Book Review Editor of *Art History*, and has published widely on aspects of nineteenth-century art, including *Manet* (1986) and *Unknown Impressionists* (1988).

MARSHALL BERMAN teaches Political Theory and Urbanism at the City University of New York. He is the author of *All That Is Solid Melts into Air: The Experience of Modernity* (1982), an earlier book, *The Politics of Authenticity*, and many articles on politics and culture. He is on the editorial board of *Dissent* magazine, and the advisory board of *Tikkun*.

BRYAN CHEYETTE is a lecturer in English at Queen Mary and Westfield College, University of London. He is the author of *Constructions of "the Jew" in English Literature and Society: Racial Representations, 1875–1945* (1993) and has edited a book of essays on English and American literary anti-Semitism for Stanford University Press. He is currently working on a critical history of British-Jewish literature in the twentieth century.

DR. MICHÈLE C. CONE, Research Associate at the Institute of French Studies, New York University, is best known for *Artists under Vichy* (1992) and "Abstract Art as a Veil: Tricolor Painting in Vichy France," *The Art Bulletin*, June 1992. She also writes and lectures on contemporary art, and is the author of *The Roots and Routes of Art in the 20th Century* (1975).

STEVEN CONNOR is Professor of Modern Literature and Theory at Birkbeck College, University of London. He has written widely about nineteenth- and twentieth-century literature and culture, and is the author of *Postmodernist Culture: An Introduction to Theories of the Contemporary* (1989) and *Theory and Cultural Value* (1992).

BARRY CURTIS is Head of the School of the History and Theory of Visual Culture at Middlesex University. He is an editor of *BLOCK* and has published on film, British cultural theory, and architecture. His most recent writings appear in *Watching Europe* (Amsterdam Cultural Studies Foundation, 1993), *Travellers' Tales* (1994), and in the journal *Art History* (1995).

SANDER L. GILMAN is Henry R. Luce Professor of the Liberal Arts in Human Biology at the University of Chicago. He is a cultural and literary historian and the author or editor of over forty books, the most recent in English–*Freud, Race, and Gender* and *The Case of Sigmund Freud*–having appeared in 1993. He is the author of the basic study of the visual stereotyping of the mentally ill, *Seeing the Insane* (1982), as well as the standard study of the subject, *Jewish Self-Hatred: Anti-Semitism and the Hidden Language of the Jews* (1986).

ROMY GOLAN is Assistant Professor in the History of Art Department at Yale University. Her publications include "Matta, Duchamp et le mythe: un nouveau paradigme pour la dernière phase du Surrealisme," in *Les Classiques du XXème Siècle: Matta* (1985); *The Circle of Montparnasse: Jewish Artists in Paris 1905–1945* (1985), co-authored with Kenneth E. Silver; and *Modernity and Nostalgia: Art and Politics in France between the Wars* (1995).

JULIA KRISTEVA is a practising psychoanalyst and professor of literature and linguistics both at the University of Paris and Columbia University, New York. She has written numerous articles on both subjects, two novels, and books including *Pouvoir de l'horreur (Powers of Horror*, 1982), *Etrangers à nous-mêmes (Strangers to Ourselves*, 1988), and *Le Temps sensible: Proust et l'expérience littéraire* (1994).

GALE B. MURRAY is Judson Bemis Professor in Humanities and Professor of Art History at Colorado College in Colorado Springs. She is the author of *Toulouse-Lautrec: The Formative Years, 1878–1891* (1991) and editor of *Toulouse-Lautrec: A Retrospective* (1992).

CAROL OCKMAN is Professor of Art History at Williams College. She has written on Ingres, portraiture, and feminist methodology. Her *Ingres's Eroticized Bodies: Retracing the Serpentine Line* (1995) includes a chapter on ethnic stereotyping in Ingres's portrait of the Baronne de Rothschild.

CLAIRE PAJACZKOWSKA is a Senior Lecturer in Visual Culture at Middlesex University. She has translated a number of books and articles on psychoanalysis and visual culture from the French and has written for *Screen, Free Associations, BLOCK,* and *Heresies*. Her most recent articles appear in *What She Wants* (1994) and *Travellers' Tales* (1994).

ADRIAN RIFKIN is Professor of Fine Art at the University of Leeds. He has written and made radio programs on nineteenth- and twentieth-century culture, popular entertainment, photography, art, and aesthetics, and published *Street Noises: Parisian Pleasure 1900–1940* (1993). He is currently completing *Staging an Artist: Ingres between Then and Now* and a series of essays under the title *Gay Poetics*.

JULIET STEYN is currently Course Leader, MA, Art Criticism and Theory at the Kent Institute of Art and Design at Canterbury. She is at present editing *Other than Identity*. Her Ph.D. thesis was titled *The Jew in Britain: Assumptions of Identity*. Recent publications include "Inside-Out: Assumption of English Modernism in the Whitechapel Gallery, London, 1914," in *Art Apart*, edited by Marcia Pointon (1994).

SUSAN R. SULEIMAN is Professor of Romance and Comparative Literatures at Harvard University. Her books include *Subversive Intent: Gender, Politics, and the Avant-Garde* (1990), and *Risking Who One Is: Encounter with Contemporary Art and Literature* (1994). Her earlier study, *Authoritarian Fiction*, was reissued with a new preface in 1993.

JUDITH WECHSLER, National Endowment for the Humanities Professor of Art History, Tufts University, has written *A Human Comedy: Physiognomy and Caricature in 19th Century Paris* (1982), *The Interpretation of Cézanne* (1981), and articles and catalogue essays on nineteenth- and twentieth-century art.

JAMES E. YOUNG is Professor of English and Judaic Studies at the University of Massachusetts at Amherst. He is the author of *The Texture of Memory: Holocaust Memorials and Meaning* (1993) and *Writing and Rewriting the Holocaust* (1988). He was also guest curator for "The Art of Memory," an exhibition at the Jewish Museum in New York City (1994) and editor of the accompanying catalogue, *The Art of Memory* (1994).

Index